The Corporate Responsibility Code Book

Deborah Leipziger

Deborah Leipziger is a consultant in the field of corporate social responsibility, and advises companies on the development and implementation of codes of conduct and standards. Her clients have included the UN's Global Compact, Warwick University and Social Accountability International. She is an adviser to Morley Fund Management, assisting them on their approach to socially responsible investment. Deborah played a key role in the development of the Social Accountability 8000 standard and its Guidance Document. She is the author of *SA8000: The Definitive Guide to the New Social Standard* (FT Prentice Hall, 2001), and the co-author of *Living Corporate Citizenship* (FT, 2002) and *Corporate Citizenship: Successful Strategies of Responsible Companies* (FT, 1998). Deborah resides in The Hague, with her husband and three daughters.

thehague@wanadoo.nl

The landscape of corporate responsibility is rapidly changing. To make **The Corporate Responsibility Code Book** an even more invaluable resource as codes evolve, regular updates will be available on the Greenleaf Publishing website, at **www.greenleaf-publishing.com/catalogue/crcbpdt.htm**.

THE CORPORATE RESPONSIBILITY
code book

Deborah Leipziger

Greenleaf
PUBLISHING
2 0 0 3

This book is dedicated to my three daughters, Natasha Lara, Alexandra Nicole and Jacqueline Lucia, my triple bottom line, and to my husband Daryl Mundis, my inspiration through all that he does to create a more just world.

© 2003 Greenleaf Publishing Limited

Published by Greenleaf Publishing Limited
Aizlewood's Mill
Nursery Street
Sheffield S3 8GG
UK

Printed on paper made from at least 75% post-consumer waste using TCF and ECF bleaching.
Printed and bound by The Cromwell Press, UK.
Cover by LaliAbril.com.

British Library Cataloguing in Publication Data:
 A catalogue record for this book is available from the British Library.

ISBN 1874719780

Contents

Foreword

Keith Jones, Chief Executive, Morley Fund Management

The field of corporate responsibility has come a long way in a few years. Investors and company managements alike are realising that corporate governance and social and environmental performance are important elements of sustained financial profitability. However, in comparison to financial information, corporate responsibility communication is embryonic. Good communication needs a common standardised language, an understanding of what needs to be communicated and how to do this. As investors we look to codes and standards for the essential grammar of this language. These codes and standards must be reliable, relevant and challenging, yet not so onerous or inflexible that only the largest companies will take them up, nor an exercise in meaningless box ticking and additional bureaucracy.

I believe that the emergence of corporate responsibility, from being a niche interest of environmentalists and pressure groups to one of public concern, has, in part, stemmed from recent examples of corporate irresponsibility and destruction of shareholder value, but also, and more positively, from growing evidence that good corporate responsibility is good business.

In recognition of this link, Morley Fund Management has been at the forefront of promoting good corporate responsibility. We have been effective in raising standards of corporate governance and environmental reporting among many UK listed companies, as well as engaging with companies on issues such as access to life-saving drugs in developing countries and on transparency of payments in the oil and mining sectors. These initiatives reflect my conviction that with share ownership comes a responsibility to engage with companies on all issues that may significantly impact company profitability or the society and environment in which they operate.

However, there are many challenges in the analysis of these so-called 'softer' issues. Which indicators are important for a particular sector? How should they be measured? Can the measurements be trusted? How to differentiate 'greenwash', or fig leaves, from substance? As with accounting and communication of financial information, a dialogue needs to develop between companies and investors (and indeed other stakeholders) to determine how and what to report on. A balance needs to be struck between the demands for information and the resources available to companies. Standards that are too onerous will be practical only for larger companies and won't gain traction; equally, standards that are too diluted become irrelevant.

This book is timely, as the debate has progressed from the 'Why should we report on these issues?' to the 'How should we?' Clear and effective codes will address some of the frustrations felt on both sides: by the companies complaining of questionnaire fatigue; and from the inability of those seeking information to get beyond the glossy brochure. Companies are realising that public trust has been eroded and they need to rebuild this by making explicit how they put their corporate responsibility policies into practice both to investors and wider society.

The task Deborah has undertaken is extremely valuable. From her contributions to the Morley Advisory Committee on socially responsible investment, it is obvious that she has a deep understanding of the practical challenges of corporate responsibility reporting as well as far-reaching experience in the development of codes and standards that are appropriate to the companies concerned. This is crucial to her analysis of the strengths and weaknesses of current standards.

I certainly look forward to continued growth in the scope and quality of corporate responsibility reporting, not only for the improvement in societal well-being it will deliver but also as a valuable investment tool to distinguish high-quality sustainable companies from their peers.

A note to readers

What's in a name?

As I wrote this book I was constantly reminded of the phrase 'things are seldom what they seem'. Corporate responsibility (CR) codes and standards are seldom what they seem. The reader should be advised that the terminology of CR tools is still being developed. The terms 'code', 'standard' and 'norm' are often used interchangeably and imprecisely. Another example of this imprecision is in the use of the term 'voluntary'. Although many company codes on labour issues are described as 'voluntary', they often require companies to conform to existing laws. Even the use of terms such as 'sustainable development' and 'accountability' within the title of codes and standards can be imprecise. The International Chamber of Commerce (ICC) Charter on Sustainable Development is far more about environment than sustainable development writ large. Social Accountability 8000 is more about labour rights than social accountability writ large. The field of corporate responsibility is still evolving and developing its own *lingua franca*.

Codes are in the eye of the beholder

Much of what is written about CR tools is public relations and marketing—an attempt to gain more members and attain critical mass. In this book, I seek to break through the 'spin' to objectively describe principles and codes; but, in reading my descriptions of the strengths and weaknesses of the initiatives, keep in mind that for some a code might be too rigorous and yet for others the same code might be too lenient.

This book seeks to provide clarity in a very broad and complex field, by offering manageable and useful information. *The Corporate Responsibility Code Book* is a reference guide for companies, non-governmental organisations (NGOs), trade unions and students. This book will be useful for companies trying to decide between several different approaches; for NGOs or civil-society groups trying to decide which codes to lobby companies to adhere to; and for activists, who can use this volume to call attention to cases where companies are not living up to the standards that they have committed themselves to in writing. But, mostly, this is a useful reference book to check what issues are included in which tools, and which are absent. Each profile is meant to stand alone so in some cases there may be some repetition.

It has been a challenge to narrow the field from the thousands of codes and standards into 32 key tools. There are a great many useful tools that are not included here but that may be included in a future edition. Another challenge has been to describe a constantly moving target, as each of the initiatives described herein are evolving. For this reason, regular updates will be made available on the Greenleaf Publishing website at www.greenleaf-publishing.com/catalogue/crcbpdt.htm.

Deborah Leipziger
October 2003

Acknowledgements

This book is based on interviews with a wide range of experts from various countries and sectors. I am grateful to the following people for their time and wisdom:

Adrian Henriques
Shareen Hertel
Geoffrey Chandler
Gemma Crijns
Laura Donovan
John Elkington
Jan Jonker
Hilary Sutcliffe
Deborah Smith
Rory Sullivan
Simone de Colle
Malcolm McIntosh

Dorothy Mackenzie
Andrew Wilson
Katherine Hagen
Reino Fridh
David Vidal
Anita Normark
Eileen Kaufman
Sumi Dhanarajan
Jane Nelson
Mark Wade
Allen White

The following people reviewed the profiles of their organisations:

Mats Isaksson, OECD
Jonathan Cohen, AccountAbility
Mattias Stausberg, Global Compact
Kathryn Gordon, OECD
Mark Wade, Shell
Reg Green, ICEM
Dan Rees, Ethical Trading Initiative
Ineke Zeldenrust, Clean Clothes Campaign
Anne Lally, Fair Labor Association

David Weissbrodt, UN Working Group on the Working Methods and Activities of Transnational Corporations
Eileen Kaufman, Social Accountability International
Teodorina Lessidrenska, Global Reporting Initiative
Sharlie Mello, Global Sullivan Principles
Susan Cote-Freeman, Transparency International
Jill Rosenblum, The Natural Step

I am thankful to the standard-setters who have allowed Greenleaf Publishing to reproduce the standards in this volume. Each of the standard-setters was invited to comment on the introductory remarks that precede its principles, code or standard. I am grateful to them for their feedback.

My friends have supported me through this endeavour and deserve recognition. A special thank you goes to Shareen Hertel for her thoughtful advice, encouragement and wisdom. I am also very grateful to Jan Jonker for his encouragement and introductions.

I am grateful to my dear friends, Monica Sallouti, Jessica Holmes, Robin Schaap, Nancy Bennet, Oshani Perera, Gail Whiteman, Nancy Combs, Ann Marie Armbruster, Alice Winkler, Marie Kagaju, Maritza Saxon and Karin Green, for their faith in me.

Most of all, I am thankful to my husband and in-house counsel Daryl Mundis for his sound advice, patience, sense of humour, wisdom and unflagging support. I am grateful to my daughters, Natasha Lara, Jacqueline Lucia and Alexandra Nicole, for illustrating the recycled early drafts of this book. I am, as always, grateful to my parents for teaching me to love books and the written word.

Finally, I would like to thank John Stuart, Dean Bargh and their team at Greenleaf Publishing for their support and sound advice.

Introduction

There is no single code or standard, no panacea that will lead to corporate responsibility. Each company is different, with its own challenges, corporate culture, unique set of stakeholders and management systems. Corporate responsibility is a journey for which there is no single map but hundreds of guides. Codes and standards are maps that can be combined in new ways for different journeys. In my lectures around the world, I am asked the question, 'What are the best standards for companies seeking to be socially responsible?' Over the course of more than a decade, I have analysed hundreds of codes of conduct and standards to answer that question. This book is a result of 12 years of inquiry into corporate responsibility.

The Corporate Responsibility Code Book is a guide for companies trying to understand the landscape of corporate responsibility. This book is a valuable tool not only for companies developing their own code but also for companies with a strong track record in corporate responsibility, seeking to understand the interrelationships among codes and standards in order to create their own vision.

Companies are seeking to integrate codes of conduct and guidelines into their corporate cultures and management systems. The challenge for corporate responsibility is that each company is different; each sector has different priorities. The very same company in one region may face different challenges in other parts of the world. And yet stakeholders, especially consumers and investors, are keen for some degree of comparability with which they can evaluate corporate performance. There are countervailing forces at work within corporate responsibility: on the one hand is the need for convergence to simplify the large numbers of codes and standards; and on the other hand there is the need to foster diversity and innovation.

Code paradoxes

It is a paradox that many of the best codes of conduct and standards are not well known and that some corporate responsibility instruments that are well disseminated are not terribly effective. The purpose of this book is to disseminate some of the best corporate responsibility instruments available and to comment on their role. Another paradox is that it is possible to have comprehensive codes of conduct that achieve nothing, and quite vague codes of conduct that are well embedded into the organisation and that foster innovation and change.

Information overload is nowhere more apparent than in the field of corporate responsibility. There are millions of pages and web pages written on codes and standards, but most of it is 'spin' put out by organisations punting to sell their code or standard. The reality is that corporate responsibility is an emerging field, a new terrain for which maps are much needed but often imprecise. Just as the early cartographers drew imaginary creatures on their maps when they came up against the edge of what they knew, there is much *terra incognita* in the field of corporate responsibility. The weaving together of codes and standards in this volume points out the *terra incognita*, the vacuums within corporate responsibility, and also the duplication.

The need for a code book

In my consulting practice I advise companies about codes of conduct and their implementation. On many occasions I am brought in after a company has already developed a policy or code and disseminated it. Disseminating a code that is poorly crafted can lead to confusion and inefficiency, causing a 'domino effect' of misunderstanding and apathy.

My clients ask, 'What is the difference between Social Accountability 8000 [SA8000] and AccountAbility 1000 [AA1000]? Which should I use?' The answer is that each code and standard is a product of the organisation that crafted it and that each of the 32 codes in this book offer valuable lessons in corporate responsibility. There is no Holy Grail in the field of corporate responsibility, only different approaches and views of the field. *The Corporate Responsibility Code Book* distils the most valuable elements of each corporate responsibility instrument in a balanced and concise way.

The Corporate Responsibility Code Book will guide companies through a critical turning point in the field of social responsibility, from rhetoric to action on codes of conduct. The goal of the book is to help companies select, develop and implement social and environmental codes of conduct. One of the first steps a company can take to become more socially responsible is to adopt a code of conduct—but taking this step without clear implementation strategies leaves companies exposed. This book will demonstrate how the world's leading companies are implementing global codes of conduct, including the Global Compact of the United

Nations, the Guidelines for Multinational Enterprises of the Organisation for Economic Co-operation and Development (OECD), SA8000 and AA1000. The codes in this book cover a wide range of issues, including human rights, labour rights, environmental management, corruption and corporate governance. This book also includes 'how-to' (or 'process') codes focusing on reporting, stakeholder engagement and assurance.

Albert Einstein wrote that 'Not everything that counts can be counted; and not everything that can be counted counts.'[1] This sentence provides a useful commentary on codes of conduct and principles and a useful refrain for readers who should question the tools presented in this volume. Do these tools allow an organisation to count and consider what is most relevant in its sector, to its stakeholders? Do the tools count that which does not need to be counted?

The instruments and tools described in this book can be seen as a dialogue between different actors in society. As the book indicates, there have been several waves of dialogue, from the 1970s, in which multinational companies were seen as the enemy to be tamed, to the 1990s where a number of leading companies became far more engaged in a process of dialogue with stakeholders. The codes and principles described in this work have served to institutionalise dialogue and to create fora for discussion among actors who had never been in discussion or between whom there was hostility. It may well be that these dialogues are the most significant contribution of these tools, and yet such contributions cannot be 'counted'.

In this book, I will answer the following questions:

- What distinguishes an outstanding code of conduct from a mediocre code of conduct?

- How can we implement an existing code of conduct?

- What are the pitfalls to avoid in implementing the code of conduct?

- How can we build on work already taking place in this field?

Dr Samuel Johnson once said 'A man may be very sincere in good principles without having good practice' (Boswell 1765: 403); the same is true for companies. At best, codes of conduct and standards can promote corporate responsibility, but they can also be used as a 'fig leaf', as an automatic response to deflect criticism. It is ironic that many of the companies involved in corporate scandals, such as Enron and Royal Ahold, have excellent statements on social policies. If the corporate responsibility movement is to progress, it must shun hollow statements.

This book is based on interviews with the standard-setters, with the implementers of standards, with academics, with activists and with other key stakeholders from around the world. Each of the standards and codes described has been shared with the promulgators of the instrument to ensure that the information is as up to date as possible. To those standards-setters whose standards are not profiled in this

---

1 This quote was featured on the integrityworks website: www.integrityworks.com/about/about.htm, last accessed 3 October 2003.

book, I apologise. It is possible that a second edition of this book will be published with additional codes and standards. I welcome your thoughts on emerging standards that might be useful in such a volume.

Reference

Boswell, J. (1765) *Life of Johnson* (G.B. Hills edn; rev. L.F. Powell; New Haven, CT: Yale University Press [1995]).

Executive summary of corporate responsibility initiatives

The following list provides the web addresses at which the code, principle or standard may be found, the part and chapter in which it is discussed in this book, keywords and a brief description of the code, principle or standard.

AccountAbility 1000 Framework

www.accountability.org.uk

Part 9, 'Implementation', Chapter 24, page 374

Keywords   Social accounting • Ethical accounting • Auditing • Reporting • Stakeholder engagement

AccountAbility 1000 (AA1000) is a framework that defines best practice in social and ethical auditing, accounting and reporting. Stakeholder engagement is an integral aspect of AA1000. Launched in 1999, AA1000 is designed to assist companies, stakeholders, auditors, consultants and standard-setting bodies. AA1000 can be used in two ways: as an independent tool or in conjunction with other corporate responsibility (CR) standards. AA1000 provides a roadmap for companies on key CR issues, explaining points of divergence and convergence with other major standards. The AA1000 Assurance Standard was developed by the Institute for Social and Ethical AccountAbility (AccountAbility), a professional membership organisation committed to promoting accountability as a means to achieving sustainable development.

AA1000 Assurance Standard

www.accountability.org.uk

Part 9, 'Implementation', Chapter 25, page 414

Keywords Assurance • Assurance providers • AccountAbility • Principles • Quality

The AA1000 Assurance Standard includes core assurance principles, practice and quality standards, guidelines for organisations and qualifications for assurance providers. Developed by AccountAbility, the AA1000 Assurance Standard is compatible with the Global Reporting Initiative and SIGMA. The standard is based on continuous improvement.

Business Principles for Countering Bribery

www.cepaa.org/Document%20Center/AntiBribery.htm
www.transparency.org

Part 5, 'Combating corruption', Chapter 18, page 287

Keywords Bribery • Transparency International • Social Accountability International • Multi-stakeholder • Consultation • Non-governmental organisations • Policies • Procedures • Facilitation payments

Published in December 2002, the Business Principles for Countering Bribery were developed through a multi-stakeholder dialogue, including trade unions, companies, non-governmental organisations (NGOs) and academics from many countries. The convenors of the dialogue are Transparency International and Social Accountability International (SAI). Transparency International was founded in 1993 to build coalitions to fight corruption. Companies are encouraged to apply (rather than adopt) the Business Principles by initiating their own internal process of setting policies and procedures within the company through consultation with stakeholders.

CERES Principles

www.ceres.org/our_work/principles.htm

Part 4, 'From environment to sustainability', Chapter 15, page 253

Keywords Multi-stakeholder • Environment • Sustainability • Waste • Energy conservation • Protection of whistle-blowers • Valdez Principles

Founded in 1989, the Coalition for Environmentally Responsible Economies (CERES) is a network of more than 80 environmental, investor and advocacy groups promoting sustainability. CERES is best known for the CERES Principles, a set of ten principles covering the major environmental concerns facing companies, including energy conservation, reduction and disposal of waste, and risk reduction. Companies endorsing the Principles must commit publicly to those Principles, address issues raised by the CERES network and other stakeholders and report annually on their progress in meeting the CERES Principles.

Clean Clothes Campaign: Model Code

www.cleanclothes.org/codes/ccccode.htm

Part 3, 'Labour rights, Chapter 12, page 181

Keywords   Campaign • Multi-stakeholder • Garments • Europe •
Non-governmental organisations • Trade unions

The Clean Clothes Campaign (CCC) is a Europe-wide voluntary network, with affiliated groups in Austria, Belgium, France, Germany, Italy, The Netherlands, Portugal, Spain, Sweden and Switzerland. The aim of the CCC is to improve working conditions in the garment and sportswear industries.

EMAS (Eco-Management and Audit Scheme)

www.europa.eu.int/comm/environment/emas/index_en.htm

Part 4, 'From environment to sustainability', page 209

Keywords   European • Environmental management systems • Training •
Accreditation • Verification • Environmental reports

Developed in 2001 by the European Parliament and the Council of the European Union, EMAS is a voluntary initiative that seeks to promote environmental performance by organisations. A systems-based approach, EMAS requires participating organisations to regularly produce a public report on their environmental performance. These reports are verified by an independent verifier. The goal of EMAS is continuous improvement.

EMAS includes the following management systems: policies, planning, training communication, documentation, emergency preparedness, records, audit and management review.

Ethical Trading Initiative: Base Code

www.ethicaltrade.org/pub/publications/basecode/en/content.shtml

Part 3, 'Labour rights', Chapter 11, page 176

Keywords   Labour rights • Tripartite • Good practice • Development

The Ethical Trading Initiative (ETI) seeks to improve the lives of workers in global supply chains by creating a forum to identify and promote good practice in the implementation of codes of conduct. The initiative is tripartite, consisting of membership groups from three sectors: companies, NGOs and trade unions. The ETI is funded by the UK government's Department for International Development and by its members, who pay dues. In pursuit of its aims, the ETI conducts experimental projects into aspects of code implementation, hosts seminars, events and conferences and has a research and publications programme.

Fair Labor Association: Workplace Code of Conduct

www.fairlabor.org/html/amendctr.html

Part 3, 'Labour rights', Chapter 10, page 168

Keywords Labour rights • Brands • Independent monitoring • Verification

The Fair Labor Association (FLA) is a network of companies, human rights and labour organisations, colleges and universities seeking to improve working conditions. The FLA accredits independent monitors to inspect factories. It works with companies to improve internal monitoring systems. Companies are expected to implement systems to ensure that the FLA Workplace Code of Conduct is upheld throughout their supply chains. The FLA accredits, selects, hires and pays monitors to conduct independent and external monitoring visits in 5% of participating company factories.

Global Compact

www.unglobalcompact.org $\rightarrow$ **'About the GC'**

Part 1, 'Global initiatives', Chapter 4, page 72

Keywords UN Secretary-General • Environment • Human rights • Labour •
UN agencies • Development • Partnerships • Learning network

The UN Global Compact is an initiative of UN Secretary-General, Kofi Annan, 'to give a human face to globalisation' (Annan 1999). Launched in July 2000, the Compact addresses environment, human rights and workers' rights. The Global Compact unites global principles with local networks. The Compact is a global, multi-stakeholder, multi-issue network with more than 40 regional and national sub-networks. As a voluntary initiative, the Global Compact convenes all key social actors: companies, labour, civil-society organisations and governments.

Global Reporting Initiative

www.globalreporting.org/guidelines/2002.asp

Part 9, 'Implementation', Chapter 26, page 425

Keywords Sustainability • Guidelines • Reporting • Social reports • Environment •
Framework • Indicators • Multi-stakeholder

The Global Reporting Initiative (GRI) has pioneered sustainability reporting guidelines that serve as a framework for economic, social and environmental reporting.

The GRI's mission is 'to elevate the quality of reporting to a higher level of comparability, consistency and utility' (GRI 2002: 9). In 1997, CERES, in collaboration with the Tellus Institute, convened the GRI.

Global Sullivan Principles of Corporate Social Responsibility

www.globalsullivanprinciples.org/principles.htm

Part 1, 'Global initiatives', Chapter 3, page 68

Keywords   Reverend Leon Sullivan • US companies • Environment • Supply chain • Human rights • Bribery

In 1999, Reverend Leon Sullivan launched the Global Sullivan Principles (GSP) after consultation with companies and stakeholders, with the aim of encouraging companies to 'support economic, social and political justice wherever they do business'.[1]

ICC Business Charter for Sustainable Development

www.iccwbo.org/home/environment_and_energy/charter.asp

Part 4, 'From environment to sustainability', page 204

Keywords   Integrated management • Education • Research • Prior assessment • Precautionary approach • Transfer of technology • Compliance • Reporting • Emergency preparedness

Launched in 1991, the International Chamber of Commerce (ICC) Business Charter was developed by business leaders. The Charter includes 16 principles which focus on how to make the environment a corporate priority. Among the key issues are: integrated management, education, research, prior assessment, precautionary approach, transfer of technology, compliance, reporting and emergency preparedness.

International Labour Organisation: Tripartite Declaration of Principles concerning Multinational Enterprises and Social Policy

www.ilo.org/public/english/standards/norm/sources/mne.htm

Part 3, 'Labour rights', Chapter 8, page 137

Keywords   Labour rights • Development • Training • International Labour Organisation (ILO) • ILO conventions

Launched in 1977, the Tripartite Declaration of Principles Concerning Multinational Enterprises and Social Policy is directed towards companies, govern-

---

1   Quoted at www.globalsullivanprinciples.org.

ments, trade unions and employers' organisations. The Declaration refers to 28 ILO conventions and 28 recommendations negotiated within a multilateral framework.

ISO 14001

www.iso.ch/iso/en/prods-services/otherpubs/iso14000/index.html

Part 9, 'Implementation', Chapter 27, page 478

Keywords   Environmental management systems • International Organisation for Standardisation (ISO) • Auditors • Certification • Standard

ISO 14001 is the key element in a family of standards for creating environmental management systems (EMSs). An EMS is 'the part of the overall management system that includes organisational structure, planning activities, responsibilities, practices, procedures, processes and resources for developing, implementing, achieving, reviewing and maintaining the environmental policy'.[2]

The International Organisation for Standardisation (ISO) has developed over 13,000 standards, working with standard-setting bodies in 145 countries. As with all ISO standards, companies that have successfully undergone an ISO 14001 audit by a trained auditor receive an ISO 14001 certificate. Elements of the ISO series—particularly ISO 14001—can also be used internally, without external auditors.

Johnson & Johnson Credo

www.jnj.com/our_company/our_credo

Part 7, 'Company codes of conduct', Chapter 21, page 341

Keywords   Customers • Employees • Communities • Environment • Compensation • Stockholders • Suppliers • Distributors

Written in 1943, the Johnson & Johnson Credo contains the key values of the company, including equal opportunity, environmental protection and quality.

The Credo defines the company's stakeholders, including doctors, nurses, patients, mothers, fathers and other customers, as well as employees, communities, stockholders, suppliers and distributors. The Credo has been translated into 36 languages.

2   ISO definitions are available at www.iso14000.com/Implementation/definitions.htm.

Marine Stewardship Council's Principles and Criteria for Sustainable Fishing

www.msc.org/assets/docs/fishery%20certification?MSCprinciples&criteria.doc

Part 8, 'Framework, sectoral and regional agreements', Chapter 23, Section 23.6.3, page 363

Keywords Fisheries • Certification • Logo • Unilever • Sustainable harvesting

Founded in 1997 by Unilever, the Marine Stewardship Council (MSC) became an independent organisation in 1999. The MSC is a multi-stakeholder organisation that promotes environmentally responsible stewardship of the world's most renewable food source. The MSC accredits certifiers to ensure that fish are harvested in a sustainable manner. Facilities that pass the audit receive the MSC certificate and can use the MSC product label on their products.

The Natural Step Principles

www.naturalstep.org/learn/principles.php

Part 4, 'From environment to sustainability', Chapter 16, page 259

Keywords Sustainability • Environment • Human needs • Systems • Redesign • Sweden • Thermodynamics • Vision • Assessment

The Natural Step Principles were developed by scientists and are based on the laws of thermodynamics.[3] The Principles focus on systems, requiring the organisations working with The Natural Step to redefine their relationship to the environment. The Natural Step provides companies with tools for visioning and assessment and with a framework for action.

Norms on the Responsibilities of Transnational Corporations and Other Business Enterprises with Regard to Human Rights

www1.umn.edu/humanrts/links/commentary-Aug2003.html

Part 2, 'Human rights', Chapter 7, page 106

Keywords Human rights • Labour rights • Environment • Development • Anti-bribery • Corruption • Consumer protection

The Norms are very comprehensive, integrating human rights, labour rights, environment, development, anti-bribery issues and consumer protection. The Norms have been developed by the UN Working Group on the Working Methods and Activities of Transnational Corporations, which is part of the Sub-Commission on the Promotion and Protection of Human Rights of the UN Commission on Human Rights. The Sub-Commission adopted the Norms on 13 August 2003, but they still

---

3 For more on the history of The Natural Step, see Robèrt 2002.

need to be put to and endorsed by the 53 nation Human Rights Commission, which meets in early March 2004.

Agreement between the Norwegian Oil and Petrochemical Workers' Union, of the International Federation of Chemical, Energy, Mine and General Workers' Unions, and Statoil

www.icem.org/agreements/statoil/statagren.html

Part 8, 'Framework, sectoral and regional agreements', Chapter 22, Section 22.6, page 351

Keywords   Labour • Human rights • Environment • Trade unions • Global Compact • Global union federation • Petroleum • ILO conventions • Subcontractors

In 1998, Statoil signed an agreement with the Norwegian Oil and Petrochemical Workers' Union (NOPEF) on behalf of the International Federation of Chemical, Energy, Mine and General Workers' Unions (ICEM). The agreement covers labour, human rights and the environment. The goal of the agreement is 'to create an open channel of information between ICEM and Statoil management about industrial relations issues in order to continuously improve and develop good work practice in Statoil's world-wide operations' (Statoil undated). The most significant aspect of the agreement is that it sets a global policy to guide and empower decisions at the local level.

OECD Convention for Combating Bribery of Foreign Officials in International Business Transactions

www.oecd.org/document/21/0,2340,en_2649_34855_2017813_1_1_1_1_,00.html

Part 5, 'Combating corruption', Chapter 17, page 269

Keywords   Bribery • Foreign public officials • Criminalise • Facilitation payments • Functional equivalence

Launched in 1997, the OECD Convention on Combating Bribery is a landmark agreement, defining key terms and developing a legal framework for addressing bribery. The Convention has been ratified by all 30 members of the OECD and by a growing number of non-members as well. The Convention applies to bribery of foreign government officials anywhere, regardless of where the incident takes place.

OECD Guidelines for Multinational Enterprises

www.oecd.org/department/0,2688,en_2649_34889_1_1_1_1_1,00.html

Part 1, 'Global initiatives', Chapter 2, page 52

Keywords   Environment • Technology • Science • Taxation • Labour rights • National Contact Points

The OECD Guidelines for Multinational Enterprises are among the most comprehensive of corporate responsibility (CR) tools, addressing a range of issues unparalleled in any single CR instrument. The Guidelines address science, technology and taxation—issues that are not common denominators among CR tools. Given their comprehensive nature, the Guidelines are useful in setting a context for companies on CR. In a sense, they provide for companies a map of the CR issues they may encounter.

OECD Principles of Corporate Governance

www.oecd.org/document/62/0,2340,en_2649_34795_1912830_1_1_1_1,00.html

Part 6, 'Corporate governance', Chapter 19, page 324

Keywords   Shareholders • Stakeholders • Disclosure • Transparency •
Board of directors • Corporate governance

Endorsed in 1999 by the OECD, the Principles of Corporate Governance represent the first initiative by an intergovernmental organisation to develop guiding principles in the field of corporate governance. The OECD Principles are directed to a wide audience, including governments, companies, investors and business groups.

Responsible Care®

www.icca-chem.org/section02a.html

Part 8, 'Framework, sectoral and regional agreements', Chapter 23, Section 23.6.2, page 362

Keywords   Chemical industry • Policy • Employee involvement • Experience sharing •
Safety • Product stewardship • Resource conservation •
Stakeholder engagement • Management systems • Self-assessment

The chemical industry's voluntary initiative, Responsible Care, was first conceived in Canada in 1985 to address public concern about the manufacture, distribution and use of chemicals. Since 1992, when Agenda 21 was adopted, the number of national chemical industry associations embracing the initiative has grown from 6 to 47. Under Responsible Care, the worldwide chemical industry is committed to continual improvement in all aspects of health, safety and environmental performance and to open communication about its activities and achievements.

Rio Declaration on Environment and Development

www.un.org/documents/ga/conf151/aconf15126-1annex1.htm

Part 4, 'From environment to sustainability', Chapter 14, page 245

Keywords   Sustainable development • Poverty • Sovereignty • Technology transfer •
Compensation • Precautionary principle • Environmental impact assessment •
Women • Youth • Indigenous peoples

In 1992 the Earth Summit (UN Conference on Environment and Development [UNCED]) was held in Rio de Janeiro, where heads of state adopted the Rio Declaration. The Rio Principles enshrined in the declaration define the right of people to development and gives signatories the responsibility to safeguard the environment for future generations.

Shell Business Principles

www.shell.com → **About Shell** → **How We Work** → **Business Principles**

Part 7, 'Company codes of conduct', Chapter 20, page 334

Keywords   Economic principles • Business integrity • Political activities •
Health, safety and environment • Community • Competition • Stakeholders

First published in 1976, but since amended, Shell's Business Principles cover a very wide range of issues, including economic principles, business integrity, political activities, health, safety, environment, community and competition. One of the most significant aspects of the Principles is the section on 'responsibilities', in which Shell identifies its five key stakeholders: shareholders, customers, employees, those with whom they do business and society.

SIGMA: 'Sustainability: Integrated Guidelines for Management'

www.projectsigma.com/guidelines/SIGMAguidelines.pdf

Part 9, 'Implementation', Chapter 28, page 497

Keywords   Sustainability • Guidelines • Management • Integration • Core functions

The 'Sustainability: Integrated Guidelines for Management' (SIGMA) project sets out a framework for companies seeking to become more sustainable. Launched in 1999, the SIGMA project is a partnership between Forum for the Future, Account-Ability and the British Standards Institution (BSI). The SIGMA project contains a set of principles, a framework for mainstreaming sustainability into the core functions of a company, and a toolkit.

Social Accountability 8000

www.sa-intl.org/SA8000/SA8000.htm

Part 3, 'Labour rights', Chapter 9, page 155

Keywords   Labour rights • Accreditation • Certification • Management systems •
Multi-sectoral • Multi-stakeholder

Social Accountability 8000 (SA8000) is a global and verifiable standard designed to make workplaces more humane. The standard combines key elements of the International Labour Organisation (ILO) conventions with the management systems of

ISO. SA8000 is a certification standard developed, overseen and updated through multi-stakeholder dialogue with trade unions, companies, NGOs and academics.

Universal Declaration of Human Rights

www.un.org/Overview/rights.html

Part 2, 'Human rights', Chapter 5, page 85

Keywords   United Nations • Human rights • Foundation standard • Slavery • Freedom of opinion • Freedom of expression

The Universal Declaration of Human Rights (UDHR) is one of the most significant documents ever drafted. It enshrines the concept of human rights broadly, to include not only political rights but also social and economic rights. Universally accepted, the UDHR has formed the basis of many constitutions around the world. Moreover, the UDHR is cited in many of the corporate responsibility codes and principles contained in this book as a foundation standard. Adopted by the UN General Assembly in 1948, the UDHR was unanimously adopted by the then 48 member states of the United Nations.

Voluntary Principles on Security and Human Rights

www.state.gov/www/global/human_rights/001220_fsdrl_principles.html

Part 2, 'Human rights', Chapter 6, page 95

Keywords   Governments • Extractive sector • Private security forces • Non-governmental organisations • Human rights

The Voluntary Principles on Security and Human Rights represent an unprecedented step in the field of corporate responsibility. Convened by the US and UK governments, a consensus was reached by NGOs, companies and a trade union on principles in the difficult area of human rights and security in the extractive sector (i.e. in the mining and petroleum sector). The agreement sets an important precedent for other sectoral discussions. First released in December 2000, the agreement is noteworthy because it was convened by governments and included key stakeholders.

References

Annan, K. (1999) Speech made by the UN Secretary-General, Kofi Annan, at the World Economic Forum in Davos, Switzerland, on 31 January 1999 (www.un.org/News/Press/docs/1999/19990201.sgsm6881.html).

GRI (Global Reporting Initiative) (2002) *Sustainability Reporting Guidelines* (Boston, MA: GRI).

Robèrt, K.-H. (2002) *The Natural Step Story: Seeding a Quiet Revolution* (Gabriola Island, BC, Canada: New Society Publishers).

Statoil (undated) *The Exchange of Information and the Development of Good Working Practice within Statoil Worldwide Operations* (submission to the Global Compact Learning Forum; Stavanger, Norway: Statoil).

1
Values, principles, norms, codes and standards

Corporate social responsibility is a journey, and codes and standards can serve as a map to guide companies towards greater transparency and accountability. Statements of values and principles serve as a magnetic north for companies, orienting companies in times of crisis as well as through times of opportunity.[1] Such tools are not an end in themselves, but a beginning. Creation of a code of conduct without implementation is a dangerous pursuit, raising expectations among company stakeholders, such as consumers, investors, employees and local communities. A statement of values or principles or the creation of a code or standard represents the proverbial line in the sand for a company, a call to action.

In this book, a wide range of voluntary corporate responsibility (CR) instruments are examined, including:

- Principles
- Codes of conduct
- Standards
- Norms
- Guidelines
- Framework agreements

There are many other types of CR instruments, including labelling initiatives, stakeholder dialogue and so on, but in this book we look at documents that guide behaviour.

---

1 I am grateful to Mark Wade, of Shell, for this metaphor, which he credits to the World Business Council for Sustainable Development.

1.1 Definitions

In corporate responsibility, there is a continuum from values, through principles and codes, to standards (see Fig. 1; Box 1.1): it is necessary to delineate values and principles before articulating codes and standards.

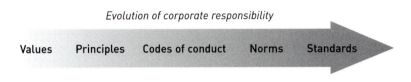

Evolution of corporate responsibility

Values   Principles   Codes of conduct   Norms   Standards

Figure 1.1 The corporate responsibility continuum

- *Value:* 'any object or quality desirable as a means or as an end in itself' (*American College Dictionary* 1970); for example: corporate responsibility values include diversity and honesty

- *Principle:* 'fundamental truth or law as the basis of reasoning or action; a personal code of conduct' (*Concise Oxford Dictionary* 1995).

- *Code of conduct:* 'a set of rules' (*Concise Oxford Dictionary* 1995) or a 'formal statement of the values and business practices of a corporation. A code may be a short mission statement, or it may be a sophisticated document that requires compliance with articulated standards and have a complicated enforcement mechanism' (www.codesofconduct.org).

- *Norm:* 'model or pattern' (*American College Dictionary* 1970); norms tend to be internationally agreed.

- *Standard:* 'an authoritative model or measure, a pattern for guidance, by comparison with which the quality, excellence, correctness, etc. of other things [e.g. the corporate responsibility of a company] may be determined' (*American College Dictionary* 1970); or 'a set of principles, code of conduct or process system established by a third party whereby adoption of that standard leads to a prescribed level of performance being achieved' (Smith 2002: 21).

Box 1.1 The corporate responsibility continuum: definitions

Codes and standards differ in several ways. A code of conduct is specific to a firm or industry, whereas a standard is applicable across a wide range of sectors and geographic regions. Another major difference is the degree to which monitoring, auditing and reporting occur in companies adhering to codes and in those adopting standards. A code of conduct is generally subject only to internal scrutiny by the company, whereas companies adhering to standards are accountable to a broader constituency. According to Shareen Hertel of Columbia University, who has studied workers' rights in Mexico and Bangladesh, 'with standards, governments, firms and civil society can institutionalise the standard, as it is amenable to varying governance and implementation frameworks'.[2] A standard generally includes some form of consensus forged among different stakeholders. In this analysis, codes and standards are voluntary (for a comparison of codes and standards, see Table 1.1).

Code of conduct	*Standard*
Internal or firm-specific	Applied broadly, across geographic regions and/or sectors
Entails limited accountability	Entails greater accountability (i.e. in terms of reporting and scrutiny)
Requires internal consensus and possibly some external consultation	Requires some degree of consensus among stakeholders, and, therefore, is more accountable

Table 1.1 A comparison of codes of conduct and standards

Although the term 'standard' is used frequently in the field of corporate responsibility, a better term might be 'norm'. In its technical definition, the term 'standard' implies that companies can and should achieve a uniform output. For example, there are standards that specify the gauge for train tracks to ensure uniformity. Given the significant differences between companies, arising from sectoral, regional, cultural and historical differences, it is unlikely that standardisation is possible or even desirable. According to Gemma Crijns of Nyenrode University, the majority of the so-called CR standards are, in fact, a series of norms.[3] The ability of norms to catalyse and encourage different approaches among companies is a theme of this book and a challenge for the field of corporate responsibility.

1.2 Categories of codes and standards

Given that the definitions of codes and standards are often vague and blurred, one of the best ways to define codes is to categorise them (see Fig. 1.2). It is important to note that, throughout this book, codes and standards may fall into more than

2 Interview with Shareen Hertel, Columbia University, New York, 8 January 2003.
3 Gemma Crijns, Nyenrode University, Breukelen, The Netherlands, communication with the author, 2003.

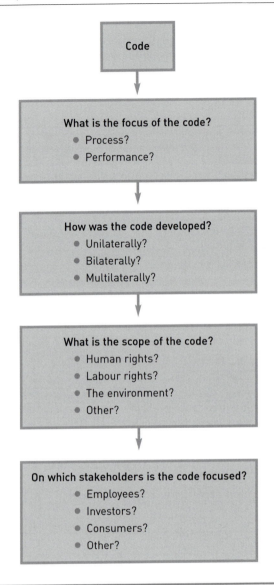

Figure 1.2 Classification of codes

one category, given their complexity and cross-cutting nature. Codes and standards can be distinguished by:

- Their focus or purpose (i.e. whether they are focused on process and/or performance)

- The way in which they were developed (i.e. unilaterally, bilaterally or multilaterally)

- Their scope (i.e. whether they cover human rights, labour and/or environment)

- Their stakeholder focus (i.e. whether they are focused on employees, investors, consumers and so on, or whether they are multi-stakeholder tools)

These different types of category are important in comparing codes and standards, in gaining an understanding of how codes complement one another and in determining which may be considered as competitive.

1.2.1 Classification by focus

CR codes and standards can be divided into two key categories—those that focus on performance (or outcome) and those that focus on process (or method) (see Fig. 1.3):

- **Performance-oriented codes** define minimum standards of what constitutes socially responsible behaviour. For example, companies should prohibit child labour and discrimination. Among the key performance instruments are the OECD Guidelines for Multinational Enterprises (also a foundation standard) and the Global Compact. These tools relate to the focus of corporate responsibility and the desired outcomes that companies are working towards.

- **Process-oriented standards and guidelines** define the procedures a company should follow, such as social reporting and stakeholder consultation. Among the key examples of process-oriented tools are the Global Reporting Initiative (GRI), the AccountAbility 1000 series (AA1000) and ISO 14001. These instruments relate to the 'how' of corporate social responsibility.

However, it is important to note that these categories are not mutually exclusive. Some standards, such as Social Accountability (SA8000), may include both process and performance requirements (see the area of overlap between the two circles in Fig. 1.3).

Among the process-oriented and performance-oriented, some standards may be regarded as being foundation and/or certification standards:

- **Foundation standards** lay the groundwork for a new field, defining best practice in an emerging area. The various ILO conventions and the OECD

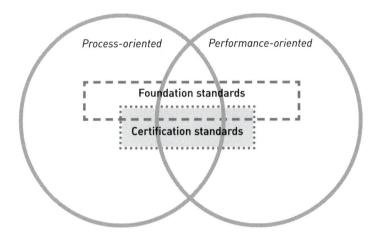

Figure 1.3 Classification of codes, standards and guidelines according to focus

Guidelines for Multinational Enterprises are examples of foundation standards.

● **Certification standards** are systems that award a certificate to organisations that comply with certain criteria and that pass an external and independent audit. SA8000 and ISO 14001 are examples of certification standards.

In this book, the discussions of codes and standards will utilise this terminology.

1.2.2 **Classification by method of development**

As illustrated in Figure 1.2, codes, standards and guidelines may be classified according to the way in which they have been crafted:

● **Unilateral codes** are developed by a company. Usually, there is some level of dialogue with key stakeholders, but the company has ultimate responsibility for the code. These 'branded' codes include Nike's Code of Conduct[4] and the Shell Business Principles (Chapter 20).

● **Bilateral codes** are signed between two parties. A framework agreement between a trade union and a company is an example of a bilateral code.

4 www.nike.com/nikebiz/nikebiz.jhtml?page=25&cat=compliance&subcat=code

The Ikea Framework Agreement[5] and the Statoil Framework Agreement (Chapter 22, Section 22.6) are examples.

- **Multilateral or multi-stakeholder codes** are developed by a network of organisations through extensive negotiations. Examples are SA8000 and the Ethical Trading Initiative Base Code.

With regard to multilateral codes, according to the World Bank (2003: 12):

> Multi-stakeholder initiatives are efforts that bring diverse stake-holders together around a set of agreed principles in the area of labour, human rights or the environment. These initiatives vary in their mission, some focusing on shared learning around best practice and others with more focused monitoring or certification programmes.

1.2.3 Classification by scope

Corporate responsibility includes a very wide range of issues; however, most CR initiatives address only a portion of them. The following provides a listing of some of the key issues in CR, with a sample of the tools that address them:

Corporate governance

- OECD Principles of Corporate Governance

Combating bribery

- OECD Convention on Countering Bribery
- Business Principles for Countering Bribery

Environment

- CERES Principles
- The Natural Step

Labour

- ILO Tripartite Declaration of Principles Concerning Multinational Enterprises and Social Policy
- Social Accountability 8000

Human rights

- Universal Declaration of Human Rights

---

5 www.icem.org

1.2.4 Classification by stakeholder focus

Different standards and codes are targeted at different groups of stakeholders. Most of the initiatives addressed in this book focus on employees and suppliers. However, companies can choose to apply a code or norm among one group of stakeholders but not others. For example, a company may implement a code of conduct in its supply chain but not in its own facilities

The following is a partial listing of the diversity of stakeholders referenced within the key tools presented within this book:

Employees

- SA8000

- Shell's Business Principles

- Johnson & Johnson Credo

Suppliers

- SA8000

- Workplace Code of Conduct of the Fair Labor Association

- Base Code of the Ethical Trading Initiative

- Model Code of the Clean Clothes Campaign

Customers

- Shell's Business Principles

- SIGMA

Trade unions

- SA8000

- Agreement between NOPEF/ICEM and Statoil

- Workplace Code of Conduct of the Fair Labor Association

- Base Code of the Ethical Trading Initiative

- Model Code of the Clean Clothes Campaign

Governments

- OECD Convention on Countering Bribery

- Business Principles for Countering Bribery

Society/community

- SIGMA

- Shell's Business Principles

Shareholders

- Shell's Business Principles

1.2.5 Classification by sector

Different sectors face different types of issues, constraints and pressure from stake-holders. As a result, many industries are developing sectoral initiatives; for example, the Voluntary Principles on Security and Human Rights were developed by the extractive sector in a multi-stakeholder setting (see Chapter 6). Responsible Care® addresses the CR issues within the chemical industry (see Chapter 23, Section 23.6.2).

1.2.6 Classification by region

There are some CR tools developed for and within a regional context. One example is the Asia–Pacific Economic Co-operation Code of Business Conduct (see Chapter 23, Section 23.7.1). While these initiatives can be useful in galvanising support from a region, global tools, because of their universality, tend to be more useful in a globalised world.

1.3 How can codes of conduct help companies?

Codes and guidelines can serve different goals, in the short, medium and long term. In the short term, codes can assist with crisis management; in the medium term, codes can prevent a crisis; in the long term, a code that is effectively implemented can enhance stakeholder (including shareholder) value, promote trust, enhance business performance and help to forestall crises.[6]

An effective code of conduct or standard can:

- Raise awareness about corporate responsibility within the company

- Help companies to set strategies and objectives

- Assist companies with implementation and control of values

- Help companies avoid risk

- Foster dialogue and partnerships between companies and key stake-holders

- Enhance unity and identity among divergent companies

6 Interview with Shareen Hertel, Columbia University, New York, 8 January 2003.

1.3.1 Raising awareness of corporate responsibility

A code of conduct can raise consciousness about corporate responsibility within a company, serving as an important signal to employees, investors and consumers.[7] Codes are essential for communicating consistently with employees, in that codes clarify expectations,[8] especially on bribery and corruption issues. According to John Elkington, founder of SustainAbility, codes can make organisations 'pay attention and think. They can legitimise new demands that would otherwise be dismissed, and help codify and simplify complex issues whose very complexity is an alibi for inaction'.[9]

Most companies use their websites to communicate their values, principles and codes. Like an outstanding CR policy, a well-implemented code of conduct can serve to differentiate a company in a crowded marketplace.

1.3.2 Setting strategies and objectives

A code of conduct or standard can assist a company in managing change in a highly complex business environment. Companies such as Aviva[10] and Morley Fund Management[11] in the United Kingdom are looking to their business principles to guide them in creating social and environmental goals and objectives.

1.3.3 Assisting with implementation and control

Codes of conduct and standards oriented towards process contain useful guides for implementing and controlling social and environmental standards. SA8000 provides useful management systems which are helpful in implementing codes and social standards, including 'training programmes, communications, elected representatives, management representatives with adequate budgets, clear lines of authority, management reviews, control of suppliers, and planning as well as policies, procedures, forms, checklists for recording compliance with each portion of the standard. By integrating SA8000 into these systems, SA8000 becomes part of the culture of the company' (Leipziger 2001: 59). Among the process tools discussed in this book are: AA1000, the Global Reporting Initiative, ISO 14001 and SIGMA.

1.3.4 Avoiding risk

Codes can assist a company in limiting its risk of being caught in a scandal, but only if the code is well implemented. An code that is no more than ornamental can actually increase risk. In the words of Geoffrey Chandler, formerly with Shell and Amnesty International's Business Group:

7   Part 9 provides more information on effective tools for raising awareness.
8   Interview with Hilary Sutcliffe, Director of Shared View Social Responsibility, 17 January 2003
9   Interview with John Elkington, SustainAbility, 2 February 2003.
10 www.aviva.com/responsibility/index.htm
11 www.morleyfm.com/sri_frameset.htm

Genuine codes, genuinely implemented, reduce risk in today's critical world. A code that is no more than a public relations front increases risk because its fraudulence will readily be exposed. Companies complain that when they proclaim what they are trying to do in terms of principles they are more vigorously scrutinised to see if they live up to them. Well that's life. If they don't want scrutiny, try hiding and see what that leads to. If their actions stand up to scrutiny they will gain greatly in terms of reputation.[12]

1.3.5 Fostering dialogue and partnerships with key stakeholders

One of the most valuable aspects of developing a code of conduct concerns the dialogue and consultations with trade unions, non-governmental organisations (NGOs) and employees that may occur in such a process. Opening up the channels of communication is a valuable by-product of code development. This type of sustained dialogue between a company and its stakeholders is essential for developing trust. According to Shareen Hertel, 'a code can assist a company in building an invaluable reservoir of goodwill'.[13]

1.3.6 Enhancing unity and identity among divergent companies

In a global world, principles and values can contribute to a company's brand and corporate culture. For example, Nokia states that:

> the values and principles incorporated into the Nokia Way are at the very heart of our distinctive culture—and they unite our whole company, across the world (www.nokia.com).

The Nokia Values include customer satisfaction, respect for the individual, achievement and continuous learning.

For multinational companies with global operations, the setting of values, principles and codes can be a mechanism for building a common, shared, sense of identity within the company.

Holcim, one of the world's largest cement companies, has operations in over 70 countries. Holcim management viewed the development of a code of conduct to implement its CR policy as an opportunity to build bridges between its far-flung operations at a time when the company was re-branding from Holderbank to Holcim (www.holcim.com).

12   Interview with Geoffrey Chandler, 8 January 2003.
13   Interview with Shareen Hertel, Columbia University, New York, 8 January 2003.

1.4 The DNA of an outstanding code of conduct or standard

An outstanding code of conduct or standard has several characteristics:

- It is clear and concise, not complex.
- It is flexible and dynamic.
- It must be written with implementation in mind.
- It should reference key standards.
- It should elicit strong support from stakeholders.
- It should contain mechanisms for addressing complaints and resolving disputes.
- It should be based on a genuine desire to change.

1.4.1 Clarity and conciseness

An outstanding code does not seek to do too much. Clear and concise, it provides definitions for key terms. Clarity is one of the key variables, as the people tasked with implementing the code in a factory itself may not have a formal education. Clarity is essential for successful implementation of a code, as people will often see what they want to see in it. (This is also why companies need to invest in high-quality translations of codes into local languages, as is the case with Shell's Business Principles, which are now available in 51 languages, covering the first languages of 99% of its employees.[14])

1.4.2 Flexibility and dynamism

CR instruments need to be flexible and responsive. Thus, it is important not only that there be revisions to codes and standards but that the revisions do not occur too frequently. An outstanding code will promote innovation and 'breakthrough approaches'[15] in the workplace, and, as such, it too must be open to change. Flexibility need not be interpreted only in terms of changes to the standard itself; sometimes, highlighting issues in training or in guidance materials is a useful substitute to altering the standard (for more on training, see Part 9).

14   Personal communication with Mark Wade, Shell.
15   I am indebted to John Elkington for this useful phrase.

1.4.3 Written with implementation in mind

A standard should define a clear process for achieving compliance and for demonstrating how this compliance is to be achieved.[16] Standard-setters need to develop clear guidance material for people implementing standards. Likewise, a company that sets a code of conduct for its suppliers should also provide guidance and training on implementation. When it comes to standards, 'the devil is in the details'.

1.4.4 Reference to key standards

A code of conduct or standard should benefit from the experience of other standards, including normative standards such as the Universal Declaration of Human Rights and specific conventions of the International Labour Organisation. Standards do not occur in a vacuum.

1.4.5 Stakeholder support

Stakeholders need to be involved in the development of the code. Stakeholder participation is necessary not only to make the code or standard more legitimate but also to enhance its implementation. Stakeholders need to feel a sense of ownership of the code and its success.

According to Jane Nelson of the International Business Leaders' Forum, a strong code or standard must involve the private sector in its development.[17]

1.4.6 Complaints and dispute resolution

Disputes will arise in most CR systems, given different cultures and different interpretations of CR instruments. The existence of disputes may be an indicator that the system is in fact being taken seriously by stakeholders. Complaints may constitute important feedback for the system and can signal a need to address issues differently. However, few standards and codes contain formal, written procedures for addressing complaints or for resolving disputes.

An effective system for handling problems can avoid negative publicity, which can seriously threaten an emerging standard.

1.4.7 Desire to change

An outstanding code or standard is not enough in itself to make a difference. The key variable for a successful implementation process is the desire of the company to change. According to human rights expert Rory Sullivan:

16   Interview with Deborah Smith, EQ Management Ltd, Shoreham Beach, West Sussex, UK, 14 January 2003.
17   Interview with Jane Nelson, International Business Leaders' Forum, London, 11 April 2003.

It is not the code itself that determines success. The key variable is the commitment of the company to change. If the company wants to be leading-edge a code can help it to achieve leading-edge results. If a company is just adopting a code in order to quell the concerns of the press or a pressure group, then the results will be mediocre.[18]

1.5 Bringing a code of conduct or guidelines to life

To bring a code of conduct to life there is a need to:

- Train to raise awareness

- Gain strong support at a senior level

- Provide text in appropriate translations

- Provide incentives to implement the code or guidelines

1.5.1 Training to raise awareness

Training is necessary at all levels in implementing a code or guidelines. Workers, managers, auditors and suppliers will all benefit from training. Training creates a supporting scaffold for change.

1.5.2 Strong support from senior leadership

In order to succeed, codes and principles must have the support of the chief executive officer (CEO) and/or the board of directors. CR initiatives that emerge from external or public relations are of questionable value. Because of this, Responsible Care and the Global Compact require a letter of personal commitment from the CEO.

1.5.3 Translation of text

In order to be effective, codes need to be accessible to stakeholders. Companies, standard-setters and governments need to invest in translating codes and standards into key languages. In some cases, workers may be illiterate. Some companies, such as Chiquita, have developed easy-to-understand versions of their codes, with cartoon drawings that explain issues to workers with little formal education.[19]

---

18 Interview with Rory Sullivan, Director of Investor Responsibility, Insight Investment (Member of the Amnesty International Business Group, United Kingdom), London, 21 January 2003.

19 www.chiquita.com/chiquita/nitro.asp?category=corpres&subcategory=values&file=CRvaluesmenu.asp

1.5.4 Incentives

Incentives are critical. Incentives to embed CR policies include factoring CR goals into a manager's performance evaluation and use of CR performance as a criteria for bonuses and wage rises. These types of incentives send a powerful signal that the company is changing.

1.6 Guidelines for reviewing corporate responsibility tools

The following chapters of this book contain the text of 32 CR instruments. In analysing these codes and standards, there are several factors to consider:

- The origins
- The date
- The focus
- The signatories

1.6.1 The origins

The nature of the organisation (or organisations) that developed or launched the code is a very important consideration. Foremost among these considerations is the type of organisation. For example, an employers' organisation will have to satisfy a wide range of companies, which can result in a watered-down code that meets the lowest common denominator. Yet such standards developed through a multi-stakeholder process will demonstrate that consensus has been reached.

1.6.2 The date

There are several waves of codes. Codes and standards dating from the 1970s were developed at a time when multinational corporations were 'under fire', in part for their activities in countries such as Chile and South Africa. The OECD Guidelines and the ILO Tripartite Declaration were greatly influenced by the era in which they were developed.

1.6.3 The focus

We need to look at who is at the centre of the code. Employees? Customers? Investors? Stakeholders in general? The driving forces behind the code are very important factors in understanding the DNA of a code.

1.6.4 Signatories

Here, we need to look at whether the standard has reached a critical mass and what the signatories reveal about the standard. For example, are all of the signatories located in certain regions or specific sectors? Are the companies at risk in some way?

*   *   *

In the following chapters, readers will encounter 32 sets of principles, codes, standards, norms and other initiatives. While they are all different, they represent important markers on the journey to make companies responsible.

References

American College Dictionary (1970) *The American College Dictionary* (New York: Random House).

Concise Oxford Dictionary (1995) *The Concise Oxford Dictionary* (Oxford, UK: Clarendon Press, 9th edn).

Leipziger, D. (2001) *SA8000: The Definitive Guide to the New Social Standard* (London: FT).

Smith, D. (2002) *Demonstrating Corporate Values: Which Standard for your Company?* (London: Institute of Business Ethics).

World Bank (2003) *Terms of Reference: Study of Options for Strengthening CSR Implementation among Suppliers in Global Supply Chains* (Washington, DC: World Bank Group, 25 March 2003).

Part 1
Global initiatives

This part covers global principles that are being adopted around the world and that address a wide range of issues. These principles serve as a useful framework for companies on some of the major issues within the field of corporate responsibility.

The major global initiatives examined in this part are, in the order in which they were launched:

- OECD Guidelines for Multinational Enterprises

- Global Sullivan Principles

- UN Global Compact

The Millennium Development Goals are also included at the end of Chapter 4 as a reference to the UN Global Compact.

A number of other initiatives have developed a global following, including the AccountAbility 1000 framework (AA1000), Social Accountability 8000 (SA8000), ISO 14001, the Global Reporting Initiative (GRI) and others. These initiatives will be addressed in subsequent parts of the book, either by issue area or by focus (SA8000 can be found in Chapter 9, in Part 3, on labour rights; AA1000, the GRI, and ISO 14001 can be found in Chapters 24, 26 and 27, respectively, in Part 9, on process standards [implementation]).

2
The OECD Guidelines for Multinational Enterprises

This is the value added of the Guidelines for all: for enterprises as a useful point of reference, for stakeholders as a high quality vehicle for dialogue, and for developing countries as a partnership and co-operation-building instrument.

Corrine Dreyfus, European Commission[1]

The basic approach of the Guidelines is that internationally agreed guidelines can help to prevent misunderstandings and build an atmosphere of confidence and predictability between business, labour, and governments.

OECD[2]

Type   Foundation and performance standard

Strength   Comprehensiveness

Keywords   Environment • Technology • Science • Taxation • Labour rights • National contact points

2.1 Background

The OECD Guidelines for Multinational Enterprises (hereinafter referred to as the Guidelines), part of the OECD Declaration on International Investment and Multinational Enterprises (OECD 2000), feature recommendations from governments to

1   Dreyfus 2001: 120.
2   OECD 2002.

companies. Unique among corporate responsibility (CR) tools in its comprehensive nature, the set of Guidelines addresses all aspects of corporate behaviour, from taxation and competition to consumer interests and science and technology. The Guidelines are voluntary and non-binding.

To understand the objectives of the Guidelines, it is necessary to review the role of the OECD. The Organisation for Economic Co-operation and Development (OECD) promotes policies that contribute to economic growth and development. Founded in 1961, the OECD is a membership organisation for governments from 30 countries.[3] The OECD has made a significant contribution to corporate social responsibility by developing several CR-related principles, including the OECD Principles of Corporate Governance (see Part 6, Chapter 19) and the OECD Convention on Combating Bribery of Foreign Public Officials in International Business Transactions (see Part 5, Chapter 17).

The objectives of the Guidelines are (see page 57):

1. To ensure that the operations of these enterprises are in harmony with government policies

2. To strengthen the basis of mutual confidence between enterprises and the societies in which they operate

3. To help improve the foreign investment climate

4. To enhance the contribution to sustainable development made by multinational enterprises

The Guidelines were adopted in 1976; as such they are part of the first wave of CR tools. Since then, the Guidelines have been revised to include sustainable development issues and the core labour standards. The Guidelines provide an important foundation for many codes and standards.

2.2 Strengths and weaknesses

The Guidelines are among the most comprehensive of CR tools, addressing a range of issues unparalleled in any single CR instrument. The Guidelines address science, technology and taxation—issues that are not common denominators among CR tools. Given their comprehensive nature, the Guidelines are useful in setting a context on CR for companies. In a sense, the Guidelines are a map for companies of the CR issues they may encounter.

---

3   The member countries are, in alphabetical order: Australia, Austria, Belgium, Canada, the Czech Republic, Denmark, Finland, France, Germany, Greece, Hungary, Iceland, Republic of Ireland, Italy, Japan, Korea, Luxembourg, Mexico, The Netherlands, New Zealand, Norway, Poland, Portugal, the Slovak Republic, Spain, Sweden, Switzerland, Turkey, the United Kingdom, and the USA. The European Commission also takes part in the work of the OECD. In addition, Argentina, Brazil and Chile have declared their commitment to the Guidelines but are not OECD members.

The Guidelines encourage companies to 'observe standards of employment and industrial relations not less favourable than those observed by comparable employers in the host country' (see page 63). In many regions, observance of local norms would be insufficient to meet basic standards set by the International Labour Organisation (ILO). The ILO participated in the negotiations and views the Guidelines as being compatible with its own conventions and declarations. The words 'not less favourable' mean that companies are asked to observe the other recommendations on human rights, core labour standards and supply chain codes.

The OECD requires each member state to appoint a National Contact Point (NCP) to promote the Guidelines. The NCP also addresses issues that may arise from the Guidelines, by assessing the problem and assisting the parties to reach an agreement through mediation. The Committee on International Investment and Multinational Enterprises (CIME) reviews the reports of the NCPs.

The institutional capacity of the CIME and the NCPs enhances the potential of the Guidelines to be used effectively. For example, when a major multinational corporation abruptly announced its decision to close its French operations, the French trade union contacted the NCP. According to Corrine Dreyfus of the European Commission,

> The architecture of this follow-up mechanism [NCPs] is unique, especially inasmuch as it involves the public authorities stepping in to promote dialogue and to help find solutions. This architecture is embedded in the commitment of adhering countries (Dreyfus 2001: 120).

Although the NCPs provide local infrastructure to the Guidelines, Anne-Christine Habbard of the International Federation for Human Rights (FIDH) states that the FIDH in France is disappointed in the NCPs' enforcement of the Guidelines (Habbard 2001: 101).

2.3 Companies to which the Guidelines for Multinational Enterprises apply

The Guidelines are a useful starting point and checklist for all companies, but they are especially so for multinational corporations. However, as the Guidelines do not contain management systems, it is best they be used in conjunction with process standards.

2.4 Questions posed and answered

The Guidelines answer the following questions:

● How can multinational corporations operate in harmony with local practice?

● Which common principles for corporate behaviour of multinational corporations will promote sustainable economic growth?

2.5 The promise and the challenge

The revisions to the Guidelines in 2000 re-energised the CIME and the NCPs, making the Guidelines more relevant than ever. However, a great deal of work still needs to be done to make the Guidelines better known. The Polish NCP stated that:

> despite many efforts aimed at making the Guidelines better known by the parties concerned, they are still not widely recognised in Poland as an effective instrument for assuring the appropriate standards of business conduct (quoted in OECD 2001: 17).

In the same OECD report (OECD 2001: 17) it was concluded that 'the same observation would probably be valid for many other adhering countries as well'. In the 'Summary Report of the Chair of the Meeting on the Activities of the NCPs' in the 2002 Annual Report on the Guidelines (OECD 2002) it is suggested that the visibility of the instrument is growing but that much remains to be done to ensure that the Guidelines reach their full potential as a vital tool for the international community and for host societies.

There are signs that more OECD member states are using the Guidelines in new ways. Although it is common for member states to inform investors about the Guidelines, the Dutch government is the first to require companies seeking export credits to take notice of the Guidelines. Also, the French organisation in charge of managing export credits and investment guarantees (COFACE [Compagnie Française pour l'Assurance du Commerce Extérieur] asks companies to sign a letter acknowledging that they are aware of the Guidelines.

References

Dreyfus, C. (2001) 'Enhancing the Contribution of the OECD Guidelines for Multinational Enterprises: Lessons to be Learned', in *OECD Annual Report 2001* (Paris: OECD): 120.

Habbard, A.C. (2001) 'The Integration of Human Rights in Corporate Principles: OECD Guidelines for Multinational Enterprises: Global Instruments for Corporate Responsibility', in *OECD Annual Report 2001* (Paris: OECD): 101.

OECD (Organisation for Economic Co-operation and Development) (2000) *OECD Declaration on International Investment and Multinational Enterprises* (Paris: OECD, 27 June 2000).

—— (2001) 'OECD Guidelines for Multinational Enterprises: Global Instruments for Corporate Responsibility', in *OECD Annual Report 2001* (Paris: OECD): 17.

—— (2002) *OECD Guidelines for Multinational Enterprises: Global Instruments for Corporate Responsibility* (Paris: OECD).

Additional resources

Further reading

OECD (Organisation for Economic Co-operation and Development) (2000) *The OECD Guidelines for Multinational Enterprises: Meeting of the OECD Council at Ministerial Level* (Paris: OECD).

Website

OECD (Organisation for Economic Co-operation and Development): www.oecd.org.

Note: Many National Contact Points have developed handbooks for implementation of the Guidelines. These range from simple to very in-depth guides. For a list of National Contact Points, go to the OECD website.

The OECD Guidelines for Multinational Enterprises*

PART I: THE OECD GUIDELINES FOR MULTINATIONAL ENTERPRISES

Preface

1. The OECD *Guidelines for Multinational Enterprises* (the *Guidelines*) are recommendations addressed by governments to multinational enterprises. They provide voluntary principles and standards for responsible business conduct consistent with applicable laws. The *Guidelines* aim to ensure that the operations of these enterprises are in harmony with government policies, to strengthen the basis of mutual confidence between enterprises and the societies in which they operate, to help improve the foreign investment climate and to enhance the contribution to sustainable development made by multinational enterprises. The *Guidelines* are part of the OECD *Declaration on International Investment and Multinational Enterprises* the other elements of which relate to national treatment, conflicting requirements on enterprises, and international investment incentives and disincentives.

2. International business has experienced far-reaching structural change and the *Guidelines* themselves have evolved to reflect these changes. With the rise of service and knowledge-intensive industries, service and technology enterprises have entered the international marketplace. Large enterprises still account for a major share of international investment, and there is a trend toward large-scale international mergers. At the same time, foreign investment by small- and medium-sized enterprises has also increased and these enterprises now play a significant role on the international scene. Multinational enterprises, like their domestic counterparts, have evolved to encompass a broader range of business arrangements and organisational forms. Strategic alliances and closer relations with suppliers and contractors tend to blur the boundaries of the enterprise.

3. The rapid evolution in the structure of multinational enterprises is also reflected in their operations in the developing world, where foreign direct investment has grown rapidly. In developing countries, multinational enterprises have diversified

---

*   The Preface and the ten guidelines reprinted with permission from *The OECD Guidelines for Multinational Enterprises*, © OECD 1994.

beyond primary production and extractive industries into manufacturing, assembly, domestic market development and services.

4. The activities of multinational enterprises, through international trade and investment, have strengthened and deepened the ties that join OECD economies to each other and to the rest of the world. These activities bring substantial benefits to home and host countries. These benefits accrue when multinational enterprises supply the products and services that consumers want to buy at competitive prices and when they provide fair returns to suppliers of capital. Their trade and investment activities contribute to the efficient use of capital, technology and human and natural resources. They facilitate the transfer of technology among the regions of the world and the development of technologies that reflect local conditions. Through both formal training and on-the-job learning enterprises also promote the development of human capital in host countries.

5. The nature, scope and speed of economic changes have presented new strategic challenges for enterprises and their stakeholders. Multinational enterprises have the opportunity to implement best practice policies for sustainable development that seek to ensure coherence between social, economic and environmental objectives. The ability of multinational enterprises to promote sustainable development is greatly enhanced when trade and investment are conducted in a context of open, competitive and appropriately regulated markets.

6. Many multinational enterprises have demonstrated that respect for high standards of business conduct can enhance growth. Today's competitive forces are intense and multinational enterprises face a variety of legal, social and regulatory settings. In this context, some enterprises may be tempted to neglect appropriate standards and principles of conduct in an attempt to gain undue competitive advantage. Such practices by the few may call into question the reputation of the many and may give rise to public concerns.

7. Many enterprises have responded to these public concerns by developing internal programmes, guidance and management systems that underpin their commitment to good corporate citizenship, good practices and good business and employee conduct. Some of them have called upon consulting, auditing and certification services, contributing to the accumulation of expertise in these areas. These efforts have also promoted social dialogue on what constitutes good business conduct. The *Guidelines* clarify the shared expectations for business conduct of the governments adhering to them and provide a point of reference for enterprises. Thus, the *Guidelines* both complement and reinforce private efforts to define and implement responsible business conduct.

8. Governments are co-operating with each other and with other actors to strengthen the international legal and policy framework in which business is conducted. The post-war period has seen the development of this framework, starting with the adoption in 1948 of the Universal Declaration of Human Rights. Recent instruments include the ILO Declaration on Fundamental Principles and Rights at Work, the Rio Declaration on Environment and Development and Agenda 21 and the Copenhagen Declaration for Social Development.

9. The OECD has also been contributing to the international policy framework. Recent developments include the adoption of the Convention on Combating Bribery of Foreign Public Officials in International Business Transactions and of the OECD Principles of Corporate Governance, the OECD Guidelines for Consumer Protection in the Context of Electronic Commerce, and ongoing work on the OECD Guidelines on Transfer Pricing for Multinational Enterprises and Tax Administrations.

10. The common aim of the governments adhering to the *Guidelines* is to encourage the positive contributions that multinational enterprises can make to economic, environmental and social progress and to minimise the difficulties to which their various operations may give rise. In working towards this goal, governments find themselves in partnership with the many businesses, trade unions and other non-governmental organisations that are working in their own ways toward the same end. Governments can help by providing effective domestic policy frameworks that include stable macroeconomic policy, non-discriminatory treatment of firms, appropriate regulation and prudential supervision, an impartial system of courts and law enforcement and efficient and honest public administration. Governments can also help by maintaining and promoting appropriate standards and policies in support of sustainable development and by engaging in ongoing reforms to ensure that public sector activity is efficient and effective. Governments adhering to the *Guidelines* are committed to continual improvement of both domestic and international policies with a view to improving the welfare and living standards of all people.

I. Concepts and Principles

1. The *Guidelines* are recommendations jointly addressed by governments to multinational enterprises. They provide principles and standards of good practice consistent with applicable laws. Observance of the *Guidelines* by enterprises is voluntary and not legally enforceable.

2. Since the operations of multinational enterprises extend throughout the world, international co-operation in this field should extend to all countries. Governments adhering to the *Guidelines* encourage the enterprises operating on their territories to observe the *Guidelines* wherever they operate, while taking into account the particular circumstances of each host country.

3. A precise definition of multinational enterprises is not required for the purposes of the *Guidelines*. These usually comprise companies or other entities established in more than one country and so linked that they may co-ordinate their operations in various ways. While one or more of these entities may be able to exercise a significant influence over the activities of others, their degree of autonomy within the enterprise may vary widely from one multinational enterprise to another. Ownership may be private, state or mixed. The *Guidelines* are addressed to all the entities within the multinational enterprise (parent companies and/or local entities). According to the actual distribution of responsibilities among them, the different entities are expected to co-operate and to assist one another to facilitate observance of the *Guidelines*.

4. The *Guidelines* are not aimed at introducing differences of treatment between multinational and domestic enterprises; they reflect good practice for all. Accordingly, multinational and domestic enterprises are subject to the same expectations in respect of their conduct wherever the *Guidelines* are relevant to both.

5. Governments wish to encourage the widest possible observance of the *Guidelines*. While it is acknowledged that small- and medium-sized enterprises may not have the same capacities as larger enterprises, governments adhering to the *Guidelines* nevertheless encourage them to observe the *Guidelines* recommendations to the fullest extent possible.

6. Governments adhering to the *Guidelines* should not use them for protectionist purposes nor use them in a way that calls into question the comparative advantage of any country where multinational enterprises invest.

7. Governments have the right to prescribe the conditions under which multinational enterprises operate within their jurisdictions, subject to international law. The entities of a multinational enterprise located in various countries are subject to the laws applicable in these countries. When multinational enterprises are subject to conflicting requirements by adhering countries, the governments concerned will co-operate in good faith with a view to resolving problems that may arise.

8. Governments adhering to the *Guidelines* set them forth with the understanding that they will fulfil their responsibilities to treat enterprises equitably and in accordance with international law and with their contractual obligations.

9. The use of appropriate international dispute settlement mechanisms, including arbitration, is encouraged as a means of facilitating the resolution of legal problems arising between enterprises and host country governments.

10. Governments adhering to the *Guidelines* will promote them and encourage their use. They will establish National Contact Points that promote the *Guidelines* and act as a forum for discussion of all matters relating to the *Guidelines*. The adhering Governments will also participate in appropriate review and consultation procedures to address issues concerning interpretation of the *Guidelines* in a changing world.

II. General Policies

Enterprises should take fully into account established policies in the countries in which they operate, and consider the views of other stakeholders. In this regard, enterprises should:

1. Contribute to economic, social and environmental progress with a view to achieving sustainable development.

2. Respect the human rights of those affected by their activities consistent with the host government's international obligations and commitments.

3. Encourage local capacity building through close co-operation with the local community, including business interests, as well as developing the enterprise's activities in domestic and foreign markets, consistent with the need for sound commercial practice.

4. Encourage human capital formation, in particular by creating employment opportunities and facilitating training opportunities for employees.

5. Refrain from seeking or accepting exemptions not contemplated in the statutory or regulatory framework related to environmental, health, safety, labour, taxation, financial incentives, or other issues.

6. Support and uphold good corporate governance principles and develop and apply good corporate governance practices.

7. Develop and apply effective self-regulatory practices and management systems that foster a relationship of confidence and mutual trust between enterprises and the societies in which they operate.

8. Promote employee awareness of, and compliance with, company policies through appropriate dissemination of these policies, including through training programmes.

9. Refrain from discriminatory or disciplinary action against employees who make bona fide reports to management or, as appropriate, to the competent public authorities, on practices that contravene the law, the *Guidelines* or the enterprise's policies.

10. Encourage, where practicable, business partners, including suppliers and sub-contractors, to apply principles of corporate conduct compatible with the *Guidelines.*

11. Abstain from any improper involvement in local political activities.

III. Disclosure

1. Enterprises should ensure that timely, regular, reliable and relevant information is disclosed regarding their activities, structure, financial situation and performance. This information should be disclosed for the enterprise as a whole and, where appropriate, along business lines or geographic areas. Disclosure policies of enterprises should be tailored to the nature, size and location of the enterprise, with due regard taken of costs, business confidentiality and other competitive concerns.

2. Enterprises should apply high quality standards for disclosure, accounting, and audit. Enterprises are also encouraged to apply high quality standards for non-financial information including environmental and social reporting where they exist. The standards or policies under which both financial and non-financial information are compiled and published should be reported.

3. Enterprises should disclose basic information showing their name, location, and structure, the name, address and telephone number of the parent enterprise and

its main affiliates, its percentage ownership, direct and indirect in these affiliates, including shareholdings between them.

4. Enterprises should also disclose material information on:

   a) The financial and operating results of the company.

   b) Company objectives.

   c) Major share ownership and voting right.

   d) Members of the board and key executives, and their remuneration.

   e) Material foreseeable risk factors.

   f) Material issues regarding employees and other stakeholders.

   g) Governance structures and policies.

5. Enterprises are encouraged to communicate additional information that could include:

   a) Value statements or statements of business conduct intended for public disclosure including information on the social, ethical and environmental policies of the enterprise and other codes of conduct to which the company subscribes. In addition, the date of adoption, the countries and entities to which such statements apply and its performance in relation to these statements may be communicated.

   b) Information on systems for managing risks and complying with laws, and on statements or codes of business conduct.

   c) Information on relationships with employees and other stakeholders.

IV. Employment and Industrial Relations

Enterprises should, within the framework of applicable law, regulations and prevailing labour relations and employment practices:

1. a) Respect the right of their employees to be represented by trade unions and other bona fide representatives of employees, and engage in constructive negotiations, either individually or through employers' associations, with such representatives with a view to reaching agreements on employment conditions;

   b) Contribute to the effective abolition of child labour.

   c) Contribute to the elimination of all forms of forced or compulsory labour.

   d) Not discriminate against their employees with respect to employment or occupation on such grounds as race, colour, sex, religion, political opinion, national extraction or social origin, unless selectivity concerning employee characteristics furthers established governmental policies which specifically promote greater equality of employment opportunity or relates to the inherent requirements of a job.

2. a) Provide facilities to employee representatives as may be necessary to assist in the development of effective collective agreements.

b) Provide information to employee representatives which is needed for meaningful negotiations on conditions of employment.

c) Promote consultation and co-operation between employers and employees and their representatives on matters of mutual concern.

3. Provide information to employees and their representatives which enables them to obtain a true and fair view of the performance of the entity or, where appropriate, the enterprise as a whole.

4. a) Observe standards of employment and industrial relations not less favourable than those observed by comparable employers in the host country.

b) Take adequate steps to ensure occupational health and safety in their operations.

5. In their operations, to the greatest extent practicable, employ local personnel and provide training with a view to improving skill levels, in co-operation with employee representatives and, where appropriate, relevant governmental authorities.

6. In considering changes in their operations which would have major effects upon the livelihood of their employees, in particular in the case of the closure of an entity involving collective lay-offs or dismissals, provide reasonable notice of such changes to representatives of their employees, and, where appropriate, to the relevant governmental authorities, and co-operate with the employee representatives and appropriate governmental authorities so as to mitigate to the maximum extent practicable adverse effects. In light of the specific circumstances of each case, it would be appropriate if management were able to give such notice prior to the final decision being taken. Other means may also be employed to provide meaningful co-operation to mitigate the effects of such decisions.

7. In the context of bona fide negotiations with representatives of employees on conditions of employment, or while employees are exercising a right to organise, not threaten to transfer the whole or part of an operating unit from the country concerned nor transfer employees from the enterprises' component entilies in other countries in order to influence unfairly those negotiations or to hinder the exercise of a right to organise.

8. Enable authorised representatives of their employees to negotiate on collective bargaining or labour-management relations issues and allow the parties to consult on matters of mutual concern with representatives of management who are authorised to take decisions on these matters.

V. Environment

Enterprises should, within the framework of laws, regulations and administrative practices in the countries in which they operate, and in consideration of relevant international agreements, principles, objectives, and standards, take due account of the need to protect the environment, public health and safety, and generally to conduct their activities in a manner contributing to the wider goal of sustainable development. In particular, enterprises should:

1. Establish and maintain a system of environmental management appropriate to the enterprise, including:

   a) Collection and evaluation of adequate and timely information regarding the environmental, health, and safety impacts of their activities.

   b) Establishment of measurable objectives and, where appropriate, targets for improved environmental performance, including periodically reviewing the continuing relevance of these objectives; and

   c) Regular monitoring and verification of progress toward environmental, health, and safety objectives or targets.

2. Taking into account concerns about cost, business confidentiality, and the protection of intellectual property rights:

   a) Provide the public and employees with adequate and timely information on the potential environment, health and safety impacts of the activities of the enterprise, which could include reporting on progress in improving environmental performance; and

   b) Engage in adequate and timely communication and consultation with the communities directly affected by the environmental, health and safety policies of the enterprise and by their implementation.

3. Assess, and address in decision-making, the foreseeable environmental, health, and safety-related impacts associated with the processes, goods and services of the enterprise over their full life cycle. Where these proposed activities may have significant environmental, health, or safety impacts, and where they are subject to a decision of a competent authority, prepare an appropriate environmental impact assessment.

4. Consistent with the scientific and technical understanding of the risks, where there are threats of serious damage to the environment, taking also into account human health and safety, not use the lack of full scientific certainty as a reason for postponing cost-effective measures to prevent or minimise such damage.

5. Maintain contingency plans for preventing, mitigating, and controlling serious environmental and health damage from their operations, including accidents and emergencies; and mechanisms for immediate reporting to the competent authorities.

6. Continually seek to improve corporate environmental performance, by encouraging, where appropriate, such activities as:

   a) Adoption of technologies and operating procedures in all parts of the enterprise that reflect standards concerning environmental performance in the best performing part of the enterprise.

   b) Development and provision of products or services that have no undue environmental impacts; are safe in their intended use; are efficient in their consumption of energy and natural resources; can be reused, recycled, or disposed of safely.

c) Promoting higher levels of awareness among customers of the environmental implications of using the products and services of the enterprise; and

d) Research on ways of improving the environmental performance of the enterprise over the longer term.

7. Provide adequate education and training to employees in environmental health and safety matters, including the handling of hazardous materials and the prevention of environmental accidents, as well as more general environmental management areas, such as environmental impact assessment procedures, public relations, and environmental technologies.

8. Contribute to the development of environmentally meaningful and economically efficient public policy, for example, by means of partnerships or initiatives that will enhance environmental awareness and protection.

VI. Combating Bribery

Enterprises should not, directly or indirectly, offer, promise, give, or demand a bribe or other undue advantage to obtain or retain business or other improper advantage. Nor should enterprises be solicited or expected to render a bribe or other undue advantage. In particular, enterprises should:

1. Not offer, nor give in to demands, to pay public officials or the employees of business partners any portion of a contract payment. They should not use sub-contracts, purchase orders or consulting agreements as means of channelling payments to public officials, to employees of business partners or to their relatives or business associates.

2. Ensure that remuneration of agents is appropriate and for legitimate services only. Where relevant, a list of agents employed in connection with transactions with public bodies and state-owned enterprises should be kept and made available to competent authorities.

3. Enhance the transparency of their activities in the fight against bribery and extortion. Measures could include making public commitments against bribery and extortion and disclosing the management systems the company has adopted in order to honour these commitments. The enterprise should also foster openness and dialogue with the public so as to promote its awareness of and co-operation with the fight against bribery and extortion.

4. Promote employee awareness of and compliance with company policies against bribery and extortion through appropriate dissemination of these policies and through training programmes and disciplinary procedures.

5. Adopt management control systems that discourage bribery and corrupt practices, and adopt financial and tax accounting and auditing practices that prevent the establishment of "off the books" or secret accounts or the creation of documents which do not properly and fairly record the transactions to which they relate.

6. Not make illegal contributions to candidates for public office or to political parties or to other political organisations. Contributions should fully comply with public disclosure requirements and should be reported to senior management.

VII. Consumer Interests

When dealing with consumers, enterprises should act in accordance with fair business, marketing and advertising practices and should take all reasonable steps to ensure the safety and quality of the goods or services they provide. In particular, they should:

1. Ensure that the goods or services they provide meet all agreed and legally required standards for consumer health and safety, including health warnings and product safety and information labels.

2. As appropriate to the goods or services, provide accurate and clear information regarding their content, safe use, maintenance, storage, and disposal sufficient to enable consumers to make informed decisions.

3. Provide transparent and effective procedures that address consumer complaints and contribute to fair and timely resolution of consumer disputes without undue cost or burden.

4. Not make representations or omissions, nor engage in any other practices, that are deceptive, misleading, fraudulent, or unfair.

5. Respect consumer privacy and provide protection for personal data.

6. Co-operate fully and in a transparent manner with public authorities in the prevention or removal of serious threats to public health and safety deriving from the consumption or use of their products.

VIII. Science and Technology

Enterprises should:

1. Endeavour to ensure that their activities are compatible with the science and technology (S&T) policies and plans of the countries in which they operate and as appropriate contribute to the development of local and national innovative capacity.

2. Adopt, where practicable in the course of their business activities, practices that permit the transfer and rapid diffusion of technologies and know-how, with due regard to the protection of intellectual property rights.

3. When appropriate, perform science and technology development work in host countries to address local market needs, as well as employ host country person- nel in an S&T capacity and encourage their training, taking into account commer- cial needs.

4. When granting licenses for the use of intellectual property rights or when otherwise transferring technology, do so on reasonable terms and conditions and

in a manner that contributes to the long term development prospects of the host country.

5. Where relevant to commercial objectives, develop ties with local universities, public research institutions, and participate in co-operative research projects with local industry or industry associations.

IX. Competition

Enterprises should, within the framework of applicable laws and regulations, conduct their activities in a competitive manner. In particular, enterprises should:

1. Refrain from entering into or carrying out anti-competitive agreements among competitors:

    a) To fix prices.

    b) To make rigged bids (collusive tenders).

    c) To establish output restrictions or quotas; or

    d) To share or divide markets by allocating customers, suppliers, territories or lines of commerce.

2. Conduct all of their activities in a manner consistent with all applicable competition laws, taking into account the applicability of the competition laws of jurisdictions whose economies would be likely to be harmed by anti-competitive activity on their part.

3. Co-operate with the competition authorities of such jurisdictions by, among other things and subject to applicable law and appropriate safeguards, providing as prompt and complete responses as practicable to requests for information.

4. Promote employee awareness of the importance of compliance with all applicable competition laws and policies.

X. Taxation

It is important that enterprises contribute to the public finances of host countries by making timely payment of their tax liabilities. In particular, enterprises should comply with the tax laws and regulations in all countries in which they operate and should exert every effort to act in accordance with both the letter and the spirit of those laws and regulations. This would include such measures as providing to the relevant authorities the information necessary for the correct determination of taxes to be assessed in connection with their operations and conforming transfer pricing prac-tices to the arm's length principle.

3
The Global Sullivan Principles
of Social Responsibility

The high standards of the Global Sullivan Principles provide an important model for ethical behaviour of every corporation that operates worldwide.

Roger C. Beach, Unocal Chairman and
Chief Executive Officer[1]

Type Performance standard

Strength The idealism and aspirations of Reverend Sullivan

Keywords Reverend Leon Sullivan • US companies • Environment • Supply chain • Human rights • Bribery

3.1 Background

According to the Reverend Leon Sullivan, the aim of the Global Sullivan Principles (GSP) is to encourage companies to 'support economic, social and political justice wherever they do business'.[2] In 1999, Sullivan launched the GSP after consultation with companies and stakeholders. An African-American who fought to combat apartheid in South Africa, Sullivan founded the Sullivan Principles in 1977 which convinced US companies operating in South Africa to afford all their South African workers the same rights granted to US employees, regardless of race. One of the most significant aspects of the Sullivan Principles, from a legal point of view, is that

1 Unocal news report, 'Unocal supports Global Sullivan Principles for corporate responsibility', 3 November 1999, www.unocal.com/uclnews/99news/110399.htm.
2 Quoted at www.globalsullivanprinciples.org.

they encourage companies to violate an unjust law, setting an important precedent.

Sullivan died in 2001, but the initiative continues under strong leadership. Several hundred companies around the world have adopted the GSP, including Avon, Chevron, Shell and The Coca-Cola Company.[3] The GSP have also attracted a wide range of small and medium-sized companies in the USA, as well as universities and local governments. Each endorsing organisation makes a commitment to the GSP and submits a report describing the progress it is making, including the establishment of policies, training, procedures and reporting.

3.2 Strengths and weaknesses

The distinguishing feature of the GSP is their aspirational element, which provides vision and leadership. Where some codes of conduct are thought to be too managerialist, the GSP provide a vision of companies as a force for social justice. For a code to succeed, it must capture the imagination and vision of companies. The GSP, through the charismatic leadership of Sullivan, have succeeded in inspiring companies. A significant part of the GSP is their message to companies that they should promote the principles to their suppliers, customers and other business associates. The GSP are aspirational in nature and do not include any kind of verification. Accountability is promoted through reporting. Like the Global Compact (see Chapter 4), the GSP provide a framework with which companies can align their own codes of conduct and initiatives.

One of the major weaknesses of the GSP is that they do not mention the right to collective bargaining. Another problem is that they do not define some of the terms they use, such as 'female abuse' and 'basic needs'.

3.3 Companies to which the Global Sullivan Principles apply

The GSP apply to all workers, in all industries and in all countries. However, the majority of the organisations adopting the GSP are based in the USA. Given the aspirational nature of the GSP, companies are advised to use them in conjunction with process standards, such as AA1000 and GRI, as well as standards that include some element of external verification, such as SA8000.

---

3 www.globalsullivanprinciples.org/Endorser_list_Oct9.PDF

3.4 Questions posed and answered

The GSP answer the following question:

- To what should socially responsible companies aspire?

3.5 The promise and the challenge

One of the key challenges for the GSP will be leadership and capacity-building in the wake of Leon Sullivan's death. Another key challenge will be to attract a global following. It is unclear to what extent reporting by endorsers will be seen as sufficient and credible in a cynical world.

Additional resource

Website

Global Sullivan Principles: www.globalsullivanprinciples.org

The Global Sullivan Principles
of Social Responsibility*

As a company which endorses the Global Sullivan Principles we will respect the law, and as a responsible member of society we will apply these Principles with integrity consistent with the legitimate role of business. We will develop and implement company policies, procedures, training and internal reporting structures to ensure commitment to these Principles throughout our organization. We believe the application of these Principles will achieve greater tolerance and better understanding among peoples, and advance the culture of peace.

Accordingly, we will:

- Express our support for universal human rights and, particularly, those of our employees, the communities within which we operate, and parties with whom we do business.

- Promote equal opportunity for our employees at all levels of the company with respect to issues such as color, race, gender, age, ethnicity or religious beliefs, and operate without unacceptable worker treatment such as the exploitation of children, physical punishment, female abuse, involuntary servitude, or other forms of abuse.

- Respect our employees' voluntary freedom of association.

- Compensate our employees to enable them to meet at least their basic needs and provide the opportunity to improve their skill and capability in order to raise their social and economic opportunities.

- Provide a safe and healthy workplace; protect human health and the environment; and promote sustainable development.

- Promote fair competition including respect for intellectual and other property rights, and not offer, pay or accept bribes.

- Work with governments and communities in which we do business to improve the quality of life in those communities—their educational, cultural, economic and social well being—and seek to provide training and opportunities for workers from disadvantaged backgrounds.

- Promote the application of these Principles by those with whom we do business.

We will be transparent in our implementation of these Principles and provide information which demonstrates publicly our commitment to them.

---

* Reproduced with permission by the Global Sullivan Principles.

4
The UN Global Compact

Amnesty International [AI] believes initiatives like the UN Global Compact are worthwhile because, at a minimum, they encourage companies to make a commitment to human rights. This gives AI—and other [non-governmental organisations]—a clear opportunity to hold these companies to that commitment. We also believe that the possibilities for dialogue on human rights issues within the Global Compact framework have some value.

Amnesty International, Economic Relations Briefing[1]

UBS supports the Global Compact and is convinced that by adopting its principles it not only contributes to its stated objectives, but also creates value for its shareholders.

UBS[2]

Type   Performance-oriented tool

Strength Its global scope

Keywords UN Secretary-General • Environment • Labour • Human rights • UN agencies • Development • Partnerships • Learning network

4.1 Background

The UN Global Compact is an initiative of UN Secretary-General, Kofi Annan, 'to give a human face to globalisation' (Annan 1999). Launched in 2000, the Compact

1 Quoted on the Amnesty International website, at http://web.amnesty.org/pages/ec-globalcompact-eng.
2 Quoted on the UBS website, at www.ubs.com/e/about/ubs_environment/commitments/globalcompact.html.

addresses the environment, human rights and workers' rights. The Compact unites global principles with local networks to create fluid networks. The Compact is a global multi-stakeholder, multi-issue network with more than 40 regional and national sub-networks. As a voluntary initiative, the Global Compact convenes all the key social actors: companies, labour, civil-society organisations and governments. At the time of writing (mid-2003), more than 1,000 companies were participating in the initiative. Participating companies are asked to communicate in their annual reports and/or other prominent public reports (e.g. sustainability reports) on progress made in implementing the nine principles.

The Global Compact is the first initiative on corporate responsibility aimed at companies to emerge from the UN Secretary-General's office. The initiative benefits from the engagement of several UN bodies, including the ILO, The UN Development Programme (UNDP), the UN Environment Programme (UNEP), and the Office of the UN High Commissioner for Human Rights. In May 2003, the UN Industrial Development Organisation (UNIDO) joined the Global Compact as the fifth UN core agency. These core agencies provide expertise and operational support (see Fig. 4.1).

The Global Compact differs from nearly all other corporate responsibility (CR) initiatives in that it seeks to promote development through good corporate citizenship. Members of the Global Compact commit 'to join with the United Nations in partnership projects of benefit to developing countries, particularly the least developed, which the forces of globalisation have largely marginalised' (Ruggie 2002: 31).

The Global Compact is a voluntary initiative, with a clear focus on learning and dialogue; it is not a code or a system for verification. In the words of one of its key architects, John Ruggie, the Global Compact has 'explicitly adopted a learning approach to inducing corporate change, as opposed to a regulatory approach; and it comprises a network form of organisation, as opposed to the traditional hierarchic/bureaucratic form' (Ruggie 2002: 28).

The nine principles of the Global Compact are derived from the Universal Declaration of Human Rights, the ILO's Fundamental Principles on Rights at Work (ILO 1998) and the Rio Declaration on Environment and Development.

4.2 Strengths and weaknesses

No other CR initiative has the moral authority and convening power of the UN Secretary-General. With these assets, the Global Compact has succeeded in promoting corporate responsibility broadly through networks around the world. The Compact has also mobilised an impressive database of corporate activities on corporate responsibility. Perhaps its greatest achievement has been to rally support for corporate responsibility in many countries where this is a relatively new concept. The Global Compact is a truly global initiative, with the majority of participating companies coming from the South, and with a large number of active networks in developing countries.

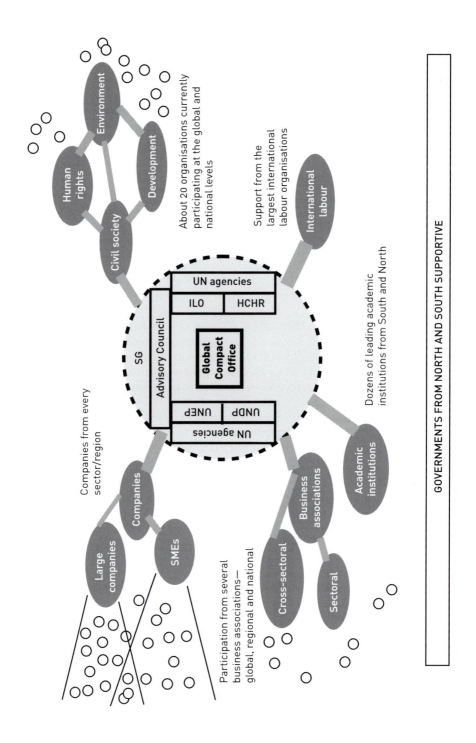

Figure 4.1 The Global Compact Constellation

By focusing on development, the Compact provides a new direction for corporate responsibility, giving voice to the poor and tackling such issues as the digital divide and HIV/AIDS. The partnership projects should contribute to the Millennium Development Goals, to which all 189 member states of the US have committed themselves by 2015 (these appear at the end of this chapter, page 81). The support of key UN bodies in this regard provides legitimacy and significant expertise.

The Compact has produced accessible handbooks for companies, available on its website. *A Guide to the Global Compact* (see 'Additional resources' on page 79) is an excellent tool for all companies seeking to implement CR policies, including useful definitions and examples.

If the principles of the Global Compact lack the specificity of AA1000 and SA8000 it is because they were designed to meet the needs of a very global and diverse constituency of governments and businesses. The key difference is that the Compact was never intended to supplant any regulatory initiatives. Instead, it complements them. The Global Compact Office does not have the mandate or the resources to monitor company activity. The general nature of the principles can be perceived as both a strength and a weakness. It is easier to attract a critical mass of companies with general principles than with highly specialised criteria. Moreover, general principles make it easier for companies to integrate the Compact into their own internal codes or policies. By developing a general standard, and by forging alliances with highly specialised initiatives such as SA8000 and GRI, the Compact is able to build a critical mass.

The flexible structure of the Compact is both a source of great strength and a source of weakness. As a series of 'nested networks', it is a flexible instrument for promoting corporate responsibility at a global level. Figure 4.2 demonstrates the architecture of the Global Compact. It is a useful framework for other initiatives to co-ordinate with, an umbrella under which many actors and initiatives can be united. Its critics question whether companies submitting case studies to the UN Secretariat are, in fact, creating new CR projects or are submitting initiatives that were already under way before the Compact was announced. Other critics are concerned that companies with poor social and environmental records will be able to benefit from their association with the Compact, in effect 'blue-washing' their image (HRW 2000: 1-2). For example, Nestlé, which has long been criticised for marketing infant formula to mothers in the developing world, has joined the Compact. This presents a dilemma in that UNICEF, a UN body, has been one of the critics of Nestlé (Freedman and Stecklow 2000; www.babymilkaction.org), but it also represents an opportunity for dialogue.

Another criticism of the Compact is its lack of assurance systems (Roth 2000). However, its architect, John Ruggie, responds that large-scale verification by the United Nations is not feasible (Ruggie 2002: 32). The Global Compact has developed strong partnerships with other key initiatives, such as SA8000 (Chapter 9), to promote independent certification, and with the Global Reporting Initiative (Chapter 26), to promote reporting.

Engagement mechanisms	Operational concepts	
Learning forums	● Example submission (mandatory)	
	● Business case studies	
	● Supportive research/analytical work	
	● Informal, issue-specific networks	
	● Annual conferences	
	Annual topic	**Working groups**
Policy dialogues	Role of business in zones of conflict	● Transparency ● Conflict impact assessment and risk management ● Multi-stakeholder partnerships ● Revenue-sharing regimes
	Business and sustainable development	● Sustainable investment (LDCs) ● Sustainable entrepreneurship ● Corporate management and sustainability ● Investors and sustainability
Partnership projects	**Suggested parameters**	
	● Should be inspired by the Global Compact	
	● Should contribute to the Millennium Development Goals	
	● Should be carried out with other actors such as UN agencies, labour, NGOs and public-sector entities	
	● Should allow network participants to offer a substantial example of how they enact the principles (thus providing added incentives for them to do so)	
	● Projects involving several companies are particularly encouraged	
Outreach and network building	**Replication of global structure** ● National Learning Forums ● National Policy Dialogues ● National Partnership Projects	
Global Compact governance	● Building strategic alliances	
	● Innovating operational concepts	
	● Inter-agency co-ordination	
	● Advocacy and policy coherence of UN officials	

	● Global Compact Advisory Council
	  i) protecting integrity
	  ii) issue leadership	

Figure 4.2 Summary of Global Compact activities

4.3 Companies to which the Global Compact applies

The Global Compact is well suited to companies making their first inroads into the field of CR. Companies with a well-established record in CR may seek to join the UN Global Compact to further promote their work in CR. The Global Compact is creating strong networks in Brazil and India and throughout Eastern Europe.

4.4 Questions posed and answered

The UN Global Compact poses several questions (McIntosh *et al.* 2003: 115):

- What are the principles that define responsible corporate behaviour?
- How can corporate citizenship promote development?
- How can the United Nations and governments begin to create mechanisms to address the governance of a globalised world?
- What constitutes best practice in corporate citizenship?

4.5 The promise and the challenge

The Global Compact has one of the most ambitious objectives of any of the initiatives described in this book: to make the world economy more sustainable and inclusive (United Nations 2003: 4). The brainchild of the very popular UN Secretary-General, Kofi Annan, the Global Compact has the ability to convene CEOs from around the world to promote corporate responsibility and development. The Compact is forging new types of alliances and partnerships while promoting corporate responsibility globally.

Like any new, global, initiative, the Compact faces challenges. One of the questions it must address is whether or not all companies can join the Compact or whether there should be some kind of a screen. Could a tobacco company join the Compact? At this point, none is on the list, but it is not clear whether the Compact will develop exclusion criteria. According to Georg Kell of the UN Secretary-General's Office:

> the Global Compact is not about sinners and saints. There will always be companies that lead and companies that follow. We want to keep the door open. But we need some safeguards (quoted in United Nations 2003: 8).

According to *Ethical Performance* (2002), companies that have signed up to the UN Global Compact but have not delivered on their pledge to implement the nine principles may face expulsion. The Global Compact explains that this article was controversial as it misrepresented several issues (see www.unglobalcompact,.org). The integrity of the Global Compact initiative is critically important to its mission. Therefore, the Global Compact Office is continuing to build in integrity measures. Efforts are under way to handle dilemmas through dialogue (www.unglobalcompact. org).

At the Learning Forum held in 2002 in Berlin there was discussion about a tenth principle to address transparency, not only of business but for all organisations. Although no conclusion had been reached by early 2003, there is a great deal of interest in such a principle (Waddock 2002: 4-5).

Another key challenge for the Global Compact, and for many of the initiatives described in this book, is the need to promote the principles among small and medium-sized enterprises (SMEs). SMEs have fewer resources to devote to corporate responsibility than do multinational corporations, and may face less pressure from consumers and investors than do large enterprises.[3] UNIDO's role as the Compact's fifth core agency will be to address the specific concerns and needs of SMEs.

The Global Compact has had only partial success in attracting US-based companies. This may be due, in part, to the cynicism that many Americans feel towards the United Nations.

References

Annan, K. (1999) Speech made by the UN Secretary-General, Kofi Annan, at the World Economic Forum in Davos, Switzerland, 31 January 1999 (www.un.org/News/Press/docs/1999/19990201.sgsm6881.html).

Ethical Performance (2002) News Alert, 8 April 2002, www.ethicalcorp.com.

Freedman, A.M., and S. Stecklow (2000) 'Bottled up: As Unicef battles baby-formula makers, African infants sicken', Wall Street Journal, 12 December 2000: A1.

HRW (Human Rights Watch) (2000) 'Business and Human Rights: The Role of the International Community', in World Report 2000 (New York: HRW, www.hrw.org): 1-2.

ILO (International Labour Organisation) (1998) Fundamental Principles on Rights at Work (Adopted by the International Labour Conference at its 86th session, Geneva, 18 June 1988; Geneva: ILO).

McIntosh, M., D. Leipziger and G. Coleman (2003) Living Corporate Citizenship: Strategic Routes to Socially Responsible Business (London: FT Pearson).

Roth, K. (2000) Letter from Human Rights Watch to Kofi Annan, 28 July 2000, www.hrw.org/advocacy/corporations.

Ruggie, J.G. (2002) 'The Theory and Practice of Learning Networks: Corporate Social Responsibility and the Global Compact', Journal of Corporate Citizenship 5 (Spring 2002): 27-36.

United Nations (2003) 'Guide to the Global Compact: A Practical Understanding of the Vision and Nine Principles', United Nations, www.unglobalcompact.org.

Waddock, S. (2002) 'Learning from Experience: The UN Global Compact Learning Forum 2002', available at www.unglobalcompact.org.

3 ILD (Institute for Leadership Development), 'SMEs in the Global Compact', www. ildglobal.org/newsite/ild/smes/smes.htm

Additional resources

Further reading

McIntosh, M., S. Waddock and G. Kell (2004) *Learning to Talk: The Early Years of the* UN *Global Compact* (Sheffield, UK: Greenleaf Publishing, forthcoming).

Website

UN Global Compact: www.unglobalcompact.org. This website contains the following publications online:

- *The Comprehensive Guide to the Global Compact*
- *A Guide to the Global Compact: A Practical Understanding of the Vision and Nine Principles*
- *The Global Compact Performance Model*
- *Reports from Learning Fora*

The Global Compact's Nine Principles

The Global Compact's principles in the areas of human rights, labour and the environment enjoy universal consensus being derived from:

- The Universal Declaration of Human Rights;
- The International Labour Organization's Declaration on Fundamental Principles and Rights at Work; and
- The Rio Declaration on Environment and Development.

The nine principles are:

Human Rights

- **Principle 1:** Businesses are asked to support and respect the protection of international human rights within their sphere of influence; and
- **Principle 2:** make sure their own corporations are not complicit in human rights abuses.

Labour

- **Principle 3:** Businesses are asked to uphold the freedom of association and the effective recognition of the right to collective bargaining;
- **Principle 4:** the elimination of all forms of forced and compulsory labour;
- **Principle 5:** the effective abolition of child labour; and
- **Principle 6:** the elimination of discrimination in respect of employment and occupation.

Environment

- **Principle 7:** Businesses are asked to support a precautionary approach to environmental challenges;
- **Principle 8:** undertake initiatives to promote greater environmental responsibility; and
- **Principle 9:** encourage the development and diffusion of environmentally friendly technologies.

The Millennium Development Goals

1. Eradicate extreme poverty and hunger

- Reduce by half the proportion of people living on less than a dollar a day
- Reduce by half the proportion of people who suffer from hunger

2. Achieve universal primary education

- Ensure that all boys and girls complete a full course of primary schooling

3. Promote gender equality and empower women

- Eliminate gender disparity in primary and secondary education preferably by 2005, and at all levels by 2015

4. Reduce child mortality

- Reduce by two thirds the mortality rate among children under five

5. Improve maternal health

- Reduce by three quarters the maternal mortality ratio

6. Combat HIV/AIDS, malaria and other diseases

- Halt and begin to reverse the spread of HIV/AIDS
- Halt and begin to reverse the incidence of malaria and other major diseases

7. Ensure environmental sustainability

- Integrate the principles of sustainable development into country policies and programmes; reverse loss of environmental resources
- Reduce by half the proportion of people without sustainable access to safe drinking water
- Achieve significant improvement in lives of at least 100 million slum dwellers, by 2020

8. Develop a global partnership for development

- Develop further an open trading and financial system that is rule-based, predictable and non-discriminatory. Includes a commitment to good governance, development and poverty reduction—nationally and internationally

- Address the least developed countries' special needs. This includes tariff- and quota-free access for their exports; enhanced debt relief for heavily indebted poor countries; cancellation of official bilateral debt; and more generous official development assistance for countries committed to poverty reduction

- Address the special needs of landlocked and small island developing States

- Deal comprehensively with developing countries' debt problems through national and international measures to make debt sustainable in the long term

- In cooperation with the developing countries, develop decent and productive work for youth

- In cooperation with pharmaceutical companies, provide access to affordable essential drugs in developing countries

- In cooperation with the private sector, make available the benefits of new technologies—especially information and communications technologies

By the year 2015, all 191 United Nations Member States have pledged to meet the above goals

Part 2
Human rights

Where, after all, do universal human rights begin? In small places, close to home—so close and so small that they cannot be seen on any maps of the world. Yet they are the world of the individual person; the neighbourhood he lives in; the school or college he attends; the factory, farm or office where he works. Such are the places where every man, woman and child seeks equal justice, equal opportunity, equal dignity without discrimination. Unless these rights have meaning there, they have little meaning any-where. Without concerned citizen action to uphold them close to home, we shall look in vain for progress in the larger world.

Eleanor Roosevelt [1]

Human rights are those rights enshrined in the Universal Declaration of Human Rights. As used in this book, the term 'human rights' conveys the broadest scope of that term to include political, social, economic, cultural and civil (previously known as civic) rights.

There are various types of human rights. Civil and political rights include freedom of religion, freedom of association and protection from torture, slavery and discrimination. Economic, cultural and social rights include the right to

---

1 At the presentation of 'In Your Hands: A Guide for Community Action for the Tenth Anniversary of the Universal Declaration of Human Rights', 27 March 1958, United Nations, New York (www.udhr.org/history/inyour.htm).

education, the right to adequate working conditions and the right to participate in cultural activities. In addition, over the past few years consideration of solidarity rights has been emerging to include issues that require international co-operation, such as environmental protection and the right to development (for more information, see Novib 1997).

The beginning of any discussion on human rights is the Universal Declaration of Human Rights (UDHR). Drafted in 1948, the Universal Declaration has been endorsed by all member countries of the United Nations. The Declaration is addressed to 'every individual and every organ of society'—and so business is urged to comply with the Universal Declaration, or as Goran Lindahl, former president and chief executive officer (CEO) of ABB, has stated, businesses 'must now act as co-guarantors of human rights' (quoted in Frankental and House 2001: 5).

Part 2 of this book includes the texts of three key documents in the field of human rights:[2]

- Universal Declaration of Human Rights

- Voluntary Principles on Security and Human Rights

- Norms on the Responsibilities of Transnational Corporations and Other Business Enterprises with Regard to Human Rights

References

Frankental, P., and F. House (2001) *Human Rights: Is it Any of Your Business?* (London: Amnesty International, and Prince of Wales Business Leaders' Forum, April 2001).

Novib (1997) *Human Rights and Development: Novib's Challenges in the Field of Human Rights* (The Hague: Novib, December 1997).

2   The fundamental labour conventions of the International Labour Organisation (ILO) are discussed in Chapter 8, in Part 3 on labour rights.

5
The Universal Declaration of Human Rights

The Universal Declaration of Human Rights is the first comprehensive international proclamation of the basic rights of the individual. It ranks with the Magna Carta, the French Declaration of the Rights of Man and of the Citizen, and the American Declaration of Independence as a milestone in mankind's struggle for freedom and human dignity.

Thomas Buergenthal, Judge, International Court of Justice[1]

The Universal Declaration is the internationally accepted framework for human rights created by the United Nations . . . This framework should form the basis of a company's human rights policy . . . Business should comply within the company's full chain of operation with each particular right.

International Business Leaders' Forum[2]

Type   Foundation initiative

Strength   Its legitimacy

Keywords United Nations • Human rights • Foundation standard • Slavery • Freedom of opinion • Freedom of expression

1 Buergenthal 1998: 91.
2 IBLF 2003.

5.1 Background

The Universal Declaration of Human Rights (UDHR) is one of the most significant documents ever drafted. It enshrines the concept of human rights broadly, to include not only political rights but also social and economic rights. Universally accepted, the UDHR has formed the basis of many constitutions around the world. Moreover, the UDHR is cited in many of the corporate responsibility (CR) codes and principles contained in this book as a foundation standard.

Adopted by the UN General Assembly in 1948, the UDHR was unanimously adopted by the then 48 member states of the United Nations. In 1993, 171 governments adopted the Vienna Declaration,[3] which reaffirms support for the Universal Declaration. The UDHR is not legally binding but is accepted as customary law. The UDHR is elaborated on in two UN international covenants—one on civil and political rights,[4] and one on social, economic and cultural rights.[5] These two covenants are binding for states that decide to become a party to these treaties.

5.2 Strengths and weaknesses

One of the greatest strengths of the UDHR is its acceptance around the world as a cornerstone of human rights. The clarity of its composition is also a great strength. Despite the fact that it is already over half a century old, it remains as relevant in 2003 as it was in 1948.

The drafters of the UDHR were predominantly of Western background, leading some critics to argue that the concept of human rights is a 'Western' notion. To refute this argument, it is worth noting that very few governments have filed significant reservations on any of the human rights treaties (which are based on the UDHR) they have ratified, despite being allowed to do so under international law (for more information on this debate, see Avery 1997). The UDHR has also been criticised for its lack of focus on minorities and indigenous peoples. However, subsequent UN documents have compensated for the oversight (van Boven 1998: 78). According to Gemma Crijns of Nyenrode University, formerly with Amnesty International, approximately 80 conventions, declarations and resolutions have been developed from the UDHR on a variety of human rights issues.[6]

According to Geoffrey Chandler (2001):

> The Universal Declaration on its own, however, is not easily translatable into immediate corporate action which is why [Amnesty

3   www.unhchr.ch/html/menu3/b/a_cescr.htm
4   International Covenant on Civil and Political Rights (1966): www.unhchr.ch/html/menu3/b/a_ccpr.htm.
5   International Covenant on Economic, Social and Cultural Rights (1966): www.unhchr.ch/html/menu3/b/a_cescr.htm.
6   Personal communication with Gemma Crijns, Nyenrode University, Breukelen, The Netherlands, 2003.

International asks] companies to support it explicitly as a starting point, so expressing a commitment in principle to human rights, but then apply its relevant sections to their own operations.

5.3 Companies to which the Universal Declaration of Human Rights applies

The UDHR calls on 'every organ of society' to follow its underlying principles. Hence, business is included in the UDHR, along with individuals and states. A growing number of multinational companies refer to the Declaration on their websites and within their own statements of principles, including Aviva, BP, British Telecommunications (BT), Shell and Vodafone. BT provides its employees with access to the UDHR and uses it in its training.[7] Others, such as Novo Nordisk (www.novonordisk.com), have conducted a review of their operations against the Declaration and redefined their focus. For example, Novo Nordisk has realised that it needs to do more to promote the right to health, especially with regard to diabetes care, as well as enhance its work to promote diversity.[8]

5.4 Questions posed and answered

The UDHR poses and answers a fundamental question: What are human rights?

5.5 The challenge and the promise

One of the challenges in the human rights field is to translate the UDHR into business principles. Social and economic rights are being translated into business codes, but civil and political rights are rarely included in business principles. The Danish Centre on Human Rights (www.humanrightsbusiness.org) is working to translate the articles of the UDHR into business principles, with the support of companies and stakeholders. It currently uses approximately 1,400 indicators; however, indicators are selected according to each user, based on the company type and area of operations. As a result, a small company operating with only a handful of employees in Denmark may receive around 20 indicators; and a large global

---

7 See ww.btplc.com/Betterworld/Humanrights/Humanrights.htm.
8 See www.novonordisk.com/sustainability/positions/human_rights.asp.

company with thousands of employees around the world may receive close to a thousand indicators.[9]

References

Avery, C. (1997) 'Business and Human Rights: Five Common Misconceptions', http://208.55.16.210/Misconceptions.htm.

Buergenthal, T. (1998) 'Centerpiece of the Human Rights Revolution', in B. van der Heijden and B. Tahzib-Lie (eds.), *Reflections on the Universal Declaration of Human Rights: A Fiftieth Anniversary Anthology* (Dordrecht, Netherlands: Martinius Nijhoff): 91-94.

Chandler, G. (2001) 'Companies and Human Rights: Recent Developments', http://208.55.16.210/Chandler-UN-Guidelines.htm, 5 April 2001.

IBLF (International Business Leaders' Forum) (2003) 'Business and Human Rights', www.iblf.org/csr/csrwebassist.nsf/content/a1a2a3d4.html.

Van Boven, T. (1998) 'A Universal Declaration of Human Responsibilities?', in B. van der Heijden and B. Tahzib-Lie (eds.), *Reflections on the Universal Declaration of Human Rights: A Fiftieth Anniversary Anthology* (Dordrecht, Netherlands: Martinius Nijhoff): 73-79.

Additional resources

Websites

Business and Human Rights Resource Centre: www.business-humanrights.org

Human Rights and Business Project of the Danish Institute for Human Rights: www.humanrightsbusiness.org

Universal Declaration of Human Rights: www.udhr.org

9   E-mail to author from Margaret Jungk, Danish Centre for Human Rights, 8 October 2003.

The Universal Declaration of Human Rights

PREAMBLE

Whereas recognition of the inherent dignity and of the equal and inalienable rights of all members of the human family is the foundation of freedom, justice and peace in the world,

Whereas disregard and contempt for human rights have resulted in barbarous acts which have outraged the conscience of mankind, and the advent of a world in which human beings shall enjoy freedom of speech and belief and freedom from fear and want has been proclaimed as the highest aspiration of the common people,

Whereas it is essential, if man is not to be compelled to have recourse, as a last resort, to rebellion against tyranny and oppression, that human rights should be protected by the rule of law,

Whereas it is essential to promote the development of friendly relations between nations,

Whereas the peoples of the United Nations have in the Charter reaffirmed their faith in fundamental human rights, in the dignity and worth of the human person and in the equal rights of men and women and have determined to promote social progress and better standards of life in larger freedom,

Whereas Member States have pledged themselves to achieve, in co-operation with the United Nations, the promotion of universal respect for and observance of human rights and fundamental freedoms,

Whereas a common understanding of these rights and freedoms is of the greatest importance for the full realization of this pledge,

Now, Therefore THE GENERAL ASSEMBLY proclaims THIS UNIVERSAL DECLARATION OF HUMAN RIGHTS as a common standard of achievement for all peoples and all nations, to the end that every individual and every organ of society, keeping this Declaration constantly in mind, shall strive by teaching and education to promote respect for these rights and freedoms and by progressive measures, national and international, to secure their universal and effective recognition and observance, both among the peoples of Member States themselves and among the peoples of territories under their jurisdiction.

Article 1.

All human beings are born free and equal in dignity and rights. They are endowed with reason and conscience and should act towards one another in a spirit of brotherhood.

Article 2.

Everyone is entitled to all the rights and freedoms set forth in this Declaration, without distinction of any kind, such as race, colour, sex, language, religion, political or other opinion, national or social origin, property, birth or other status. Furthermore, no distinction shall be made on the basis of the political, jurisdictional or international status of the country or territory to which a person belongs, whether it be independent, trust, non-self-governing or under any other limitation of sovereignty.

Article 3.

Everyone has the right to life, liberty and security of person.

Article 4.

No one shall be held in slavery or servitude; slavery and the slave trade shall be prohibited in all their forms.

Article 5.

No one shall be subjected to torture or to cruel, inhuman or degrading treatment or punishment.

Article 6.

Everyone has the right to recognition everywhere as a person before the law.

Article 7.

All are equal before the law and are entitled without any discrimination to equal protection of the law. All are entitled to equal protection against any discrimination in violation of this Declaration and against any incitement to such discrimination.

Article 8.

Everyone has the right to an effective remedy by the competent national tribunals for acts violating the fundamental rights granted him by the constitution or by law.

Article 9.

No one shall be subjected to arbitrary arrest, detention or exile.

Article 10.

Everyone is entitled in full equality to a fair and public hearing by an independent and impartial tribunal, in the determination of his rights and obligations and of any criminal charge against him.

Article 11.

(1) Everyone charged with a penal offence has the right to be presumed innocent until proved guilty according to law in a public trial at which he has had all the guarantees necessary for his defence.

(2) No one shall be held guilty of any penal offence on account of any act or omission which did not constitute a penal offence, under national or international law, at the time when it was committed. Nor shall a heavier penalty be imposed than the one that was applicable at the time the penal offence was committed.

Article 12.

No one shall be subjected to arbitrary interference with his privacy, family, home or correspondence, nor to attacks upon his honour and reputation. Everyone has the right to the protection of the law against such interference or attacks.

Article 13.

(1) Everyone has the right to freedom of movement and residence within the borders of each state.

(2) Everyone has the right to leave any country, including his own, and to return to his country.

Article 14.

(1) Everyone has the right to seek and to enjoy in other countries asylum from persecution.

(2) This right may not be invoked in the case of prosecutions genuinely arising from non-political crimes or from acts contrary to the purposes and principles of the United Nations.

Article 15.

(1) Everyone has the right to a nationality.

(2) No one shall be arbitrarily deprived of his nationality nor denied the right to change his nationality.

Article 16.

(1) Men and women of full age, without any limitation due to race, nationality or religion, have the right to marry and to found a family. They are entitled to equal rights as to marriage, during marriage and at its dissolution.

(2) Marriage shall be entered into only with the free and full consent of the intending spouses.

(3) The family is the natural and fundamental group unit of society and is entitled to protection by society and the State.

Article 17.

(1) Everyone has the right to own property alone as well as in association with others.

(2) No one shall be arbitrarily deprived of his property.

Article 18.

Everyone has the right to freedom of thought, conscience and religion; this right includes freedom to change his religion or belief, and freedom, either alone or in community with others and in public or private, to manifest his religion or belief in teaching, practice, worship and observance.

Article 19.

Everyone has the right to freedom of opinion and expression; this right includes freedom to hold opinions without interference and to seek, receive and impart information and ideas through any media and regardless of frontiers.

Article 20.

(1) Everyone has the right to freedom of peaceful assembly and association.

(2) No one may be compelled to belong to an association.

Article 21.

(1) Everyone has the right to take part in the government of his country, directly or through freely chosen representatives.

(2) Everyone has the right of equal access to public service in his country.

(3) The will of the people shall be the basis of the authority of government; this will shall be expressed in periodic and genuine elections which shall be by universal and equal suffrage and shall be held by secret vote or by equivalent free voting procedures.

Article 22.

Everyone, as a member of society, has the right to social security and is entitled to realization, through national effort and international co-operation and in accordance with the organization and resources of each State, of the economic, social and cultural rights indispensable for his dignity and the free development of his personality.

Article 23.

(1) Everyone has the right to work, to free choice of employment, to just and favourable conditions of work and to protection against unemployment.

(2) Everyone, without any discrimination, has the right to equal pay for equal work.

(3) Everyone who works has the right to just and favourable remuneration ensuring for himself and his family an existence worthy of human dignity, and supplemented, if necessary, by other means of social protection.

(4) Everyone has the right to form and to join trade unions for the protection of his interests.

Article 24.

Everyone has the right to rest and leisure, including reasonable limitation of working hours and periodic holidays with pay.

Article 25.

(1) Everyone has the right to a standard of living adequate for the health and well-being of himself and of his family, including food, clothing, housing and medical care and necessary social services, and the right to security in the event of unemployment, sickness, disability, widowhood, old age or other lack of livelihood in circumstances beyond his control.

(2) Motherhood and childhood are entitled to special care and assistance. All children, whether born in or out of wedlock, shall enjoy the same social protection.

Article 26.

(1) Everyone has the right to education. Education shall be free, at least in the elementary and fundamental stages. Elementary education shall be compulsory. Technical and professional education shall be made generally available and higher education shall be equally accessible to all on the basis of merit.

(2) Education shall be directed to the full development of the human personality and to the strengthening of respect for human rights and fundamental freedoms. It shall promote understanding, tolerance and friendship among all nations, racial or religious groups, and shall further the activities of the United Nations for the maintenance of peace.

(3) Parents have a prior right to choose the kind of education that shall be given to their children.

Article 27.

(1) Everyone has the right freely to participate in the cultural life of the community, to enjoy the arts and to share in scientific advancement and its benefits.

(2) Everyone has the right to the protection of the moral and material interests resulting from any scientific, literary or artistic production of which he is the author.

Article 28.

Everyone is entitled to a social and international order in which the rights and freedoms set forth in this Declaration can be fully realized.

Article 29.

(1) Everyone has duties to the community in which alone the free and full development of his personality is possible.

(2) In the exercise of his rights and freedoms, everyone shall be subject only to such limitations as are determined by law solely for the purpose of securing due recognition and respect for the rights and freedoms of others and of meeting the just requirements of morality, public order and the general welfare in a democratic society.

(3) These rights and freedoms may in no case be exercised contrary to the purposes and principles of the United Nations.

Article 30.

Nothing in this Declaration may be interpreted as implying for any State, group or person any right to engage in any activity or to perform any act aimed at the destruction of any of the rights and freedoms set forth herein.

6
The Voluntary Principles on Security and Human Rights

> In an area where no standards exist, we see the development of some guiding principles as a positive first step. But this is only the beginning of the process. The business, human rights and government communities all still have a lot of talking to do.
>
> *Kenneth Roth, Human Rights Watch*[1]

> The Voluntary Principles are a very creative effort by governments, non-governmental organisations and extractive industry companies working in remote areas of developing nations to establish practical standards and best practices for providing security while supporting the universally recognised human rights of local residents. While the issues remain complex, the initiative is already clarifying and improving relationships and practices for subscribing companies and their neighbours, and it is hoped this will lead to more such agreements to enhance the benefits and minimise the negatives of globalisation.
>
> *Judge Gabrielle Kirk McDonald*[2]

Type   Performance-oriented principles, sectoral

Strength The ability to institutionalise dialogue

Keywords Governments • Extractive sector • Private security forces •
Non-governmental organisations • Human rights

---

1 Human Rights Watch, 'Human Rights Principles for Oil and Mining Companies Welcomed', New York, www.hrw.org/press/2000/12/oil1221.htm, 21 December 2000.
2 E-mail to author from Judge McDonald, 7 May 2003. Judge McDonald represented Freeport McMoran in the negotiations of the Voluntary Principles.

6.1 Background

The Voluntary Principles represent an unprecedented step in the field of corporate responsibility. Convened by the US and UK governments, non-governmental organisations (NGOs), companies and a trade union reached a consensus on principles in the difficult area of human rights and security for the extractive sector (i.e. mining and petroleum). The agreement sets an important precedent for other sectoral discussions. First released in December of 2000, the agreement is noteworthy because it was convened by governments and included key stakeholders.

The participants include:

● **Governments**: the US and UK governments (the Dutch and Norwegian governments have joined subsequently)

● **Companies**: BP, Chevron, Conoco, Freeport McMoRan, Rio Tinto, Shell and Texaco (ExxonMobil and Occidental Petroleum have joined subsequently)

● **NGOs**: Amnesty International, Business for Social Responsibility, the Council on Economic Priorities, Fund for Peace, Human Rights Watch, International Alert, International Federation of Chemical, Energy, Mine, and General Workers' Unions, Lawyers Committee for Human Rights and the International Business Leaders' Forum

The Voluntary Principles address the issue of security forces, including:

● The criteria companies need to consider in assessing the risk to human rights in forming security agreements

● The relationship between a company's security and state security, such as the army or police

● The relationship between the company's security force and private armies

By narrowing the debate to include only security arrangements, the negotiations bypassed more difficult areas of debate that could have polarised the process, such as whether or not to conduct business in countries with severe human rights violations.

The Voluntary Principles are based, in part, on the UN Code of Conduct for Law Enforcement Officials[3] and the UN Basic Principles on the Use of Force and Firearms by Law Enforcement Officials.[4]

---

3   Adopted by the General Assembly, 17 December 1979: www.unhchr.ch/html/menu3/b/h_comp42.htm.

4   Adopted by the UN Congress on the Prevention of Crime and Treatment of Offenders, 7 September 1990: www.unhchr.ch/html/menu3/b/h_comp43.htm.

6.2 Strengths and weaknesses

The role of governments as convenors is an emerging trend in corporate citizenship. The US and UK governments are concerned with the reputation of their companies abroad and with the security of their citizens abroad.[5] According to Bennett Freeman, one of the architects of the Voluntary Principles:

> One key to success was the willingness of the two governments to use their convening authority and diplomatic capacity not only to facilitate the dialogue between companies and NGOs, but to draft and announce a standard that would advance the interests of the companies, NGOs and governments alike (Freeman 2001: 6).

Like all ground-breaking agreements, the Principles have been criticised. One of the criticisms is that the Principles are voluntary—a similar criticism is made of the UN Global Compact (see Chapter 4), the OECD Principles (Chapter 19) and SA8000 (Chapter 9). There is widespread agreement that the companies would not have been able to commit to binding principles for fear of litigation. A second criticism levelled at the Principles is the absence of involvement of other key governments affected by this issue, especially governments in the South. After all, the governments of Ecuador, Colombia and Nigeria are but a few of those that have a significant interest with regard to the extractive industries. The US and UK governments opted to broker an agreement and then work with other governments to gain their approval. The goal of the initiative was to reach an agreement within a one-year time-period, which would have been difficult had more governments been involved.

6.3 Companies to which the Voluntary Principles on Security and Human Rights apply

The Principles specifically apply to the extractive sector, including mining and petroleum. However, as crime and terrorism are on the rise, the Principles could apply to companies who need to hire guards to ensure the safety of their staff.

6.4 Questions posed and answered

What criteria should 'companies take into account as they assess the risk to human rights in their security arrangements?' What are the optimal forms for the 'rela-

---

5   For an excellent overview of US interests in promoting human rights and corporate social responsibility, see Freeman 2001.

tionships between companies and security forces, both military and police?' (Freeman 2002: 2).

6.5 The challenge and the promise

The challenge for companies involved will be to operationalise the Principles. Another important challenge is to bring additional governments, especially from the South, into the discussion.

References

Freeman, B. (2001) 'Corporate Responsibility and Human Rights', transcript of speech available at www.lse.ac.uk/collections/globalDimensions/seminars/ humanRightsAndCorporateResponsibility/freemanTranscript.htm.
—— (2002) 'Finding Common Ground: The Voluntary Principles on Security and Human Rights', text of a draft speech provided to the author in Oslo.

The Voluntary Principles on Security and Human Rights

The Governments of the United States and the United Kingdom, companies in the extractive and energy sectors ("Companies"), and non-governmental organizations, all with an interest in human rights and corporate social responsibility, have engaged in a dialogue on security and human rights.

The participants recognize the importance of the promotion and protection of human rights throughout the world and the constructive role business and civil society— including non-governmental organizations, labor/trade unions, and local communities—can play in advancing these goals. Through this dialogue, the participants have developed the following set of voluntary principles to guide Companies in maintaining the safety and security of their operations within an operating framework that ensures respect for human rights and fundamental freedoms. Mindful of these goals, the participants agree to the importance of continuing this dialogue and keeping under review these principles to ensure their continuing relevance and efficacy.

Acknowledging that security is a fundamental need, shared by individuals, communities, businesses, and governments alike, and acknowledging the difficult security issues faced by Companies operating globally, we recognize that security and respect for human rights can and should be consistent;

Understanding that governments have the primary responsibility to promote and protect human rights and that all parties to a conflict are obliged to observe applicable international humanitarian law, we recognize that we share the common goal of promoting respect for human rights, particularly those set forth in the Universal Declaration of Human Rights, and international humanitarian law;

Emphasizing the importance of safeguarding the integrity of company personnel and property, Companies recognize a commitment to act in a manner consistent with the laws of the countries within which they are present, to be mindful of the highest applicable international standards, and to promote the observance of applicable international law enforcement principles (e.g., the UN Code of Conduct for Law Enforcement Officials and the UN Basic Principles on the Use of Force and Firearms by Law Enforcement Officials), particularly with regard to the use of force;

Taking note of the effect that Companies' activities may have on local communities, we recognize the value of engaging with civil society and host and home governments to contribute to the welfare of the local community while mitigating any potential for conflict where possible;

Understanding that useful, credible information is a vital component of security and human rights, we recognize the importance of sharing and understanding our respective experiences regarding, *inter alia*, best security practices and procedures, country human rights situations, and public and private security, subject to confidentiality constraints;

Acknowledging that home governments and multilateral institutions may, on occasion, assist host governments with security sector reform, developing institutional capacities and strengthening the rule of law, we recognize the important role Companies and civil society can play in supporting these efforts;

We hereby express our support for the following voluntary principles regarding security and human rights in the extractive sector, which fall into three categories, risk assessment, relations with public security, and relations with private security:

RISK ASSESSMENT

The ability to assess accurately risks present in a Company's operating environment is critical to the security of personnel, local communities and assets; the success of the Company's short and long-term operations; and to the promotion and protection of human rights. In some circumstances, this is relatively simple; in others, it is important to obtain extensive background information from different sources; monitoring and adapting to changing, complex political, economic, law enforcement, military and social situations; and maintaining productive relations with local communities and government officials.

The quality of complicated risk assessments is largely dependent on the assembling of regularly updated, credible information from a broad range of perspectives—local and national governments, security firms, other companies, home governments, multilateral institutions, and civil society knowledgeable about local conditions. This information may be most effective when shared to the fullest extent possible (bearing in mind confidentiality considerations) between Companies, concerned civil society, and governments.

Bearing in mind these general principles, we recognize that accurate, effective risk assessments should consider the following factors:

- **Identification of security risks.** Security risks can result from political, economic, civil or social factors. Moreover, certain personnel and assets may be at greater risk than others. Identification of security risks allows a Company to take measures to minimize risk and to assess whether Company actions may heighten risk.

- **Potential for violence.** Depending on the environment, violence can be widespread or limited to particular regions, and it can develop with little or no warning. Civil society, home and host government representatives, and other sources should be consulted to identify risks presented by the potential for violence. Risk assessments should examine patterns of violence in areas of Company operations for educational, predictive, and preventative purposes.

- **Human rights records.** Risk assessments should consider the available human rights records of public security forces, paramilitaries, local and national law enforcement, as well as the reputation of private security. Awareness of past abuses and allegations can help Companies to avoid recurrences as well as to promote accountability. Also, identification of the capability of the above entities to respond to situations of violence in a lawful manner (i.e., consistent with applicable international standards) allows Companies to develop appropriate measures in operating environments.

- **Rule of law.** Risk assessments should consider the local prosecuting authority and judiciary's capacity to hold accountable those responsible for human rights abuses and for those responsible for violations of international humanitarian law in a manner that respects the rights of the accused.

- **Conflict analysis.** Identification of and understanding the root causes and nature of local conflicts, as well as the level of adherence to human rights and international humanitarian law standards by key actors, can be instructive for the development of strategies for managing relations between the Company, local communities, Company employees and their unions, and host governments. Risk assessments should also consider the potential for future conflicts.

- **Equipment transfers.** Where Companies provide equipment (including lethal and non-lethal equipment) to public or private security, they should consider the risk of such transfers, any relevant export licensing requirements, and the feasibility of measures to mitigate foreseeable negative consequences, including adequate controls to prevent misappropriation or diversion of equipment which may lead to human rights abuses. In making risk assessments, companies should consider any relevant past incidents involving previous equipment transfers.

INTERACTIONS BETWEEN COMPANIES AND PUBLIC SECURITY

Although governments have the primary role of maintaining law and order, security and respect for human rights, Companies have an interest in ensuring that actions taken by governments, particularly the actions of public security providers, are consistent with the protection and promotion of human rights. In cases where there is a need to supplement security provided by host governments, Companies may be required or expected to contribute to, or otherwise reimburse, the costs of protecting Company facilities and personnel borne by public security. While public security is expected to act in a manner consistent with local and national laws as well as with human rights standards and international humanitarian law, within this context abuses may nevertheless occur.

In an effort to reduce the risk of such abuses and to promote respect for human rights generally, we have identified the following voluntary principles to guide relationships between Companies and public security regarding security provided to Companies:

Security Arrangements

- Companies should consult regularly with host governments and local communities about the impact of their security arrangements on those communities.

- Companies should communicate their policies regarding ethical conduct and human rights to public security providers, and express their desire that security be provided in a manner consistent with those policies by personnel with adequate and effective training.

- Companies should encourage host governments to permit making security arrangements transparent and accessible to the public, subject to any overriding safety and security concerns.

Deployment and Conduct

- The primary role of public security should be to maintain the rule of law, including safeguarding human rights and deterring acts that threaten Company personnel and facilities. The type and number of public security forces deployed should be competent, appropriate and proportional to the threat.

- Equipment imports and exports should comply with all applicable law and regulations. Companies that provide equipment to public security should take all appropriate and lawful measures to mitigate any foreseeable negative consequences, including human rights abuses and violations of international humanitarian law.

- Companies should use their influence to promote the following principles with public security: (a) individuals credibly implicated in human rights abuses should not provide security services for Companies; (b) force should be used only when strictly necessary and to an extent proportional to the threat; and (c) the rights of individuals should not be violated while exercising the right to exercise freedom of association and peaceful assembly, the right to engage in collective bargaining, or other related rights of Company employees as recognized by the Universal Declaration of Human Rights and the ILO Declaration on Fundamental Principles and Rights at Work.

- In cases where physical force is used by public security, such incidents should be reported to the appropriate authorities and to the Company. Where force is used, medical aid should be provided to injured persons, including to offenders.

Consultation and Advice

- Companies should hold structured meetings with public security on a regular basis to discuss security, human rights and related work-place safety issues. Companies should also consult regularly with other Companies, host and home governments, and civil society to discuss security and human rights. Where Companies operating in the same region have common concerns, they should consider collectively raising those concerns with the host and home governments.

- In their consultations with host governments, Companies should take all appropriate measures to promote observance of applicable international law enforcement principles, particularly those reflected in the UN Code of Conduct for Law Enforcement Officials and the UN Basic Principles on the Use of Force and Firearms.

- Companies should support efforts by governments, civil society and multilateral institutions to provide human rights training and education for public security as well as their efforts to strengthen state institutions to ensure accountability and respect for human rights.

Responses to Human Rights Abuses

- Companies should record and report any credible allegations of human rights abuses by public security in their areas of operation to appropriate host government authorities. Where appropriate, Companies should urge investigation and that action be taken to prevent any recurrence.

- Companies should actively monitor the status of investigations and press for their proper resolution.

- Companies should, to the extent reasonable, monitor the use of equipment provided by the Company and to investigate properly situations in which such equipment is used in an inappropriate manner.

- Every effort should be made to ensure that information used as the basis for allegations of human rights abuses is credible and based on reliable evidence. The security and safety of sources should be protected. Additional or more accurate information that may alter previous allegations should be made available as appropriate to concerned parties.

INTERACTIONS BETWEEN COMPANIES AND PRIVATE SECURITY

Where host governments are unable or unwilling to provide adequate security to protect a Company's personnel or assets, it may be necessary to engage private security providers as a complement to public security. In this context, private security may have to coordinate with state forces, (law enforcement, in particular) to carry weapons and to consider the defensive local use of force. Given the risks associated with such activities, we recognize the following voluntary principles to guide private security conduct:

- Private security should observe the policies of the contracting Company regarding ethical conduct and human rights; the law and professional standards of the country in which they operate; emerging best practices developed by industry, civil society, and governments; and promote the observance of international humanitarian law.

- Private security should maintain high levels of technical and professional proficiency, particularly with regard to the local use of force and firearms.

- Private security should act in a lawful manner. They should exercise restraint and caution in a manner consistent with applicable international guidelines regarding the local use of force, including the UN Principles on the Use of Force and Firearms by Law Enforcement Officials and the UN Code of Conduct for Law Enforcement Officials, as well as with emerging best practices developed by Companies, civil society, and governments.

- Private security should have policies regarding appropriate conduct and the local use of force (e.g., rules of engagement). Practice under these policies should be capable of being monitored by Companies or, where appropriate, by independent third parties. Such monitoring should encompass detailed investigations into allegations of abusive or unlawful acts; the availability of disciplinary measures sufficient to prevent and deter; and procedures for reporting allegations to relevant local law enforcement authorities when appropriate.

- All allegations of human rights abuses by private security should be recorded. Credible allegations should be properly investigated. In those cases where allegations against private security providers are forwarded to the relevant law enforcement authorities, Companies should actively monitor the status of investigations and press for their proper resolution.

- Consistent with their function, private security should provide only preventative and defensive services and should not engage in activities exclusively the responsibility of state military or law enforcement authorities. Companies should designate services, technology and equipment capable of offensive and defensive purposes as being for defensive use only.

- Private security should (a) not employ individuals credibly implicated in human rights abuses to provide security services; (b) use force only when strictly necessary and to an extent proportional to the threat; and (c) not violate the rights of individuals while exercising the right to exercise freedom of association and peaceful assembly, to engage in collective bargaining, or other related rights of Company employees as recognized by the Universal Declaration of Human Rights and the ILO Declaration on Fundamental Principles and Rights at Work.

- In cases where physical force is used, private security should properly investigate and report the incident to the Company. Private security should refer the matter to local authorities and/or take disciplinary action where appropriate. Where force is used, medical aid should be provided to injured persons, including to offenders.

- Private security should maintain the confidentiality of information obtained as a result of its position as security provider, except where to do so would jeopardize the principles contained herein.

To minimize the risk that private security exceed their authority as providers of security, and to promote respect for human rights generally, we have developed the following additional voluntary principles and guidelines:

- Where appropriate, Companies should include the principles outlined above as contractual provisions in agreements with private security providers and ensure that private security personnel are adequately trained to respect the rights of employees and the local community. To the extent practicable, agreements between Companies and private security should require investigation of unlawful or abusive behavior and appropriate disciplinary action. Agreements should also permit termination of the relationship by Companies where there is credible evidence of unlawful or abusive behavior by private security personnel.

- Companies should consult and monitor private security providers to ensure they fulfil their obligation to provide security in a manner consistent with the principles outlined above. Where appropriate, Companies should seek to employ private security providers that are representative of the local population.

- Companies should review the background of private security they intend to employ, particularly with regard to the use of excessive force. Such reviews should include an assessment of previous services provided to the host government and whether these services raise concern about the private security firm's dual role as a private security provider and government contractor.

- Companies should consult with other Companies, home country officials, host country officials, and civil society regarding experiences with private security. Where appropriate and lawful, Companies should facilitate the exchange of information about unlawful activity and abuses committed by private security providers.

7

The Norms on the Responsibilities of Transnational Corporations and Other Business Enterprises with Regard to Human Rights

> The world is rightly asking that companies should be more accountable. And there is today a multiplicity of codes and guidelines reflecting this demand. But none [touches] the totality of what is required. What we need is a comprehensive and authoritative instrument for this purpose. It seems to me that only the UN can provide this. What we have before us today in these Guidelines [Norms] is such an instrument—it is the logical extension of the Universal Declaration into corporate practice which would be complementary to the Secretary-General's Global Compact.
>
> *Sir Geoffrey Chandler*[1]

Type   Performance-oriented standard, process-oriented standard

Strength Comprehensiveness

Keywords Human rights • Labour rights • Environment • Development • Anti-bribery • Corruption • Consumer protection

7.1 Background

The Norms on the Responsibilities of Transnational Corporations and Other Business Enterprises with Regard to Human Rights (hereafter referred to as the Norms) are very comprehensive, integrating human rights, labour rights, the environ-

---

1 Chandler 2001.

ment, development, anti-bribery issues and consumer protection. David Weissbrodt of the UN Working Group on the Working Methods and Activities of Transnational Corporations played a key role in the development of the Norms (Weissbrodt 2000). The Working Group is part of the Sub-Commission on the Promotion and Protection of Human Rights of the UN Commission on Human Rights (UNCHR). Unlike the UNCHR and the General Assembly, the representatives of the Sub-Commission on the Promotion and Protection of Human Rights are not representing governments but serve in their individual capacity as experts. The Norms were adopted by the Sub-Commission on 13 August 2003, but still need to be put to and endorsed by the 53 nation Human Rights Commission, in early March 2004.

The Norms represent an important milestone in the field of corporate responsibility, for several reasons. First, the Norms operationalise the Universal Declaration of Human Rights (see Chapter 5) for companies. Second, the Norms have benefited from the experiences of hundreds of existing codes and standards, building on the lessons learned from earlier initiatives. Third, the Norms address issues that have not been seen in voluntary codes in the past, such as war crimes. Last, the Norms set an important context for human rights issues, articulating that states have the primary responsibility to promote human rights. This is important, as many codes of conduct leave governments out of the equation altogether. The Norms state clearly the responsibility of companies to 'inform themselves of the human rights impact of their principle activities and major proposed activities' (see page 113).

The Norms represent a turning point in that they project corporate responsibility (CR) issues into a legal framework. Although some of the conventions and codes cited by the Norms are non-binding, some of them are binding, such as those relating to war crimes. According to the Lawyers' Committee on Human Rights,

> [the Norms] present the most comprehensive, action-oriented restatement to date of existing human rights laws applicable to global business. Taken as a whole, they confirm in fundamentally new ways (i) the many laws that do indeed apply, and then (ii) how they apply and can be implemented with respect to business conduct (LCHR 2002).

7.2 Strengths and weaknesses

The majority of the codes and principles in this book deal with only a fraction of CR issues. Often, it is the spotlight of media attention that drives the content of codes. The result is that many key issues are excluded. The comprehensive nature of the Norms sets forth a complete agenda for companies, despite their title suggesting that they deal exclusively with human rights.

Human Rights Watch and Amnesty International have praised the Working Group on the Working Methods and Activities of Transnational Corporations for its transparent nature. Hundreds of non-governmental organisations (NGOs), academics and trade unions have commented on the Norms. The companies providing input have been fewer in number than their NGO counterparts.

According to Katherine Hagen (2002: 6), a former deputy director general for the International Labour Organisation (ILO), the Norms are significant because they are being discussed within the UN Human Rights Commission. Another strength is the large number of codes and principles to which the Norms refer, including company codes of conduct, sector codes and NGO codes of conduct.

Sumithra Dhanarajan, a policy adviser at Oxfam, believes that an effective code must be written from the point of view of the potential victims of human rights abuses.[2] The Norms may be one of the few standards that take this perspective (LCHR 2002).

Some companies remain sceptical about the Norms in the sense that there was a lack of corporate involvement in their development. Many companies, however, have been involved in the drafting process. Perhaps a greater involvement of companies in the process will allay some of the concerns of the corporate sector.

7.3 Companies to which the Norms on the Responsibilities of Transnational Corporations and Other Business Enterprises with Regard to Human Rights apply

The Norms are directed not only at transnational corporations (TNCs) but also at 'other business enterprises', such as the suppliers, contractors and subcontractors of the TNCs.

7.4 Questions posed and answered

The Norms pose many questions, perhaps more than any other tool presented in this book. Among the key questions posed and answered are:

- What are the responsibilities of states in promoting human rights?
- What is the role of companies in protecting the right of security of persons?
- What is discrimination?
- How can companies respect national sovereignty and human rights?
- What are the obligations of companies in relation to consumer protection?

2   Interview with Sumithra Dhanarajan, Policy Advisor, Private Sector, Oxfam, UK, 8 April 2003.

- What are the obligations of companies in relation to intellectual property rights?

7.5 The challenge and the promise

The challenge for the Norms will be to create momentum amid apathy. The Norms represent a new vehicle and a broad forum for discussion. In its testimony on the Norms, Human Rights Watch proposed that the Working Group on the Working Methods and Activities of Transnational Corporations could create

> a permanent forum that could later evolve into a formal complaints mechanism, to receive, consider and assess information from local communities, companies, governments, NGOs, trade unions and other interested parties regarding corporate conduct and its impact on the enjoyment of human rights (HRW 2002).

Other commentators have recommended that domestic courts could play a role in the Norms and that annual reports on the progress of the Norms could be implemented.[3] The Norms have opened a political space for action and discussion that was not previously available.

References

Chandler, G. (2001) Statement, regarding the Draft Universal Human Rights Guidelines for Companies, to the Working Group on the Working Methods and Activities of Transnational Corporations, UN Sub-Commission on the Promotion and Protection of Human Rights. Geneva, 31 July 2001; copy available at http://208.55.16.210/Chandler-statement.htm.

Hagen, K. (2002) 'Overview of the Global Reporting Initiative and other Similar Initiatives', Hagen Resources International (HRI), www.hrigeneva.com/websitedocs/pdf%20docs/gri.pdf.

HRW (Human Rights Watch) (2002) Statement to the Working Group on the Working Methods and Activities of Transnational Corporations, UN Sub-Commission on the Promotion and Protection of Human Rights', August 2002; copy available at http://208.55.16.210/HRW-statement-Aug-2002.htm.

LCHR (Lawyers' Committee for Human Rights) (2002) Statement to the UN Sub-Commission on the Protection and Promotion of Human Rights, 1 August 2002; see http://208.55.16.210/Lawyers-Committee-1-Aug-2002-statement.htm.

Weissbrodt, D. (2000) *Proposed Draft Human Rights Code of Conduct for Companies* (working paper, addendum; draft human rights code of conduct for companies, with source materials, 25 May 2000; www.unhchr.ch/Huridocda/Huridoca.nsf/0/13e40a9bc4e3be3fc1256912003c5797?Opendocument).

---

3 See www.ishr.ch/About%20UN/Reports%20and%20Analysis/Sub%2054%20-%20ESC%2orights.htm

Commentary on the Norms on the Responsibilities of Transnational Corporations and Other Business Enterprises with Regard to Human Rights

UN Doc. E/CN.4/Sub.2/2003/38/Rev.2 (2003)

Preamble

Bearing in mind the principles and obligations under the Charter of the United Nations, in particular the preamble and Articles 1, 2, 55, and 56, inter alia to promote universal respect for, and observance of, human rights and fundamental freedoms,

Recalling that the Universal Declaration of Human Rights proclaims a common standard of achievement for all peoples and all nations, to the end that Governments, other organs of society and individuals shall strive, by teaching and education, to promote respect for human rights and freedoms, and, by progressive measures, to secure universal and effective recognition and observance, including of equal rights of women and men and the promotion of social progress and better standards of life in larger freedom,

Recognizing that even though States have the primary responsibility to promote, secure the fulfillment of, respect, ensure respect of and protect human rights, transnational corporations and other business enterprises, as organs of society, are also responsible for promoting and securing the human rights set forth in the Universal Declaration of Human Rights,

Realizing that transnational corporations and other business enterprises, their officers and persons working for them are also obligated to respect generally recognized responsibilities and norms contained in United Nations treaties and other international instruments such as the Convention on the Prevention and Punishment of the Crime of Genocide; the Convention against Torture and Other Cruel, Inhuman or Degrading Treatment or Punishment; the Slavery Convention and the Supplementary Convention on the Abolition of Slavery, the Slave Trade, and Institutions and Practices Similar to Slavery; the International Convention on the Elimination of All Forms of Racial Discrimination; the Convention on the Elimination of All Forms of Discrimination against Women; the International Covenant on Economic, Social and Cultural

Rights; the International Covenant on Civil and Political Rights; the Convention on the Rights of the Child; the International Convention on the Protection of the Rights of All Migrant Workers and Members of Their Families; the four Geneva Conventions of 12 August 1949 and two Additional Protocols thereto for the protection of victims of war; the Declaration on the Right and Responsibility of Individuals, Groups and Organs of Society to Promote and Protect Universally Recognized Human Rights and Fundamental Freedoms; the Rome Statute of the International Criminal Court; the United Nations Convention against Transnational Organized Crime; the Convention on Biological Diversity; the International Convention on Civil Liability for Oil Pollution Damage; the Convention on Civil Liability for Damage Resulting from Activities Dangerous to the Environment; the Declaration on the Right to Development; the Rio Declaration on the Environment and Development; the Plan of Implementation of the World Summit on Sustainable Development; the United Nations Millennium Declaration; the Universal Declaration on the Human Genome and Human Rights; the International Code of Marketing of Breast-milk Substitutes adopted by the World Health Assembly; the Ethical Criteria for Medical Drug Promotion and the "Health for All in the Twenty-First Century" policy of the World Health Organization; the Convention against Discrimination in Education of the United Nations Educational, Scientific, and Cultural Organization; conventions and recommendations of the International Labour Organization; the Convention and Protocol relating to the Status of Refugees; the African Charter on Human and Peoples' Rights; the American Convention on Human Rights; the European Convention for the Protection of Human Rights and Fundamental Freedoms; the Charter of Fundamental Rights of the European Union; the Convention on Combating Bribery of Foreign Public Officials in International Business Transactions of the Organisation for Economic Cooperation and Development; and other instruments,

Taking into account the standards set forth in the Tripartite Declaration of Principles Concerning Multinational Enterprises and Social Policy and the Declaration on Fundamental Principles and Rights at Work of the International Labour Organization,

Aware of the Guidelines for Multinational Enterprises and the Committee on International Investment and Multinational Enterprises of the Organisation for Economic Cooperation and Development,

Aware also of the United Nations Global Compact initiative which challenges business leaders to "embrace and enact" nine basic principles with respect to human rights, including labour rights and the environment,

Conscious of the fact that the Governing Body Subcommittee on Multinational Enterprises and Social Policy, the Committee of Experts on the Application of Standards, as well as Committee on Freedom of Association of the International Labour Organization have named business enterprises implicated in States' failure to comply with Conventions No. 87 concerning the Freedom of Association and Protection of the Right to Organize and No. 98 concerning the Application of the Principles of the Right to Organize and Bargain Collectively, and seeking to supplement and assist their efforts to encourage transnational corporations and other business enterprises to protect human rights,

Conscious also of the Commentary on the Norms on the responsibilities of transnational corporations and other business enterprises with regard to human rights, and finding it a useful interpretation and elaboration of the standards contained in the Norms,

Taking note of global trends which have increased the influence of transnational corporations and other business enterprises on the economies of most countries and in international economic relations, and of the growing number of other business enterprises which operate across national boundaries in a variety of arrangements resulting in economic activities beyond the actual capacities of any one national system,

Noting that transnational corporations and other business enterprises have the capacity to foster economic well-being, development, technological improvement and wealth, as well as the capacity to cause harmful impacts on the human rights and lives of individuals through their core business practices and operations, including employment practices, environmental policies, relationships with suppliers and consumers, interactions with Governments and other activities,

Noting also that new international human rights issues and concerns are continually emerging and that transnational corporations and other business enterprises often are involved in these issues and concerns, such that further standard-setting and implementation are required at this time and in the future,

Acknowledging the universality, indivisibility, interdependence and interrelatedness of human rights, including the right to development, which entitles every human person and all peoples to participate in, contribute to and enjoy economic, social, cultural and political development in which all human rights and fundamental freedoms can be fully realized,

Reaffirming that transnational corporations and other business enterprises, their officers—including managers, members of corporate boards or directors and other executives—and persons working for them, inter alia, human rights obligations and responsibilities and that these human rights norms will contribute to the making and development of international law as to those responsibilities and obligations,

Solemnly proclaims these Norms on the Responsibilities of Transnational Corporations and Other Business Enterprises with Regard to Human Rights and urges that every effort be made so that they become generally known and respected.

A. General obligations

1. States have the primary responsibility to promote, secure the fulfillment of, respect, ensure respect of and protect human rights recognized in international as well as national law, including ensuring that transnational corporations and other business enterprises respect human rights. Within their respective spheres of activity and influence, transnational corporations and other business enterprises have the obligation to promote, secure the fulfillment of, respect, ensure respect of and protect human rights recognized in international as well as national law, including the rights and interests of indigenous peoples and other vulnerable groups.

Commentary

(a) This paragraph reflects the primary approach of the Norms and the remainder of the Norms shall be read in the light of this paragraph. The obligation of transnational corporations and other business enterprises under these Norms applies equally to activities occurring in the home country or territory of the transnational corporation or other business enterprise, and in any country in which the business is engaged in activities.

(b) Transnational corporations and other business enterprises shall have the responsibility to use due diligence in ensuring that their activities do not contribute directly or indirectly to human abuses, and that they do not directly or indirectly benefit from abuses of which they were aware or ought to have been aware. Transnational corporations and other business enterprises shall further refrain from activities that would undermine the rule of law as well as governmental and other efforts to promote and ensure respect for human rights, and shall use their influence in order to help promote and ensure respect for human rights. Transnational corporations and other business enterprises shall inform themselves of the human rights impact of their principal activities and major proposed activities so that they can further avoid complicity in human rights abuses. The Norms may not be used by States as an excuse for failing to take action to protect human rights, for example, through the enforcement of existing laws.

B. Right to equal opportunity and non-discriminatory treatment

2. Transnational corporations and other business enterprises shall ensure equality of opportunity and treatment, as provided in the relevant international instruments and national legislation as well as international human rights law, for the purpose of eliminating discrimination based on race, colour, sex, language, religion, political opinion, national or social origin, social status, indigenous status, disability, age—except for children, who may be given greater protection—or other status of the individual unrelated to the inherent requirements to perform the job or of complying with special measures designed to overcome past discrimination against certain groups.

Commentary

(a) Transnational corporations and other business enterprises shall treat each worker with equality, respect and dignity. Examples of the other sorts of status on the basis of which discrimination should be eliminated are health status (including HIV/AIDS, disability), marital status, capacity to bear children, pregnancy and sexual orientation. No worker shall be subject to direct or indirect physical, sexual, racial, psychological, verbal, or any other discriminatory form of harassment or abuse as defined above. No worker shall be subject to intimidation or degrading treatment or be disciplined without fair procedures. Transnational corporations and other business enterprises shall establish a work environment in which it is clear that such discrimination will not be tolerated. These responsibilities shall be carried out in accordance with the Code of Practice on HIV/AIDS and the World of Work and the Code of Practice on Managing Disability in the Workplace of the International Labour Convention (ILO) and other relevant international instruments.

(b) Discrimination means any distinction, exclusion, or preference made on the above-stated bases, which has the effect of nullifying or impairing equality of opportunity or treatment in employment or occupation. All policies of transnational corporations and other business enterprises, including, but not limited to, those relating to recruitment, hiring, discharge, pay, promotion and training, shall be non-discriminatory.

(c) Particular attention should be devoted to the consequences of business activities that may affect the rights of women and particularly in regard to conditions of work.

(d) Transnational corporations and other business enterprises shall treat other stakeholders, such as indigenous peoples and communities, with respect and dignity, and on a basis of equality.

C. Right to security of persons

3. Transnational corporations and other business enterprises shall not engage in nor benefit from war crimes, crimes against humanity, genocide, torture, forced disappearance, forced or compulsory labour, hostage-taking, extrajudicial, summary or arbitrary executions, other violations of humanitarian law and other international crimes against the human person as defined by international law, in particular human rights and humanitarian law.

Commentary

(a) Transnational corporations and other business enterprises which produce and/or supply military, security, or police products/services shall take stringent measures to prevent those products and services from being used to commit human rights or humanitarian law violations and to comply with evolving best practices in this regard.

(b) Transnational corporations and other business enterprises shall not produce or sell weapons that have been declared illegal under international law. Transnational corporations and other business enterprises shall not engage in trade that is known to lead to human rights or humanitarian law violations.

4. Security arrangements for transnational corporations and other business enterprises shall observe international human rights norms as well as the laws and professional standards of the country or countries in which they operate.

Commentary

(a) Transnational corporations and other business enterprises, their officers, workers, contractors, subcontractors, suppliers, licensees and distributors, and natural or other legal persons that enter into any agreement with the transnational corporation or business enterprise shall observe international human rights norms, particularly as set forth in the Convention against Torture and Other Cruel, Inhuman or Degrading Treatment or Punishment; the Rome Statute of the International Criminal Court; the United Nations Basic Principles on the Use of Force and Firearms by Law Enforcement Officials; the United Nations Code of Conduct for Law Enforcement Officials; and emerging best practices developed by the industry, civil society and Governments.

(b) Business security arrangements shall be used only for preventive or defensive services and they shall not be used for activities that are exclusively the responsibility of the State military or law enforcement services. Security personnel shall only use force when strictly necessary and only to the extent proportional to the threat.

(c) Security personnel shall not violate the rights of individuals while exercising the rights to freedom of association and peaceful assembly, to engage in collective bargaining, or to enjoy other related rights of workers and employers, such as are recognized by the International Bill of Human Rights and the Declaration on Fundamental Principles and Rights at Work of the ILO.

(d) Transnational corporations and other business enterprises shall establish policies to prohibit the hiring of individuals, private militias and paramilitary groups, or working with units of State security forces or contract security firms that are known to have been responsible for human rights or humanitarian law violations. Transnational corporations and other business enterprises shall engage with due diligence in investigations of potential security guards or other security providers before they are hired and ensure that guards in their employ are adequately trained, guided by and follow relevant international limitations with regard, for example, to the use of force and firearms. If a transnational corporation or other business enterprise contracts with a State security force or a private security firm, the relevant provisions of these Norms (paragraphs 3 and 4 as well as the related commentary) shall be incorporated into the contract and at least those provisions should be made available upon request to stakeholders in order to ensure compliance.(

(e) Transnational corporations and other business enterprises using public security forces shall consult regularly with host Governments and, where appropriate, non-governmental organizations and communities concerning the impact of their security arrangements on local communities. Transnational corporations and other business enterprises shall communicate their policies regarding ethical conduct and human rights, and express their desire that security be provided in a manner consistent with those policies by personnel with adequate and effective training.

D. Rights of workers

5. Transnational corporations and other business enterprises shall not use forced or compulsory labour as forbidden by the relevant international instruments and national legislation as well as international human rights and humanitarian law.

Commentary

(a) Transnational corporations and other business enterprises shall not use forced or compulsory labour, as forbidden in the ILO Forced Labour Convention, 1930 (No. 29) and the Abolition of Forced Labour Convention, 1957 (No. 105) and other relevant international human rights instruments. Workers shall be recruited, paid, and provided with just and favourable conditions of work. They shall take all feasible measures to prevent workers falling into debt bondage and other contemporary forms of slavery.

(b) Workers shall have the option to leave employment and the employer shall facilitate such departure by providing all the necessary documentation and assistance.

(c) Employers shall have resort to prison labour only in the conditions spelled out in ILO Convention No. 29, which allows such labour only as a consequence of a conviction in a court of law provided that the work or service is carried out under the supervision and control of a public authority and that the person concerned is not hired out to or placed at the disposal of private individuals, companies or associations.

6. Transnational corporations and other business enterprises shall respect the rights of children to be protected from economic exploitation as forbidden by the relevant international instruments and national legislation as well as international human rights and humanitarian law.

Commentary

(a) Economic exploitation of children includes employment or work in any occupation before a child completes compulsory schooling and, except for light work, before the child reaches 15 years of age or the end of compulsory schooling. Economic exploitation also includes the employment of children in a manner that is harmful to their health or development, will prevent children from attending school or performing school-related responsibilities, or otherwise is not consistent with human rights standards such as the Minimum Age Convention (No. 138) and Recommendation (No. 146), the Worst Forms of Child Labour Convention (No. 182) and Recommendation (No. 190) and the Convention on the Rights of the Child. Economic exploitation does not include work done by children in schools for general, vocational, or technical education or in other training institutions.

(b) Transnational corporations and other business enterprises shall not employ any person under the age of 18 in any type of work that by its nature or circumstances is hazardous, interferes with the child's education, or is carried out in a way likely to jeopardize the health, safety, or morals of young persons.

(c) Transnational corporations and other business enterprises may employ persons aged 13 to 15 years in light work if national laws or regulations permit. Light work is defined as work which is not likely to be harmful to the health or development of the child, and will not prejudice school attendance, participation in vocational orientation, training programmes approved by competent authority, or the child's capacity to benefit from the instruction received.

(d) Transnational corporations and other business enterprises shall consult with Governments on the design and implementation of national action programmes to eliminate the worst forms of child labour consistent with ILO Convention No. 182. Transnational corporations and other business enterprises using child labour shall create and implement a plan to eliminate child labour. Such a plan shall assess what will happen to children when they are no longer employed in the business and include measures such as withdrawing children from the workplace in tandem with the provision of suitable opportunities for schooling, vocational training and other social protection for the children and their families, for example by employing the parents or older siblings or engaging in other measures consistent with ILO Recommendations Nos. 146 and 190.

7. Transnational corporations and other business enterprises shall provide a safe and healthy working environment as set forth in relevant international instruments and national legislation as well as international human rights and humanitarian law.

Commentary

(a) Transnational corporations and other business enterprises bear responsibility for the occupational health and safety of their workers and shall provide a working environment in accordance with the national requirements of the countries in which they are located and with international standards such as those found in the International Covenant on Economic, Social and Cultural Rights; ILO Conventions Nos. 110 (Plantations, 1958) 115 (Radiation Protection Convention, 1960), 119 (Guarding of Machinery Convention, 1963), 120 (Hygiene (Commerce and Offices) Convention, 1964), 127 (Maximum Weight Convention, 1967), 136 (Benzene Convention, 1971), 139 (Occupational Cancer Convention, 1974), 147 (Merchant Shipping, 1976), 148 (Working Environment (Air Pollution, Noise and Vibration) Convention, 1977), 155 (Occupational Safety and Health Convention, 1981), 161 (Occupational Health Services Convention, 1985), 162 (Asbestos Convention, 1986), 167 (Safety and Health in Construction Convention, 1988), 170 (Chemicals Convention, 1990), 174 (Prevention of Major Industrial Accidents Convention, 1993), 176 (Safety and Health in Mines Convention, 1995), 183 (Maternity Protection, 2000) and other relevant recommendations; as well as ensuring their application under ILO Conventions Nos. 81 (Labour Inspection Convention, 1947), 129 (Labour Inspection (Agriculture) Convention, 1969), 135 (Workers' Representatives Convention, 1971), and their successor conventions. Such a safe and healthy work environment for women and men shall aid in the prevention of accidents and injuries arising out of, linked with, or occurring within the course of work. Transnational corporations and other business enterprises shall also take into account the particular needs of migrant workers as set forth in the Migrant Workers (Supplementary Provisions) Convention, 1975 (No. 143) and the International Convention on the Protection of the Rights of All Migrant Workers and Members of Their Families.

(b) Consistent with paragraph 15 (a), transnational corporations and other business enterprises shall make available information about the health and safety standards relevant to their local activities. The information shall also include arrangements for training in safe working practices and details on the effects of all substances used in manufacturing processes. In particular, and additionally consistent with paragraph 15 (e), transnational corporations and other business enterprises shall make known any special hazards that tasks or conditions of work involve and the related measures available to protect the workers.

(c) Transnational corporations and other business enterprises shall provide, where necessary, measures to deal with emergencies and accidents, including first-aid arrangements. They also shall provide, at their expense, personal protective clothing and equipment when necessary. Further, they shall incur expenses for occupational health and safety measures.

(d) Transnational corporations and other business enterprises shall consult and cooperate fully with health, safety and labour authorities, workers' representatives and their organizations and established safety and health organizations on matters of occupational health and safety. They shall cooperate in the work of international organizations concerned with the preparation and adoption of international safety and health standards. Where appropriate, matters relating to safety and health should be incorporated in agreements with the representatives of the workers and their organizations. Transnational corporations and other business enterprises shall examine the causes of safety and health hazards in their industry and work to implement improvements and solutions to those conditions, including the provision of safe equipment at least consistent with industry standards. Further, they shall monitor the working environment and the health of workers liable to exposure to specified hazards and risks. Transnational corporations and other business enterprises shall investigate work-related accidents, keep records of incidents stating their cause and remedial measures taken to prevent similar accidents, ensure the provision of remedies for the injured, and otherwise act in accordance with paragraph 16 (e).

(e) Consistent with paragraph 16 (e), transnational corporations and other business enterprises shall also: (i) respect the right of workers to remove themselves from work situations in which there is a reasonable basis for concern about present, imminent and serious danger to life or health; (ii) not subject them to consequences as a result; and further (iii) not require them to return to work situations as long as the condition continues.

(f) Transnational corporations and other business enterprises shall not require any worker to work more than 48 hours per week or more than 10 hours in one day. Voluntary overtime for workers shall not exceed 12 hours per week and shall not be expected on a regular basis. Compensation for such overtime shall be at a rate higher than the normal rate. Each worker shall be given at least one day off in every seven-day period. These protections may be adjusted to meet the different needs of management personnel; construction, exploration and similar workers who work for short periods (e.g. a week or two) followed by a comparable period of rest; and professionals who have clearly indicated their personal desire to work more hours.

8. Transnational corporations and other business enterprises shall provide workers with remuneration that ensures an adequate standard of living for them and their families. Such remuneration shall take due account of their needs for adequate living conditions with a view towards progressive improvement.

Commentary

(a) Transnational corporations and other business enterprises shall provide workers with fair and reasonable remuneration for work done or to be done, freely agreed upon or fixed by national laws or regulations (whichever is higher), payable regularly and at short intervals in legal tender, so as to ensure an adequate standard of living for workers and their families. Operations in the least developed countries shall take particular care to provide just wages. Wages shall be paid, consistent with international standards such as the Protection of Wages Convention, 1949 (No. 95). Wages are a contractual obligation of employers that are to be honoured even into insolvency in accordance with Workers' Claims (Employer's Insolvency) Convention, 1992 (No. 173).

(b) Transnational corporations and other business enterprises shall not deduct from a worker's wages already earned as a disciplinary measure, nor shall any deduction from wages be permitted under conditions or to an extent other than as prescribed by national laws or regulations, or fixed by a collective agreement or arbitration award. Transnational corporations and other business enterprises shall also avoid taking actions to undermine the value of employee benefits, including pensions, deferred compensation and health care.

(c) Transnational corporations and other business enterprises shall keep detailed written records on each worker's hours of work and wages paid. Workers shall be informed in an appropriate and easily understandable manner before they enter employment and when any changes take place as to the conditions in respect of wages, salaries and additional emoluments under which they are employed. At the time of each payment of wages, workers shall receive a wage statement informing them of such particulars relating to the pay period concerned as the gross amount of wages earned, any deduction which may have been made, including the reasons therefore, and the net amount of wages due.

(d) Transnational corporations and other business enterprises shall not limit in any manner the freedom of workers to dispose of their wages, nor shall they exert any coercion on workers to make use of company stores or services, where such stores exist. In cases in which the partial payment of wages in the form of allowances in kind is authorized by national laws or regulations, collective agreements, or arbitration awards, transnational corporations and other business enterprises shall ensure that such allowances are appropriate for the personal use and benefit of workers and their families and that the value attributed to such allowances is fair and reasonable.

(e) In determining a wage policy and rates of remuneration, transnational corporations and other business enterprises shall ensure the application of the principle of equal remuneration for work of equal value and the principle of equality of opportunity and treatment in respect of employment and occupation, in accordance with international standards such as the Equal Remuneration Convention, 1951 (No. 100), The Discrimination in Employment and Occupation Convention, 1958 (No. 111) and the Workers with Family Responsibilities Convention, 1981 (No. 156).

9. Transnational corporations and other business enterprises shall ensure freedom of association and effective recognition of the right to collective bargaining by protecting the right to establish and, subject only to the rules of the organization concerned, to join organizations of their own choosing without distinction, previous authorization, or interference, for the protection of their employment interests and for other collective bargaining purposes as provided in national legislation and the relevant conventions of the International Labour Organization.

Commentary

(a) Transnational corporations and other business enterprises shall respect workers' and employers' freedom of association consistent with the Freedom of Association and Protection of the Right to Organize Convention, 1948 (No. 87) and other international human rights law. They shall respect the rights of workers' organizations to function independently and without interference, including with respect to the right of workers' organizations to draw up their constitutions and rules, to elect their representatives, to organize their administration and activities and to formulate their programmes. Further, they shall refrain from discriminating against workers by reason of trade union membership or participation in trade union activities, and shall refrain from any interference that restricts these rights or impedes their lawful exercise. They shall ensure that the existence of workers' representatives does not undermine the position of the union established consistent with international standards, and that workers' representatives are entitled to bargain collectively only where there is no such union in the company. Where appropriate in the local circumstances, multinational enterprises shall support representative employers' organizations.

(b) Transnational corporations and other business enterprises shall recognize workers' organizations for the purpose of collective bargaining consistent with the Right to Organize and Collective Bargaining Convention, 1949 (No. 98) and other international human rights law. They shall respect the right of workers to strike, to submit grievances, including grievances as to compliance with these Norms, to fair and impartial persons who have the authority to redress any abuses found, and to be protected from suffering prejudice for using those procedures, consistent with the norms contained in the Collective Bargaining Convention, 1981 (No. 154).

(c) Transnational corporations and other business enterprises shall enable representatives of their workers to conduct negotiations on their terms and conditions of employment with representatives of management who are authorized to make decisions about the issues under negotiation. They shall further give workers and their representatives access to information, facilities and other resources, and ensure internal communications, consistent with international standards such as the Workers' Representatives Convention, 1971 (No. 135) and the Communications within the Undertaking Recommendation, 1967 (No. 129) that are relevant and necessary for their representatives to conduct negotiations effectively and without unnecessary harm to legitimate interests of employers.

(d) Transnational corporations and other business enterprises shall abide by provisions in collective bargaining agreements that provide for the settlement of disputes arising over their interpretation and application and also by decisions of tribunals or other mechanisms empowered to make determinations on such matters. Transnational corporations and other business enterprises jointly with the representatives and organizations of workers shall seek to establish voluntary conciliation machinery, appropriate to national conditions, which may include provisions for voluntary arbitration, to assist in the prevention and settlement of industrial disputes between employers and workers.

(e) Transnational corporations and other business enterprises shall take particular care to protect the rights of workers from procedures in countries that do not fully implement international standards regarding freedom of association, the right to organize and the right to bargain collectively.

E. Respect for national sovereignty and human rights

10. Transnational corporations and other business enterprises shall recognize and respect applicable norms of international law, national laws and regulations, as well as administrative practices, the rule of law, the public interest, development objectives, social, economic and cultural policies including transparency, accountability and prohibition of corruption, and authority of the countries in which the enterprises operate.

Commentary

(a) Transnational corporations and other business enterprises, within the limits of their resources and capabilities, shall encourage social progress and development by expanding economic opportunities—particularly in developing countries and, most importantly, in the least developed countries.

(b) Transnational corporations and other business enterprises shall respect the right to development, which all peoples are entitled to participate in and contribute to, and the right to enjoy economic, social, cultural and political development in which all human rights and fundamental freedoms can be fully realized and in which sustainable development can be achieved so as to protect the rights of future generations.

(c) Transnational corporations and other business enterprises shall respect the rights of local communities affected by their activities and the rights of indigenous peoples and communities consistent with international human rights standards such as the Indigenous and Tribal Peoples Convention, 1989 (No. 169). They shall particularly respect the rights of indigenous peoples and similar communities to own, occupy, develop, control, protect and use their lands, other natural resources, and cultural and intellectual property. They shall also respect the principle of free, prior and informed consent of the indigenous peoples and communities to be affected by their development projects. Indigenous peoples and communities shall not be deprived of their own means of subsistence, nor shall they be removed from lands which they occupy in a manner inconsistent with Convention No. 169. Further, they shall avoid endangering the health, environment, culture and institutions of indigenous peoples and communities in the context of projects, including road building in or near indigenous peoples and communities. Transnational corporations and other business enterprises shall use particular care in situations in which indigenous lands, resources, or rights thereto have not been adequately demarcated or defined.

(d) Transnational corporations and other business enterprises shall respect, protect and apply intellectual property rights in a manner that contributes to the promotion of technological innovation and to the transfer and dissemination of technology, to the mutual advantage of producers and users of technological knowledge, in a manner conducive to social and economic welfare, such as the protection of public health, and to a balance of rights and obligations.

11. Transnational corporations and other business enterprises shall not offer, promise, give, accept, condone, knowingly benefit from, or demand a bribe or other improper advantage, nor shall they be solicited or expected to give a bribe or other improper advantage to any Government, public official, candidate for elective post, any member of the armed forces or security forces, or any other individual or organization. Transnational corporations and other business enterprises shall refrain from any activity which supports, solicits, or encourages States or any other entities to abuse human rights. They shall further seek to ensure that the goods and services they provide will not be used to abuse human rights.

Commentary

(a) Transnational corporations and other business enterprises shall enhance the transparency of their activities in regard to payments made to Governments and public officials; openly fight against bribery, extortion and other forms of corruption; and cooperate with State authorities responsible for combating corruption.

(b) Transnational corporations and other business enterprises shall not receive payment, reimbursement, or other benefit in the form of natural resources without the approval of the recognized Government of the State of origin of such resources.

(c) Transnational corporations and other business enterprises shall assure that the information in their financial statements fairly presents in all material respects the financial condition, results of operations and cash flows of the business.

12. Transnational corporations and other business enterprises shall respect economic, social and cultural rights as well as civil and political rights and contribute to their realization, in particular the rights to development, adequate food and drinking water, the highest attainable standard of physical and mental health, adequate housing, privacy, education, freedom of thought, conscience, and religion and freedom of opinion and expression, and shall refrain from actions which obstruct or impede the realization of those rights.

Commentary

(a) Transnational corporations and other business enterprises shall observe standards that promote the availability, accessibility, acceptability and quality of the right to health, for example as identified in article 12 of the International Covenant on Economic, Social and Cultural Rights, general comment No. 14 on the right to the highest attainable standard of health adopted by the Committee on Economic, Social and Cultural Rights and the relevant standards established by the World Health Organization.

(b) Transnational corporations and other business enterprises shall observe standards which promote the availability of food in a quantity and of a quality sufficient to satisfy the dietary needs of individuals, free from adverse substances, acceptable within a given culture, accessible in ways that are sustainable and do not interfere with the enjoyment of other human rights, and are otherwise in accordance with international standards such as article 11 of the International Covenant on Economic, Social and Cultural Rights and general comment No. 12 on the right to adequate food adopted by the Committee on Economic, Social and Cultural Rights. Transnational corporations and other business enterprises shall further observe standards which protect the right to water and are otherwise in accordance with general comment No. 15 adopted by the Committee on Economic, Social and Cultural Rights on the right to water.

(c) Transnational corporations and other business enterprises shall further observe standards which protect the right to adequate housing and are otherwise in accordance with article 11 of the International Covenant on Economic, Social and Cultural Rights and general comment No. 7 adopted by the Committee on Economic, Social and Cultural Rights on the right to adequate housing: forced evictions. Transnational corporations and other business enterprises shall not forcibly evict individuals, families and/or communities against their will from their homes and/or land which they occupy without having had recourse to, and access to, appropriate forms of legal or other protection pursuant to international human rights law.

(d) Transnational corporations and other business enterprises shall observe standards that protect other economic, social and cultural rights and are otherwise in accordance with the International Covenant on Economic, Social and Cultural Rights and the relevant general comments adopted by the Committee on

Economic, Social and Cultural Rights, paying particular attention to the implementation of norms stated in paragraphs 16 (g) and (i).

(e) Transnational corporations and other business enterprises shall observe standards that protect civil and political rights and are otherwise in accordance with the International Covenant on Civil and Political Rights and the relevant general comments adopted by the Human Rights Committee.

F. Obligations with regard to consumer protection

13. Transnational corporations and other business enterprises shall act in accordance with fair business, marketing and advertising practices and shall take all necessary steps to ensure the safety and quality of the goods and services they provide, including observance of the precautionary principle. Nor shall they produce, distribute, market, or advertise harmful or potentially harmful products for use by consumers.

Commentary

(a) Transnational corporations and other business enterprises shall adhere to the relevant international standards of business practice regarding competition and anti-trust matters, such as The Set of Multilaterally Agreed Equitable Principles and Rules for the Control of Restrictive Business Practices of the United Nations Conference on Trade and Development. A transnational corporation or other business enterprise shall encourage the development and maintenance of fair, transparent and open competition by not entering into arrangements with competing businesses to directly or indirectly fix prices, divide territories, or create monopoly positions.

(b) Transnational corporations and other business enterprises shall observe relevant international standards for the protection of consumers, such as the United Nations Guidelines for Consumer Protection, and relevant international standards for the promotion of specific products, such as the International Code of Marketing of Breast-milk Substitutes adopted by the World Health Assembly and the Ethical Criteria for Medical Drug Promotion of the World Health Organization. Transnational corporations and other business enterprises shall ensure that all marketing claims are independently verifiable, satisfy reasonable and relevant legal levels of truthfulness, and are not misleading. Further, they shall not target children when advertising potentially harmful products.

(c) Transnational corporations and other business enterprises shall ensure that all goods and services they produce, distribute, or market are capable of use for the purposes claimed, safe for intended and reasonably foreseeable uses, do not endanger the life or health of consumers, and are regularly monitored and tested to ensure compliance with these standards, in the context of reasonable usage and custom. They shall adhere to relevant international standards so as to avoid variations in the quality of products that would have detrimental effects on consumers, especially in States lacking specific regulations on product quality.

They shall further respect the precautionary principle when dealing, for example, with preliminary risk assessments that may indicate unacceptable effects on health or the environment. Further, they shall not use the lack of full scientific certainty as a reason to delay the introduction of cost-effective measures intended to prevent such effects.

(d) Any information provided by a transnational corporation or other business enterprise with regard to the purchase, use, content, maintenance, storage and disposal of its products and services shall be provided in a clear, comprehensible and prominently visible manner and in the language officially recognized by the country in which such products or services are provided. Transnational corporations and other business enterprises, when appropriate, shall also provide information regarding the appropriate recycling, reusability and disposal of its products and services.

(e) Consistent with paragraph 15 (e), where a product is potentially harmful to the consumer, transnational corporations and other business enterprises shall disclose all appropriate information on the contents and possible hazardous effects of the products they produce through proper labeling, informative and accurate advertising and other appropriate methods. In particular, they shall warn if death or serious injury is probable from a defect, use, or misuse. Transnational corporations and other business enterprises shall supply appropriate information of potentially harmful products to the relevant authorities. This information shall include the characteristics of products or services that may cause injury to the health and safety of consumers, workers, or others, and information regarding restrictions, warnings and other regulatory measures imposed by several countries as to these products or services on the grounds of health and safety protection.

G. Obligations with regard to environmental protection

14. Transnational corporations and other business enterprises shall carry out their activities in accordance with national laws, regulations, administrative practices and policies relating to the preservation of the environment of the countries in which they operate, as well as in accordance with relevant international agreements, principles, objectives, responsibilities and standards with regard to the environment as well as human rights, public health and safety, bioethics and the precautionary principle, and shall generally conduct their activities in a manner contributing to the wider goal of sustainable development.

Commentary

(a) Transnational corporations and other business enterprises shall respect the right to a clean and healthy environment in the light of the relationship between the environment and human rights; concerns for intergenerational equity; internationally recognized environmental standards, for example with regard to air pollution, water pollution, land use, biodiversity and hazardous wastes; and the wider goal of sustainable development, that is, development that meets the needs of the present without compromising the ability of future generations to meet their own needs.

(b) Transnational corporations and other business enterprises shall be responsible for the environmental and human health impact of all of their activities, including any products or services they introduce into commerce, such as packaging, transportation and by-products of the manufacturing process.

(c) Consistent with paragraph 16 (i), in decision-making processes and on a periodic basis (preferably annually or biannually), transnational corporations and other business enterprises shall assess the impact of their activities on the environment and human health including impacts from siting decisions, natural resource extraction activities, the production and sale of products or services, and the generation, storage, transport and disposal of hazardous and toxic substances. Transnational corporations and other business enterprises shall ensure that the burden of negative environmental consequences shall not fall on vulnerable racial, ethnic and socio-economic groups.

(d) Assessments shall, inter alia, address particularly the impact of proposed activities on certain groups, such as children, older persons, indigenous peoples and communities (particularly in regard to their land and natural resources), and/or women. Transnational corporations and other business enterprises shall distribute such reports in a timely manner and in a manner that is accessible to the United Nations Environmental Programme, the ILO, other interested international bodies, the national Government hosting each company, the national Government where the business maintains its principal office and other affected groups. The reports shall be accessible to the general public.

(e) Transnational corporations and other business enterprises shall respect the prevention principle, for example by preventing and/or mitigating deleterious impacts identified in any assessment. They shall also respect the precautionary principle when dealing, for example, with preliminary risk assessments that may indicate unacceptable effects on health or the environment. Further, they shall not use the lack of full scientific certainty as a reason to delay the introduction of cost-effective measures intended to prevent such effects.

(f) Upon the expiration of the useful life of their products or services, transnational corporations and other business enterprises shall ensure effective means of collecting or arranging for the collection of the remains of the product or services for recycling, reuse and/or environmentally responsible disposal.

(g) Transnational corporations and other business enterprises shall take appropriate measures in their activities to reduce the risk of accidents and damage to the environment by adopting best management practices and technologies. In particular, they shall use best management practices and appropriate technologies and enable their component entities to meet these environmental objectives through the sharing of technology, knowledge and assistance, as well as through environmental management systems, sustainability reporting, and reporting of anticipated or actual releases of hazardous and toxic substances. In addition, they shall educate and train workers to ensure their compliance with these objectives.

H. General provisions of implementation

15. As an initial step towards implementing these Norms, each transnational corporation or other business enterprise shall adopt, disseminate and implement internal rules of operation in compliance with the Norms. Further, they shall periodically report on and take other measures fully to implement the Norms and to provide at least for the prompt implementation of the protections set forth in the Norms. Each transnational corporation or other business enterprise shall apply and incorporate these Norms in their contracts or other arrangements and dealings with contractors, subcontractors, suppliers, licensees, distributors, or natural or other legal persons that enter into any agreement with the transnational corporation or business enterprise in order to ensure respect for and implementation of the Norms.

Commentary

(a) Each transnational corporation or other business enterprise shall disseminate its internal rules of operation or similar measures, as well as implementation procedures, and make them available to all relevant stakeholders. The internal rules of operation or similar measures shall be communicated in oral and written form in the language of workers, trade unions, contractors, subcontractors, suppliers, licensees, distributors, natural or other legal persons that enter into contracts with the transnational corporation or other business enterprise, customers and other stakeholders in the transnational corporation or other business enterprise.

(b) Once internal rules of operation or similar measures have been adopted and disseminated, transnational corporations and other business enterprises shall—to the extent of their resources and capabilities—provide effective training for their managers as well as workers and their representatives in practices relevant to the Norms.

(c) Transnational corporations and other business enterprises shall ensure that they only do business with (including purchasing from and selling to) contractors, subcontractors, suppliers, licensees, distributors, and natural or other legal persons that follow these or substantially similar Norms. Transnational corporations and other business enterprises using or considering entering into business relationships with contractors, subcontractors, suppliers, licensees, distributors, or natural or other legal persons that do not comply with the Norms shall initially work with them to reform or decrease violations, but if they will not change, the enterprise shall cease doing business with them.

(d) Transnational corporations and other business enterprises shall enhance the transparency of their activities by disclosing timely, relevant, regular and reliable information regarding their activities, structure, financial situation and performance. They shall also make known the location of their offices, subsidiaries and factories, so as to facilitate measures to ensure that the enterprises, products and services are being produced under conditions that respect these Norms.

(e) Transnational corporations and other business enterprises shall inform in a timely manner everyone who may be affected by conditions caused by the enterprises that might endanger health, safety, or the environment.

(f) Each transnational corporation or other business shall endeavour to improve continually its further implementation of these Norms.

16. Transnational corporations and other business enterprises shall be subject to periodic monitoring and verification by United Nations, other international and national mechanisms already in existence or yet to be created, regarding application of the Norms. This monitoring shall be transparent and independent and take into account input from stakeholders (including non-governmental organizations) and as a result of complaints of violations of these Norms. Further, transnational corporations and other business enterprises shall conduct periodic evaluations concerning the impact of their own activities on human rights under these Norms.

Commentary

(a) These Norms shall be monitored and implemented through amplification and interpretation of intergovernmental, regional, national and local standards with regard to the conduct of transnational corporations and other business enterprises.

(b) United Nations human rights treaty bodies should monitor implementation of these Norms through the creation of additional reporting requirements for States and the adoption of general comments and recommendations interpreting treaty obligations. The United Nations and its specialized agencies should also monitor implementation by using the Norms as the basis for procurement determinations concerning products and services to be purchased and with which transnational corporations and other business enterprises develop partnerships in the field. Country rapporteurs and thematic procedures of the United Nations, Commission on Human Rights should monitor implementation by using the Norms and other relevant international standards for raising concerns about actions by transnational corporations and other business enterprises within their respective mandates. The Commission on Human Rights should consider establishing a group of experts, a special rapporteur, or working group of the Commission to receive information and take effective action when enterprises fail to comply with the Norms. The Sub-Commission on the Promotion and Protection of Human Rights and its relevant working group should also monitor compliance with the Norms and developing best practices by receiving information from non-governmental organizations, unions, individuals and others, and then by allowing transnational corporations or other business enterprises an opportunity to respond. Further, the Sub-Commission, its working group and other United Nations bodies are invited to develop additional techniques for implementing and monitoring these Norms and other effective mechanisms and to ensure access is given to NGOs, unions, individuals and others.

(c) Trade unions are encouraged to use the Norms as a basis for negotiating agreements with transnational corporations and other business enterprises and monitoring compliance of these entities. NGOs are also encouraged to use the Norms as the basis for their expectations of the conduct of the transnational corporation or other business enterprise and monitoring compliance. Further, monitoring could take place by using the Norms as the basis for benchmarks of ethical investment initiatives and for other benchmarks of compliance. The Norms shall also be monitored through industry groups.

(d) Transnational corporations and other business enterprises shall ensure that the monitoring process is transparent, for example by making available to relevant stakeholders the workplaces observed, remediation efforts undertaken and other results of monitoring. They shall further ensure that any monitoring seeks to obtain and incorporate input from relevant stakeholders. Further, they shall ensure such monitoring by their contractors, subcontractors, suppliers, licensees, distributors, and any other natural or legal persons with whom they have entered into any agreement, to the extent possible.

(e) Transnational corporations and other business enterprises shall provide legitimate and confidential avenues through which workers can file complaints with regard to violations of these Norms. To the extent possible, they shall make known to the complainant any actions taken as a result of the investigation. Further, they shall not discipline or take other action against workers or others who submit complaints or who assert that any company has failed to comply with these Norms.

(f) Transnational corporations and other business enterprises receiving claims of violations of these Norms shall make a record of each claim and obtain an independent investigation of the claim or call upon other proper authorities. They shall actively monitor the status of investigations, press for their full resolution and take action to prevent recurrences.

(g) Each transnational corporation or other business enterprise shall engage in an annual or other periodic assessment of its compliance with the Norms, taking into account comments from and encourage the participation of indigenous peoples and communities to determine how best to respect their rights. The results of the assessment shall be made available to stakeholders to the same extent as the annual report of the transnational corporation or other business enterprise.

(h) Assessments revealing inadequate compliance with the Norms shall also include plans of action or methods of reparation and redress that the transnational corporation or other business enterprise will pursue in order to fulfill the Norms. See also paragraph 18.

(i) Before a transnational corporation or other business enterprise pursues a major initiative or project, it shall, to the extent of its resources and capabilities, study the human rights impact of that project in the light of these Norms. The impact statement shall include a description of the action, its need, anticipated benefits, an analysis of any human rights impact related to the action, an analysis of reasonable alternatives to the action, and identification of ways to reduce any negative human rights consequences. A transnational corporation or other business enterprise shall make available the results of that study to relevant stakeholders and shall consider any reactions from stakeholders.

17. States should establish and reinforce the necessary legal and administrative framework for ensuring that the Norms and other relevant national and international laws are implemented by transnational corporations and other business enterprises.

Commentary

(a) Governments should implement and monitor the use of the Norms, for example, by making them widely available and using them as a model for legislation or administrative provisions with regard to the activities of each enterprise doing business in their country, including through the use of labour inspections, ombudspersons, national human rights commissions, or other national human rights mechanisms.

18. Transnational corporations and other business enterprises shall provide prompt, effective and adequate reparation to those persons, entities and communities that have been adversely affected by failures to comply with these Norms through, inter alia, reparations, restitution, compensation and rehabilitation for any damage done or property taken. In connection with determining damages, in regard to criminal sanctions, and in all other respects, these Norms shall be applied by national courts and/or international tribunals, pursuant to national and international law.

19. Nothing in these Norms shall be construed as diminishing, restricting, or adversely affecting the human rights obligations of States under national and international law, nor shall they be construed as diminishing, restricting, or adversely affecting more protective human rights norms, nor shall they be construed as diminishing, restricting, or adversely affecting other obligations or responsibilities of transnational corporations and other business enterprises in fields other than human rights.

Commentary

(a) This savings clause is intended to ensure that transnational corporations and other business enterprises will pursue the course of conduct that is the most protective of human rights—whether found in these Norms or in other relevant sources. If more protective standards are recognized or emerge in international or State law or in industry or business practices, those more protective standards shall be pursued. This savings clause is styled after similar savings clauses found in such instruments as the Convention on the Rights of the Child (art. 41). This provision and similar references in the Norms to national and international law are also based upon the Vienna Convention on the Law of Treaties (art. 27), in that a State may not invoke the provisions of its internal law as justification for its failure to comply with a treaty, the Norms, or other international law norms.

(b) Transnational corporations and other business enterprises are encouraged to express their own commitment to respecting, ensuring respect for, preventing abuses of, and promoting internationally recognized human rights by adopting their own internal human rights rules of operation which are even more conducive to the promotion and protection of human rights than those contained in these Norms.

I. Definitions

20. The term "transnational corporation" refers to an economic entity operating in more than one country or a cluster of economic entities operating in two or more countries—whatever their legal form, whether in their home country or country of activity, and whether taken individually or collectively.

21. The phrase "other business enterprise" includes any business entity, regardless of the international or domestic nature of its activities, including a transnational corporation, contractor, subcontractor, supplier, licensee or distributor; the corporate, partnership, or other legal form used to establish the business entity; and the nature of the ownership of the entity. These Norms shall be presumed to apply, as a matter of practice, if the business enterprise has any relation with a transnational corporation, the impact of its activities is not entirely local, or the activities involve violations of the right to security as indicated in paragraphs 3 and 4.

22. The term "stakeholder" includes stockholders, other owners, workers and their representatives, as well as any other individual or group that is affected by the activities of transnational corporations or other business enterprises. The term "stakeholder" shall be interpreted functionally in the light of the objectives of these Norms and include indirect stakeholders when their interests are or will be substantially affected by the activities of the transnational corporation or business enterprise. In addition to parties directly affected by the activities of business enterprises, stakeholders can include parties which are indirectly affected by the activities of transnational corporations and other business enterprises such as consumer groups, customers, Governments, neighbouring communities, indigenous peoples and communities, non-governmental organizations, public and private lending institutions, suppliers, trade associations and others.

23. The phrases "human rights" and "international human rights" include civil, cultural, economic, political and social rights, as set forth in the International Bill of Human Rights and other human rights treaties, as well as the right to development and rights recognized by international humanitarian law, international refugee law, international labour law, and other relevant instruments adopted within the United Nations system.

Part 3
Labour rights

The International Labour Organisation (ILO, www.ilo.org) provides a key starting point for understanding initiatives in the field of workers' rights. Established in 1919, the ILO promotes social justice and internationally recognised human and labour rights. The ILO is the only agency of the United Nations to have a tripartite structure, in which three parties—governments, trade unions and employer organisations—play an equal role. The tripartite nature of the ILO ensures that a wide range of perspectives is taken into account.

The ILO formulates labour standards by developing conventions and recommendations on minimum standards. These conventions are international treaties which governments decide whether or not to sign and ratify. Once a country has ratified a convention, the convention becomes legally binding in that country. Recommendations are not legally binding.

To date, the ILO has adopted more than 180 conventions and 185 recommendations. Of these conventions, there are four 'core conventions' (ILO 1998: 7):

● Freedom of association and the effective recognition of the right to collective bargaining

● The elimination of all form of forced and compulsory labour

● The effective abolition of child labour

● The elimination of discrimination with respect to employment and occupation

These core conventions are an integral part of many standards and, as such, are foundation standards. The ILO conventions are ratified by countries that commit themselves to ensuring that their domestic legislation conforms to their obligations under the conventions.

The ILO Declaration on Fundamental Principles and Rights at Work is an important landmark for workers' rights. Adopted in 1998, the Principles require all member states of the ILO to respect the fundamental (core) conventions listed above, *even if those countries have not ratified the conventions*.

Although it is states that commit to the conventions, many of the countries with the worst records for protecting workers' rights are unable to guarantee those rights because of a lack of inspectors and because of the forces of globalisation that cause countries to compete with one another to offer low wages.

Part 3 contains the text of the following principles, codes and standards on labour rights:

- ILO Tripartite Declaration of Principles Concerning Multinational Enterprises and Social Policy

- Social Accountability 8000

- Workplace Code of Conduct of the Fair Labor Association

- Base Code of the Ethical Trading Initiative

- Model Code of the Clean Clothes Campaign

There is also a brief chapter (Chapter 13) listing other major initiatives in the field of labour rights in the clothing industry.

A note on the challenges and problems of multi-sectoral approaches

The late 1990s saw the rise of new types of initiatives to promote workers' rights, including multi-stakeholder initiatives convened by non-governmental organisations (NGOs), often with the financial support of governments. Among these initiatives are those discussed in this part: Social Accountability 8000, the Ethical Trading Initiative, the Fair Labor Association and the Clean Clothes Campaign. These labour initiatives share several points of convergence:

- They are based on ILO conventions and are thus quite similar; it is the implementation and monitoring systems that differ and the frameworks and models that underpin the codes.

- They utilise management systems, such as training, job descriptions and review processes, to embed new policies within the organisation(s).

- They all have benefited from multi-stakeholder discussions and/or partnerships.

- Most approaches apply the highest standard in cases where there are conflicting standards, such as the use of international rather than national codes of conduct.

Human rights include positive and negative rights—positive rights are the 'dos'; negative rights are the 'don'ts'. The multi-stakeholder standards discussed in this part include positive and negative rights, prohibiting child labour, forced labour and discrimination, while promoting wages that support basic needs. According to research conducted by Shareen Hertel of the Human Rights Programme at Columbia University, grass-roots leaders in Mexico and Bangladesh favour a greater inclusion of positive rights in codes of conduct, rather than just prohibitions.[1]

The key divergences between initiatives address the following issues:

- Is the initiative regional or global?

- Is the initiative sectoral or multi-sectoral?

- Where does the ultimate accountability lie—at the factory or retailer or branding company?

- Who carries out the audits—NGOs, professional auditors or focus groups?

- What type of monitoring is involved—internal and/or external?

- Is a living wage required?

- Is there systematic surveillance and implementation of corrective actions?

- Are site visits to workplaces announced or unannounced?

The key initiatives are those presented in Part 3. In 2003, the multi-stakeholder organisations involved in the initiatives covered in Part 3—together with the Fair Wear Foundation and the Worker Rights Consortium—decided to work together on a trial project 'to evaluate the effective implementation of a common approach to observing the provisions of voluntary codes of labour practice'.[2] Collaboration between initiatives is a positive development that can promote clarity and cohesion in a splintered field.

The challenges and promises of these initiatives are quite similar, so in this part of the book the section on challenges and initiatives consists of an explanation of the key points of divergence from (or convergence with) the other initiatives discussed in this part. The type of approach taken for each of the initiatives covered in this part may be summarised as follows:

- Social Accountability 8000: accreditation and certification standard

- Workplace Code of Conduct of the Fair Labor Association: accreditation and certification standard

---

1 Correspondence between Deborah Leipziger and Shareen Hertel, 25 November 2002.
2 'Multistakeholder Organisations Decide on Trial Collaboration', joint communiqué issued from the meeting on 24 February 2003; document shared by Dan Rees of the Ethical Trading Initiative.

- Base Code of the Ethical Trading Initiative: membership and learning network

- Model Code of the Clean Clothes Campaign: campaign

Reference

ILO (International Labour Organisation) (1998) *ILO Declaration on Fundamental Principles and Rights at Work and its Follow-up* (Geneva: ILO).

8
International Labour Organisation: Tripartite Declaration of Principles concerning Multinational Enterprises and Social Policy

> BP . . . will respect the 2000 International Labour Organisation Tripartite Declaration of Principles concerning Multinational Enterprises and Social Policy.
>
> *BP*[1]

Type   Performance-oriented foundation standard

Strength Integrates key ILO conventions and recommendations

Keywords Labour rights • Development • Training • ILO • ILO conventions

8.1 Background

Launched in 1977, the Tripartite Declaration of Principles concerning Multinational Enterprises and Social Policy (hereafter referred to as the Declaration) is directed towards companies, governments, trade unions and employer organisations. The Declaration is often cited, but it is not as relevant today as many other standards. However, it remains an important precursor in the field of corporate responsibility (CR) codes and standards.

---

1   www.bp.com/company_overview/business_pol/ethical_conduct/policy_expect.asp, ©
    1999–2003 BP plc.

One way in which standards can be understood is to view them on a time-line, in which the early codes of the 1970s, such as the OECD Guidelines for Multinational Enterprises (Chapter 2) and the Declaration, are precursors of the more recent standards such as the UN Global Compact (Chapter 4). The Declaration is significant for several reasons. First, the Declaration refers to 28 ILO conventions, and as many recommendations, that were negotiated within a multilateral framework. Second, the Declaration includes procedures for examining disputes[2] that arise in the implementation of the Declaration. A government or trade union can seek to establish whether or not the behaviour of a company is in accordance with the Declaration. To cite an example, Belgium has brought a case to the ILO Committee on Multinational Enterprises concerning a closure of a Michelin plant in which workers were not given adequate warning. The Committee concluded that multinational companies should not close factories without consulting workers (Gallin 1997). Like the OECD Guidelines (Chapter 2), procedures exist for challenging company behaviour but are rarely used.

8.2 Strengths and weaknesses

Like the OECD Guidelines (Chapter 2), which influenced the Declaration, companies are encouraged to observe standards comparable to the host country in which they operate. For many parts of the developing world, the observance of local norms could still involve poor working conditions.

The Declaration is very much a product of its era—a time when multinational corporations were heavily criticised for their political activities in Chile and elsewhere (Vernon 1977). As such, it is a bit dated.

The key strength of the ILO Declaration is that it defines the obligations of governments as well as companies in promoting social and economic development.

8.3 Companies to which the Tripartite Declaration of Principles concerning Multinational Enterprises and Social Policy applies

The Declaration focuses on multinational enterprises. However, the Declaration is very clear that

> the principles laid down in this Declaration do not aim at introducing or maintaining inequalities of treatment between multinational and national enterprises. They reflect good practice for all (ILO 2001: 4; see also page 143).

2   See http://training.itcilo.it/ils/foa/library/tridecl/procedure_en.htm.

8.4 Questions posed and answered

The Declaration asks:

- How can multinational enterprises promote development and the needs of developing countries?

- What are the obligations of governments in promoting training? Equal opportunity? And other frameworks to promote social and environmental development?

8.5 The promise and the challenge

On the promises and challenges of this and the other initiatives discussed in Part 3 on labour rights, see the introductory text (pages 133-36).

With its focus on development, the Declaration is a precursor to the Global Compact (Chapter 4).

References

Gallin, D. (1997) 'The Tripartite Declaration on Multinational Enterprises', a comment in answer to a request for interpretation on the 20th anniversary of the Global Labour Institute, www.global-labour.org/tripartite_declaration_ilo.htm.

ILO (International Labour Organisation) (2001) *Tripartite Declaration of Principles concerning Multinational Enterprises and Social Policy* (Geneva: ILO).

Vernon, R. (1977) *Storm over the Multinationals: The Real Issues* (Cambridge, MA: Harvard University Press, June 1977).

Tripartite Declaration of Principles concerning Multinational Enterprises and Social Policy*

including

- *List* of international labour Conventions and Recommendations referred to in the *Tripartite Declaration of Principles concerning Multinational Enterprises and Social Policy, and*

- *Addendum* to the *Tripartite Declaration of Principles concerning Multinational Enterprises and Social Policy*

(Declaration adopted by the Governing Body of the International Labour Office at its 204th Session (Geneva, November 1977)).

The Governing Body of the International Labour Office:

Recalling that the International Labour Organization for many years has been involved with certain social issues related to the activities of multinational enterprises;

Noting in particular that various Industrial Committees, Regional Conferences, and the International Labour Conference since the mid-1960s have requested appropriate action by the Governing Body in the field of multinational enterprises and social policy;

Having been informed of the activities of other international bodies, in particular the UN Commission on Transnational Corporations and the Organization for Economic Cooperation and Development (OECD);

Considering that the ILO, with its unique tripartite structure, its competence, and its long-standing experience in the social field, has an essential role to play in evolving principles for the guidance of governments, workers' and employers' organizations, and multinational enterprises themselves;

Recalling that it convened a Tripartite Meeting of Experts on the Relationship between Multinational Enterprises and Social Policy in 1972, which recommended an ILO programme of research and study, and a Tripartite Advisory Meeting on the Relationship of Multinational Enterprises and Social Policy in 1976 for the purpose of reviewing the ILO programme of research and suggesting appropriate ILO action in the social and labour field;

---

* Reprinted with permission from the *Tripartite Declaration of Principles Concerning Multinational Enterprises and Social Policy,* © International Labour Organization, 2002.

Bearing in mind the deliberations of the World Employment Conference;

Having thereafter decided to establish a tripartite group to prepare a Draft Tripartite Declaration of Principles covering all of the areas of ILO concern which relate to the social aspects of the activities of multinational enterprises, including employment creation in the developing countries, all the while bearing in mind the recommendations made by the Tripartite Advisory Meeting held in 1976;

Having also decided to reconvene the Tripartite Advisory Meeting to consider the Draft Declaration of Principles as prepared by the tripartite group;

Having considered the Report and the Draft Declaration of Principles submitted to it by the reconvened Tripartite Advisory Meeting;

Hereby approves the following Declaration which may be cited as the Tripartite Declaration of Principles concerning Multinational Enterprises and Social Policy, adopted by the Governing Body of the International Labour Office, and invites governments of States Members of the ILO, the employers' and workers' organizations concerned and the multinational enterprises operating in their territories to observe the principles embodied therein.

1. Multinational enterprises play an important part in the economies of most countries and in international economic relations. This is of increasing interest to governments as well as to employers and workers and their respective organizations. Through international direct investment and other means such enterprises can bring substantial benefits to home and host countries by contributing to the more efficient utilization of capital, technology and labour. Within the framework of development policies established by governments, they can also make an important contribution to the promotion of economic and social welfare; to the improvement of living standards and the satisfaction of basic needs; to the creation of employment opportunities, both directly and indirectly; and to the enjoyment of basic human rights, including freedom of association, throughout the world. On the other hand, the advances made by multinational enterprises in organizing their operations beyond the national framework may lead to abuse of concentrations of economic power and to conflicts with national policy objectives and with the interest of the workers. In addition, the complexity of multinational enterprises and the difficulty of clearly perceiving their diverse structures, operations and policies sometimes give rise to concern either in the home or in the host countries, or in both.

2. The aim of this Tripartite Declaration of Principles is to encourage the positive contribution which multinational enterprises can make to economic and social progress and to minimize and resolve the difficulties to which their various operations may give rise, taking into account the United Nations resolutions advocating the Establishment of a New International Economic Order.

3. This aim will be furthered by appropriate laws and policies, measures and actions adopted by the governments and by cooperation among the governments and the employers' and workers' organizations of all countries.

4. The principles set out in this Declaration are commended to the governments, the employers' and workers' organizations of home and host countries and to the multinational enterprises themselves.

5. These principles are intended to guide the governments, the employers' and workers' organizations and the multinational enterprises in taking such measures and actions and adopting such social policies, including those based on the principles laid down in the Constitution and the relevant Conventions and Recommendations of the ILO, as would further social progress.

6. To serve its purpose this Declaration does not require a precise legal definition of multinational enterprises; this paragraph is designed to facilitate the understanding of the Declaration and not to provide such a definition. Multinational enterprises include enterprises, whether they are of public, mixed or private ownership, which own or control production, distribution, services or other facilities outside the country in which they are based. The degree of autonomy of entities within multinational enterprises in relation to each other varies widely from one such enterprise to another, depending on the nature of the links between such entities and their fields of activity and having regard to the great diversity in the form of ownership, in the size, in the nature and location of the operations of the enterprises concerned. Unless otherwise specified, the term "multinational enterprise" is used in this Declaration to designate the various entities (parent companies or local entities or both or the organization as a whole) according to the distribution of responsibilities among them, in the expectation that they will cooperate and provide assistance to one another as necessary to facilitate observance of the principles laid down in the Declaration.

7. This Declaration sets out principles in the fields of employment, training, conditions of work and life and industrial relations which governments, employers' and workers' organizations and multinational enterprises are recommended to observe on a voluntary basis; its provisions shall not limit or otherwise affect obligations arising out of ratification of any ILO Convention.

General policies

8. All the parties concerned by this Declaration should respect the sovereign rights of States, obey the national laws and regulations, give due consideration to local practices and respect relevant international standards. They should respect the Universal Declaration of Human Rights and the corresponding International Covenants adopted by the General Assembly of the United Nations as well as the Constitution of the International Labour Organization and its principles according to which freedom of expression and association are essential to sustained progress. They should also honour commitments which they have freely entered into, in conformity with the national law and accepted international obligations.

9. Governments which have not yet ratified Conventions Nos. 87, 98, 111 and 122 are urged to do so and in any event to apply, to the greatest extent possible, through their national policies, the principles embodied therein and in Recommendations Nos. 111, 119 and 122[1]. Without prejudice to the obligation of governments to ensure compliance with Conventions they have ratified, in countries in which the Conventions and Recommendations cited in this paragraph are not complied with, all parties should refer to them for guidance in their social policy.

10. Multinational enterprises should take fully into account established general policy objectives of the countries in which they operate. Their activities should be in harmony with the development priorities and social aims and structure of the country in which they operate. To this effect, consultations should be held between multinational enterprises, the government and, wherever appropriate, the national employers' and workers' organizations concerned.

11. The principles laid down in this Declaration do not aim at introducing or maintaining inequalities of treatment between multinational and national enterprises. They reflect good practice for all. Multinational and national enterprises, wherever the principles of this Declaration are relevant to both, should be subject to the same expectations in respect of their conduct in general and their social practices in particular.

12. Governments of home countries should promote good social practice in accordance with this Declaration of Principles, having regard to the social and labour law, regulations and practices in host countries as well as to relevant international standards. Both host and home country governments should be prepared to have consultations with each other, whenever the need arises, on the initiative of either.

Employment promotion

13. With a view to stimulating economic growth and development, raising living standards, meeting manpower requirements and overcoming unemployment and underemployment, governments should declare and pursue, as a major goal, an active policy designed to promote full, productive and freely chosen employment[2].

14. This is particularly important in the case of host country governments in developing areas of the world where the problems of unemployment and underemployment are at their most serious. In this connection, the general conclusions adopted by the Tripartite World Conference on Employment, Income Distribution and Social Progress and the International Division of Labour (Geneva, June 1976) should be kept in mind[3].

15. Paragraphs 13 and 14 above establish the framework within which due attention should be paid, in both home and host countries, to the employment impact of multinational enterprises.

16. Multinational enterprises, particularly when operating in developing countries, should endeavour to increase employment opportunities and standards, taking into account the employment policies and objectives of the governments, as well as security of employment and the long-term development of the enterprise.

17. Before starting operations, multinational enterprises should, wherever appropriate, consult the competent authorities and the national employers' and workers' organizations in order to keep their manpower plans, as far as practicable, in harmony with national social development policies. Such consultation, as in the case of national enterprises, should continue between the multinational enterprises and all parties concerned, including the workers' organizations.

18. Multinational enterprises should give priority to the employment, occupational development, promotion and advancement of nationals of the host country at all levels in cooperation, as appropriate, with representatives of the workers employed by them or of the organizations of these workers and governmental authorities.

19. Multinational enterprises, when investing in developing countries, should have regard to the importance of using technologies which generate employment, both directly and indirectly. To the extent permitted by the nature of the process and the conditions prevailing in the economic sector concerned, they should adapt technologies to the needs and characteristics of the host countries. They should also, where possible, take part in the development of appropriate technology in host countries.

20. To promote employment in developing countries, in the context of an expanding world economy, multinational enterprises, wherever practicable, should give consideration to the conclusion of contracts with national enterprises for the manufacture of parts and equipment, to the use of local raw materials and to the progressive promotion of the local processing of raw materials. Such arrangements should not be used by multinational enterprises to avoid the responsibilities embodied in the principles of this Declaration.

Equality of opportunity and treatment

21. All governments should pursue policies designed to promote equality of opportunity and treatment in employment, with a view to eliminating any discrimination based on race, colour, sex, religion, political opinion, national extraction or social origin[4].

22. Multinational enterprises should be guided by this general principle throughout their operations without prejudice to the measures envisaged in paragraph 18 or to government policies designed to correct historical patterns of discrimination and thereby to extend equality of opportunity and treatment in employment. Multinational enterprises should accordingly make qualifications, skill and experience the basis for the recruitment, placement, training and advancement of their staff at all levels.

23. Governments should never require or encourage multinational enterprises to discriminate on any of the grounds mentioned in paragraph 21, and continuing guidance from governments, where appropriate, on the avoidance of such discrimination in employment is encouraged.

Security of employment

24. Governments should carefully study the impact of multinational enterprises on employment in different industrial sectors. Governments, as well as multinational enterprises themselves, in all countries should take suitable measures to deal with the employment and labour market impacts of the operations of multinational enterprises.

25. Multinational enterprises equally with national enterprises, through active manpower planning, should endeavour to provide stable employment for their employees and should observe freely negotiated obligations concerning employment stability and social security. In view of the flexibility which multinational enterprises may have, they should strive to assume a leading role in promoting security of employment, particularly in countries where the discontinuation of operations is likely to accentuate long-term unemployment.

26. In considering changes in operations (including those resulting from mergers, take-overs or transfers of production) which would have major employment effects, multinational enterprises should provide reasonable notice of such changes to the appropriate government authorities and representatives of the workers in their employment and their organizations so that the implications may be examined jointly in order to mitigate adverse effects to the greatest possible extent. This is particularly important in the case of the closure of an entity involving collective lay-offs or dismissals.

27. Arbitrary dismissal procedures should be avoided[5].

28. Governments, in cooperation with multinational as well as national enterprises, should provide some form of income protection for workers whose employment has been terminated[6].

Training

29. Governments, in cooperation with all the parties concerned, should develop national policies for vocational training and guidance, closely linked with employment[7]. This is the framework within which multinational enterprises should pursue their training policies.

30. In their operations, multinational enterprises should ensure that relevant training is provided for all levels of their employees in the host country, as appropriate, to meet the needs of the enterprise as well as the development policies of the country. Such training should, to the extent possible, develop generally useful skills and promote career opportunities. This responsibility should be carried out, where appropriate, in cooperation with the authorities of the country, employers' and workers' organizations and the competent local, national or international institutions.

31. Multinational enterprises operating in developing countries should participate, along with national enterprises, in programmes, including special funds, encouraged by host governments and supported by employers' and workers' organizations. These programmes should have the aim of encouraging skill formation and development as well as providing vocational guidance, and should be jointly administered by the parties which support them. Wherever practicable, multinational enterprises should make the services of skilled resource personnel available to help in training programmes organized by governments as part of a contribution to national development.

32. Multinational enterprises, with the cooperation of governments and to the extent consistent with the efficient operation of the enterprise, should afford opportunities within the enterprise as a whole to broaden the experience of local management in suitable fields such as industrial relations.

Conditions of work and life

Wages, benefits and conditions of work

33. Wages, benefits and conditions of work offered by multinational enterprises should be not less favourable to the workers than those offered by comparable employers in the country concerned.

34. When multinational enterprises operate in developing countries, where comparable employers may not exist, they should provide the best possible wages, benefits and conditions of work, within the framework of government policies[8]. These should be related to the economic position of the enterprise, but should be at least adequate to satisfy basic needs of the workers and their families. Where they provide workers with basic amenities such as housing, medical care or food, these amenities should be of a good standard[9].

35. Governments, especially in developing countries, should endeavour to adopt suitable measures to ensure that lower income groups and less developed areas benefit as much as possible from the activities of multinational enterprises.

Safety and health

36. Governments should ensure that both multinational and national enterprises provide adequate safety and health standards for their employees. Those governments which have not yet ratified the ILO Conventions on Guarding of Machinery (No. 119), Ionizing Radiation (No. 115), Benzene (No. 136) and Occupational Cancer (No. 139) are urged nevertheless to apply to the greatest extent possible the principles embodied in these Conventions and in their related Recommendations (Nos. 118, 114, 144 and 147). The Codes of Practice and Guides in the current list of ILO publications on Occupational Safety and Health should also be taken into account[10].

37. Multinational enterprises should maintain the highest standards of safety and health, in conformity with national requirements, bearing in mind their relevant experience within the enterprise as a whole, including any knowledge of special hazards. They should also make available to the representatives of the workers in the enterprise, and upon request, to the competent authorities and the workers' and employers' organizations in all countries in which they operate, information on the safety and health standards relevant to their local operations, which they observe in other countries. In particular, they should make known to those concerned any special hazards and related protective measures associated with new products and processes. They, like comparable domestic enterprises, should be expected to play a leading role in the examination of causes of industrial safety and health hazards and in the application of resulting improvements within the enterprise as a whole.

38. Multinational enterprises should cooperate in the work of international organizations concerned with the preparation and adoption of international safety and health standards.

39. In accordance with national practice, multinational enterprises should cooperate fully with the competent safety and health authorities, the representatives of the workers and their organizations, and established safety and health organizations. Where appropriate, matters relating to safety and health should be incorporated in agreements with the representatives of the workers and their organizations.

Industrial relations

40. Multinational enterprises should observe standards of industrial relations not less favourable than those observed by comparable employers in the country concerned.

Freedom of association and the right to organize

41. Workers employed by multinational enterprises as well as those employed by national enterprises should, without distinction whatsoever, have the right to establish and, subject only to the rules of the organization concerned, to join organizations of their own choosing without previous authorisation[11]. They should also enjoy adequate protection against acts of anti-union discrimination in respect of their employment[12].

42. Organizations representing multinational enterprises or the workers in their employment should enjoy adequate protection against any acts of interference by each other or each other's agents or members in their establishment, functioning or administration[13].

43. Where appropriate, in the local circumstances, multinational enterprises should support representative employers' organizations.

44. Governments, where they do not already do so, are urged to apply the principles of Convention No. 87, Article 5, in view of the importance, in relation to multinational enterprises, of permitting organizations representing such enterprises or the workers in their employment to affiliate with international organizations of employers and workers of their own choosing.

45. Where governments of host countries offer special incentives to attract foreign investment, these incentives should not include any limitation of the workers' freedom of association or the right to organize and bargain collectively.

46. Representatives of the workers in multinational enterprises should not be hindered from meeting for consultation and exchange of views among themselves, provided that the functioning of the operations of the enterprise and the normal procedures which govern relationships with representatives of the workers and their organizations are not thereby prejudiced.

47. Governments should not restrict the entry of representatives of employers' and workers' organizations who come from other countries at the invitation of the local or national organizations concerned for the purpose of consultation on matters of mutual concern, solely on the grounds that they seek entry in that capacity.

Collective bargaining

48. Workers employed by multinational enterprises should have the right, in accordance with national law and practice, to have representative organizations of their own choosing recognized for the purpose of collective bargaining.

49. Measures appropriate to national conditions should be taken, where necessary, to encourage and promote the full development and utilization of machinery for voluntary negotiation between employers or employers' organizations and workers' organizations, with a view to the regulation of terms and conditions of employment by means of collective agreements[14].

50. Multinational enterprises, as well as national enterprises, should provide workers' representatives with such facilities as may be necessary to assist in the development of effective collective agreements[15].

51. Multinational enterprises should enable duly authorized representatives of the workers in their employment in each of the countries in which they operate to conduct negotiations with representatives of management who are authorized to take decisions on the matters under negotiation.

52. Multinational enterprises, in the context of bona fide negotiations with the workers' representatives on conditions of employment, or while workers are exercising the right to organize, should not threaten to utilize a capacity to transfer the whole or part of an operating unit from the country concerned in order to influence unfairly those negotiations or to hinder the exercise of the right to organize; nor should they transfer workers from affiliates in foreign countries with a view to undermining bona fide negotiations with the workers' representatives or the workers' exercise of their right to organize.

53. Collective agreements should include provisions for the settlement of disputes arising over their interpretation and application and for ensuring mutually respected rights and responsibilities.

54. Multinational enterprises should provide workers' representatives with information required for meaningful negotiations with the entity involved and, where this accords with local law and practices, should also provide information to enable them to obtain a true and fair view of the performance of the entity or, where appropriate, of the enterprise as a whole[16].

55. Governments should supply to the representatives of workers' organizations on request, where law and practice so permit, information on the industries in which the enterprise operates, which would help in laying down objective criteria in the collective bargaining process. In this context, multinational as well as national enterprises should respond constructively to requests by governments for relevant information on their operations.

Consultation

56. In multinational as well as in national enterprises, systems devised by mutual agreement between employers and workers and their representatives should provide, in accordance with national law and practice, for regular consultation on matters of mutual concern. Such consultation should not be a substitute for collective bargaining[17].

Examination of grievances

57. Multinational as well as national enterprises should respect the right of the workers whom they employ to have all their grievances processed in a manner consistent with the following provision: any worker who, acting individually or jointly with other workers, considers that he has grounds for a grievance should have the right to submit such grievance without suffering any prejudice whatsoever as a result, and to have such grievance examined pursuant to an appropriate procedure[18]. This is particularly important whenever the multinational enterprises operate in countries which do not abide by the principles of ILO Conventions pertaining to freedom of association, to the right to organize and bargain collectively and to forced labour[19].

Settlement of industrial disputes

58. Multinational as well as national enterprises jointly with the representatives and organizations of the workers whom they employ should seek to establish voluntary conciliation machinery, appropriate to national conditions, which may include provisions for voluntary arbitration, to assist in the prevention and settlement of industrial disputes between employers and workers. The voluntary conciliation machinery should include equal representation of employers and workers[20].

List of international labour Conventions and Recommendations referred to in the Tripartite Declaration of Principles concerning Multinational Enterprises and Social Policy

(adopted by the Governing Body of the International Labour Office at its 204th Session (Geneva, November 1977))[21]

Conventions

- Convention (No. 29) concerning Forced or Compulsory Labour, 1930.

- Convention (No. 87) concerning Freedom of Association and Protection of the Right to Organize, 1948.

- Convention (No. 98) concerning the Application of the Principles of the Right to Organize and to Bargain Collectively, 1949.

- Convention (No. 100) concerning Equal Remuneration for Men and Women Workers for Work of Equal Value, 1951.

- Convention (No. 105) concerning the Abolition of Forced Labour, 1957.

- Convention (No. 110) concerning Conditions of Employment of Plantation Workers, 1958.

- Convention (No. 111) concerning Discrimination in Respect of Employment and Occupation, 1958.

- Convention (No. 115) concerning the Protection of Workers against Ionizing Radiations, 1960.

- Convention (No. 119) concerning the Guarding of Machinery, 1963.

- Convention (No. 122) concerning Employment Policy, 1964.

- Convention (No. 130) concerning Medical Care and Sickness Benefits, 1969.

- Convention (No. 135) concerning Protection and Facilities to be Afforded to Workers' Representatives in the Undertaking, 1971.

- Convention (No. 136) concerning Protection against Hazards of Poisoning arising from Benzene, 1971.

- Convention (No. 139) concerning Prevention and Control of Occupational Hazards caused by Carcinogenic Substances and Agents, 1974.

- Convention (No. 142) concerning Vocational Guidance and Vocational Training in the Development of Human Resources, 1975.

Recommendations

- Recommendation (No. 35) concerning Indirect Compulsion to Labour, 1930.

- Recommendation (No. 69) concerning Medical Care, 1944.

- Recommendation (No. 90) concerning Equal Remuneration for Men and Women Workers for Work of Equal Value, 1951.

- Recommendation (No. 92) concerning Voluntary Conciliation and Arbitration, 1951.

- Recommendation (No. 94) concerning Consultation and Cooperation between Employers and Workers at the Level of the Undertaking, 1952.

- Recommendation (No. 110) concerning Conditions of Employment of Plantation Workers, 1958.

- Recommendation (No. 111) concerning Discrimination in Respect of Employment and Occupation, 1958.

- Recommendation (No. 114) concerning the Protection of Workers against Ionizing Radiations, 1960.

- Recommendation (No. 115) concerning Workers' Housing, 1961.

- Recommendation (No. 116) concerning Reduction of Hours of Work, 1962.

- Recommendation (No. 118) concerning the Guarding of Machinery, 1963.

- Recommendation (No. 119) concerning Termination of Employment at the Initiative of the Employer, 1963.

- Recommendation (No. 122) concerning Employment Policy, 1964.

- Recommendation (No. 129) concerning Communications between Management and Workers within the Undertaking, 1967.

- Recommendation (No. 130) concerning the Examination of Grievances within the Undertaking with a View to their Settlement, 1967.

- Recommendation (No. 134) concerning Medical Care and Sickness Benefits, 1969.

- Recommendation (No. 144) concerning Protection against Hazards of Poisoning arising from Benzene, 1971.

- Recommendation (No. 147) concerning Prevention and Control of Occupational Hazards caused by Carcinogenic Substances and Agents, 1974.

- Recommendation (No. 150) concerning Vocational Guidance and Vocational Training in the Development of Human Resources, 1975.

Addendum to the Tripartite Declaration of Principles concerning Multinational Enterprises and Social Policy

(adopted by the Governing Body of the International Labour Office at its 238th Session (Geneva, November 1987) and 264th Session (November 1995))

References to Conventions and Recommendations in the Tripartite Declaration of Principles concerning Multinational Enterprises and Social Policy

A number of international labour Conventions and Recommendations containing provisions relevant to the Declaration are referred to in footnotes in the Declaration as well as in an annex. These footnotes do not affect the meaning of the provisions of the Declaration to which they refer. They should be considered as references to relevant instruments adopted by the International Labour Organization in the corresponding subject areas, which have helped shape the provisions of the Declaration.

Since the adoption of the Declaration by the Governing Body on 16 November 1977, new Conventions and Recommendations have been adopted by the International Labour Conference. This makes it necessary to include a new list of Conventions and Recommendations adopted since 1977 (including those adopted in June 1977), containing provisions relevant to the Declaration, and this list is set out below. Like the footnotes included in the Declaration at the time of its adoption, the new references do not affect the meaning of the provisions of the Declaration.

In keeping with the voluntary nature of the Declaration all of its provisions, whether derived from ILO Conventions and Recommendations or other sources, are recommendatory, except of course for provisions in Conventions which are binding on the member States which have ratified them.

List of Conventions and Recommendations adopted since 1977 (inclusive) which contain provisions relevant to the Declaration

Number and title of Convention and Recommendation	Relevant paragraphs
Conventions	
No. 148 concerning the Protection of Workers against Occupational Hazards in the Working Environment Due to Air Pollution, Noise and Vibration, 1977	36
No. 154 concerning the Promotion of Collective Bargaining, 1981	9, 49
No. 155 concerning Occupational Safety and Health and the Working Environment, 1981	36
No. 156 concerning Equal Opportunities and Equal Treatment for Men and Women Workers: Workers with Family Responsibilities, 1981	21
No. 158 concerning Termination of Employment at the Initiative of the Employer, 1982	9, 26, 27, 28
No. 161 concerning Occupational Health Services, 1985	36
No. 162 concerning Safety in the Use of Asbestos, 1986	36
No. 167 concerning Safety and Health in Construction, 1988	36
No. 168 concerning Employment Promotion and Protection against Unemployment, 1988	13
No. 170 concerning Safety in the Use of Chemicals at Work, 1990	36
No. 173 concerning the Protection of Workers' Claims in the Event of the Insolvency of their Employer, 1992	28
No. 174 concerning the Prevention of Major Industrial Accidents, 1993	36
No. 176 concerning Safety and Health in Mines, 1995	36
Recommendations	
No. 156 concerning the Protection of Workers against Occupational Hazards in the Working Environment Due to Air Pollution, Noise and Vibration, 1977	36
No. 163 concerning the Promotion of Collective Bargaining, 1981	51, 54, 55
No. 164 concerning Occupational Safety and Health and the Working Environment, 1981	36
No. 165 concerning Equal Opportunities and Equal Treatment for Men and Women Workers: Workers With Family Responsibilities, 1981	21
No. 166 concerning Termination of Employment at the Initiative of the Employer	9, 26, 27, 28
No. 169 concerning Employment Policy, 1984	9, 13
No. 171 concerning Occupational Health Services, 1985	36
No. 172 concerning Safety in the Use of Asbestos, 1986	36

Number and title of Convention and Recommendation	Relevant paragraphs
Recommendations	
No. 175 concerning Safety and Health in Construction, 1988	36
No. 176 concerning Employment Promotion and Protection against Unemployment, 1988	13
No. 177 concerning Safety in the Use of Chemicals at Work, 1990	36
No. 180 concerning the Protection of Workers' Claims in the event of the Insolvency of their Employer, 1992	28
No. 181 concerning the Prevention of Major Industrial Accidents, 1993	36
No. 183 concerning Safety and Health in Mines, 1995	36

Notes:

[1] Convention (No. 87) concerning Freedom of Association and Protection of the Right to Organize; Convention (No. 98) concerning the Application of the Principles of the Right to Organize and to Bargain Collectively; Convention (No. 111) concerning Discrimination in Respect of Employment and Occupation; Convention (No. 122) concerning Employment Policy; Recommendation (No. 111) concerning Discrimination in Respect of Employment and Occupation; Recommendation (No. 119) concerning Termination of Employment at the Initiative of the Employer; Recommendation (No. 122) concerning Employment Policy.

[2] Convention (No. 122) and Recommendation (No. 122) concerning Employment Policy.

[3] ILO, World Employment Conference, Geneva, 4-17 June 1976.

[4] Convention (No. 111) and Recommendation (No. 111) concerning Discrimination in Respect of Employment and Occupation; Convention (No. 100) and Recommendation (No. 90) concerning Equal Remuneration for Men and Women Workers for Work of Equal Value.

[5] Recommendation (No. 119) concerning Termination of Employment at the Initiative of the Employer.

[6] Recommendation (No. 119) concerning Termination of Employment at the Initiative of the Employer.

[7] Convention (No. 142) and Recommendation (No. 150) concerning Vocational Guidance and Vocational Training in the Development of Human Resources.

[8] Recommendation (No. 116) concerning Reduction of Hours of Work.

[9] Convention (No. 110) and Recommendation (No. 110) concerning Conditions of Employment of Plantation Workers; Recommendation (No. 115) concerning Workers' Housing; Recommendation (No. 69) concerning Medical Care; Convention (No. 130) and Recommendation (No. 134) concerning Medical Care and Sickness.

[10] The ILO Conventions and Recommendations referred to are listed in "Publications on Occupational Safety and Health", ILO, Geneva, 1976, pp. 1-3. An up-to-date list of Codes of Practice and Guides can be found in the latest edition.

[11] Convention No. 87, Article 2.

[12] Convention No. 98, Article 1(1).

[13] Convention No. 98, Article 2(1).

[14] Convention No. 98, Article 4.

[15] Convention (No. 135) concerning Protection and Facilities to be Afforded to Workers' Representatives in the Undertaking.

[16] Recommendation (No. 129) concerning Communications between Management and Workers within Undertakings.

[17] Recommendation (No. 94) concerning Consultation and Cooperation between Employers and Workers of the Level of Undertaking; Recommendation (No. 129) concerning Communications within the Undertaking.

[18] Recommendation (No. 130) concerning the Examination of Grievances within the Undertaking with a view to their Settlement.

[19] Convention (No. 29) concerning Forced or Compulsory Labour; Convention (No. 105) concerning the Abolition of Forced Labour; Recommendation (No. 35) concerning Indirect Compulsion to Labour.

[20] Recommendation (No. 92) concerning Voluntary Conciliation and Arbitration.

[21] It was proposed that the Office make available, on request, offprints of the international labour Conventions and Recommendations referred to in the Tripartite Declaration. ILO: Report of the Reconvened Tripartite Advisory Meeting on the Relationship of Multinational Enterprises and Social Policy, Geneva, 4-7 April 1977, GB.204/4/2, 204th Session, Geneva, 15-18 November 1977, p. 2.

9
Social Accountability 8000

SA8000, a truly global standard, is today the best management tool available to ensure social accountability.

Neil Kearney, General Secretary, International Textile, Garment and Leather Workers' Federation[1]

Social Accountability 8000 (SA8000) is the current benchmark in the field of corporate social accountability.'

Morton Winston, Amnesty International, USA[2]

I was very impressed and pleased with the Gap Analysis and then with the Audit because both processes transformed even the most skeptical of our employees into supporters of the SA8000, having realised that it is a useful instrument for both people and company to bring about positive results and better understanding. It is in this spirit that we will apply the improvements and welcome future audits.

Lorenzo Bertolli, Chief Executive, Cirio Del Monte Kenya Limited[3]

Type Performance-oriented standard, process-oriented standard, certification standard

Strength Its inclusion of management systems

Keywords Labour rights • Accreditation • Certification • Management systems • Multi-sectoral • Multi-stakeholder

---

1   Quoted in SAI 2001.
2   Quoted in SAI 2001.
3   E-mail from Lorenzo Bertolli, Chief Executive, Cirio Del Monte Kenya Limited, to Alice Tepper Marlin, President and CEO, Social Accountability International, 20 March 2003.

9.1 Background

Social Accountability 8000 (SA8000[4]) is a global and verifiable standard designed to make workplaces more humane. The standard combines key elements of the ILO conventions with the management systems of the International Organisation for Standardisation (ISO). SA8000 is a certification standard developed, overseen and updated through multi-stakeholder dialogue with trade unions, companies, non-governmental organisations (NGOs) and academics.[5]

SA8000's management systems differentiate the standard from most codes of conduct and statements of intent. Its requirement of the creation of management systems ensures that social issues are integrated into all aspects of company policy and day-to-day operations. Management systems include the need for: training programmes, communications, elected representatives, management representatives, clear lines of authority, management reviews, control of suppliers, and planning and policies. Such management systems guarantee that social policies are still in effect long after an auditor leaves the facility. The management systems of SA8000 also ensure that there will be continuous improvement to the social conditions of the workplace.

9.2 Strengths and weaknesses

SA8000 is both a process and a performance standard in a field dominated by standards that are generally one or the other. Its management systems represent an important point of differentiation. The management standards embed the standard into daily practice. Also, SA8000 certification is gaining recognition in the developing world, with factories seeking certification even without pressure from their customers.

SA8000 applies to companies around the world and across industries, serving as a common benchmark to ensure that basic rights are respected within the supply chains of those companies and industries. As of Autumn 2003, there are SA8000 certifications in 36 industries in 36 countries, impacting 171,307 workers.[6] For example, the AVE (the foreign trade association of the German retail trade) programme developed by a consortium of German retailers provides a listing of SA8000-certified facilities for its members. The global nature of SA8000 allows companies selecting suppliers to use a common system across their operations. The past decade has seen the rise of many national and sectoral standards; although such standards are useful for galvanising an industry into action, they can lead to duplication and multiple audits of the same facilities.

---

4   SA8000 is a registered trademark.
5   For more information on the implementation of SA8000 and other labour standards, see Leipziger 2001.
6   Source: Deborah Case, SAI, certified facilities update, 1 October 2003, electronic communication, internal to SAI.

SA8000 has developed extensive training programmes to promote worker rights. Training is very important in helping to promote the awareness necessary for sustainable improvements to be achieved. There are many types of training being offered and developed: for workers on how to use SA8000 as a tool; for managers on how to follow the requirements; for supply chain managers on how to communicate the requirements and partner with suppliers to enable compliance; and for auditors.[7]

One of the key elements of a certification standard is that, if companies can be certified, they can subsequently lose that certification if they fail to live up to SA8000. Under SA8000, any individual or organisation has the right to complain that a certification is improper, triggering an investigation. Thus, certified facilities can lose their certification and accredited bodies can lose their standing to conduct SA8000 audits.

SA8000 promotes corrective action. During an SA8000 audit, the auditor alerts the facility that it needs to take corrective action in one or more areas before it can gain the SA8000 certificate. This process is critical for guaranteeing continuous improvement.

SA8000 leads to business benefits. Social Accountability International (SAI) has sent questionnaires to all certified facilities to test whether some benefits assumed to occur are in fact being realised, such as the generation of new sales, fewer days lost to injury, the creation of higher-quality products and services, productivity increases and greater retention of workers. The results were positive: over half the respondents reported benefits in each of the above-listed categories. SAI has also surveyed certified facilities regarding the perceived costs and benefits of earning certification.

Since its inception, researchers have studied and written about the use of SA8000 certification in action in India, South Africa, the Philippines, Thailand, the USA and Kenya, providing examples of the problems met and solutions found in use of the SA8000 standard as a tool for workplace improvement (see Leipziger and Kaufman 2003).

Criticism of SA8000 varies and sometimes appears contradictory. For example, some criticise SA8000 for being very rigorous, whereas others regard it as being too lenient. For some, it is a strength that SA8000 requires investment, whereas others regard SA8000 as 'expensive'.

Many of the criticisms made of SA8000 may also be made regarding other major workplace standards. For example, all management standards are biased in favour of companies that have established management systems and that are certified to other management standards, such as ISO 14001 (Chapter 27). As such, it is easier for large companies to implement SA8000 than it is for smaller companies. More research needs to be done on how small and medium-sized enterprises can overcome these barriers, perhaps with technical assistance from governments.

In addition, a study from the Friedrich Ebert Foundation has criticised SA8000 for not requiring the multinational companies that source from certified suppliers

---

7   Social Accountability International and the International Garment, Textile and Leather Workers' Federation (ITGLWF) are conducting training in 12 countries to make codes of conduct more useful to workers (Wick 2003).

to cover the cost of the SA8000 audit and related improvements (Wick 2003: 37). As with ISO standards, the facility being audited bears the costs of the audit under SA8000. However, a significant number of multinational companies, including Toys'R'Us (Leipziger 2001: 14) and Otto Versand (Leipziger 2001: 31), provide assistance, such as training and advice, to suppliers. In many cases, SA8000-certified companies are given priority over non-certified companies and granted longer-term contracts.

9.3 Companies to which Social Accountability 8000 applies

Although SA8000 is suited to all companies, the majority of the companies seeking certification are those where labour conditions are known to be problematic, including those in the textiles, garments, shoes, toys and agriculture sectors. Pressure from US and European buyers is generally an important factor in companies seeking certification. As it is based on the management systems of ISO, SA8000 is well suited to companies that have implemented strong management systems, especially those that have already attained ISO 14001 or ISO 9000 certification.

9.4 Questions posed and answered

SA8000 answers the following questions:

- What are the minimum standards for creating a humane work place?
- What management systems can assist in the implementation of humane working conditions?

It encourages company owners and managers to ask (Leipziger 2001: 111):

- How can I ensure that my company and members of its supply chain are respecting workers' rights?

9.5 The promise and the challenge

On the promises and challenges of this and the other initiatives discussed in Part 3 on labour rights, see the introductory text (pages 133-36).

9.5.1 Points of convergence

9.5.1.1 Training

Training is essential to the success of SA8000. In order to promote compliance, it is necessary to build awareness and capacity, and training has a role to play in this process. In addition, training of managers, workers, NGO staff and auditors is critical to fostering dialogue between stakeholders.

9.5.1.2 Auditing

One of the problems facing suppliers is that they undergo many different audits—for quality, environment and social issues. SA8000, which has been modelled on ISO management systems (Leipziger 2001: 139), can be combined with other types of audits, thus reducing costs and streamlining systems. Although use of combined audits is still in its infancy, this is an important trend, which will require investment in terms of training.

9.5.1.3 Achieving a critical mass and convergence of standards

As with other standards, one of the key challenges is to create a critical mass of certified suppliers. Another key challenge is convergence with other initiatives, which SA8000 is fostering through several initiatives,[8] including worker and manager training in China and Vietnam (www.cepaa.org).

References

Leipziger, D. (2001) *SA8000: The Definitive Guide to the New Social Standard* (London: FT Prentice Hall).

——, and E. Kaufman (2003) 'SA8000: Human Rights in the Workplace', in R. Sullivan (ed.), *Business and Human Rights: Dilemmas and Solutions* (Sheffield, UK: Greenleaf Publishing): 197-206.

SAI (Social Accountability International) (2001) *Setting Standards for a Just World* (brochure; New York: SAI).

Wick, I. (2003) *Workers' Tool or PR Ploy? A Guide to Codes of International Labour Practice* (Bonn/Siegburg: Friedrich Ebert Foundation and Südwind Institut für Ökonomie und Ökumene, 3rd rev. edn, www.fes.de).

Additional resource

Further reading

Smith, D. (2002) *Demonstrating Corporate Values: Which Standard for your Company?* (London: IBE).

8 'Multistakeholder Organisations Decide on Trial Collaboration', joint communiqué issued from the meeting on 24 February 2003; document shared by Dan Rees of the Ethical Trading Initiative.

Social Accountability 8000*

I. PURPOSE AND SCOPE

This standard specifies requirements for social accountability to enable a company to:

a) develop, maintain, and enforce policies and procedures in order to manage those issues which it can control or influence;

b) demonstrate to interested parties that policies, procedures and practices are in conformity with the requirements of this standard.

The requirements of this standard shall apply universally with regard to geographic location, industry sector and company size.

Note: Readers are advised to consult the SA8000 Guidance Document for interpretative guidance with respect to this standard.

II. NORMATIVE ELEMENTS AND THEIR INTERPRETATION

The company shall comply with national and other applicable law, other requirements to which the company subscribes, and this standard. When national and other applicable law, other requirements to which the company subscribes, and this standard address the same issue, that provision which is most stringent applies.

The company shall also respect the principles of the following international instruments:

- ILO Conventions 29 and 105 (Forced & Bonded Labour)

- ILO Convention 87 (Freedom of Association)

- ILO Convention 98 (Right to Collective Bargaining)

- ILO Conventions 100 and 111 (Equal remuneration for male and female workers for work of equal value; Discrimination)

- ILO Convention 135 (Workers' Representatives Convention)

---

* Reprinted with the permission of Social Accountability International. SA8000 is a registered trademark.

- ILO Convention 138 & Recommendation 146 (Minimum Age and Recommendation)
- ILO Convention 155 & Recommendation 164 (Occupational Safety & Health)
- ILO Convention 159 (Vocational Rehabilitation & Employment/Disabled Persons)
- ILO Convention 177 (Home Work)
- ILO Convention 182 (Worst Forms of Child Labour)
- Universal Declaration of Human Rights
- The United Nations Convention on the Rights of the Child
- The United Nations Convention to Eliminate All Forms of Discrimination Against Women

III. DEFINITIONS

1. ***Definition of company:*** The entirety of any organization or business entity responsible for implementing the requirements of this standard, including all personnel (i.e., directors, executives, management, supervisors, and non-management staff, whether directly employed, contracted or otherwise representing the company).

2. ***Definition of supplier/subcontractor:*** A business entity which provides the company with goods and/or services integral to, and utilized in/for, the production of the company's goods and/or services.

3. ***Definition of sub-supplier:*** A business entity in the supply chain which, directly or indirectly, provides the supplier with goods and/or services integral to, and utilized in/for, the production of the supplier's and/or company's goods and/or services.

4. ***Definition of remedial action:*** Action taken to make amends to a worker or former employee for a previous violation of a worker's rights as covered by SA8000.

5. ***Definition of corrective action:*** The implementation of a systemic change or solution to ensure an immediate and ongoing remedy to a nonconformance.

6. ***Definition of interested party:*** Individual or group concerned with or affected by the social performance of the company.

7. ***Definition of child:*** Any person less than 15 years of age, unless local minimum age law stipulates a higher age for work or mandatory schooling, in which case the higher age would apply. If, however, local minimum age law is set at 14 years of age in accordance with developing-country exceptions under ILO Convention 138, the lower age will apply.

8. ***Definition of young worker:*** Any worker over the age of a child as defined above and under the age of 18.

9. **Definition of child labour:** Any work by a child younger than the age(s) specified in the above definition of a child, except as provided for by ILO Recommendation 146.

10. **Definition of forced labour:** All work or service that is extracted from any person under the menace of any penalty for which said person has not offered him/herself voluntarily or for which such work or service is demanded as a means of repayment of debt.

11. **Definition of remediation of children:** All necessary support and actions to ensure the safety, health, education, and development of children who have been subjected to child labour, as defined above, and are dismissed.

12. **Definition of homeworker:** A person who carries out work for a company under direct or indirect contract, other than on a company's premises, for remuneration, which results in the provision of a product or service as specified by the employer, irrespective of who supplies the equipment, materials or other inputs used.

IV. SOCIAL ACCOUNTABILITY REQUIREMENTS

1. CHILD LABOUR

Criteria:

1.1 The company shall not engage in or support the use of child labour as defined above.

1.2 The company shall establish, document, maintain, and effectively communicate to personnel and other interested parties policies and procedures for remediation of children found to be working in situations which fit the definition of child labour above, and shall provide adequate support to enable such children to attend and remain in school until no longer a child as defined above.

1.3 The company shall establish, document, maintain, and effectively communicate to personnel and other interested parties policies and procedures for promotion of education for children covered under ILO Recommendation 146 and young workers who are subject to local compulsory education laws or are attending school, including means to ensure that no such child or young worker is employed during school hours and that combined hours of daily transportation (to and from work and school), school, and work time does not exceed 10 hours a day.

1.4 The company shall not expose children or young workers to situations in or outside of the workplace that are hazardous, unsafe, or unhealthy.

2. FORCED LABOUR

Criterion:

2.1 The company shall not engage in or support the use of forced labour, nor shall personnel be required to lodge 'deposits' or identity papers upon commencing employment with the company.

3. HEALTH AND SAFETY

Criteria:

3.1 The company, bearing in mind the prevailing knowledge of the industry and of any specific hazards, shall provide a safe and healthy working environment and shall take adequate steps to prevent accidents and injury to health arising out of, associated with or occurring in the course of work, by minimizing, so far as is reasonably practicable, the causes of hazards inherent in the working environment.

3.2 The company shall appoint a senior management representative responsible for the health and safety of all personnel, and accountable for the implementation of the Health and Safety elements of this standard.

3.3 The company shall ensure that all personnel receive regular and recorded health and safety training, and that such training is repeated for new and reassigned personnel.

3.4 The company shall establish systems to detect, avoid or respond to potential threats to the health and safety of all personnel.

3.5 The company shall provide, for use by all personnel, clean bathrooms, access to potable water, and, if appropriate, sanitary facilities for food storage.

3.6 The company shall ensure that, if provided for personnel, dormitory facilities are clean, safe, and meet the basic needs of the personnel.

4. FREEDOM OF ASSOCIATION & RIGHT TO COLLECTIVE BARGAINING

Criteria:

4.1 The company shall respect the right of all personnel to form and join trade unions of their choice and to bargain collectively.

4.2 The company shall, in those situations in which the right to freedom of association and collective bargaining are restricted under law, facilitate parallel means of independent and free association and bargaining for all such personnel.

4.3 The company shall ensure that representatives of such personnel are not the subject of discrimination and that such representatives have access to their members in the workplace.

5. DISCRIMINATION

Criteria:

5.1 The company shall not engage in or support discrimination in hiring, remuneration, access to training, promotion, termination or retirement based on race, caste, national origin, religion, disability, gender, sexual orientation, union membership, political affiliation, or age.

5.2 The company shall not interfere with the exercise of the rights of personnel to observe tenets or practices, or to meet needs relating to race, caste, national origin, religion, disability, gender, sexual orientation, union membership, or political affiliation.

5.3 The company shall not allow behaviour, including gestures, language and physical contact, that is sexually coercive, threatening, abusive or exploitative.

6. DISCIPLINARY PRACTICES

Criterion:

6.1 The company shall not engage in or support the use of corporal punishment, mental or physical coercion, and verbal abuse.

7. WORKING HOURS

Criteria:

7.1 The company shall comply with applicable laws and industry standards on working hours. The normal workweek shall be as defined by law but shall not on a regular basis exceed 48 hours. Personnel shall be provided with at least one day off in every seven-day period. All overtime work shall be reimbursed at a premium rate and under no circumstances shall exceed 12 hours per employee per week.

7.2 Other than as permitted in Section 7.3 (below), overtime work shall be voluntary.

7.3 Where the company is party to a collective bargaining agreement freely negotiated with worker organizations (as defined by the ILO) representing a significant portion of its workforce, it may require overtime work in accordance with such agreement to meet short-term business demand. Any such agreement must comply with the requirements of Section 7.1 (above).

8. REMUNERATION

Criteria:

8.1 The company shall ensure that wages paid for a standard working week shall always meet at least legal or industry minimum standards and shall be sufficient to meet basic needs of personnel and to provide some discretionary income.

8.2 The company shall ensure that deductions from wages are not made for disciplinary purposes, and shall ensure that wage and benefits composition are detailed clearly and regularly for workers; the company shall also ensure that wages and benefits are rendered in full compliance with all applicable laws and that remuneration is rendered either in cash or check form, in a manner convenient to workers.

8.3 The company shall ensure that labour-only contracting arrangements and false apprenticeship schemes are not undertaken in an effort to avoid fulfilling its obligations to personnel under applicable laws pertaining to labour and social security legislation and regulations.

9. MANAGEMENT SYSTEMS

Criteria:

Policy

9.1 Top management shall define the company's policy for social accountability and labour conditions to ensure that it:

    a) includes a commitment to conform to all requirements of this standard;

    b) includes a commitment to comply with national and other applicable law, other requirements to which the company subscribes and to respect the international instruments and their interpretation (as listed in Section II);

    c) includes a commitment to continual improvement;

    d) is effectively documented, implemented, maintained, communicated and is accessible in a comprehensible form to all personnel, including directors, executives, management, supervisors, and staff, whether directly employed, contracted or otherwise representing the company;

    e) is publicly available.

Management Review

9.2 Top management shall periodically review the adequacy, suitability, and continuing effectiveness of the company's policy, procedures and performance results vis-a-vis the requirements of this standard and other requirements to which the company subscribes. System amendments and improvements shall be implemented where appropriate.

Company Representatives

9.3 The company shall appoint a senior management representative who, irrespective of other responsibilities, shall ensure that the requirements of this standard are met.

9.4 The company shall provide for non-management personnel to choose a representative from their own group to facilitate communication with senior management on matters related to this standard.

Planning and Implementation

9.5 The company shall ensure that the requirements of this standard are understood and implemented at all levels of the organisation; methods shall include, but are not limited to:

    a) clear definition of roles, responsibilities, and authority;

b) training of new and/or temporary employees upon hiring;

c) periodic training and awareness programs for existing employees;

d) continuous monitoring of activities and results to demonstrate the effectiveness of systems implemented to meet the company's policy and the requirements of this standard.

Control of Suppliers/Subcontractors and Sub-Suppliers

9.6 The company shall establish and maintain appropriate procedures to evaluate and select suppliers/subcontractors (and, where appropriate, sub-suppliers) based on their ability to meet the requirements of this standard.

9.7 The company shall maintain appropriate records of suppliers/subcontractors (and, where appropriate, sub-suppliers') commitments to social accountability, including, but not limited to, the written commitment of those organizations to:

a) conform to all requirements of this standard (including this clause);

b) participate in the company's monitoring activities as requested;

c) promptly implement remedial and corrective action to address any nonconformance identified against the requirements of this standard;

d) promptly and completely inform the company of any and all relevant business relationship(s) with other suppliers/subcontractors and sub-suppliers.

9.8 The company shall maintain reasonable evidence that the requirements of this standard are being met by suppliers and subcontractors.

9.9 In addition to the requirements of Sections 9.6 and 9.7 above, where the company receives, handles or promotes goods and/or services from suppliers/subcontractors or sub-suppliers who are classified as homeworkers, the company shall take special steps to ensure that such homeworkers are afforded a similar level of protection as would be afforded to directly employed personnel under the requirements of this standard. Such special steps shall include but not be limited to:

a) establishing legally binding, written purchasing contracts requiring conformance to minimum criteria (in accordance with the requirements of this standard);

b) ensuring that the requirements of the written purchasing contract are understood and implemented by homeworkers and all other parties involved in the purchasing contract;

c) maintaining, on the company premises, comprehensive records detailing the identities of homeworkers; the quantities of goods produced/services provided and/or hours worked by each homeworker;

d) frequent announced and unannounced monitoring activities to verify compliance with the terms of the written purchasing contract.

Addressing Concerns and Taking Corrective Action

9.10 The company shall investigate, address, and respond to the concerns of employees and other interested parties with regard to conformance/nonconformance with the company's policy and/or the requirements of this standard; the company shall refrain from disciplining, dismissing or otherwise discriminating against any employee for providing information concerning observance of the standard.

9.11 The company shall implement remedial and corrective action and allocate adequate resources appropriate to the nature and severity of any nonconformance identified against the company's policy and/or the requirements of the standard.

Outside Communication

9.12 The company shall establish and maintain procedures to communicate regularly to all interested parties data and other information regarding performance against the requirements of this document, including, but not limited to, the results of management reviews and monitoring activities.

Access for Verification

9.13 Where required by contract, the company shall provide reasonable information and access to interested parties seeking to verify conformance to the requirements of this standard; where further required by contract, similar information and access shall also be afforded by the company's suppliers and subcontractors through the incorporation of such a requirement in the company's purchasing contracts.

Records

9.14 The company shall maintain appropriate records to demonstrate conformance to the requirements of this standard.

10
Fair Labor Association: Workplace Code of Conduct

> We've always believed that industry-wide action is essential to achieving real and lasting changes in working conditions . . . The FLA's programme . . . has the potential to make a real difference in the lives of workers across the industry and around the globe.
>
> *Susheela Jayapal, General Counsel Adidas America*[1]

Type Process-oriented standard, performance-oriented standard, certification standard

Strength Operates at brand level

Keywords Labour rights • Brands • Independent monitoring • Verification

10.1 Background

The Fair Labor Association (FLA) is a network of companies, human rights and labour organisations and colleges and universities seeking to improve working conditions. The FLA accredits independent monitors to inspect factories.

The FLA works with companies to improve internal monitoring systems. Companies are expected to implement systems to ensure that the FLA Code of Conduct is upheld throughout their supply chains. The FLA accredits, selects, hires and pays monitors to conduct independent and external monitoring visits in 5% of participating-company factories. This sample is selected through a weighted process that focuses on countries with the highest risk of labour problems.

---

1 Quoted by Rutgers (1999).

Participating companies must remediate problems found through internal and external monitoring visits (for more details, see van Heerden and Shubash 2003). These findings are posted on the website of the FLA (www.fairlabor.org) within 60 days of the monitoring visit. This system of verification through independent monitoring is reinforced through the third-party complaint system, through which trade unions, non-governmental organisations (NGOs) and companies can notify the FLA of non-compliance in any facilities producing for an FLA member company.

In 1996, US President Clinton convened the Apparel Industry Partnership to address the issue of workers' rights. The result of the negotiations was the Fair Labor Association—a non-profit organisation that accredits independent monitors to inspect factories. Among the companies participating in the FLA are Nike, Reebok, Philip–Van Heusen and Liz Claiborne.[2] Although NGOs and trade unions participated in the drafting of the FLA Code of Conduct, trade unions and the Interfaith Center on Corporate Responsibility (ICCR, www.iccr.org) have since withdrawn their support because of the absence of a living-wage requirement in the FLA Code of Conduct. The FLA also plans to deal with complaints from interested parties.

The FLA model combines both internal monitoring by the participating company in the USA, in addition to independent, external monitoring by groups accredited by the FLA. Under the FLA system, at least 30% of all contractors must undergo independent, external monitoring, with the selection of which contractors will undergo external auditing to be made on the basis of risk analysis by the FLA. At the end of three years, the participating company should have monitored each of its relevant facilities. According to the FLA website, the participating company in the USA must conduct internal monitoring, with attention to the following aspects:[3]

- The communication of standards within the workplace

- The training of company monitors

- The conducting of periodic visits and audits to ensure compliance

- The provision of factory workers with a confidential reporting mechanism

- The development of relationships with local labour, human rights or religious organisations

- The establishing of mechanisms for remedying problems and for communicating results to the FLA

Once 30% of all contractors have been independently monitored by FLA-accredited monitors, the company can use the FLA 'service mark' in its advertising, within its stores or on its products. The FLA staff evaluates the company performance in fulfilling each of its obligations (see above). Independent, external monitoring is one means by which internal compliance systems are evaluated. The

2   See www.fairlabor.org/all/companies/index.html.
3   See www.fairlabor.org/html/faqs.html.

FLA staff also can use their discretion to perform independent verification through a visit to a factory to confirm that remediation efforts have been undertaken and have been effective. In addition, companies report to the FLA on a quarterly and annual basis, and these reports are verified by yearly visits to headquarters and/or field offices to review information.

The FLA has accredited a range of organisations to conduct external monitoring against various components of its code. These organisations include large companies, such as Intertek Services (www.itsintertek.com), and small NGOs, such as Phulki, based in Bangladesh.

The FLA is also working with 185 colleges and universities participating in its programmes. Together, these universities have 1,000 collegiate licensees that manufacture goods on their behalf, such as shirts with a university 'brand', key-rings and yearbooks.

10.2 Strengths and weaknesses

Trade unions have failed to support the FLA because of its lack of commitment to introducing a living-wage requirement (see Greenhouse 1998). The FLA responds to this criticism by stating that too little is known about a living wage to include it as a standard. According to Anne Lally of the FLA, 'the logic is that if this standard cannot always be implemented, and brands take commitments seriously, how can they commit to it?'[4] The FLA is conducting a living-wage forum in Autumn 2003 to explore practical ways to tackle this complex question. In June 2003, the FLA introduced Public Reporting to enhance the transparency of the initiative.

10.3 Companies to which the Workplace Code of Conduct of the Fair Labor Association applies

The Workplace Code of Conduct applies to all companies, but is most applicable to companies that produce branded goods for the US market.

10.4 Questions posed and answered

Under what conditions should products be manufactured so as to ensure that workers' rights are being respected?

---

4   Personal communication from Anne Lally, 27 June 2003.

10.5 The promise and the challenge

On the promises and challenges of this and the other initiatives discussed in Part 3 on labour rights, see the introductory text (pages 133-36).

10.5.1 Points of divergence

10.5.1.1 Geographical target

The FLA works primarily with US companies and their contractors all over the world; it also works with some companies with European headquarters, such as Adidas (www.adidas.com). In contrast, SA8000 (Chapter 9) works with companies from around the world, and the Ethical Trading Initiative (ETI, Chapter 11) works primarily with companies producing consumer goods sold within the United Kingdom.

10.5.1.2 Focus of certification and cost

The FLA provides a certificate to participating US companies, whereas SA8000 provides a certificate to the factory where the good is produced. This may seem like a small detail but it represents a very significant difference. The Clean Clothes Campaign (CCC, Chapter 12) focuses its attention on multinational companies rather than at the factory level. This has implications for both cost and accountability.

Under both FLA and CCC, the multinational company is responsible for the cost of external monitoring, whereas under SA8000 the facility (or factory) undergoing the audit bears the costs.[5] There has been some convergence on the part of SA8000 companies to move closer to the FLA and CCC systems, although this is not required. For example, a number of SA8000 companies have begun to cover the costs associated with audits for their contractors and to assist them with their remediation efforts (e.g. Toys'R'Us [Leipziger 2001: 14] and Otto Versand [Leipziger 2001: 31]). The FLA is also exploring ways in which factories can be brought into the FLA system officially.[6]

10.5.1.3 Sectoral target

The FLA is focused primarily on the apparel and footwear industries, with licensees producing electronic and paper goods. SA8000 is not industry-specific or sector-specific, with participating companies producing toys, agriculture and a wide range of other goods and services.[7]

---

5 For cases in which companies complete their initial implementation period within three years, the FLA will reimburse a portion of the cost of inspections (www.fairlabor.org).

6 Personal communication from Anne Lally, 27 June 2003.

7 On 23 October 2001, the Board of Directors of the FLA expanded the scope of the FLA beyond the apparel and footwear industries by admitting licensees that have a line of goods that manufacture rings, yearbooks, hosiery and other items generally sold in university shops (www.fairlabor.org).

10.5.1.4 Wages

The FLA Workplace Code of Conduct requires companies to pay the prevailing wage rather than a 'living wage'.[8]

10.5.1.5 Right to organise

Although both the FLA Code and SA8000 guarantee the right of workers to organise, only SA8000 sets a requirement for countries in which the right to organise is restricted by law. In these countries, companies shall facilitate parallel means of organising under SA8000. The FLA system allows for the board of the FLA to provide guidance in this area. The FLA requires that participating companies take 'steps to ensure that employees have the ability to exercise these rights without fear of discrimination or punishment' (FLA 2001: 20).

10.5.1.6 Monitoring

The FLA, like the ETI, relies on both internal and external monitoring. The FLA will determine which factories should be monitored, based on risk analysis and company recommendation. As a result, 85% of applicable facilities will not be monitored in a given year (ILRF 1999). Internal monitoring for some companies covers 100% of the supply chain. External monitoring is simply a verification that such systems are working.

Factory visits are exclusively unannounced. This is a point of divergence with SA8000, which requires that the contractor prepare a significant amount of documentation in preparation for the audit, similar to the ISO model.

References

FLA (Fair Labor Association) (2001) 'Charter Document', amended October 2001, available at www.fairlabor.org/html/amendctr.html.

Greenhouse, G. (1998) 'Plan to Curtail Sweatshops Rejected by Union', *New York Times*, 5 November 1998 (www.sweatshopwatch.org/swatch/headlines/1998/FLA.html#nyt1).

ILRF (International Labour Rights Fund) (1999) *Assessment of Fair Labor Association Agreement of November 2, 1998* (Washington, DC: ILRF, 1 January 1999).

Leipziger, D. (2001) *SA8000: The Definitive Guide to the New Social Standard* (London: FT Prentice Hall).

Rutgers (1999) 'Adidas-Salomon Joins Fair Labor Association', 7 July 1999, at http://ur.rutgers.edu/news/ACLA/adidas.htm.

---

8   The FLA has called for further research on wages (www.fairlabor.org). The US Department of Labor issued a study on the relationship between wages and basic needs, which can be found at www.dol.gov/ILAB/media/reports/oiea/wagestudy/main.htm.

Van Heerden, A., and J.S. Shubash II (2003) 'Labor Relations and International Labor Rights: The Role of Private Labor Rights Initiatives', in *The Permanent Court of Arbitration/Peace Palace Papers*. XI. *Internationalization of Labor Dispute Settlement* (ed. International Bureau of the Permanent Court of Arbitration; Dordrecht, Netherlands: Kluwer Law International).

Additional resources

Further reading

Wick, I. (2003) *Workers' Tool or PR Ploy? A Guide to Codes of International Labour Practice* (Bonn/Siegburg: Friedrich Ebert Foundation and Südwind Institut für Ökonomie und Ökumene, 3rd rev. edn, www.fes.de).

Website

Fair Labor Association: www.fairlabor.org

Workplace Code of Conduct*

The Apparel Industry Partnership has addressed issues related to the eradication of sweatshops in the United States and abroad. On the basis of this examination, the Partnership has formulated the following set of standards defining decent and humane working conditions. The Partnership believes that consumers can have confidence that products that are manufactured in compliance with these standards are not produced under exploitative or inhumane conditions.

Forced Labor. There shall not be any use of forced labor, whether in the form of prison labor, indentured labor, bonded labor or otherwise.

Child Labor. No person shall be employed at an age younger than 15 (or 14 where the law of the country of manufacture[8] allows) or younger than the age for completing compulsory education in the country of manufacture where such age is higher than 15.

Harassment or Abuse. Every employee shall be treated with respect and dignity. No employee shall be subject to any physical, sexual, psychological or verbal harassment or abuse.

Nondiscrimination. No person shall be subject to any discrimination in employment, including hiring, salary, benefits, advancement, discipline, termination or retirement, on the basis of gender, race, religion, age, disability, sexual orientation, nationality, political opinion, or social or ethnic origin.

Health and Safety. Employers shall provide a safe and healthy working environment to prevent accidents and injury to health arising out of, linked with, or occurring in the course of work or as a result of the operation of employer facilities.

Freedom of Association and Collective Bargaining. Employers shall recognize and respect the right of employees to freedom of association and collective bargaining.

Wages and Benefits. Employers recognize that wages are essential to meeting employees' basic needs. Employers shall pay employees, as a floor, at least the mini-

---

*   Reproduced with the permission of the Fair Labor Association.

mum wage required by local law or the prevailing industry wage, whichever is higher, and shall provide legally mandated benefits.

Hours of Work. Except in extraordinary business circumstances, employees shall (i) not be required to work more than the lesser of (a) 48 hours per week and 12 hours overtime or (b) the limits on regular and overtime hours allowed by the law of the country of manufacture or, where the laws of such country do not limit the hours of work, the regular work week in such country plus 12 hours overtime and (ii) be entitled to at least one day off in every seven day period.

Overtime Compensation. In addition to their compensation for regular hours of work, employees shall be compensated for overtime hours at such premium rate as is legally required in the country of manufacture or, in those countries where such laws do not exist, at a rate at least equal to their regular hourly compensation rate.

Any Company that determines to adopt the Workplace Code of Conduct shall, in addition to complying with all applicable laws of the country of manufacture, comply with and support the Workplace Code of Conduct in accordance with the attached Principles of Monitoring and shall apply the higher standard in cases of differences or conflicts. Any Company that determines to adopt the Workplace Code of Conduct also shall require its licensees and contractors and, in the case of a retailer, its suppliers to comply with applicable local laws and with this Code in accordance with the attached Principles of Monitoring and to apply the higher standard in cases of differences or conflicts.

Note:

[8] All references to local law throughout this Code shall include regulations implemented in accordance with applicable local law.

11
Ethical Trading Initiative: Base Code

I think the Ethical Trading Initiative is an enormously important and impressive initiative . . . we are at a new point in our potential capacity to pull together the real interests of NGOs, the trade union movement and the business community, with the business community not being involved simply to do a bit of 'charitable extra' but in the mainstream of their business interests.

Claire Short, UK Member of Parliament, former Secretary of State for International Development[1]

Type   Performance-oriented initiative, process-oriented initiative

Strength Promotion of learning and good practice

Keywords Labour rights • Tripartite • Good practice • Development

11.1 Background

The Ethical Trading Initiative (ETI) seeks to improve the lives of workers in global supply chains by creating a forum to identify and promote good practice in the implementation of codes of conduct. The ETI is tripartite, consisting of membership groups from three sectors: companies, non-governmental organisations (NGOs) and trade unions. It is funded by the UK government's Department for International Development and its members, which include NGOs and companies, which pay dues.

1 Short 1998.

In pursuit of its aims, the ETI conducts experimental projects into aspects of code implementation, hosts seminars, events and conferences and has a research and publications programme. The ETI is interested in sharing the lessons learned from various different approaches to monitoring, verification and other aspects of code implementation. Among the participating companies are: Marks & Spencer, Sainsbury's, The Co-operative Wholesale Society, Chiquita International Brands and Levi Strauss & Co. along with NGOs such as Save the Children, the FairTrade Foundation and the international trade union movement.[2]

Members of the ETI provide a progress report to the ETI each year. Company members must demonstrate continued progress and improvements towards implementing the ETI Base Code in order to remain a member.

11.2 Strengths and weaknesses

The ETI has produced valuable research from its pilot studies in China, South Africa, Zimbabwe, Costa Rica and Sri Lanka. According to Dan Rees, manager of the ETI secretariat, through its pilot in Zimbabwe ETI learned that 'combining international audit firms with an aid agency approach' was key (interview with Rees, quoted in Cowe 2001).

Another major lesson learned concerns the degree of complexity and ambiguity within the field. As the pilot studies replicate the ETI tripartite model they are forging important alliances. However, working within the tripartite structure can be time-consuming[3] and expensive.

Company members report that the ETI provides a valuable forum in which to engage trade unions and NGOs. In addition, the ETI catalyses learning by sharing good practice and networking while providing a peer review of corporate progress and co-operation rather than competition.

11.3 Companies to which the Base Code of the Ethical Trading Initiative applies

The ETI and the best practices it disseminates are relevant to all companies seeking to promote better working conditions in global supply chains. The member companies are producing for the UK market, among others.

---

2 www.ethicaltrade.org/pub/members/welcome/main/index.shtml
3 Interview with Sumithra Dhanarajan, Policy Adviser, Private Sector, Oxfam United Kingdom, 8 April 2003.

11.4 Questions posed and answered

What constitutes best practice in ethical supply chains? What types of alliance can be developed to promote ethical supply chains?

11.5 The promise and the challenge

On the promises and challenges of this and the other initiatives discussed in Part 3 on labour rights, see the introductory text (pages 133-36).

11.5.1 Points of divergence

11.5.1.1 Commitment to providing regular employment

The ETI Base Code of conduct is very similar to the other codes discussed in Part 3, with one significant exception: ETI companies make a commitment to provide 'regular employment'. To quote the Base Code: 'To every extent possible work performed must be on the basis of recognised employment relationship established through national law and practice' (see page 182).

11.5.1.2 Verification

Unlike SA8000 (Chapter 9) and the Fair Labor Association (FLA, Chapter 10), the ETI does not verify brands or suppliers; rather, it focuses on the identification of good practice.

11.5.1.3 Geographical target

The companies participating in SA8000 are global, whereas the ETI is primarily designed for companies producing consumer goods sold in the United Kingdom.

11.5.1.4 Approach

ETI promotes a comparative analysis of different approaches to promoting workers' rights, whereas SA8000 is an operational system for accredited certification.

11.5.1.5 Consultation

Like the FLA, both ETI and the creators of SA8000 have consulted with a wide range of NGOs and unions around the world.

11.5.1.6 Focus

ETI has a strong focus on the context within which companies operate. According to its website, 'ETI will, where appropriate, consider the broader impact of its members' activities on human rights, environment and development issues within the wider community in which they operate' (ETI 1998: 2).

11.5.1.7 Partnership approach

The forging of new partnerships is also an important priority for the ETI and it works in partnership with industry stakeholders in all its experimental work. For example, in the Western Cape of Africa, the ETI has helped to establish the Ethical Trading Forum, which brings together producers, trade unions, NGOs and government to promote better working conditions within the field of agriculture.

References

Cowe, R. (2001) 'Hard Labour to Put Code into Practice', *Financial Times*, 12 June 2001: 12.

ETI (Ethical Trade Initiative) (1998) 'Base Code', www.ethicaltrade.org/pub/publications/basecode/en/index.shtml.

Short, C. (1998) Speech by the Right Honourable Clare Short, MP, First Annual Conference of the Ethical Trading Initiative, 2 December 1998, www.dfid.gov.uk/News/Speeches/files/sp2dec.html.

Additional resources

Further reading

Wick, I. (2003) *Workers' Tool or PR Ploy? A Guide to Codes of International Labour Practice* (Bonn/Siegburg: Friedrich Ebert Foundation and Südwind Institut für Ökonomie und Ökumene, 3rd rev. edn, www.fes.de).

Website

Ethical Trade Initiative: www.ethicaltrade.org

The Base Code
Ethical Trading Initiative*

1. EMPLOYMENT IS FREELY CHOSEN

1.1 There is no forced, bonded or involuntary prison labour.

1.2 Workers are not required to lodge "deposits" or their identity papers with their employer and are free to leave their employer after reasonable notice.

2. FREEDOM OF ASSOCIATION AND THE RIGHT TO COLLECTIVE BARGAINING ARE RESPECTED

2.1 Workers, without distinction, have the right to join or form trade unions of their own choosing and to bargain collectively.

2.2 The employer adopts an open attitude towards the activities of trade unions and their organisational activities.

2.3 Workers' representatives are not discriminated against and have access to carry out their representative functions in the workplace.

2.4 Where the right to freedom of association and collective bargaining is restricted under law, the employer facilitates, and does not hinder, the development of parallel means for independent and free association and bargaining.

3. WORKING CONDITIONS ARE SAFE AND HYGIENIC

3.1 A safe and hygienic working environment shall be provided, bearing in mind the prevailing knowledge of the industry and of any specific hazards. Adequate steps shall be taken to prevent accidents and injury to health arising out of, associated with, or occurring in the course of work, by minimising, so far as is reasonably practicable, the causes of hazards inherent in the working environment.

3.2 Workers shall receive regular and recorded health and safety training, and such training shall be repeated for new or reassigned workers.

---

* Reproduced with the permission of the Ethical Trading Initiative.

3.3 Access to clean toilet facilities and to potable water, and, if appropriate, sanitary facilities for food storage shall be provided.

3.4 Accommodation, where provided, shall be clean, safe, and meet the basic needs of the workers.

3.5 The company observing the code shall assign responsibility for health and safety to a senior management representative.

4. CHILD LABOUR SHALL NOT BE USED

4.1 There shall be no new recruitment of child labour.

4.2 Companies shall develop or participate in and contribute to policies and programmes which provide for the transition of any child found to be performing child labour to enable her or him to attend and remain in quality education until no longer a child; "child" and "child labour" being defined in the appendices.

4.3 Children and young persons under 18 shall not be employed at night or in hazardous conditions.

4.4 These policies and procedures shall conform to the provisions of the relevant ILO standards.

5. LIVING WAGES ARE PAID

5.1 Wages and benefits paid for a standard working week meet, at a minimum, national legal standards or industry benchmark standards, whichever is higher. In any event wages should always be enough to meet basic needs and to provide some discretionary income.

5.2 All workers shall be provided with written and understandable information about their employment conditions in respect to wages before they enter employment and about the particulars of their wages for the pay period concerned each time that they are paid.

5.3 Deductions from wages as a disciplinary measure shall not be permitted nor shall any deductions from wages not provided for by national law be permitted without the expressed permission of the worker concerned. All disciplinary measures should be recorded.

6. WORKING HOURS ARE NOT EXCESSIVE

6.1 Working hours comply with national laws and benchmark industry standards, whichever affords greater protection.

6.2 In any event, workers shall not on a regular basis be required to work in excess of 48 hours per week and shall be provided with at least one day off for every 7 day period on average. Overtime shall be voluntary, shall not exceed

12 hours per week, shall not be demanded on a regular basis and shall always be compensated at a premium rate.

7. NO DISCRIMINATION IS PRACTISED

7.1 There is no discrimination in hiring, compensation, access to training, promotion, termination or retirement based on race, caste, national origin, religion, age, disability, gender, marital status, sexual orientation, union membership or political affiliation.

8. REGULAR EMPLOYMENT IS PROVIDED

8.1 To every extent possible work performed must be on the basis of recognised employment relationship established through national law and practice.

8.2 Obligations to employees under labour or social security laws and regulations arising from the regular employment relationship shall not be avoided through the use of labour-only contracting, sub-contracting, or home-working arrangements, or through apprenticeship schemes where there is no real intent to impart skills or provide regular employment, nor shall any such obligations be avoided through the excessive use of fixed-term contracts of employment.

9. NO HARSH OR INHUMANE TREATMENT IS ALLOWED

9.1 Physical abuse or discipline, the threat of physical abuse, sexual or other harassment and verbal abuse or other forms of intimidation shall be prohibited.

The provisions of this code constitute minimum and not maximum standards, and this code should not be used to prevent companies from exceeding these standards. Companies applying this code are expected to comply with national and other applicable law and, where the provisions of law and this Base Code address the same subject, to apply that provision which affords the greater protection.

12
Clean Clothes Campaign: Model Code

The most useful aspect of the Clean Clothes Campaign is its strong link to grass-roots organisations. Most multistakeholder initiatives do not have a grass-roots base.

Gemma Crijns, Nyenrode University and Amnesty International Business Group, The Netherlands[1]

Type   Performance-oriented standard

Strength It is a campaigning tool linked to grass-roots organisations

Keywords Campaign • Consumers • Multi-stakeholder • Garments • Europe • Non-governmental organisations • Trade unions

12.1 Background

The Clean Clothes Campaign (CCC) is a Europe-wide voluntary network with affiliated groups in Austria, Belgium, France, Germany, Italy, The Netherlands, Portugal, Spain, Sweden and Switzerland. The aim of the CCC is to improve working conditions in the garment and sportswear industries. The initiative is the oldest of the initiatives described in this part, having its origins in 1990 in The Netherlands. Unlike the other initiatives described here, the key focus is on consumer awareness, along with dialogue with companies.

In Sweden and Switzerland, the CCC has engaged directly with companies willing to accept its principles in projects aimed at developing a better understanding of code monitoring and verification and will continue to do so.

1 Personal communication with Gemma Crijns, Nyenrode University, Breukelen, The Netherlands, 2003.

The CCC has developed a code of conduct that is based on ILO conventions. To understand the CCC, it is necessary to comprehend its structure. Each national group functions autonomously as a network of activists and non-governmental organisations (NGOs), including human rights groups, women's groups, community leaders, trade unions and researchers. The international partner network of the campaign consists of NGOs and trade unions in the majority of countries producing for the European market. These networks organise campaigns for consumers, such as postcards urging companies to adopt CCC's code of conduct. These campaigns are highly effective in attracting the attention of companies.

The CCC seeks to create tripartite bodies to oversee monitoring and verification and to set standards for company membership. These tripartite groups are to include trade unions, NGOs and companies or industry associations; these groups will be responsible for carrying out a joint review of information from the auditors.

12.2 Strengths and weaknesses

The Clean Clothes Campaign is successful in mobilising consumer awareness which leads companies to the negotiating table.

> Besides functioning as a mass mobilisation and solidarity organisation, the CCC also acts as a stakeholder in multiparty negotiations with companies. Although these dual functions are considered fundamental pillars of CCC work, they are difficult to combine. Progress has therefore been slow in the field of negotiations with companies. Once the experience gained in pilot projects is evaluated . . . the results show how much additional substance in needed to make the CCC Code more concrete (Wick 2003: 31).

12.3 Companies to which the Model Code of the Clean Clothes Campaign applies

The Model Code applies to companies producing and selling garments and footwear.

12.4 Questions posed and answered

- What are the responsibilities of companies (producing branded products) and factories in promoting workers' rights?

- What are the basic principles of monitoring supply chains to ensure the basic rights of workers?

12.5 The promise and the challenge

A dual strategy of campaigning against abuses in specific companies and, at the same time, trying to engage with companies is a challenge. According to a study of codes, the combination of these two functions has led to slow progress in negotiating with companies (Wick 2003: 35).

12.5.1 Points of divergence

12.5.1.1 Focus area
The CCC is a campaign and as such it conducts advocacy work to promote change within companies. It also conducts research and solidarity work with groups around the world.

12.5.1.2 Targets
The CCC code not only addresses multinational companies but also focuses on the factory level, unlike the Fair Labor Association (FLA, Chapter 10), which works primarily with US companies, and Social Accountability (SA8000, Chapter 9), which works at the factory level.

12.5.1.3 Sectoral target
The CCC focuses exclusively on the garment industry.

12.5.1.4 Monitoring
Like FLA, the visits are unannounced, in contrast to SA8000, where they are announced.

Reference

Wick, I. (2003) *Workers' Tool or PR Ploy? A Guide to Codes of International Labour Practice* (Bonn/Siegburg: Friedrich Ebert Foundation and Südwind Institut für Ökonomie und Ökumene, 3rd rev. edn, www.fes.de).

Additional resource

Website
Clean Clothes Campaign: www.cleanclothes.org

Code of Labour Practices for the Apparel Industry including Sportswear*

February 1998

I. INTRODUCTION

Statement of purpose

The Clean Clothes Campaign is dedicated to advancing the interests of workers in the apparel and sportswear industry and the concerns of consumers who purchase products made and sold by this industry. The Campaign seeks an end to the oppression, exploitation and abuse of workers in this industry, most of who are women. The Campaign also seeks to provide consumers with accurate information concerning the working conditions under which the apparel and sportswear they purchase are made. The Clean Clothes Campaign seeks to achieve its aims through a variety of means including a code of labour practice that would be adopted and implemented by companies, industry associations and employer organisations. The code, which is a concise statement of minimum standards with respect to labour practices, is meant to be accompanied by a commitment by the companies adopting it to take positive actions in applying it. Companies are expected to insist on compliance with the code by any of their contractors, subcontractors, suppliers and licensees organising production that would fall under the scope of the code.

Companies adopting the code will be expected to engage an independent institution established for the purpose of monitoring compliance with the code, in assisting companies in implementing the code and in providing consumers with information concerning the labour practices in the industry.

This code of labour practice sets forth minimum standards for wages, working time and working conditions and provides for observance of all of the core standards of the International Labour Organisation including Conventions 29, 87, 98, 100, 105, 111 and 138. These are minimum standards that are meant to apply throughout the industry and in all countries. The code is not a trade protectionist measure. It is not meant to be used as a means to close the markets of some countries at the expense of workers in other countries.

---

* Reproduced with the permission of the Clean Clothes Campaign.

The code is not meant to be a substitute for international intergovernmental co-operation nor for international legislation. Although the code does seek to afford workers protection from oppression, abuse and exploitation where national laws are inadequate or are not enforced, it does not seek to become a substitute for national laws or the national labour inspectorate. The code is not a substitute for secure and independent trade unions nor should it be used as a substitute for collective bargaining.

Scope of application

The code is intended for retailers as well as manufacturers and all companies positioned in between those in the apparel and sportswear supply chain. It can also be used by industry associations or employer organisations.

The code applies to all of the company's apparel and sportswear products (including sportshoes). The code specifically applies to the following general industrial classification of economic activities within the European Community (NACE) classification codes:

- 436 knitting industry
- 451 manufacture of mass-produced footwear
- 452 production of hand-made footwear
- 453 manufacture of ready-made clothing and accessories
- 454 bespoke tailoring, dressmaking and hatmaking
- 456 manufacture of furs and of fur goods

Through the code retailers and manufacturers declare their responsibility for the working conditions under which the apparel, sportswear and shoes they sell are produced. This responsibility extends to all workers producing products for the company, regardless of their status or relationship to the company and whether or not they are employees of the company. The code would therefore apply to home-based workers and to workers who are engaged either informally or on a contracted basis.

The code applies to all of the companies' contractors, subcontractors, suppliers and licensees world-wide. The terms 'contractor', 'subcontractor', 'supplier' mean any natural or legal person who contracts with the company and is engaged in a manufacturing process, including CMT (cut-make-and-trim), assembly and packaging, which result in a finished product for the consumer. A licensee means any natural or legal person who contracts with a company to produce or distribute finished products using the name or brand image of that company.

Observance of the code must be an enforceable and enforced part of any agreement between the company and its contractors, subcontractors, suppliers and licensees.

II. CODE OF LABOUR PRACTICES

Introduction

The code provides a concise statement of minimum labour standards together with a pledge by the company to observe these standards and to require its contractors, subcontractors, suppliers and licensees to observe these standards. The code is concise in order to display it in workplaces and in order to avoid any confusion between basic principles and the application of principles. An independent institution, established to provide independent monitoring of compliance with the code and to assist companies in implementing the code, will provide an auditable checklist of practices and conditions that are consistent with the standards set forth in the code. This independent organisation will also provide a means by which questions over the meaning of the code can be resolved.

The preamble establishes three principles: First, the company accepts responsibility for its workers, including workers involved in contracting and subcontracting agreements. Second, the company pledges to observe the core ILO labour standards and to ensure that workers are provided with living wages and decent working conditions. Third, the company pledges to make observance of the code a condition of any agreements that it makes with contractors and suppliers and to require them to extend this obligation to their subcontractors.

The body of the code is based on the same core ILO conventions including prohibitions against child labour, forced or bonded labour, discrimination, freedom of association and the right to collective bargaining. This is followed by the basic labour conditions—wages, hours and working conditions (including health and safety) and their formulation in the code, also derived from ILO standards.

This section also addresses the issue of regular employment relationships. Increasingly employers avoid the obligations of the employment relationship by treating workers as "independent contractors" when in fact their situation is the same as that of regular employees. The ILO is in the process of developing an international standard on this subject.

The closing section sets out the most important obligations contractors, subcontractors, suppliers and licensees must undertake in implementing the code and pledges the company to enforce its code using a range of sanctions up to and including termination of any agreements. The closing section pledges all employers concerned to refrain from disciplinary action, dismissal or otherwise discriminating against any worker for providing information concerning observance of the code.

This part also states that the code establishes only minimum standards that must not be used as a ceiling or to discourage collective bargaining. The text of the code, when meant to be posted where workers can see it, shall also include a means by which workers can report failure to comply with the code in a confidential manner.

Preamble

1. (name of company) recognises its responsibilities to workers for the conditions under which its products or services are made and that these responsibilities extend to all workers producing products or services for (name of company) whether or not they are employees of (name of company).

2. Any workers producing products or services manufactured, sold or distributed by (name of company) must be provided with living wages and decent working conditions, and the international labour standards established by Conventions 29, 87, 98, 100, 105, 111 and 138 of the International Labour Organisation must be observed.

3. (name of company) will require its contractors, their subcontractors, suppliers and licensees to provide these conditions and observe these standards when producing or distributing products or components of products for (name of company). (name of company) will, prior to placing orders with suppliers, engaging contractors and sub-contractors or granting licenses, assess whether the provisions of this code can be met.

4. For the purposes of this code the term 'contractor', 'subcontractor' or 'supplier' shall mean any natural or legal person who contracts with (name of company), either directly or indirectly via another natural or legal person who contracts with (name of company) and is engaged in a manufacturing process, including CMT (cut-make-and-trim), assembly and packaging, which result in a finished product for the consumer. The term 'licensee' means any natural or legal person who as part of a contractual arrangement with (name of company) uses for any purpose the name of (name of company) or its recognised brand names or images.

Content

- **Employment is freely chosen.**

There shall be no use of forced, including bonded or prison, labour (ILO Conventions 29 and 105). Nor shall workers be required to lodge "deposits" or their identity papers with their employer.

- **There is no discrimination in employment.**

Equality of opportunity and treatment regardless of race, colour, sex, religion, political opinion, nationality, social origin or other distinguishing characteristic shall be provided (ILO Conventions 100 and 111).

- **Child labour is not used.**

There shall be no use of child labour. Only workers above the age of 15 years or above the compulsory school-leaving age shall be engaged (ILO Convention 138). Adequate transitional economic assistance and appropriate educational opportunities shall be provided to any replaced child workers.

- **Freedom of association and the right to collective bargaining are respected.**

The right of all workers to form and join trade unions and to bargain collectively shall be recognised (ILO Conventions 87 and 98). Workers' representatives shall not be the subject of discrimination and shall have access to all workplaces necessary to enable them to carry out their representation functions (ILO Convention 135 and Recommendation 143). Employers shall adopt a positive approach towards the activities of trade unions and an open attitude towards their organisational activities.

- **Living wages are paid.**

Wages and benefits paid for a standard working week shall meet at least legal or industry minimum standards and always be sufficient to meet basic needs of workers and their families and to provide some discretionary income.

Deductions from wages for disciplinary measures shall not be permitted nor shall any deductions from wages not provided for by national law be permitted without the expressed permission of the worker concerned. All workers shall be provided with written and understandable information about the conditions in respect of wages before they enter employment and of the particulars of their wages for the pay period concerned each time that they are paid.

- **Hours of work are not excessive.**

Hours of work shall comply with applicable laws and industry standards. In any event, workers shall not on a regular basis be required to work in excess of 48 hours per week and shall be provided with at least one day off for every 7 day period. Overtime shall be voluntary, shall not exceed 12 hours per week, shall not be demanded on a regular basis and shall always be compensated at a premium rate.

- **Working conditions are decent.**

A safe and hygienic working environment shall be provided, and best occupational health and safety practice shall be promoted, bearing in mind the prevailing knowledge of the industry and of any specific hazards. Physical abuse, threats of physical abuse, unusual punishments or discipline, sexual and other harassment, and intimidation by the employer is strictly prohibited.

- **The employment relationship is established.**

Obligations to employees under labour or social security laws and regulations arising from the regular employment relationship shall not be avoided through the use of labour-only contracting arrangements, or through apprenticeship schemes where there is no real intent to impart skills or provide regular employment. Younger workers shall be given the opportunity to participate in education and training programmes.

Closing section

Contractors, subcontractors, suppliers and licensees shall undertake to support and co-operate in the implementation and monitoring of this code by:

- providing (name of company) with relevant information concerning their operations;
- permitting inspection at any time of their workplaces and operations by approved inspectors;
  - maintaining records of the name, age, hours worked and wages paid for each worker and making these available to approved inspectors on request;
  - informing, verbally and in writing, the workers concerned of the provisions of this code; and,
  - refraining from disciplinary action, dismissal or otherwise discriminating against any worker for providing information concerning observance of this code.

Contractors, subcontractors, suppliers and licensees found to be in breach of one or more terms of this Code of Labour Practices may lose the right to produce or organise production of goods for (name of company).

Questions as to the interpretation of the meaning of the provisions of this code shall be resolved according to the procedure set forth by an independent institution established for this purpose.

The provisions of this code constitute only minimum standards and conditions for the purpose of preventing exploitation. (name of company) does not intend, will not use, and will not allow any contractor, subcontractor, supplier or licensee to use these minimum standards and conditions as maximum standards or as the only conditions permitted by (name of company) or to serve as the basis for any claim as to what standards or conditions of employment should be provided.

Specific industry standards

Specific industry standards, especially with respect to health and safety (including access to medical services) and workers' accommodation may be incorporated into the code or attached separately and referenced in the code under section # 7 "working conditions are decent". These standards may be formally recognised standards or established best practice.

III. IMPLEMENTATION

Introduction

Implementation refers to the whole range of activities that could be taken by a company to give effect to the Code of Labour Practices. In the past some companies have adopted codes as a public relations response to reports of exploitation but have failed to implement them. Companies adopting the Code of Labour Practices for the apparel and sportswear industry will be expected to agree to certain minimum conditions with respect to implementing the code. One of the most important ways in which a code can be implemented is for it to become an enforceable and enforced part of agreements with contractors, subcontractors suppliers and licensees.

Implementation and monitoring are often confused. Monitoring, which means to watch or check that the terms of the code are being respected is one aspect of implementing a code. It is expected that companies adopting the code will in their relationship with their contractors, sub-contractors, suppliers and licensees monitor their compliance with the code.

Companies adopting the code are also expected to co-operate and support a system of independent monitoring of compliance with the code. This section concerns the general obligations of the company to implement the code. The obligations of the company with respect to independent monitoring are considered in Part IV.

Obligations of the company to implement the code:

- The company agrees to take positive actions to implement the code, to incorporate the code into all of its operations and to make the code an integral part of its overall philosophy and general policy.

- The company will assign responsibility for all matters pertaining to the code within its organisation and inform the independent institution and other relevant bodies where this responsibility is assigned.

- The Board of Directors (or other governing body) of the company shall periodically review the operation of the code, including the reports of internal and external monitoring.

- The company accepts responsibility for observing the code with respect to all employees and workers that it supervises and agrees to:-
  - assign responsibility for implementing this code at each place that it owns or controls;
  - ensure that all workers are aware of the contents of the code by clearly displaying an authorised text of the code at all workplaces and by orally informing these employees in a language understood by them of the provisions of the code;
  - refrain from disciplining, dismissing or otherwise discriminating against any employee for providing information concerning observance of this code.

- The company will make observance of the code a condition of all agreements that it enters into with contractors, suppliers and licensees. These agreements will obligate these contractors, suppliers and licensees to require observance of the code in all agreements that they make with their respective subcontractors and suppliers in fulfilling their agreement with the company. Such agreements shall also oblige these contractors, subcontractors, suppliers and licensees to undertake the same obligations to implement the code as found in the preceding point.

Obligations of the company to enforce the code

Observance of the code by contractors, subcontractors and suppliers must be an enforceable and enforced condition of agreement with the company.

In order to achieve this:

- The company will ensure that all agreements it enters into concerning the production of apparel and sportswear allow for the termination of the agreement for failure to observe the code by any contractors, subcontractors and suppliers.

- The company shall authorise a procedure with fixed time limits to rectify situations where its code is not being fully observed by a contractor, subcontractor or supplier. The agreement by the contractor, subcontractor or supplier to abide by this procedure would enable the continuation of the agreement with the company. The company shall require contractors or suppliers to institute similar procedures with respect to their contractors, subcontractors or suppliers.

- Such procedures shall be authorised only where:
  - there is a reasonable expectation that the situation will be corrected and that the code will be observed in the future;
  - the period specified for correcting the situation is reasonable;
  - recognisable and unmistakable violations of the code are ceased immediately;
  - such procedures shall not be authorised more than once for the same contractor, subcontractor or supplier for the same or similar failure to comply with the code; and
  - such procedures are consistent with any recommendations or procedures set forth by the independent institution established to assist in implementing this code.

- With respect to child labour, such procedures shall require that there be no further engagement of children and that temporary measures to assist child workers such as the reduction in working time, the provision of educational opportunities and transitional economic support be instituted. In the end, child workers must be replaced by adults and, where possible, from the same family. Procedures should also include measures to assist the children concerned through provision of educational opportunities and transitional economic support.

- Contractors, subcontractors and suppliers must, as part of their agreement with the company, agree to terminate any contract or agreement for the supply or production of goods by any contractor, subcontractor or supplier that they engage not fully observing the code, or they must seek and receive approval from the company to institute a procedure with fixed time limits to rectify situations where the code is not being fully observed.

- Where there is repeated failure to observe or to ensure observance of the code by a particular contractor, subcontractor, supplier or licensee, the agreement should be terminated. Guidelines or procedures for determining when it is necessary to terminate a contract for failure to observe the code shall be set forth by an independent institution established for this purpose.

In situations where it is not clear whether a particular practice constitutes a violation of the code, relevant international labour standards of the International Labour Organisation (ILO) and any recommendations provided by the independent institution established to assist companies in implementing this code shall be sought for guidance.

IV. INDEPENDENT MONITORING, ACCREDITATION AND CERTIFICATION

Introduction

When a sufficient number of companies, industry associations or employers' organisations have adopted the code of labour practice for the apparel and sportswear industry, then they, in conjunction with appropriate trade union organisations and NGOs, shall establish jointly an independent institution, referred to in this document as "the Foundation".

The purpose of the Foundation shall be to:

- conduct, directly or indirectly through other organisations, the independent monitoring of compliance with the code;

- assist companies in implementing the code; and

- provide a means to inform consumers about observance of the code and more generally about labour conditions in the industry.

To these ends the Foundation shall:

- establish standards for the independent monitoring and for the accreditation of independent monitors;

- train, or to arrange for the training, of independent monitors;

- prepare an auditable checklist of labour practices to be used in monitoring the code;

- conduct or otherwise cause to be conducted independent monitoring of compliance by specific companies with the code of labour practice;

- receive reports of such independent monitoring and make effective recommendations based on these reports to the companies concerned;

- investigate any substantiated reports concerning compliance by participating companies and make effective recommendations based on the findings of such investigations;

- prepare and publish guidelines for participating companies on the implementation of the code;

- provide other technical assistance to companies in implementing the code, including the training of company personnel;

- prepare and publish the authorised version of code in various languages and in sufficient quantities as required by participating companies;

- establish a means to interpret the provisions of the code, provided that this means is based on the recognised jurisprudence of the International Labour Organisation;

- provide a means by which workers and any others can report on a confidential basis observance of the code;

- establish, based on independent monitoring, a system of certification concerning labour practices which can be used by consumers;

- collect information from any source on working conditions in the apparel and sportswear industry and make this information available to consumers;

- promote the code of labour practice and encourage all companies operating in the industry to adopt it; and

- establish a mechanism that can make effective recommendations with respect to any disputes arising out of the implementation or the certification process.

The Foundation shall be governed by a board consisting of equal representatives of appropriate trade union organisations and NGOs on one hand and of appropriate representatives of retailers and manufactures on the other hand. The Foundation shall be financed by contributions from participating organisations and by payments for services from contracting companies.

The principal means by which the Foundation shall conduct its work will be based on contracts with specific companies to independently monitor and certify their compliance with the code and by contracts with individuals and organisations to conduct monitoring.

It is understood that the standards for independent monitoring established by the Foundation shall be based on the best practice of the two existing professions that monitor labour practices—the labour inspectorate and the contract-enforcement practices of trade unions. It is also understood that these standards shall include ethical practices for monitors, including respect for any confidential commercial information.

It is also understood that any individuals engaged to conduct monitoring shall receive training for this purpose.

Relation between the company and the Foundation

Companies adopting the code of labour practice for the apparel and sportswear industry shall enter into an agreement with the Foundation. This agreement shall provide for the following:

- the time-frame in which the production in the different facilities should comply with all the standards in the code;

- the information the company has to give to the Monitoring Foundation;

- the payments the company should make to the Monitoring Foundation;

- the procedures for the actual monitoring and the obligations of the different parties; and

- the use of the Foundation contract by the company in its public relations.

With respect to (b) the company assumes the following obligations:

- to maintain full and up-to-date information on all contractors, subcontractors, suppliers and licensees obliged to observe this code, including the nature and location of all workplaces, and to provide this information to the Foundation or its accredited monitors in a timely manner upon request.

- to require contractors, subcontractors, suppliers and licensees to maintain records of the names, ages, hours worked, and wages paid for each worker, and make these records available for inspection by accredited monitors, and to allow the Foundation or its accredited monitors to conduct confidential interviews with workers.

- to ensure that the code is clearly displayed in all places where apparel and sportswear are produced and/or distributed by or under agreement with or for the company and provide authorised texts of the code to contractors and suppliers for their use, and the use by any contractors, subcontractors and suppliers obliged to observe this code. In all cases the text of the code so displayed shall be in languages so that the workers concerned are able to understand it. The text of the code shall be provided to each worker covered by its provisions and all workers so covered shall be orally informed in a language that they can understand of the provisions of the code.

- the code so displayed must provide information to assist workers in reporting violations of the code to the Foundation or its agents taking into account the difficulties that workers will face in doing this and the need for confidentiality in order to protect workers.

- to allow for the necessary access to independent monitors and provide them with any and all relevant information upon demand.

- to ensure and clearly demonstrate that the code is being observed by all parties obliged to observe the code, the company must allow the Foundation and its agents access to all information pertaining to the implementation of the code, and ensure that its contractors, subcontractors and suppliers give similar access to the Foundation and its agents.

Monitoring: basic principles

- monitoring must be by the actual observance of working conditions through unannounced inspection visits ("spot checks") to all workplaces covered by the code;

- the frequency of inspections must be established;

- accredited monitors must be permitted to interview workers on a confidential basis;

- in addition to regular or routine inspections, inspections shall be undertaken at specific locations following substantiated complaints, where there is sufficient reason to believe that the code is not being observed;

- inspections shall be conducted in a way which does not cause undue disruption to the performance of work in the premises being inspected;

- written reports shall be provided by accredited monitors to all parties and to the participating company concerned following each visit.

The Foundation may seek other sources of information concerning compliance with the code including consulting appropriate trade union organisations, human rights organisations, religious and other similar institutions in order to obtain additional information on a certain company or in order to investigate a certain complaint.

If violations of the code are found, the company must agree to accept the recommendation of the Foundation. This recommendation shall in the first instance be aimed at improving the existing situation. Where such improvement is not possible or satisfactory, then the Foundation can oblige companies to re-negotiate, terminate or refuse to renew their contracts with certain contractors, subcontractors and/or suppliers.

Where companies fail to observe their agreement with the Foundation it is understood that the Foundation may release any relevant information to the public and may terminate the contract between the company and the Foundation.

The independent monitoring process shall form the basis for any public claims by the Foundation or by participating companies as to the operation of the code or concerning the actual labour practices covered by the code.

13
Other major initiatives in the clothing industry

Other major initiatives in the field of labour rights include the following.

13.1 The Fair Wear Foundation

The Fair Wear Foundation (FWF, www.fairwear.nl) is a Dutch initiative to promote humane working conditions in the garment industry around the world. Business associations in the garment sector, non-governmental organisations (NGOs) and trade unions launched the FWF in May 2002. The Foundation has developed the Fair Wear Code of Labour Practice. Member companies implement the Code at each of their supplier locations, and the FWF verifies compliance with the Code.

13.2 The Global Alliance

Global Alliance (www.theglobalalliance.org) is a partnership between the International Youth Foundation, the World Bank and several major brands, including Nike and The Gap.[1] The Global Alliance seeks to add the voice of workers in the South into the debate on working conditions. To ascertain the needs of workers, the Alliance has interviewed 7,000 workers in 29 factories in three countries (Thailand, Indonesia and Vietnam).

The Global Alliance provides training to workers to help develop their skills. Examples of programmes developed to help workers include: mobile medical

---

1   www.theglobalalliance.org/section.cfm/3/22

clinics, and the provision of education on breast and cervical cancer, pregnancy and nutrition.

13.3 Worldwide Responsible Apparel Production

Worldwide Responsible Apparel Production (WRAP, www.wrapapparel.org) is a certification system that has developed the WRAP Principles. These Principles have been endorsed by the organisation representing apparel manufacturers in 14 countries. In addition to labour issues, WRAP also addresses the environment, customs compliance and drug interdiction.

13.4 The Worker Rights Consortium

The Worker Rights Consortium (WRC, www.workersrights.org) was established by US colleges and universities—along with students and labour rights experts—to assist colleges and universities in implementing codes of conduct. More than 100 colleges and universities support the WRC. Affiliates are encouraged to adopt the WRC Model Code, but they are not required to do so, as long as their own code guarantees workers' rights.

Additional resources

Further reading

ILO (International Labour Organisation) (2001) *Tripartite Declaration of Principles concerning Multinational Enterprises and Social Policy* (Geneva: ILO).

Wick, I. (2003) *Workers' Tool or PR Ploy? A Guide to Codes of International Labour Practice* (Bonn/Siegburg: Friedrich Ebert Foundation and Südwind Institut für Ökonomie und Ökumene, 3rd rev. edn, www.fes.de).

Websites

International Labour Office: www.ilo.org
Global Alliance for Workers and Communities: www.theglobalalliance.org
Worldwide Responsible Apparel Production (WRAP): www.wrapapparel.org
Worker Rights Consortium (WRC): www.workersrights.org

Part 4
From environment to sustainability

Companies are in the midst of a transition from environmental management to the broader concept of sustainability. Part 4 traces this journey by introducing the key tools in each area.

It is useful to begin by distinguishing the two concepts:

- Environmental management focuses on how an organisation addresses its physical surroundings at the local and global level. For example, environmental management addresses issues of energy consumption, biodiversity, recycling, packaging and so on.

- Sustainability is a much broader concept, encompassing the environmental issues covered by environmental management but also addressing social and economic issues. Sustainable development was described in the Brundtland Report as 'development that meets the needs of the present without compromising the ability of future generations to meet their needs' (WCED 1987). Although this provides a useful starting point for discussion, and is often quoted in company environmental reports, it raises as many questions as it answers. According to Professor Thomas Gladwin of New York University (1997), sustainability transcends this definition to include 'equity, justice, alleviation of poverty and redistribution of opportunity' (quoted in Elkington 1997: 6).

Although there are more than 100 definitions of sustainability, none would be complete without a discussion of the triple bottom line:

> Sustainable development involves the simultaneous pursuit of economic prosperity, environmental quality and social equity. Companies aiming for sustainability need to perform not against a single financial bottom line but against the triple bottom line (Elkington 1997: 397).

For many companies, the triple bottom line remains a 'Holy Grail'—a remote and distant theory. The tools in this part of the book will assist companies in defining their own triple bottom line. However, just as the companies of the future must be integrationist, readers will also need to integrate this part with Part 9, on implementation.

The environment–sustainability continuum

A full description of each of the key environmental and sustainability standards would require an entire volume. Among the key principles and guidelines available (and the chapters in which they are discussed in this book) are:

- Environment
  - Rio Declaration on Environment and Development (Chapter 14)
  - Responsible Care® (Chapter 23, Section 23.6.2 and page 366)
  - Coalition for Environmentally Responsible Economies (CERES; Chapter 15)
  - Business Charter for Sustainable Development (reproduced at the end of this section, page 204)
  - ISO 14001 (Chapter 27)
  - Eco-Management and Audit Scheme (EMAS) of the European Union (reproduced at the end of this section, page 209)[1]

- Sustainability
  - The Natural Step (Chapter 16)
  - 'Sustainability: Integrated Guidelines for Management' (SIGMA; Chapter 28)
  - Global Reporting Initiative (Chapter 26)
  - The Bellagio Principles[2]

Note: details of those principles, schemes and charters listed above that are not covered in this book may be found at the websites listed in the Additional resources at the end of this introduction.

---

1 For more information on EMAS, go to http://europa.eu.int/comm/environment/emas/about/summary_en.htm, *and* http://europa.eu.int/comm/environment/emas.
2 www.iisd.org/measure/principles/bellagio1.htm

References

Elkington, J. (1997) *Cannibals with Forks: The Triple Bottom Line of 21st Century Business* (Oxford, UK: Capstone Publishing).

Gladwin, T. (1997) 'Sustainable Development: Is It Industry's Business?', *Business and the Environment*, February 1997.

WCED (World Commission on Environment and Development) (1987) *Our Common Future* (Brundtland Report; Oxford, UK: Oxford University Press).

The Business Charter for Sustainable Development

Principles for Environmental Management*

Foreword

There is widespread recognition today that environmental protection must be among the highest priorities of every business.

In its milestone 1987 report, "Our Common Future," the World Commission on Environment and Development (Brundtland Commission) emphasised the importance of environmental protection to the pursuit of sustainable development.

To help business around the world improve its environmental performance, the International Chamber of Commerce created this Business Charter for Sustainable Development. It comprises sixteen Principles for environmental management which, for business, is a vitally important aspect of sustainable development.

This Charter assists enterprises in fulfilling their commitment to environmental stewardship in a comprehensive fashion, in line with national and international guidelines and standards for environmental management. It was formally launched in April 1991 at the Second World Industry Conference on Environmental Management in Rotterdam, and continues to be widely applied and recognised around the world.

Introduction

Sustainable development involves meeting the needs of the present without compromising the ability of future generations to meet their own needs. Economic growth provides the conditions in which protection of the environment can best be achieved, and environmental protection, in balance with other human goals, is necessary to achieve growth that is sustainable.

In turn, versatile, dynamic, responsive and profitable businesses are required as the driving force for sustainable economic development and for providing the managerial,

---

*　Reprinted with permission by ICC.

technical and financial resources to contribute to the resolution of environmental challenges. Market economies, characterised by entrepreneurial initiatives, are essential to achieve this.

Business thus shares the view that there should be a common goal, not a conflict, between economic development and environmental protection, both now and for future generations.

Making market forces work in this way to protect and improve the quality of the environment—with the help of standards such as ISO 14000, and judicious use of economic instruments in a harmonious regulatory framework—is an on-going challenge that the world faces in entering the 21st century.

This challenge was recognised by the nations of the world at the 1992 United Nations Conference on Environment and Development, which called on the co-operation of business in tackling it. To this end, business leaders have launched initiatives in their individual enterprises as well as through sectoral and cross-sectoral associations.

In order that more businesses join this effort and that their environmental performance continues to improve, the International Chamber of Commerce continues to call upon enterprises and their associations to use the following Principles as a basis for pursuing such improvement and to express publicly their support for them.

Individual programmes to implement these Principles will reflect the wide diversity among enterprises in size and function.

The objective remains that the widest range of enterprises commit themselves to improving their environmental performance in accordance with these Principles, to having in place management practices to effect such improvement, to measuring their progress, and to reporting this progress as appropriate internally and externally.

Note: The term environment as used in this document also refers to environmentally related aspects of health, safety and product stewardship.

Principles

1. Corporate priority

To recognise environmental management as among the highest corporate priorities and as a key determinant to sustainable development; to establish policies, programmes and practices for conducting operations in an environmentally sound manner.

2. Integrated management

To integrate these policies, programmes and practices fully into each business as an essential element of management in all its functions.

3. Process of improvement

To continue to improve corporate policies, programmes and environmental performance, taking into account technical developments, scientific understanding, consumer needs and community expectations, with legal regulations as a starting point; and to apply the same environmental criteria internationally.

4. Employee education

To educate, train and motivate employees to conduct their activities in an environmentally responsible manner.

5. Prior assessment

To assess environmental impacts before starting a new activity or project and before decommissioning a facility or leaving a site.

6. Products and services

To develop and provide products or services that have no undue environmental impact and are safe in their intended use, that are efficient in their consumption of energy and natural resources, and that can be recycled, reused, or disposed of safely.

7. Customer advice

To advise, and where relevant educate, customers, distributors and the public in the safe use, transportation, storage and disposal of products provided; and to apply similar considerations to the provision of services.

8. Facilities and operations

To develop, design and operate facilities and conduct activities taking into consideration the efficient use of energy and materials, the sustainable use of renewable resources, the minimisation of adverse environmental impact and waste generation, and the safe and responsible disposal of residual wastes.

9. Research

To conduct or support research on the environmental impacts of raw materials, products, processes, emissions and wastes associated with the enterprise and on the means of minimizing such adverse impacts.

10. Precautionary approach

To modify the manufacture, marketing or use of products or services or the conduct of activities, consistent with scientific and technical understanding, to prevent serious or irreversible environmental degradation.

11. Contractors and suppliers

To promote the adoption of these principles by contractors acting on behalf of the enterprise, encouraging and, where appropriate, requiring improvements in their practices to make them consistent with those of the enterprise; and to encourage the wider adoption of these principles by suppliers.

12. Emergency preparedness

To develop and maintain, where significant hazards exist, emergency preparedness plans in conjunction with the emergency services, relevant authorities and the local community, recognizing potential transboundary impacts.

13. Transfer of technology

To contribute to the transfer of environmentally sound technology and management methods throughout the industrial and public sectors.

14. Contributing to the common effort

To contribute to the development of public policy and to business, governmental and intergovernmental programmes and educational initiatives that will enhance environmental awareness and protection.

15. Openness to concerns

To foster openness and dialogue with employees and the public, anticipating and responding to their concerns about the potential hazards and impacts of operations, products, wastes or services, including those of transboundary or global significance.

16. Compliance and reporting

To measure environmental performance; to conduct regular environmental audits and assessments of compliance with company requirements, legal requirements and these principles; and periodically to provide appropriate information to the Board of Directors, shareholders, employees, the authorities and the public.

Support for the Charter

The ICC undertakes to encourage member companies and others to express their support and implement the Charter and its Principles.

A list of these companies can be obtained from ICC Headquarters. The ICC also publishes regularly a Charter bulletin which provides more specific information on the Charter's Principles and different interpretations possible—an attribute of the Charter that has been widely commended.

The first edition of Business Charter for Sustainable Development was adopted by the ICC Executive Board on 27 November 1990, and first published in April 1991.

It was prepared and revised by the ICC Working Party for Sustainable Development.

Chair Peter Scupholme (British Petroleum)   **Vice-Chair** W. Ross Stevens III (Du Pont)

The ICC is indebted to numerous companies and business organisations for their input in preparing and revising the Charter.

The Business Charter for Sustainable Development provides a basic framework of reference for action by individual corporations and business organisations throughout the world. It has been recognised as a complement to environmental management systems. To this end, the ICC, the United Nations Environment Programme (UNEP) and the International Federation of Consulting Engineers (FIDIC) have developed a kit to help enterprises integrate environmental management systems in the daily management practices, a step consistent with the objectives set out in this Charter.

The Business Charter has been published in over 20 languages, including all the official languages of the United Nations.

Regulation (EC) No 761/2001 of the European Parliament and of the Council of 19 March 2001 allowing voluntary participation by organisations in a Community eco-management and audit scheme (EMAS)

THE EUROPEAN PARLIAMENT AND THE COUNCIL OF THE EUROPEAN UNION,

Having regard to the Treaty establishing the European Community, and in particular Article 175(1) thereof,

Having regard to the proposal from the Commission[1],

Having regard to the Opinion of the Economic and Social Committee[2],

After consulting the Committee of the Regions,

Acting in accordance with the procedure laid down in Article 251 of the Treaty[3], in the light of the joint text approved by the Conciliation Committee on 20 December 2000,

Whereas:

(1) Article 2 of the Treaty stipulates that the Community shall have among its tasks to promote throughout the Community sustainable growth and the Resolution of 1 February 1993[4] stresses the importance of such sustainable growth.

(2) The programme 'Towards Sustainability', presented by the Commission and approved as to its general approach by the Resolution of 1 February 1993, underlines the role and responsibilities of organisations, both to reinforce the economy and to protect the environment throughout the Community.

---

[1] OJ C 400, 22.12.1998, p. 7 and OJ C 212 E, 25.7.2000, p. 1.

[2] OJ C 209, 22.7.1999, p. 43.

[3] Opinion of the European Parliament of 15 April 1999 (OJ C 219, 30.7.1999, p. 385), confirmed on 6 May 1999 (OJ C 279, 1.10.1999, p. 253), Council Common Position of 28 February 2000 (OJ C 128, 8.5.2000, p. 1) and Decision of the European Parliament of 6 July 2000 (not yet published in the Official Journal). Decision of the European Parliament of 14 February 2001 and Decision of the Council of 12 February 2001.

[4] Resolution of the Council and the Representatives of the Governments of the Member States, meeting within the Council of 1 February 1993 on a Community programme of policy and action in relation to the environment and sustainable development (OJ C 138, 17.5.1993, p. 1).

---

* Reprinted with the permission of the European Commission. Annex IV, 'Logo', and Annex VIII, 'Registration information', have been omitted here.

(3) The programme 'Towards Sustainability' calls for broadening the range of instruments in the field of environmental protection and for using market-mechanisms to commit organisations to adopt a pro-active approach in this field beyond compliance with all relevant regulatory requirements regarding the environment.

(4) The Commission should promote a coherent approach between the legislative instruments developed at Community level in the field of environmental protection.

(5) Council Regulation (EEC) No 1836/93 of 29 June 1993 allowing voluntary participation by companies in the industrial sector in a Community eco-management and audit scheme[5] demonstrated its effectiveness in promoting improvements of the environmental performance of industry.

(6) The experience gathered from the implementation of Regulation (EEC) No 1836/93 should be used to enhance the ability of the Community eco-management and audit scheme (EMAS) to bring about an improvement in the overall environmental performance of organisations.

(7) EMAS should be made available to all organisations having environmental impacts, providing a means for them to manage these impacts and to improve their overall environmental performance.

(8) In accordance with the principles of subsidiarity and proportionality referred to in Article 5 of the Treaty, the effectiveness of EMAS in contributing to improved environmental performance of European organisations can be better achieved at Community level. This Regulation limits itself to ensuring an equal implementation of EMAS throughout the Community by providing for common rules, procedures and essential requirements regarding EMAS whilst the measures that can be adequately performed at national level are left to the Member States.

(9) Organisations should be encouraged to participate in EMAS on a voluntary basis and may gain added value in terms of regulatory control, cost savings and public image.

(10) It is important that small and medium-sized enterprises participate in EMAS and that their participation should be promoted by facilitating access to information, to existing support funds and to public institutions and by establishing or promoting technical assistance measures.

(11) The information provided by Member States should be used by the Commission to assess the need for developing specific measures aimed at greater participation in EMAS by organisations, in particular small and medium-sized enterprises.

(12) The transparency and credibility of organisations implementing environmental management systems are enhanced when their management system, audit programme and environmental statement are examined to verify that they meet

[5] OJ L 168, 10.7.1993, p. 1.

the relevant requirements of this Regulation and when the environmental statement and its subsequent updates are validated by accredited environmental verifiers.

(13) It is therefore necessary to ensure and steadily improve the competence of the environmental verifiers by providing for an independent and neutral accreditation system, retraining and an appropriate supervision of their activities in order to ensure the overall credibility of EMAS. Close cooperation between the national accreditation bodies should accordingly be set up.

(14) Organisations should be encouraged to produce and make publicly available periodic environmental statements providing the public and other interested parties with information on their environmental performance.

(15) The Member States could create incentives to encourage organisations to participate in EMAS.

(16) The Commission should provide technical support to accession candidate countries in the setting up of the necessary structures for the application of EMAS.

(17) In addition to the general requirements of the environmental management system EMAS places special significance on the following elements: legal compliance, improvement of environmental performance and also external communication and employee involvement.

(18) The Commission should adapt the Annexes to this Regulation, with the exception of Annex V, recognise European and international standards for environmental issues of relevance to EMAS and establish guidelines in partnership with EMAS interested parties for the purpose of ensuring consistent implementation of the EMAS requirements across Member States. In drafting such guidelines, the Commission should take account of Community policy on the environment and in particular Community legislation as well as international commitments where relevant.

(19) The measures necessary for the implementation of this Regulation should be adopted in accordance with Council Decision 1999/468/EC of 28 June 1999 laying down the procedures for the exercise of implementing powers conferred on the Commission[1].

(20) This Regulation should be revised, if appropriate, in the light of experience gained after a certain period of operation.

(21) The European institutions should endeavour to adopt the principles laid down in this Regulation.

(22) This Regulation takes over and replaces Regulation (EEC) 1836/93 which should therefore be repealed,

---

[1] OJ L 184, 17.7.1999, p. 23.

HAVE ADOPTED THIS REGULATION:

Article 1
The eco-management and audit scheme and its objectives

1. A Community eco-management and audit scheme allowing voluntary participation by organisations, hereafter referred to as 'EMAS', is hereby established for the evaluation and improvement of the environmental performance of organisations and the provision of relevant information to the public and other interested parties.

2. The objective of EMAS shall be to promote continual improvements in the environmental performance of organisations by:

(a) the establishment and implementation of environmental management systems by organisations as described in Annex I;

(b) the systematic, objective and periodic evaluation of the performance of such systems as described in Annex I;

(c) the provision of information on environmental performance and an open dialogue with the public and other interested parties;

(d) the active involvement of employees in the organisation and appropriate initial and advanced training that makes active participation in the tasks referred to under (a) possible. Where they so request, any employee representatives shall also be involved.

Article 2
Definitions

For the purposes of this Regulation:

(a) 'environmental policy' shall mean an organisation's overall aims and principles of action with respect to the environment including compliance with all relevant regulatory requirements regarding the environment and also a commitment to continual improvement of environmental performance; the environmental policy provides the framework for setting and reviewing environmental objectives and targets;

(b) 'continual improvement of environmental performance' shall mean the process of enhancing, year by year, the measurable results of the environmental management system related to an organisation's management of its significant environmental aspects, based on its environmental policy, objectives and targets; the enhancing of the results need not take place in all spheres of activity simultaneously;

(c) 'environmental performance' shall mean the results of an organisation's management of its environmental aspects;

(d) 'prevention of pollution' shall mean use of processes, practices, materials or products that avoid, reduce or control pollution, which may include recycling, treatment, process changes, control mechanisms, efficient use of resources and material substitution;

(e) 'environmental review' shall mean an initial comprehensive analysis of the environmental issues, impact and performance related to activities of an organisation, (Annex VII);

(f) 'environmental aspect' shall mean an element of an organisation's activities, products or services that can interact with the environment, (Annex VI); a significant environmental aspect is an environmental aspect that has or can have a significant environmental impact;

(g) 'environmental impact' shall mean any change to the environment, whether adverse or beneficial, wholly or partially resulting from an organisation's activities, products or services;

(h) 'environmental programme' shall mean a description of the measures (responsibilities and means) taken or envisaged to achieve environmental objectives and targets and the deadlines for achieving the environmental objectives and targets;

(i) 'environmental objective' shall mean an overall environ mental goal, arising from the environmental policy, that an organisation sets itself to achieve, and which is quantified where practicable;

(j) 'environmental target' shall mean a detailed performance requirement, quantified where practicable, applicable to the organisation or parts thereof, that arises from the environmental objectives and that needs to be set and met in order to achieve those objectives;

(k) 'environmental management system' shall mean the part of the overall management system that includes the organisational structure, planning activities, responsibilities, practices, procedures, processes and resources for developing, implementing, achieving, reviewing and maintaining the environmental policy;

(l) 'environmental audit' shall mean a management tool comprising a systematic, documented, periodic and objective evaluation of the performance of the organisation, management system and processes designed to protect the environment with the aim of:

    (i) facilitating management control of practices which may have an impact on the environment;

    (ii) assessing compliance with the environmental policy, including environmental objectives and targets of the organisation (Annex II);

(m) 'audit cycle' shall mean the period of time in which all the activities in an organisation are audited, (Annex II);

(n) 'auditor' shall mean an individual or a team, belonging to the organisation personnel or external to the organisation, acting on behalf of the organisation's top management, possessing, individually or collectively, the competences referred to in Annex II, point 2.4 and being sufficiently independent of the activities they audit to make an objective judgment;

(o) 'environmental statement' shall mean the information detailed in Annex III point 3.2 ((a) to (g));

(p) 'interested party' shall mean an individual or group, including authorities, concerned with or affected by the environmental performance of an organisation;

(q) 'environmental verifier' shall mean any person or organisation independent of the organisation being verified, who has obtained accreditation, in accordance with the conditions and procedures referred to in Article 4;

(r) 'accreditation system' shall mean a system for the accreditation and supervision of environmental verifiers operated by an impartial institution or organisation designated or created by the Member State (accreditation body), with sufficient resources and competency and having appropriate procedures for performing the functions defined by this Regulation for such a system;

(s) 'organisation' shall mean a company, corporation, firm, enterprise, authority or institution, or part or combination thereof, whether incorporated or not, public or private, that has its own functions and administrations. The entity to be registered as an organisation under EMAS shall be agreed with the environmental verifier and, where appropriate, the competent bodies, taking account of Commission guidance, established in accordance with the procedure laid down in Article 14(2), but shall not exceed the boundaries of one Member State. The smallest entity to be considered shall be a site. Under exceptional circumstances identified by the Commission in accordance with the procedure laid down in Article 14(2), the entity to be considered for registration under EMAS may be smaller than a site, such as a sub-division with its own functions.

(t) 'site' shall mean all land at a distinct geographic location under the management control of an organisation covering activities, products and services. This includes all infrastructure, equipment and materials;

(u) 'competent bodies' shall mean the bodies designated by Member States, whether national, regional or local, in accordance with Article 5, to perform the tasks specified in this Regulation.

Article 3
Participation in EMAS

1. EMAS shall be open to the participation of any organisation dedicated to improving its overall environmental performance.

2. In order for an organisation to be registered under EMAS it shall:

(a) Conduct an environmental review of its activities, products and services in accordance with Annex VII addressing the issues contained in Annex VI and, in the light of the results of that review, implement an environmental management system covering all the requirements referred to in Annex I, in particular the compliance with the relevant environmental legislation.

However, organisations which have a certified environmental management system, recognised according to the requirements of Article 9, do not need to conduct a formal environmental review when moving on to EMAS implementation, if the necessary information for the identification and evaluation of the environmental aspects set out in Annex VI is provided by the certified environmental management system.

(b) carry out, or cause to be carried out, environmental auditing in accordance with the requirements set out in Annex II. The audits shall be designed to assess the environmental performance of the organisation;

(c) prepare, in accordance with Annex III, point 3.2, an environmental statement. The statement shall pay particular attention to the results achieved by an organisation against its environmental objectives and targets and the requirement of continuing to improve its environmental performance, and shall consider the information needs of relevant interested parties;

(d) have the environmental review, if appropriate, management system, audit procedure and environmental statement examined to verify that they meet the relevant requirements of this Regulation and have the environmental statement validated by the environmental verifier to ensure it meets the requirements of Annex III;

(e) forward the validated environmental statement to the competent body of the Member State in which the organisation seeking registration is located and, after registration, make it publicly available.

3. In order for an organisation to maintain registration to EMAS it shall:

(a) have the environmental management system and audit programme verified in accordance with the requirements of Annex V, point 5.6;

(b) forward the yearly necessary validated updates of its environmental statement to the competent body and make them publicly available. Deviations from the frequency with which updates shall be performed can be made under circumstances laid down in Commission guidance adopted in accordance with the procedure laid down in Article 14(2), in particular for small organisations and small enterprises according to Commission Recommendation 96/280/EC[1] and when there is no operational change in the environmental management system.

Article 4
Accreditation system

1. Member States shall establish a system for the accreditation of independent environmental verifiers and for the supervision of their activities. To this end, Member States may either use existing accreditation institutions or the competent bodies referred to in Article 5 or designate or set up any other body with an appropriate status.

---

[1] OJ L 107, 30.4.1996, p. 4.

Member States shall ensure that the composition of these systems is such as to guarantee their independence and neutrality in the execution of their tasks.

2. Member States shall ensure that these systems are fully operational within 12 months following the date of entry into force of this Regulation.

3. Member States shall ensure appropriate consultation of parties involved, in setting up and directing the accreditation systems.

4. The accreditation of environmental verifiers and supervision of their activities shall be in accordance with the requirements of Annex V.

5. Environmental verifiers accredited in one Member State may perform verification activities in any other Member State in accordance with the requirements laid down in Annex V. The start of the verification activity shall be notified to the Member State in which it is being performed and the activity shall be subject to supervision by the latter's accreditation system.

6. Member States shall inform the Commission of the measures taken pursuant to this Article and communicate relevant changes in the structure and procedures of the accreditation systems.

7. The Commission shall, in accordance with the procedure laid down in Article 14(2), promote collaboration between Member States in order, in particular, to avoid inconsistency between Annex V and the criteria, conditions and procedures which the national accreditation bodies apply for the accreditation and supervision of environmental verifiers to ensure a consistent quality of environmental verifiers.

8. A forum, constituted of all accreditation bodies, shall be set up by the accreditation bodies with the aim of providing the Commission with the elements and means to fulfil its obligation under paragraph (7). It shall meet at least once per year in the presence of a representative of the Commission.

The forum shall as appropriate develop guidance on issues in the field of accreditation, competence and supervision of environmental verifiers. Guidance documents produced shall be submitted to the procedure laid down in Article 14(2).

In order to ensure a harmonised development of the functioning of accreditation bodies and the verification process in all the Member States, the forum shall develop procedures for a peer review process. The aim of the peer review shall be to ensure that the accreditation systems of Member States meet the requirements of this Regulation. A report of the peer review activities shall be transmitted to the Commission which shall forward it for information to the Committee referred to in Article 14(1) and make it publicly available.

Article 5
Competent bodies

1. Within 3 months of the entry into force of this Regulation, each Member State shall designate the competent body responsible for carrying out the tasks provided for in this Regulation, in particular in Articles 6 and 7 and shall inform the Commission thereof.

2. Member States shall ensure that the composition of the competent bodies is such as to guarantee their independence and neutrality and that the competent bodies apply the provisions of this Regulation in a consistent manner.

3. Member States shall have guidelines for suspension and deletion of the registration of organisations, for the use of competent bodies. Competent bodies shall, in particular, have procedures for:

- considering observations from interested parties concerning registered organisations, and
- refusal of registration, deletion or suspension of organisations from registration.

4. The competent body shall be responsible for the registration of organisations under EMAS. It shall therefore control the entry and maintenance of organisations on the register.

5. Competent bodies from all Member States shall meet, at least once per year in the presence of a representative of the Commission. The objective of these meetings is to ensure the consistency of procedures relating to the registration of organisations under EMAS, including suspension and deletion of registration. A peer review process shall be put in place by the competent bodies for the purpose of developing a common understanding of their practical approach towards registration. A report of the peer review activities shall be transmitted to the Commission which shall forward it for information to the Committee referred to in Article 14(1), and make it publicly available.

Article 6
Registration of organisations

Registration of organisations shall be dealt with by competent bodies on the basis of the following cases:

1. If a competent body
   - has received a validated environmental statement and
   - has received a completed form, which includes at least the minimum information set out in Annex VIII, from the organisation and
   - has received any registration fee that may be payable under Article 16 and
   - is satisfied, on the basis of evidence received, and in particular through inquiries made at the competent enforcement authority regarding the compliance of the organisation with the relevant environmental legislation, that the organisation meets all the requirements of this Regulation,

it shall register the applicant organisation and give it a registration number. The competent body shall inform the organisation's management that the organisation appears on the register.

2. If a competent body receives a supervision report from the accreditation body which gives evidence that the activities of the environmental verifier were not performed adequately enough to ensure that the requirements of this Regulation are met by the applicant organisation, registration shall be refused or suspended as appropriate until assurance of the organisation's compliance with EMAS is obtained.

3. If an organisation fails to submit to a competent body, within three months of being required to do so,

- the yearly validated updates of the environmental statement, or
- a completed form, which includes at least the minimum information set out in Annex VIII from the organisation, or
- any relevant registration fees,

the organisation shall be suspended or deleted from the register, as appropriate, depending on the nature and scope of the failure. The competent body shall inform the organisation's management of the reasons for the measures taken.

4. If, at any time, a competent body concludes, on the basis of evidence received, that the organisation is no longer complying with one or more of the conditions of this Regulation, the organisation shall be suspended or deleted from the register, as appropriate, depending on the nature and scope of the failure.

If a competent body is informed by the competent enforcement authority of a breach by the organisation of relevant regulatory requirements regarding environmental protection, it shall refuse registration of that organisation or suspend it from the register as appropriate.

5. Refusal of registration, suspension or deletion of organisations from the register shall require the consultation of the appropriate interested parties, in order to provide the competent body with the necessary elements of evidence for taking its decision. The competent body shall inform the organisation's management of the reasons for the measures taken and of the process of discussion with the competent enforcement authority.

6. Refusal or suspension shall be lifted if the competent body has received satisfactory information that the organisation is in compliance with the requirements of EMAS or if it has received satisfactory information from the competent enforcement authority that the breach has been rectified and that the organisation has made satisfactory arrangements with the aim of ensuring that it does not recur.

Article 7
List of registered organisations and environmental verifiers

1. The accreditation body shall establish, revise and update a list of environmental verifiers and their scope of accreditation in their Member State and shall directly, or via the national authorities as decided by the Member State concerned, communicate changes in this list each month to the Commission and to the competent body.

2. The competent bodies shall establish and maintain a list of registered organisations in their Member State and update this list on a monthly basis. The competent bodies shall directly, or via the national authorities as decided by the Member State concerned, communicate changes in this list each month to the Commission and may organise a system of information exchanges by economic sector and area of competence in the network of delegated local bodies.

3. The register of environmental verifiers and EMAS registered organisations shall be maintained by the Commission which shall make it publicly available.

Article 8
Logo

1. Organisations participating in EMAS may use the logo set out in Annex IV only if they have a current EMAS registration. Technical specifications regarding the reproduction of the logo shall be adopted in accordance with the procedure laid down in Article 14(2) and published by the Commission.

2. The EMAS logo may be used by organisations in the following cases:

(a) on validated information as described in Annex III, point 3.5, under circumstances defined in Commission guidance adopted under the procedure laid down in Article 14(2) which shall ensure that there is no confusion with environmental product labels (version 2 of the logo, as given in Annex IV, shall be used in this case);

(b) on validated environmental statements (version 2 of the logo, as given in Annex IV, shall be used in this case);

(c) on registered organisations' letterheads (version 1 of the logo, as given in Annex IV, shall be used in this case);

(d) on information advertising an organisation's participation in EMAS (version 1 of the logo, as given in Annex IV, shall be used in this case);

(e) on or in adverts for products, activities and services, only under circumstances defined in Commission guidance adopted in accordance with Article 14(2) which shall ensure that there is no confusion with environmental product labels.

3. The logo shall not be used in the following cases:

(a) on products or their packaging,

(b) in conjunction with comparative claims concerning other products, activities and services.

The Commission shall however, as a part of the evaluation provided for in Article 15(3), consider under which exceptional circumstances the logo may be used and, for these cases, shall adopt rules in accordance with the procedure laid down in Article 14(2) which shall ensure that there is no confusion with environmental product labels.

Article 9
Relationship with European and international standards

1. Organisations implementing European or international standards for environmental issues relevant to EMAS and certified, according to appropriate certification procedures, as complying with those standards shall be considered as meeting the corresponding requirements of this Regulation, provided that:

(a) the standards are recognised by the Commission acting in accordance with the procedure laid down in Article 14(2);

(b) the accreditation requirements for the certification bodies are recognised by the Commission acting in accordance with the procedure laid down in Article 14(2).

The references of the recognised standards (including the relevant sections of EMAS to which they apply) and recognised accreditation requirements shall be published in the *Official Journal of the European Communities*.

2. To enable organisations referred to in paragraph 1 to be registered under EMAS, the organisations concerned shall demonstrate to the environmental verifier compliance with requirements not covered by the recognised standards.

Article 10
Relationship with other environmental legislation in the Community

1. EMAS shall be without prejudice to:

(a) Community law, or

(b) national laws or technical standards not governed by Community law and

(c) the duties of organisations under those laws and standards regarding environmental controls.

2. Member States should consider how registration under EMAS in accordance with this Regulation may be taken into account in the implementation and enforcement of environmental legislation in order to avoid unnecessary duplication of effort by both organisations and competent enforcement authorities.

Member States shall inform the Commission of the measures taken in this regard. The Commission shall transmit the information received from Member States to the European Parliament and to the Council as soon as available and at least on a three-yearly basis.

Article 11
Promotion of organisations' participation, in particular of small and medium-sized enterprises

1. Member States shall promote organisations' participation in EMAS and shall, in particular, consider the need to ensure the participation of small and medium-sized enterprises (SMEs) by

- facilitating access to information, support funds, public institutions and public procurement, without prejudice to the Community rules governing public procurement,
- establishing or promoting technical assistance measures, especially in conjunction with initiatives from appropriate professional or local points of contact (e.g. local authorities, chambers of commerce, trade or craft associations),
- ensuring that reasonable registration fees encourage higher participation.

In order to promote participation of SMEs, including those concentrated in well defined geographical areas, local authorities, in participation with industrial associations, chambers of commerce and interested parties may provide assistance in the identification of significant environmental impacts. SMEs may then use this in defining their environmental programme and setting the objectives and targets of their EMAS management system. In addition, programmes designed to encourage the participation of SMEs, such as a step by step approach which will eventually lead to EMAS registration, may be developed at regional or national level. The system shall operate with the objective of avoiding unnecessary administrative burden for participants, in particular small organisations.

2. In order to encourage organisations' participation in EMAS the Commission and other institutions of the Community as well as other public authorities at national level should consider, without prejudice to Community law, how registration under EMAS may be taken into account when setting criteria for their procurement policies.

3. Member States shall inform the Commission of the measures taken under this Article. The Commission shall transmit the information received from Member States to the European Parliament and to the Council as soon as available and at least on a three-yearly basis.

Article 12
Information

1. Each Member State shall take appropriate measures to ensure that:

(a) organisations are informed of the content of this Regulation;

(b) the public is informed of the objectives and principal components of EMAS.

Member States shall, where appropriate, in cooperation with, amongst others, industrial associations, consumer organisations, environmental organisations, trade unions and local institutions, in particular use professional publications, local journals, promotion campaigns or any other functional means to promote general awareness of EMAS.

2. Member States shall inform the Commission of the measures taken under this Article.

3. The Commission shall be responsible for promoting EMAS at Community level. It shall, in particular, examine in consultation with the members of the Committee referred to in Article 14(1) the possibility of disseminating best practice by appropriate ways and means.

Article 13
Infringements

Member States shall take appropriate legal or administrative measures in case of non-compliance with the provisions of this Regulation and communicate these measures to the Commission.

Article 14
Committee

1. The Commission shall be assisted by a committee.

2. Where reference is made to this paragraph, Articles 5 and 7 of Decision 1999/468/EC shall apply, having regard to the provisions of Article 8 thereof.

The period referred to in Article 5(6) of Decision 1999/468/EC shall be set at three months.

3. The Committee shall adopt its rules of procedure.

Article 15
Revision

1. The Commission shall review EMAS in the light of the experience gained during its operation and international developments no later than five years after the entry into force of this Regulation, and shall, if necessary, propose to the European Parliament and Council the appropriate amendments.

2. All the Annexes to this Regulation, with the exception of Annex V, shall be adapted by the Commission, acting in accordance with the procedure laid down in Article 14(2) in the light of experience gained in the operation of EMAS and in response to identified needs for guidance on EMAS requirements.

3. The Commission shall in particular evaluate, in cooperation with the Member States, no later than 5 years after the entry into force of this Regulation, the use, recognition and interpretation, especially by the public and other interested parties, of the EMAS logo and assess whether there is a need to revise the logo and the requirements for its use.

Article 16
Costs and fees

1. A system of fees in accordance with arrangements established by Member States may be set up for the administrative costs incurred in connection with the registration procedures for organisations and the accreditation and supervision of environmental verifiers and other related costs of EMAS.

2. Member States shall inform the Commission of the measures taken under this Article.

Article 17
Repeal of Regulation (EEC) No 1836/93

1. Regulation (EEC) No 1836/93 shall be repealed as from the date of entry into force of this Regulation, subject to paragraphs 2 to 5 of this Article.

2. National accreditation systems and competent bodies set up pursuant to Regulation (EEC) No 1836/93 shall remain in force. Member States shall modify the procedures followed by accreditation systems and competent bodies under the corresponding provisions of this Regulation. Member States shall ensure that these systems are fully operational within 12 months following the date of entry into force of this Regulation.

3. Environmental verifiers accredited in accordance with Regulation (EEC) No 1836/93 may continue to perform their activities in accordance with the requirements established by this Regulation.

4. Sites registered in accordance with Regulation (EEC) No 1836/93 will remain on the EMAS register. The new requirements of this Regulation shall be checked at the time of the next verification of a site. If the next verification is to be carried out sooner than 6 months after entry into force of this Regulation, the date of the next verification may be extended by 6 months in agreement with the environmental verifier and the competent bodies.

5. Paragraphs 3 and 4 shall also apply to environmental verifiers accredited and sites registered in accordance with Article 14 of Regulation (EEC) No 1836/93, provided that the responsible accreditation bodies and competent bodies have agreed that the environmental verifiers and registered sites comply with all the requirements of Regulation (EEC) No 1836/93 and notify this to the Commission.

Article 18
Entry into force

This Regulation shall enter into force on the third day following that of its publication in the *Official Journal of the European Communities*.

This Regulation shall be binding in its entirety and directly applicable in all Member States.

Done at Brussels, 19 March 2001.

The European Parliament	*For the Council*
The President	*The President*
N. FONTAINE	A. LINDH

ANNEX I

A. ENVIRONMENTAL MANAGEMENT SYSTEM REQUIREMENTS

The environmental Management system shall be implemented according to the requirements given below (section 4 of EN ISO 14001:1996)*:

I-A Environmental Management System Requirements

I-A.1. *General requirements*

The organisation shall establish and maintain an environmental management system, the requirements of which are described in this annex.

I-A.2. *Environmental policy*

Top management shall define the organisation's environmental policy and ensure that it

(a) is appropriate to the nature, scale and environmental impacts of its activities, products and services;

(b) includes a commitment to continual improvement and prevention of pollution;

(c) includes a commitment to comply with relevant environmental legislation and regulations, and with other requirements to which the organisation subscribes;

(d) provides the framework for setting and reviewing environmental objectives and targets;

(e) is documented, implemented and maintained and communicated to all employees;

(f) is available to the public.

I-A.3. *Planning*

I-A.3.1. *Environmental aspects*

The organisation shall establish and maintain (a) procedure(s) to identify the environmental aspects of its activities, products or services that it can control and over which it can be expected to have an influence, in order to determine those which have or can have significant impacts on the environment. The organisation shall ensure that the aspects related to these significant impacts are considered in setting its environmental objectives.

The organisation shall keep this information up-to-date.

---

* The use of the text of the national standard reproduced in this Annex is made with the permission of CEN. The full text of the national standard can be purchased from the national standard bodies the list of which is given in this Annex.

I-A.3.2. *Legal and other requirements*

The organisation shall establish and maintain a procedure to identify and have access to legal and other requirements to which the organisation subscribes, that are applicable to the environmental aspects of its activities, products or services.

I-A.3.3. *Objectives and targets*

The organisation shall establish and maintain documented environmental objectives and targets, at each relevant function and level within the organisation.

When establishing and reviewing its objectives, an organisation shall consider the legal and other requirements, its significant environmental aspects, its technological options and its financial, operational and business requirements, and the views of interested parties.

The objectives and targets shall be consistent with the environmental policy, including the commitment to prevention of pollution.

I-A.3.4. *Environmental management programme(s)*

The organisation shall establish and maintain (a) programme(s) for achieving its objectives and targets. It shall include

(a) designation of responsibility for achieving objectives and targets at each relevant function and level of the organisation;

(b) the means and timeframe by which they are to be achieved.

If a project relates to new developments and new or modified activities, products or services, programme(s) shall be amended where relevant to ensure that environmental management applies to such projects.

I-A.4. *Implementation and operation*

I-A.4.1. *Structure and responsibility*

Roles, responsibility and authorities shall be defined, documented and communicated in order to facilitate effective environmental management.

Management shall provide resources essential to the implementation and control of the environmental management system. Resources include human resources and specialised skills, technology and financial resources.

The organisation's top management shall appoint (a) specific management representative(s) who, irrespective of other responsibilities, shall have defined roles, responsibilities and authority for

(a) ensuring that environmental management system requirements are established, implemented and maintained in accordance with this International Standard;

(b) reporting on the performance of the environmental management system to top management for review and as a basis for improvement of the environmental management system.

I-A.4.2. *Training, awareness and competence*

The organisation shall identify training needs. It shall require that all personnel whose work may create a significant impact upon the environment, have received appropriate training.

It shall establish and maintain procedures to make its employees or members at each relevant function and level aware of

(a) the importance of conformance with the environmental policy and procedures and with the requirements of the environmental management system;

(b) the significant environmental impacts, actual or potential, of their work activities and the environmental benefits of improved personal performance;

(c) their roles and responsibilities in achieving conformance with the environmental policy and procedures and with the requirements of the environmental management system, including emergency preparedness and response requirements;

(d) the potential consequences of departure from specified operating procedures.

Personnel performing the tasks which can cause significant environmental impacts shall be competent on the basis of appropriate education, training and/or experience.

I-A.4.3. *Communication*

With regard to its environmental aspects and environmental management system, the organisation shall establish and maintain procedures for

(a) internal communication between the various levels and functions of the organisation;

(b) receiving, documenting and responding to relevant communication from external interested parties.

The organisation shall consider processes for external communication on its significant environmental aspects and record its decision.

I-A.4.4. *Environmental management system documentation*

The organisation shall establish and maintain information, in paper or electronic form, to

(a) describe the core elements of the management system and their interaction;

(b) provide direction to related documentation.

I-A.4.5. *Document control*

The organisation shall establish and maintain procedures for controlling all documents required by this International Standard to ensure that

(a) they can be located;

(b) they are periodically reviewed, revised as necessary and approved for adequacy by authorised personnel;

(c) the current versions of relevant documents are available at all locations where operations essential to the effective functioning of the environmental management system are performed;

(d) obsolete documents are promptly removed from all points of issue and points of use, or otherwise assured against unintended use;

(e) any obsolete documents retained for legal and/or knowledge preservation purposes are suitably identified.

Documentation shall be legible, dated (with dates of revision) and readily identifiable, maintained in an orderly manner and retained for a specified period. Procedures and responsibilities shall be established and maintained concerning the creation and modification of the various types of document.

I-A.4.6. *Operational control*

The organisation shall identify those operations and activities that are associated with the identified significant environmental aspects in line with its policy, objectives and targets. The organisation shall plan these activities, including maintenance, in order to ensure that they are carried out under specified conditions by

(a) establishing and maintaining documented procedures to cover situations where their absence could lead to deviations from the environmental policy and the objectives and targets;

(b) stipulating operating criteria in the procedures;

(c) establishing and maintaining procedures related to the identifiable significant environmental aspects of goods and services used by the organisation and communicating relevant procedures and requirements to suppliers and contractors.

I-A.4.7. *Emergency preparedness and response*

The organisation shall establish and maintain procedures to identify potential for and respond to accidents and emergency situations, and for preventing and mitigating the environmental impacts that may be associated with them.

The organisation shall review and revise, where necessary, its emergency preparedness and response procedures, in particular, after the occurrence of accidents or emergency situations.

The organisation shall also periodically test such procedures where practicable.

I-A.5. *Checking and corrective action*

I-A.5.1. *Monitoring and measurement*

The organisation shall establish and maintain documented procedures to monitor and measure, on a regular basis, the key characteristics of its operations and activities that can have a significant impact on the environment. This shall include the recording of information to track performance, relevant operational controls and conformance with the organisation's environmental objectives and targets. Monitoring equipment shall be calibrated and maintained and records of this process shall be retained according to the organisation's procedures.

The organisation shall establish and maintain a documented procedure for periodically evaluating compliance with relevant environmental legislation and regulations.

I-A.5.2. *Nonconformance and corrective and preventive action*

The organisation shall establish and maintain procedures for defining responsibility and authority for handling and investigating nonconformance, taking action to mitigate any impacts caused and for initiating and completing corrective and preventive action.

Any corrective or preventive action taken to eliminate the causes of actual and potential nonconformances shall be appropriate to the magnitude of problems and commensurate with the environmental impact encountered.

The organisation shall implement and record any changes in the documented procedures resulting from corrective and preventive action.

I-A.5.3. *Records*

The organisation shall establish and maintain procedures for the identification, maintenance and disposition of environmental records. These records shall include training records and the results of audits and reviews.

Environmental records shall be legible, identifiable and traceable to the activity, product or service involved. Environmental records shall be stored and maintained in such a way that they are readily retrievable and protected against damage, deterioration or loss. Their retention times shall be established and recorded.

Records shall be maintained, as appropriate to the system and to the organisation, to demonstrate conformance to the requirements of this International Standard.

I-A.5.4. *Environmental management system audit*

The organisation shall establish and maintain (a) programme(s) and procedures for periodic environmental management system audits to be carried out, in order to

(a) determine whether or not the environmental management system

   (1) conforms to planned arrangements for environmental management including the requirements of this International Standard; and

   (2) has been properly implemented and maintained; and

228

(b)   provide information on the results of audits to management

The organisation's audit programme, including any schedule, shall be based on the environmental importance of the activity concerned and the results of previous audits. In order to be comprehensive, the audit procedures shall cover the audit scope, frequency and methodologies, as well as the responsibilities and requirements for conducting audits and reporting results.

I-A.6. *Management review*

The organisation's top management shall, at intervals that it determines, review the environmental management system, to ensure its continuing suitability, adequacy and effectiveness. The management review process shall ensure that the necessary information is collected to allow management to carry out this evaluation. This review shall be documented.

The management review shall address the possible need for changes to policy, objectives and other elements of the environmental management system, in the light of environmental management system audit results, changing circumstances and the commitment to continual improvement.

List of national standard bodies

B:	IBN/BIN (Institut Belge de Normalisation/Belgisch Instituut voor Normalisatie)
DK:	DS (Dansk Standard)
D:	DIN (Deutsches Institut für Normung e.V.)
EL:	ELOT (Ελληνικός οργανισμός τυποποίησης)
E:	AENOR (Asociación Española de Normalización y Certificación)
F:	AFNOR (Association Française de Normalisation)
IRL:	NSAI (National Standards Authority of Ireland)
I:	UNI (Ente Nazionale Italiano di Unificazione)
L:	EE (Service de l'Energie de l'Etat) (Luxembourg)
NL:	NEN (Nederlands Normalisatie-Instituut)
A:	ON (Österreichisches Normungsinstitut)
P:	IPQ (Instituto Português da Qualidade)
FIN:	SFS (Suomen Standardisoimisliitto r.y)
S:	SIS (Standardiseringen i Sverige)
UK:	BSI (British Standards Institution).

B. ISSUES TO BE ADDRESSED BY ORGANISATIONS IMPLEMENTING EMAS

1. Legal compliance

Organisations shall be able to demonstrate that they:

(a) have identified, and know the implications to the organisation of, all relevant environmental legislation;

(b) provide for legal compliance with environmental legislation; and

(c) have procedures in place that enable the organisation to meet these requirements on an ongoing basis.

2. Performance

Organisations shall be able to demonstrate that the management system and the audit procedures address the actual environmental performance of the organisation with respect to the aspects identified from Annex VI. The performance of the organisation against its objectives and targets shall be evaluated as part of the management review process. The organisation shall also commit itself to the continual improvement of its environmental performance. In doing so, the organisation may base its action on local, regional and national environmental programmes.

The means to achieve the objectives and targets cannot be environmental objectives. If the organisation comprises one or more sites, each of the sites to which EMAS applies shall comply with all the requirements of EMAS including the continual improvement of environmental performance as defined in Article 2(b).

3. External communication and relations

Organisations shall be able to demonstrate an open dialogue with the public and other interested parties including local communities and customers with regard to the environmental impact of their activities, products and services in order to identify the public's and other interested parties' concerns.

4. Employee involvement

In addition to the requirements in Annex I—Section A employees shall be involved in the process aimed at continually improving the organisation's environmental performance. Appropriate forms of participation such as the suggestion-book system or project-based group works or environmental committees should be used for this purpose. Organisations shall take note of Commission guidance on best practice in this field. Where they so request, any employee representatives shall also be involved.

ANNEX II

REQUIREMENTS CONCERNING INTERNAL ENVIRONMENTAL AUDITING

2.1. General requirements

Internal audits ensure that the activities carried out by an organisation are being conducted in accordance with established procedures. The audit may also identify any problems with those established procedures or any opportunities for improving those procedures. The scope of audits carried out within an organisation may vary from the audit of a simple procedure to the audit of complex activities. Over a period of time all activities in a particular organisation shall be subject to an audit. The period of time taken to complete audits of all activities is known as the audit cycle. For small non-complex organisations, it may be possible to audit all activities at one time. For these organisations the audit cycle is the interval between these audits.

Internal audits shall be carried out by persons sufficiently independent of the activity being audited to ensure an impartial view. They may be carried out by employees of the organisation or by external parties (employees from other organisations, employees from other parts of the same organisation or consultants).

2.2. Objectives

The organisation's environmental auditing programme shall define in writing the objectives of each audit or audit cycle including the audit frequency for each activity.

The objectives shall include, in particular, assessing the management systems in place, and determining conformity with the organisation's policy and programme, which shall include compliance with relevant environmental regulatory requirements.

2.3. Scope

The overall scope of the individual audits, or of each stage of an audit cycle where appropriate, shall be clearly defined and shall explicitly specify the:

1. subject areas covered;
2. activities to be audited;
3. environmental criteria to be considered;
4. period covered by the audit.

Environmental audit includes assessment of the factual data necessary to evaluate performance.

2.4. Organisation and resources

Environmental audits shall be performed by persons or groups of persons with appropriate knowledge of the sectors and fields audited, including knowledge and experience on the relevant environmental, management, technical and regulatory issues, and sufficient training and proficiency in the specific skills of auditing to achieve the stated objectives. The resources and time allocated to the audit shall be commensurate with the scope and objectives of the audit.

The top organisation management shall support the auditing.

The auditors shall be sufficiently independent of the activities they audit to make an objective and impartial judgment.

2.5. Planning and preparation for an audit

Each audit shall be planned and prepared with the objectives, in particular, of:

- ensuring the appropriate resources are allocated,
- ensuring that each individual involved in the audit process (including auditors, management, and staff) understands his or her role and responsibilities.

Preparation shall include familiarisation with activities of the organisation and with the environmental management system established there and review of the findings and conclusions of previous audits.

2.6. Audit activities

Audit activities shall include discussions with personnel, inspection of operating conditions and equipment and reviewing of records, written procedures and other relevant documentation, with the objective of evaluating the environmental performance of the activity being audited to determine whether it meets the applicable standards, regulations or objectives and targets set and whether the system in place to manage environmental responsibilities is effective and appropriate. Inter alia, spot-checking of compliance with these criteria should be used to determine the effectiveness of the entire management system.

The following steps, in particular, shall be included in the audit process:

(a) understanding of the management systems;

(b) assessing strengths and weaknesses of the management systems;

(c) gathering relevant evidence;

(d) evaluating audit findings;

(e) preparing audit conclusions;

(f) reporting audit findings and conclusions.

2.7. Reporting audit findings and conclusions

1. A written audit report of the appropriate form and content shall be prepared by the auditors to ensure full, formal submission of the findings and conclusions of the audit, at the end of each audit and audit cycle.

The findings and conclusions of the audit shall be formally communicated to the top organisation management.

2. The fundamental objectives of a written audit report are:

    (a)   to document the scope of the audit;

    (b)   to provide management with information on the state of compliance with the organisations' environmental policy and the environmental progress at the organisation;

    (c)   to provide management with information on the effectiveness and reliability of the arrangements for monitoring environmental impacts of the organisation;

    (d)   to demonstrate the need for corrective action, where appropriate.

2.8. Audit follow-up

The audit process shall culminate in the preparation and implementation of a plan of appropriate corrective action.

Appropriate mechanisms shall be in place and in operation to ensure that the audit results are followed up.

2.9. Audit frequency

The audit or audit cycle shall be completed, as appropriate, at intervals no longer than 3 years. The frequency with which any activity is audited will vary depending upon the

(a)   nature, scale and complexity of the activities;

(b)   significance of associated environmental impacts;

(c)   importance and urgency of the problems detected by previous audits;

(d)   history of environmental problems.

More complex activities with a more significant environmental impact shall be audited more frequently.

An organisation shall define its own audit programme and audit frequency taking account of Commission guidance adopted in accordance with the procedure laid down in Article 14(2).

ANNEX III

ENVIRONMENTAL STATEMENT

3.1. Introduction

The aim of the environmental statement is to provide environmental information to the public and other interested parties regarding the environmental impact and perfor- mance and the continual improvement of environmental performance of the organ- isation. It is also a vehicle to address the concerns of interested parties identified as a result of Annex I—Section B.3 and considered as significant by the organisation (Annex VI, point 6.4). Environmental information shall be presented in a clear and coherent manner in printed form for those who have no other means of obtaining this information. Upon its first registration and every three years thereafter, the organ- isation is required to make available the information detailed under point 3.2 in a consolidated printed version.

The Commission shall adopt guidance about the environmental statement in accor- dance with the procedure laid down in Article 14(2).

3.2. Environmental statement

Upon its first registration an organisation shall produce environmental information, taking into account the criteria of point 3.5 to be referred to as the environmental statement, to be validated by the environmental verifier. This information shall be submitted to the competent body following validation, and then be made publicly available. The environmental statement is a tool for communication and dialogue with the public and other interested parties regarding environmental performance. The organisation shall consider the information needs of the public and other interested parties when writing and designing the environmental statement.

The minimum requirements for this information shall be as follows:

(a) a clear and unambiguous description of the organisation registering under EMAS and a summary of its activities, products and services and its relationship to any parent organisations as appropriate;

(b) the environmental policy and a brief description of the environmental man- agement system of the organisation;

(c) a description of all the significant direct and indirect environmental aspects which result in significant environmental impacts of the organisation and an explanation of the nature of the impacts as related to these aspects (Annex VI);

(d) a description of the environmental objectives and targets in relation to the significant environmental aspects and impacts;

(e) a summary of the data available on the performance of the organisation against its environmental objectives and targets with respect to its significant environ- mental impacts. The summary may include figures on pollutant emissions, waste generation, consumption of raw material, energy and water, noise as well as other aspects indicated in Annex VI. The data should allow for year-by-year comparison to assess the development of the environmental performance of the organisation;

(f) other factors regarding environmental performance including performance against legal provisions with respect to their significant environmental impacts;

(g) the name and accreditation number of the environmental verifier and the date of validation.

3.3. Criteria for environmental performance reporting

The raw data generated by an environmental management system will be used in a number of different ways to show the environmental performance of an organisation. For this purpose organisations may use relevant existing environmental performance indicators, making sure that the indicators chosen:

(a) give an accurate appraisal of the organisation's performance;

(b) are understandable and unambiguous;

(c) allow for year on year comparison to assess the development of the environmental performance of the organisation;

(d) allow for comparison with sector, national or regional benchmarks as appropriate;

(e) allow for comparison with regulatory requirements as appropriate.

3.4. Maintenance of publicly available information

The organisation shall update the information detailed in point 3.2 and shall have any changes validated by an environmental verifier, on a yearly basis. Deviations from the frequency with which updates shall be performed may be made under circumstances laid down in Commission guidance adopted in accordance with the procedure laid down in Article 14(2). After validation changes shall also be submitted to the competent body and be made publicly available.

3.5. Publication of information

Organisations may wish to address different audiences or interested parties with the information generated by its environmental management system and use only selected information from the environmental statement. Any environmental information published by an organisation may bear the EMAS logo provided it has been validated by an environmental verifier as being:

(a) accurate and non deceptive;

(b) substantiated and verifiable;

(c) relevant and used in an appropriate context or setting;

(d) representative of the overall environmental performance of the organisation;

(e) unlikely to result in misinterpretation;

(f) significant in relation to the overall environmental impact,

and makes reference to the organisation's latest environmental statement from which it was drawn.

3.6. Public availability

The information generated in point 3.2(a) to (g) which forms the environmental statement for an organisation and the updated information specified in point 3.4 shall be available to the public and other interested parties. The environmental statement shall be made accessible to the public. To this end, organisations are encouraged to use all methods available (electronic publication, libraries etc.) The organisation shall be able to demonstrate to the environmental verifier that anybody interested in the organisation's environmental performance can easily and freely be given access to the information required in point 3.2(a) to (g) and point 3.4.

3.7. Local accountability

Organisations registering under EMAS may wish to produce one corporate environmental statement covering a number of different geographic locations. The intention of EMAS is to ensure local accountability and thus organisations shall ensure that the significant environmental impacts of each site are clearly identified and reported within the corporate statement.

ANNEX V

ACCREDITATION, SUPERVISION AND FUNCTION OF THE ENVIRONMENTAL VERIFIERS

5.1. General

The accreditation of environmental verifiers shall be based on the general principles of competence set out in this Annex. Accreditation bodies may choose to accredit individuals, organisations or both, as environmental verifiers. The procedural requirements and detailed criteria for accrediting environmental verifiers are defined pursuant to Article 4 by national accreditation systems in accordance with these principles. Conformity with these principles shall be ensured through the peer review process established by Article 4.

5.2. Requirements for the accreditation of environmental verifiers

5.2.1. *The following competence constitutes the minimum requirements with which an environmental verifier, individual or organisation, shall comply:*

(a) knowledge and understanding of the Regulation, the general functioning of environmental management systems, relevant standards and guidance issued by the Commission, under Article 4 and 14(2), for the use of this Regulation;

(b) knowledge and understanding of the legislative, regulatory and administrative requirements relevant to the activity subject to verification;

(c) knowledge and understanding of environmental issues, including the environmental dimension of sustainable development;

(d) knowledge and understanding of the technical aspects, relevant to environmental issues, of the activity subject to verification;

(e) understanding of the general functioning of the activity subject to verification in order to assess the appropriateness of the management system;

(f) knowledge and understanding of environmental auditing requirements and methodology;

(g) knowledge of information audit (Environmental Statement).

Appropriate evidence of the verifier's knowledge and of his/her/its relevant experience and technical capacities in the abovementioned fields should be provided to the accreditation body to which the candidate verifier has applied for accreditation

In addition, the environmental verifier shall be independent, in particular of the organisation's auditor or consultant, impartial and objective in performing his or her activities.

The individual environmental verifier or verification organisation shall ensure that he or she or the organisation and its staff is free of any commercial, financial or other pressures which might influence their judgment or endanger trust in their independence of judgment and integrity in relation to their activities, and that they comply with any rules applicable in this respect.

The environmental verifier shall have documented methodologies and procedures, including quality control mechanisms and confidentiality provisions, for the verification requirements of this Regulation. In case the environmental verifier is an organisation, the environmental verifier shall have and make available on request an organisation chart detailing structures and responsibilities within the organisation and a statement of legal status, ownership and funding sources.

5.2.2. *Scope of accreditation*

The scope of accreditation of environmental verifiers shall be defined according to the classification of economic activities (NACE codes) as established by Council Regulation (EEC) 3037/90[1]. The scope of accreditation shall be limited by the competence of the environmental verifier. The scope of accreditation shall also take into account the size and complexity of the activity, where appropriate; this will be assured through supervision.

5.2.3. *Additional requirements for the accreditation of individual environmental verifiers performing verifications on their own*

Individual environmental verifiers performing verification on their own, in addition to complying with the requirements of point 5.2.1 and 5.2.2 shall have:

- all the necessary competence to perform verifications, in their accredited fields,
- a limited scope of accreditation dependant on their personal competence.

Compliance with these requirements shall be ensured through the assessment carried out prior to the accreditation and through the supervisory role of the accreditation body.

5.3. Supervision of environmental verifiers

5.3.1. *Supervision of environmental verifiers carried out by the accreditation body which granted their accreditation*

The environmental verifier shall immediately inform the accreditation body of all changes which have a bearing on the accreditation or its scope.

Provision shall be made, at regular intervals not exceeding 24 months, to ensure that the environmental verifier continues to comply with the accreditation requirements and to monitor the quality of the verifications undertaken. Supervision may consist of office audit, witnessing in organisations, questionnaires, review of environmental statements validated by the environmental verifiers and review of verification report. It should be proportionate with the activity undertaken by the environmental verifier.

Any decision taken by the accreditation body to terminate or suspend accreditation or curtail the scope of accreditation shall be taken only after the environmental verifier has had the possibility of a hearing.

5.3.2. *Supervision of environmental verifiers performing verification activities in a Member State other than that where their accreditation was granted*

An environmental verifier accredited in one Member State, before performing verification activities in another Member State, shall provide to the accreditation body of the latter Member State, at least four weeks in advance, notification of:

- his or her accreditation details, competences and team composition if appropriate,

---

[1] OJ L 293, 24.10.1990, p. 1. Regulation as amended by Regulation (EEC) No 761/93 (OJ L 83, 3.4.1993, p. 1).

- when and where the verification will occur: address and contact details of the organisation, measures taken to deal with legal and language knowledge if necessary.

The accreditation body may request further clarification of the necessary legal and language knowledge as detailed above.

This notification shall be communicated before each new verification.

The accreditation body shall not require other conditions which would prejudice the right of the environmental verifier to provide services in a Member State other than the one where accreditation was granted. In particular, discriminatory fees for notification shall not be charged. The accreditation body shall also not use the notification procedure to delay the arrival of the environmental verifier. Any difficulty to supervise the environmental verifier on the date communicated shall be adequately justified. If costs for supervision arise, the accreditation body is allowed to charge appropriate fees.

If the supervising accreditation body is not satisfied with the quality of the work done by the environmental verifier, the supervision report shall be transmitted to the environmental verifier concerned, the accreditation body which granted the accreditation, to the competent body where the organisation being verified is located and, in case of any further dispute, to the forum of accreditation body.

Organisations may not refuse the right of accreditation bodies to supervise the environmental verifier through witnessed assessments during the verification process.

5.4. The function of environmental verifiers

5.4.1. *The function of the environmental verifier is to check, without prejudice to the enforcement powers of Member States in respect of regulatory requirements:*

(a) compliance with all the requirements of this Regulation: initial environmental review if appropriate, environmental management system, environmental audit and its results and the environmental statement;

(b) the reliability, credibility and correctness of the data and information in:

- the environmental statement (Annex III, point 3.2 and point 3.3),
- environmental information to be validated (Annex III, point 3.4).

The environmental verifier shall, in particular, investigate in a sound professional manner, the technical validity of the initial environmental review, if appropriate, or audit or other procedures carried out by the organisation, without unnecessarily duplicating those procedures. Inter alia, the environmental verifier should use spot-checks to determine whether the results of the internal audit are reliable.

5.4.2. *At the time of the first verification, the environmental verifier shall, in particular, check that the following requirements are met by the organisation:*

(a) a fully operational environmental management system in accordance with Annex I;

(b) a fully planned audit programme, which had already begun in accordance with Annex II so that at least areas with the most significant environmental impact have been covered;

(c) completion of one management review;

(d) the preparation of an environmental statement in accordance with Annex III, point 3.2.

5.4.3. *Legal compliance*

The environmental verifier shall ensure that an organisation has procedures in place to control those aspects of its operations subject to relevant Community or national laws and that these procedures are capable of delivering compliance. The checks of the audit, shall in particular, provide for evidence of the capability of the procedures in place to deliver legal compliance.

The environmental verifier shall not validate the environmental statement, if during the verification process he observes, for example through spot-checks, that the organisation is not in legal compliance.

5.4.4. *Organisation definition*

When verifying the environmental management system and validating the environmental statement, the environmental verifier shall ensure that the components of the organisation are unambiguously defined and corresponds to a real division of the activities. The content of the statement shall clearly cover the different parts of the organisation to which EMAS applies.

5.5. Conditions for the environmental verifier to perform his/her activities

5.5.1. The environmental verifier shall operate within his/her scope of accreditation, on the basis of a written agreement with the organisation which defines the scope of the work, enables the environmental verifier to operate in an independent professional manner and commits the organisation to providing the necessary cooperation.

5.5.2. The verification shall involve examination of documentation, a visit to the organisation including, in particular, interviews with personnel, preparation of a report to the organisations' management and the organisations' solution of the issues raised by the report.

5.5.3. The documentation to be examined in advance of the visit shall include basic information about the organisation and activities there, the environmental policy and programme, the description of the environmental management system in operation in the organisation, details of the environmental review or audit carried out, the report on that review or audit and on any corrective action taken afterwards, and the draft environmental statement.

5.5.4. The environmental verifier shall prepare a report for the organisation's management. This report shall specify:

(a) all issues relevant to the work carried out by the environmental verifier;

(b) the starting point of the organisation towards implementation of an environmental management system;

(c) in general, cases of nonconformity with the provisions of this Regulation, and in particular:

- technical defects in the environmental review, or audit method, or environmental management system, or any other relevant process,
- points of disagreement with the draft environmental statement, together with details of the amendments or additions that should be made to the environmental statement,

(d) the comparison with the previous statements and the performance assessment of the organisation.

5.6. Verification frequency

In consultation with the organisation the environmental verifier shall design a programme to ensure that all elements required for registration with EMAS are verified in a period not exceeding 36 months. In addition the environmental verifier shall at intervals not exceeding 12 months validate any updated information in the environmental statement. Deviations from the frequency with which updates shall be performed may be made under circumstances laid down in Commission guidance adopted in accordance with the procedure laid down in Article 14(2).

ANNEX VI

ENVIRONMENTAL ASPECTS

6.1. General

An organisation shall consider all environmental aspects of its activities, products and services and decide, on the basis of criteria taking into account the Community legislation, which of its environmental aspects have a significant impact, as a basis for setting its environmental objectives and targets. These criteria shall be publicly available.

An organisation shall consider both direct and indirect environmental aspects of its activities, products and services.

6.2. Direct environmental aspects

These cover the activities of an organisation over which it has management control and may include, but is not limited to:

(a)   emissions to air;

(b)   releases to water;

(c)   avoidance, recycling, reuse, transportation and disposal of solid and other wastes, particularly hazardous wastes;

(d)   use and contamination of land;

(e)   use of natural resources and raw materials (including energy);

(f)   local issues (noise, vibration, odour, dust, visual appearance, etc.);

(g)   transport issues (both for goods and services and employees);

(h)   risks of environmental accidents and impacts arising, or likely to arise, as consequences of incidents, accidents and potential emergency situations;

(i)   effects on biodiversity.

6.3. Indirect environmental aspects

As a result of the activities, products and services of an organisation there may be significant environmental aspects over which it may not have full management control.

These may include, but are not limited to:

(a)   product related issues (design, development, packaging, transportation, use and waste recovery/disposal);

(b)   capital investments, granting loans and insurance services;

(c)   new markets;

(d)   choice and composition of services (e.g. transport or the catering trade);

(e)   administrative and planning decisions;

(f)   product range compositions;

(g)   the environmental performance and practices of contractors, subcontractors and suppliers.

Organisations must be able to demonstrate that the significant environmental aspects associated with their procurement procedures have been identified and that significant impacts associated with these aspects are addressed within the management system. The organisation should endeavour to ensure that the suppliers and those acting on the organisation's behalf comply with the organisation's environmental policy within the remit of the activities carried out for the contract.

In the case of these indirect environmental aspects, an organisation shall consider how much influence it can have over these aspects, and what measures can be taken to reduce the impact.

6.4. Significance

It is the responsibility of the organisation to define criteria for assessing the significance of the environmental aspects of its activities, products and services, to determine which have a significant environmental impact. The criteria developed by an organisation shall be comprehensive, capable of independent checking, reproducible and made publicly available.

Considerations in establishing the criteria for assessing the significance of an organisation's environmental aspects may include, but are not limited to:

(a)   information about the condition of the environment to identify activities, products and services of the organisation that may have an environmental impact;

(b)   the organisation's existing data on material and energy inputs, discharges, wastes and emissions in terms of risk;

(c)   views of interested parties;

(d)   environmental activities of the organisation that are regulated;

(e)   procurement activities;

(f)   design, development, manufacturing, distribution, servicing, use, re-use, recycling and disposal of the organisation's products;

(g)   those activities of the organisation with the most significant environmental costs, and environmental benefits.

In assessing the significance of the environmental impacts of the organisation's activities the organisation shall think not only of normal operating conditions but also of start-up and shutdown conditions and of reasonably foreseeable emergency conditions. Account shall be taken of past, present and planned activities.

ANNEX VII

ENVIRONMENTAL REVIEW

7.1. General

An organisation that has not supplied the necessary information needed to identify and assess the significant environmental aspects according to Annex VI must establish its current position with regard to the environment by means of a review. The aim should be to consider all environmental aspects of the organisation as a basis for establishing the environmental management system.

7.2. Requirements

The review should cover five key areas:

(a) legislative, regulatory and other requirements to which the organisation subscribes;

(b) an identification of all environmental aspects with a significant environmental impact in accordance with Annex VI, qualified and quantified as appropriate, and compiling a register of those identified as significant;

(c) a description of the criteria for assessing the significance of the environmental impact in accordance with Annex VI, point 6.4;

(d) an examination of all existing environmental management practices and procedures;

(e) an evaluation of feedback from the investigation of previous incidents.

14

The Rio Declaration on
Environment and Development

[The Rio Declaration] . . . contains 27 norms for state and inter-
state behaviour, many of which have never been universally
accepted before . . . To be practical, they need to be applied in a
way which reflects the cultural, political and economic nature of
the country and the different communities within it. They work best
when applied together . . .

Luc Hens, Vrije Universiteit Brussel[1]

Type Performance-oriented treaty

Strength Provides definitions of key concepts and principles in environment and
development

Keywords Sustainable development • Poverty • Sovereignty • Technology transfer •
Compensation • Precautionary approach • Precautionary principle •
Environmental impact assessment • Women • Youth • Indigenous people

14.1 **Background**

In 1992 the UN Conference on Environment and Development (UNCED) signalled
a major turning point in environmental issues. It was at UNCED that environmental issues entered the mainstream. Also known as the Earth Summit, the
UNCED serves as a critical marker, a pivotal point in history that divided those
events before and after so that one can refer to events and issues before and after

---

1 Source: 'The Rio Conference and Thereafter', www.vub.ac.be/MEKO/publications/
rioconf.doc, page 8.

UNCED. UNCED produced several key documents, including the Rio Declaration on Environment and Development and Agenda 21, a plan of action for organisations of all sizes.

Although the Rio Declaration is addressed to nation-states, it introduced key concepts that are echoed in many of the tools presented in this book, including the Global Compact (Chapter 4).

The Rio Declaration defined two key principles—the precautionary principle and the polluter-pays principle—that are key elements of many environmental standards.

14.2 Strengths and weaknesses

The Rio Conference 'provides an important basis for environmental principles in international law',[2] enshrining many key concepts and definitions.

14.3 Companies to which the Rio Declaration on Environment and Development applies

The Rio Declaration is addressed to states, not companies. However, concepts such as the precautionary principle described in the Rio Declaration also apply to companies.

14.4 Questions posed and answered

What is the role of states in promoting environment and development?

14.5 The promise and the challenge

The Rio Declaration emphasises the importance of addressing the needs of women, youth and indigenous peoples.

---

2 *Ibid.*: 10.

Additional resources

Further reading

United Nations (1993) *Rio Declaration: Agenda 21* (New York: United Nations).

Website

Rio Declaration on Environment and Development:
www.un.org/documents/ga/conf151/aconf15126-1annex1.htm

The Rio Declaration on Environment and Development*

The United Nations Conference on Environment and Development,

Having met at Rio de Janeiro from 3 to 14 June 1992,

Reaffirming the Declaration of the United Nations Conference on the Human Environment, adopted at Stockholm on 16 June 1972, and seeking to build upon it,

With the goal of establishing a new and equitable global partnership through the creation of new levels of cooperation among States, key sectors of societies and people,

Working towards international agreements which respect the interests of all and protect the integrity of the global environmental and developmental system,

Recognizing the integral and interdependent nature of the Earth, our home,

Proclaims that:

Principle 1

Human beings are at the centre of concerns for sustainable development. They are entitled to a healthy and productive life in harmony with nature.

Principle 2

States have, in accordance with the Charter of the United Nations and the principles of international law, the sovereign right to exploit their own resources pursuant to their own environmental and developmental policies, and the responsibility to ensure that activities within their jurisdiction or control do not cause damage to the environment of other States or of areas beyond the limits of national jurisdiction.

---

* *Source:* Report of the United Nations Conference on the Human Environment, Stockholm, 5-16 June 1972 (United Nations publication, Sales No. E.73.II.A.14 and corrigendum), chap. I.

This document was posted online by the United Nations Department of Economic and Social Affairs (DESA). Reproduction and dissemination of the document—in electronic and/or printed format—is encouraged, provided acknowledgement is made of the role of the United Nations in making it available.

Date last updated: 12 January, 2000 by DESA/DSD.

Principle 3

The right to development must be fulfilled so as to equitably meet developmental and environmental needs of present and future generations.

Principle 4

In order to achieve sustainable development, environmental protection shall constitute an integral part of the development process and cannot be considered in isolation from it.

Principle 5

All States and all people shall cooperate in the essential task of eradicating poverty as an indispensable requirement for sustainable development, in order to decrease the disparities in standards of living and better meet the needs of the majority of the people of the world.

Principle 6

The special situation and needs of developing countries, particularly the least developed and those most environmentally vulnerable, shall be given special priority. International actions in the field of environment and development should also address the interests and needs of all countries.

Principle 7

States shall cooperate in a spirit of global partnership to conserve, protect and restore the health and integrity of the Earth's ecosystem. In view of the different contributions to global environmental degradation, States have common but differentiated responsibilities. The developed countries acknowledge the responsibility that they bear in the international pursuit of sustainable development in view of the pressures their societies place on the global environment and of the technologies and financial resources they command.

Principle 8

To achieve sustainable development and a higher quality of life for all people, States should reduce and eliminate unsustainable patterns of production and consumption and promote appropriate demographic policies.

Principle 9

States should cooperate to strengthen endogenous capacity-building for sustainable development by improving scientific understanding through exchanges of scientific and technological knowledge, and by enhancing the development, adaptation, diffusion and transfer of technologies, including new and innovative technologies.

Principle 10

Environmental issues are best handled with the participation of all concerned citizens, at the relevant level. At the national level, each individual shall have appropriate access to information concerning the environment that is held by public authorities, including information on hazardous materials and activities in their communities, and the opportunity to participate in decision-making processes. States shall facilitate and encourage public awareness and participation by making information widely available. Effective access to judicial and administrative proceedings, including redress and remedy, shall be provided.

Principle 11

States shall enact effective environmental legislation. Environmental standards, management objectives and priorities should reflect the environmental and developmental context to which they apply. Standards applied by some countries may be inappropriate and of unwarranted economic and social cost to other countries, in particular developing countries.

Principle 12

States should cooperate to promote a supportive and open international economic system that would lead to economic growth and sustainable development in all countries, to better address the problems of environmental degradation. Trade policy measures for environmental purposes should not constitute a means of arbitrary or unjustifiable discrimination or a disguised restriction on international trade. Unilateral actions to deal with environmental challenges outside the jurisdiction of the importing country should be avoided. Environmental measures addressing transboundary or global environmental problems should, as far as possible, be based on an international consensus.

Principle 13

States shall develop national law regarding liability and compensation for the victims of pollution and other environmental damage. States shall also cooperate in an expeditious and more determined manner to develop further international law regarding liability and compensation for adverse effects of environmental damage caused by activities within their jurisdiction or control to areas beyond their jurisdiction.

Principle 14

States should effectively cooperate to discourage or prevent the relocation and transfer to other States of any activities and substances that cause severe environmental degradation or are found to be harmful to human health.

Principle 15

In order to protect the environment, the precautionary approach shall be widely applied by States according to their capabilities. Where there are threats of serious or irreversible damage, lack of full scientific certainty shall not be used as a reason for postponing cost-effective measures to prevent environmental degradation.

Principle 16

National authorities should endeavour to promote the internalization of environmental costs and the use of economic instruments, taking into account the approach that the polluter should, in principle, bear the cost of pollution, with due regard to the public interest and without distorting international trade and investment.

Principle 17

Environmental impact assessment, as a national instrument, shall be undertaken for proposed activities that are likely to have a significant adverse impact on the environment and are subject to a decision of a competent national authority.

Principle 18

States shall immediately notify other States of any natural disasters or other emergencies that are likely to produce sudden harmful effects on the environment of those States. Every effort shall be made by the international community to help States so afflicted.

Principle 19

States shall provide prior and timely notification and relevant information to potentially affected States on activities that may have a significant adverse transboundary environmental effect and shall consult with those States at an early stage and in good faith.

Principle 20

Women have a vital role in environmental management and development. Their full participation is therefore essential to achieve sustainable development.

Principle 21

The creativity, ideals and courage of the youth of the world should be mobilized to forge a global partnership in order to achieve sustainable development and ensure a better future for all.

Principle 22

Indigenous people and their communities and other local communities have a vital role in environmental management and development because of their knowledge and traditional practices. States should recognize and duly support their identity, culture and interests and enable their effective participation in the achievement of sustainable development.

Principle 23

The environment and natural resources of people under oppression, domination and occupation shall be protected.

Principle 24

Warfare is inherently destructive of sustainable development. States shall therefore respect international law providing protection for the environment in times of armed conflict and cooperate in its further development, as necessary.

Principle 25

Peace, development and environmental protection are interdependent and indivisible.

Principle 26

States shall resolve all their environmental disputes peacefully and by appropriate means in accordance with the Charter of the United Nations.

Principle 27

States and people shall cooperate in good faith and in a spirit of partnership in the fulfilment of the principles embodied in this Declaration and in the further development of international law in the field of sustainable development.

15
The CERES Principles

More and more of the players who shape the global business and financial landscape—large investors, and foundations, environmental and public interest organisations, big corporations and small business—have endorsed the CERES Principles.

William C. Thompson, Jr, New York City Comptroller[1]

Type   Multi-stakeholder, aspirational, reporting requirements; performance- and process-oriented (to a lesser extent)

Strength Engagement with companies

Keywords Multi-stakeholder • Environment • Sustainability • Waste • Energy conservation • Protection of whistle-blowers • Valdez Principles

15.1 Background

Founded in 1989, the Coalition for Environmentally Responsible Economies (CERES) is a network of more than 80 environmental, investor and advocacy groups promoting sustainability. CERES is best known for the CERES Principles, a set of ten principles covering the major environmental concerns facing companies, including energy conservation, reduction and disposal of waste, and risk reduction. The CERES Principles were originally known as the Valdez Principles, which were launched in 1989 as a response to the environmental disaster of the *Exxon Valdez* oil tanker.

1 Welcoming Remarks at the 2003 CERES Conference: Advancing Sustainable Governance, New York City, 1 April 2003, quoted in full in http://ceres.org/conference/william_ thompson.html.

Endorsing companies must commit publicly to the Principles, address issues raised by the CERES network and other stakeholders and report annually on their progress in meeting the CERES Principles. Over 70 companies have endorsed the CERES Principles, with Sunoco being the first *Fortune* 500 signatory, joining in 1993.[2] Coca-Cola, the Ford Motor Company, General Motors and Polaroid are among some of the most well-known companies that have endorsed the CERES Principles. The Body Shop is the only company not headquartered in the USA to join the CERES network.

15.2 Strengths and weaknesses

One of the greatest strengths of the CERES Principles is the degree to which CERES engages with companies in ongoing dialogue. Unlike the case with the majority of the principles and standards profiled in this book, a company cannot unilaterally decide to adopt the CERES Principles: 'endorsing the Principles is a two-way process—commitment by a company and acceptance by the CERES Board of Directors'.[3] In its dialogue with a company, the Board raises problems that the CERES network has identified.

Although the Principles are aspirational in nature, the dialogue between the company and CERES allows for greater specificity, and during this dialogue companies can interpret how the Principles apply to their own operations.

Another factor that differentiates the CERES Principles from other key initiatives is that it includes a wide range of investors that can pressure companies to endorse the Principles. The nine investors within the CERES network represent more than US$300 billion in investments, constituting a powerful lever for endorsers. The reports published by the participating companies provide standardised data for investors and other stakeholders.

The engagement between companies and stakeholders within CERES is one of the hallmarks of the CERES Principles, building trust and preventing conflict:

> One of the greatest advantages CERES offers is that differences are discussed privately and in person rather than through the media or in courtrooms. Such conversations are conducted in the spirit of mutual respect and consensus-building. CERES participants consider this trust-based approach to conflict resolution to be one of the most valuable contributions of the organisation, along with public disclosure of environment-related data through the CERES report.[4]

The CERES Principles are among the few initiatives profiled in this book that include a clause to protect whistle-blowers. This is very important to safeguard those employees who disclose damaging information from suffering retaliation for going public with information. The Principles state that 'we will not take any action

2   www.ceres.org/about/endorsing_companies.htm
3   See page 1 of the CERES website answering frequently asked questions (FAQs), 'About Us: Frequently Asked Questions', www.ceres.org/about/questions.htm.
4   *Ibid.*: 3.

against employees for reporting dangerous incidents or conditions to management or to appropriate authorities' (see page 257).

15.3 Companies to which the CERES Principles apply

The CERES Principles operate within a US framework and so are best suited to companies headquartered in the USA. CERES has developed special reporting requirements for small companies, making it more appealing now to companies of all sizes.

15.4 Questions posed and answered

What measures can companies take to promote sustainability of their products and operations?

15.5 The promise and the challenge

CERES is a US-based organisation addressing global issues. It would be a challenge for an organisation such as CERES to expand globally and still maintain its cohesive network and sense of trust. Along with the US Environment Programme (UNEP), CERES helped to launch the Global Reporting Initiative (GRI, Chapter 26). CERES asks participating companies to publish a report 'consistent with the core expectations of the . . . Sustainability Reporting Guidelines of the GRI'.[5] Hence, CERES maintains its US roots and identity, but with a global reporting mechanism.

Additional resource

Website
Coalition for Environmentally Responsible Economies: www.ceres.org

5   *Ibid.*: 5.

The CERES Principles*

PRINCIPLES

Protection of the Biosphere

We will reduce and make continual progress toward eliminating the release of any substance that may cause environmental damage to the air, water, or the earth or its inhabitants. We will safeguard all habitats affected by our operations and will protect open spaces and wilderness, while preserving biodiversity.

Sustainable Use of Natural Resources

We will make sustainable use of renewable natural resources, such as water, soils and forests. We will conserve non-renewable natural resources through efficient use and careful planning.

Reduction and Disposal of Wastes

We will reduce and where possible eliminate waste through source reduction and recycling. All waste will be handled and disposed of through safe and responsible methods.

Energy Conservation

We will conserve energy and improve the energy efficiency of our internal operations and of the goods and services we sell. We will make every effort to use environmentally safe and sustainable energy sources.

Risk Reduction

We will strive to minimize the environmental, health and safety risks to our employees and the communities in which we operate through safe technologies, facilities and operating procedures, and by being prepared for emergencies.

---

* Reproduced with the permission of the Coalition for Responsible Economies (CERES).

Safe Products and Services

We will reduce and where possible eliminate the use, manufacture or sale of products and services that cause environmental damage or health or safety hazards. We will inform our customers of the environmental impacts of our products or services and try to correct unsafe use.

Environmental Restoration

We will promptly and responsibly correct conditions we have caused that endanger health, safety or the environment. To the extent feasible, we will redress injuries we have caused to persons or damage we have caused to the environment and will restore the environment.

Informing the Public

We will inform in a timely manner everyone who may be affected by conditions caused by our company that might endanger health, safety or the environment. We will regularly seek advice and counsel through dialogue with persons in communities near our facilities. We will not take any action against employees for reporting dangerous incidents or conditions to management or to appropriate authorities.

Management Commitment

We will implement these Principles and sustain a process that ensures that the Board of Directors and Chief Executive Officer are fully informed about pertinent environmental issues and are fully responsible for environmental policy. In selecting our Board of Directors, we will consider demonstrated environmental commitment as a factor.

Audits and Reports

We will conduct an annual self-evaluation of our progress in implementing these Principles. We will support the timely creation of generally accepted environmental audit procedures. We will annually complete the CERES Report, which will be made available to the public.

Disclaimer: These Principles establish an environmental ethic with criteria by which investors and others can assess the environmental performance of companies. Companies that endorse these Principles pledge to go voluntarily beyond the requirements of the law. The terms "may" and "might" in Principles one and eight are not meant to encompass every imaginable consequence, no matter how remote. Rather, these Principles obligate endorsers to behave as prudent persons who are not governed by conflicting interests and who possess a strong commitment to environmental excellence and to human health and safety. These Principles are not intended to create new legal liabilities, expand existing rights or obligations, waive legal defenses, or otherwise affect the legal position of any endorsing company, and are not intended to be used against an endorser in any legal proceeding for any purpose.

Endorsing Company Statement

By adopting these Principles, we publicly affirm our belief that corporations have a responsibility for the environment, and must conduct all aspects of their business as responsible stewards of the environment by operating in a manner that protects the Earth. We believe that corporations must not compromise the ability of future generations to sustain themselves.

We will update our practices constantly in light of advances in technology and new understandings in health and environmental science. In collaboration with CERES, we will promote a dynamic process to ensure that the Principles are interpreted in a way that accommodates changing technologies and environmental realities. We intend to make consistent, measurable progress in implementing these Principles and to apply them to all aspects of our operations throughout the world.

16
The Natural Step

The Natural Step provides an elegant framework, a compass, to guide us on the road ahead and is a powerful tool for all seeking a new mental model to move their business into a sustainable future.

Maurice Strong, Secretary-General, 1992 UN Earth Summit[1]

Type   General principles; performance-oriented

Strength It requires a new vision, a redesigning of the company's approach to environmental and social issues

Keywords Sustainability • Environment • Human needs • Systems • Redesign • Sweden • Thermodynamics • Vision • Assessment

16.1 Background

Founded in Sweden by Dr Karl-Henrik Robèrt, a leading cancer specialist, The Natural Step (TNS) addresses the systemic causes of environmental problems. Robèrt noticed that the increase in cases of childhood leukaemia was linked to environmental problems. TNS principles were developed by scientists and are based on the laws of thermodynamics (for more background on TNS, see Robèrt 2002). The principles focus on systems, requiring the organisations working with TNS to redefine their relationship to the environment and society.

TNS provides companies with tools for visioning, assessment and a framework for action. The Buckminster Fuller Institute in the UK compares TNS to 'a pair of glasses that allow . . . [a company] to see its manufacturing processes with com-

---

1   Quoted at www.naturalstep.org/about/what_others_say.php.

pletely new eyes, a new vantage point that highlight[s] the potential towards sustainability'.[2]

With offices in ten countries, TNS has gone from being a Swedish approach to one that is gaining momentum among companies based in the USA, the United Kingdom, Japan, Australia, Israel, New Zealand, South Africa, Canada and Brazil. Nike, Ikea, McDonald's Sweden, Home Depot, Electrolux and Interface are among the most well-known companies using the TNS principles and approach.[3]

TNS compares the current environmental reality to a funnel, in which a growing population and consumption patterns demand more and more life-supporting resources, causing a decrease in the amount of resources available, leading to new limitations for companies as the funnel narrows (see Fig. 16.1). Put simply, an ever-greater number of people are competing for essential resources that are being depleted. As companies 'hit the walls' of the funnel, they will face increasing financial pressures.

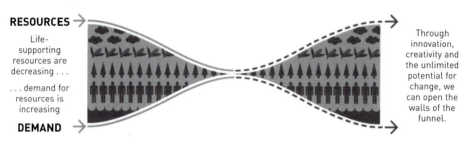

RESOURCES →
Life-supporting resources are decreasing . . .

. . . demand for resources is increasing

DEMAND →

Through innovation, creativity and the unlimited potential for change, we can open the walls of the funnel.

Figure 16.1 Opening the walls of the funnel

Source: www.naturalstep.org/learn/understand_sust.php; reprinted with permission by The Natural Step

By applying TNS principles and approach, companies can pioneer sustainable solutions and work to restore the Earth's balance. TNS is best understood by providing examples of how companies apply it. Ikea Sweden was one of the first global companies to implement TNS. As a result of working with TNS, Ikea began to 'reconceptualise . . . and redesign the relationship between Ikea and the environment' (TNS 2001). To raise awareness about the environment within the company, Ikea initiated an environmental training programme for 90% of its then 20,000 employees. Specialists were given advanced training. Rather than presenting Ikea with an answer on how to address environmental issues within the company, Ikea staff were asked to develop their own answers and model. Adopting TNS principles and approach required rethinking the Ikea business model. Instead of developing an eco-friendly product line that would have marginalised green issues, Ikea decided to mainstream environmental issues into strategy, investment decisions, transport, product design and specifications, and supply chain management.

2   Buckminster Fuller Institute, www.bfi.org/news/naturalStep.htm.
3   www.naturalstep.org/about/clients.php

16.2 Strengths and weaknesses

The approach of TNS is both theoretical and practical. Its theoretical underpinnings, based on the laws of thermodynamics, lend it credibility. In addition, TNS principles benefit from being general enough in nature that organisations in different sectors can adopt them and make them their own. In an interview with Michael Toms of New Dimensions World Broadcasting Network, Robèrt, founder of TNS, stated that:

> Instead of telling them what to do, we say, 'How could this be applied to your business or in your world?' That allows them to . . . put the details onto this basic structure which is non-negotiable. This sparks creativity, and recruits enthusiasm into the process instead of defence mechanisms. Any expert in his field of expertise is much more clever than you are. If you give him the overall principles, therefore, and then ask him for advice instead of telling him what to do he finds much smarter solutions than Greenpeace or I or anybody can do (Toms 1994).

The sustainability framework of TNS is absolute; as such it can be audited. It is possible for companies to track their performance with regard to meeting TNS sustainability principles.

According to Forum for the Future, there are business benefits associated with implementing the framework of TNS:

> The Natural Step has assisted many companies and organisations to develop strategic sustainability initiatives. These initiatives have helped them to achieve greater effectiveness, competitive advantage, bottom line results, security, employee satisfaction and public acceptance.[4]

Interface, the first US company to pioneer full-scale application of the approach of TNS, estimates that it has saved US$120 million as a result of implementing the framework.[5]

16.3 Companies to which The Natural Step applies

At the time of writing (September 2003) hundreds of companies, communities and individuals around the world have adopted the framework of TNS. Since the principles are general in nature, they can be adopted in any organisation, large or small.

---

4 See www.forumforthefuture.org.uk/aboutus/default.asp?pageid=115.
5 See www.bfi.org/news/naturalStep.htm.

16.4 Questions posed and answered

TNS asks:

- How can an organisation view its operations and impact within a systems framework?

16.5 The challenge and the promise

One of the key challenges for TNS, and for many initiatives profiled in this book, is to build capacity and scale up activities, especially in the developing world.

Because of its adaptability and strengths, TNS has influenced a wide range of other, more recent, initiatives in the field of corporate responsibility, including the SIGMA principles (Chapter 28). The framework of TNS complements many sustainability tools and resources, such as ISO 14001 (Chapter 27) and the Global Reporting Initiative (Chapter 26).

References

Robèrt, K.-H. (2002) *The Natural Step Story: Seeding a Quiet Revolution* (Gabriola Island, BC, Canada: New Society Publishers).

TNS (The Natural Step) (2001) 'Organizational Case Summary: Ikea', www.naturalstep.org/learn/docs/cs/case_ikea.pdf.

Toms, M. (1994) 'The Natural Step to a Sustainable Future: A Conversation with Karl-Henrik Robèrt MD', www.newdimensions.org/online-journal/articles/natural-step.html.

Additional resource

Website

The Natural Step: www.naturalstep.org; the text of the principles may be found at www.naturalstep.org/learn/principles.php.

The Natural Step Principles*

FOUR SIMPLE PRINCIPLES OF SUSTAINABILITY

Sustainability is fundamentally about maintaining human life on the planet and, thus, addressing human needs is an essential element of creating a sustainable society. Therefore, one of The Natural Step's principles of sustainability is to meet human needs worldwide.

The other three principles focus on interactions between humans and the planet. They are rooted in an understanding that contemporary life is fundamentally supported by natural processes, such as the capturing of energy from the sun by photosynthetic organisms and the purification of air and water. These processes are essential to maintaining human life. However, as a society we are systematically altering the ecosystem structures and functions that provide life-supporting services and resources that we need to survive.

Based on this understanding, The Natural Step sustainability principles are based on science and supported by the analyses that ecosystem functions and processes are altered when:

1. Society mines and disperses materials at a faster rate than they are re-deposited back into the Earth's crust (examples of these materials are oil, coal and metals such as mercury and lead);

2. Society produces substances faster than they can be broken down by natural processes, if they can be broken down at all (examples of such substances include dioxins, DDT and PCBs); and,

3. Society depletes or degrades resources at a faster rate than they are replenished (for example, over-harvesting trees or fish), or by other forms of ecosystem manipulation (for example, paving over fertile land or causing soil erosion).

By considering these three ways in which human life-supporting structures and functions are being altered, The Natural Step has defined three basic principles for maintaining essential ecological processes.

We also recognize that social and economic dynamics fundamentally drive the actions that lead to ecosystem changes. Therefore, the fourth principle focuses on the impor-

---

* Reproduced with the permission of The Natural Step.

tance of meeting human needs worldwide as an integral and essential part of sustainability.

From this assessment, The Natural Step's sustainability principles, also known as "conditions" that must be met in order to have a sustainable society, are as follows:

In a sustainable society, nature is not subject to systematically increasing:

1. concentrations of substances extracted from the earth's crust;

2. concentrations of substances produced by society;

3. degradation by physical means

   and, in that society . . .

4. human needs are met worldwide.

How can we—company, organization, individual, family, government, school—employ the principles?

1. eliminate our contribution to systematic increases in concentrations of substances from the Earth's crust.
This means substituting certain minerals that are scarce in nature with others that are more abundant, using all mined materials efficiently, and systematically reducing dependence on fossil fuels.

2. eliminate our contribution to systematic increases in concentrations of substances produced by society.
This means systematically substituting certain persistent and unnatural compounds with ones that are normally abundant or break down more easily in nature, and using all substances produced by society efficiently.

3. eliminate our contribution to systematic physical degradation of nature through over-harvesting, depletion, foreign introductions and other forms of modification.
This means drawing resources only from well-managed ecosystems, systematically pursuing the most productive and efficient use both of those resources and land, and exercising caution in all kinds of modification of nature.

4. contribute as much as we can to the goal of meeting human needs in our society and worldwide, going over and above all the substitution and dematerialization measures taken in meeting the first three objectives.
This means using all of our resources efficiently, fairly and responsibly so that the needs of all people on whom we have an impact, and the future needs of people who are not yet born, stand the best chance of being met.

Part 5
Combating corruption

Corruption respects no borders, knows no economic distinctions
and infects all forms of government. In the long run, no country
can afford the social, political or economic costs that corruption
entails.

OECD[1]

There is a significant difference between Part 5 and the other parts of this book.
Whereas most corporate responsibility (CR) issues are voluntary, violators of anti-
corruption norms may face criminal prosecution.[2]

Bribery of public officials may be defined as:

> the promise or giving of any undue payment or other advantages,
> whether directly or through intermediaries to a public official, for
> himself [or herself] or for a third party, to influence the official to act
> or refrain from acting in the performance of his or her official duties
> in order to obtain or retain business' (CCBIBT 1997; quoted in IMF
> 2001).

---

1 OECD 2002.
2 For a thorough background on corruption, see OECD 2002; for more information on
   business and corruption, see the website of the International Business Leaders' Forum,
   at www.iblf.org.

Several companies have written into their codes of conduct a no-bribery policy.[3] Among these companies are BP,[4] Shell[5] and Unilever.[6] Anglo-American is unusual in that it does not allow facilitation payments or small bribes often required to gain licences. According to Edward Bickham, a vice-president at Anglo-American, facilitation payments represent a 'chess game that begins to lead to bribery' (*Economist* 2002: 11).

There are a wide range of codes, principles, conventions, laws and rules on corruption. These tools can be seen as a dialogue in which after a series of principles are crafted others emerge as a response to the vacuum left by the previous tools. The following list provides a brief description of the rules, principles and conventions in chronological order to capture this dialogue and sequence:

- **The 1977 Foreign Corrupt Practices Act.** The starting point for understanding codes and standards to prevent bribery is the US Foreign Corrupt Practices Act (FCPA) of 1977.[7] This legislation dramatically altered how US companies conducted their operations, encouraging them to closely monitor their activities. The FCPA placed US firms at a disadvantage relative to multinational companies that were allowed to offer bribes. This disadvantage led the USA to press for a more level playing field, which resulted in the OECD Convention on Combating Bribery of Foreign Public Officials in International Business Transactions, which is described in Chapter 17.

- **The 1977 Rules of Conduct to Combat Extortion and Bribery of the International Chamber of Commerce.** In 1977, the International Chamber of Commerce (ICC) developed the Rules of Conduct to Combat Extortion and Bribery,[8] applicable to governments, the private sector and international organisations. The ICC Rules address both the demand side and the supply side of bribery.

- **The 1999 OECD Convention on Combating Bribery of Foreign Public Officials in International Business Transactions.** In 1999, the OECD Convention on Combating Bribery of Foreign Public Officials in International Business Transactions (Chapter 17) called on members of the OECD and other nations to criminalise bribery of foreign officials. Hence it does not deal with private-to-private bribery, nor with the demand side of bribery.

- **The 2002 Business Principles for Combating Bribery.** In 2002, Transparency International and Social Accountability International launched

---

3 For information on the development of management systems to combat bribery, see ICC 2000.
4 www.bpamoco.com/environ_social/bus_ethics/corruption/index.asp
5 www.shell.com → About Shell → How We Work → Business Principles
6 www.unilever.com/environmentsociety/purpose_principles/ourprinciples/ default.asp?ComponentID=94394SourcePageID=9368#1
7 For more information on the FCPA, see Low 1998.
8 For the latest version (1999), go to www.iccwbo.org/home/statements_rules/rules/1999/ briberydoc99.asp

the Business Principles for Combating Bribery (Chapter 18). The Principles focus on private-to-private bribery and provide a framework for companies on how to develop internal management systems to prevent corrupt practices.

- **The 2003 Draft UN Convention Against Corruption.** In 2002 and 2003 there has been discussion about a draft UN Convention Against Corruption.[9] One of the key items being discussed is the role of civil society in combating corruption. A number of non-governmental organisations (NGOs), including Transparency International[10] and the ICC,[11] have posted on their websites their comments on the Draft UN Convention, highlighting another aspect of this dialogue between and among codes and standards.

As with many of the issues described in this book, combating corruption requires the alignment of an array of forces, including governments, civil society and media. In addition, it is not enough to address the supply side of the bribery equation; the demand side of corruption also needs to be addressed. The private sector can influence both the demand side and the supply side. *The Economist* (2002: 11) has called on multinational corporations to encourage governments of countries where bribery is rampant to adequately compensate their civil servants.

This section includes a discussion of two major corporate responsibility tools:

- OECD Convention on Combating Bribery of Foreign Public Officials in International Business Transactions

- Business Principles for Countering Bribery

Other important tools include the Wolfsberg Anti-Money Laundering Principles, consisting of a set of private banking principles agreed on by 11 of the largest international banks (ABN Amro NV; Banco Santander Central Hispano, SA; Bank of Tokyo-Mitsubishi, Ltd; Barclays Bank; Citigroup; Credit Suisse Group; Deutsche Bank AG; Goldman Sachs; HSBC; J.P. Morgan Chase; Société Générale; and UBS AG; see www.wolfsberg-principles.com).

References

CCBIBT (Council on Combating Bribery in International Business Transactions) (1997) 'Annex', in *Revised Recommendation of the Council on Combating Bribery in International Business Transactions* (Paris: CCBIBT, adopted on 23 May 1997).

Economist (2002) 'The Worm That Never Dies', *The Economist*, 2–8 March 2002: 11.

9 For the January 2003 draft, see www.unodc.org/pdf/crime/convention_corruption/ session_4/261_3_rev2.pdf.
10 www.transparency.org/building_coalitions/intern.institutions/un/un_ convention.html#unconvention
11 www.iccwbo.org/home/statements_rules/statements/2003/un_convention_against_ corruption.asp

FCPA (Foreign Corrupt Practices Act) (1977) Current through Pub. L 105-366 (November 10, 1998) (Washington, DC: US Government Printing Office).

ICC (International Chamber of Commerce) (2000) *Fighting Bribery: A Corporate Practices Manual* (Paris: ICC).

IMF (International Monetary Fund) (2001) *OECD Convention on Combating Bribery of Foreign Public Officials in International Business Transactions* (Policy Development and Review; Washington, DC: IMF, 18 September 2001).

Low, L. (1998) 'Transnational Corruption: New Rules for Old Temptations, New Players to Combat a Perennial Evil', in *Proceedings of the 92nd Annual Meeting: The Challenge of Non-state Actors* (Washington, DC: American Society of International Law, 1–4 April 1998).

OECD (Organisation for Economic Co-operation and Development) (2002) *No Longer Business as Usual: Fighting Bribery and Corruption* (Paris: OECD, October 2002).

17

The OECD Convention on Combating Bribery of Foreign Public Officials in International Business Transactions

> Since the OECD Convention on Combating Bribery of Foreign Officials . . . entered into force on 15 February 1999, it is no longer business as usual.
>
> *OECD*[1]

Type   Binding performance standard; foundation tool

Strength   Its universality

Keywords Bribery • Foreign public officials • Criminalise • Facilitation payments • Functional equivalence

17.1 Background

Launched in 1999, the OECD Convention on Combating Bribery of Foreign Public Officials in International Business Transactions is a landmark agreement, defining key terms and developing a legal framework for addressing bribery. To understand the objectives of the Convention, it is necessary to review the role of the OECD (the Organisation for Economic Co-operation and Development). The OECD promotes policies that contribute to economic growth and development. Founded in 1961, the OECD is a membership organisation for governments from 30 countries (for a

---

1   OECD website, www.oecd.org.

full list of member countries, see 3, on page 53). The OECD has made a significant contribution to corporate responsibility (CR) by developing several principles relating to corporate responsibility, including the OECD Principles of Corporate Governance (see Chapter 19) and the OECD Guidelines for Multinational Enterprises (see Chapter 2).

The Convention has been ratified by all 30 members of the OECD and by a growing number of non-members as well.[2] The Convention applies to bribery of foreign government officials anywhere, regardless of where the incident takes place. As a result of ratification, the 30 OECD member countries (and some non-members) have agreed to the principle of 'functional equivalence':

> The Convention requires countries to establish the bribery of foreign public officials as a **criminal offence** under their laws; and to ensure that the attempt and conspiracy to bribe foreign public officials shall be criminalised to the same extent as the bribery of national public officials (IMF 2001: 6).

The Convention is intended to serve as a deterrent to bribery.

It is important to note that the Convention criminalises offering and/or paying bribes, but not soliciting and/or accepting bribes. The Convention covers only the bribery of foreign officials and not private-to-private corruption. The Convention allows 'small facilitation payments' to low-ranking officials.

The Convention includes monitoring provisions, based on a peer review system common within the OECD framework. The OECD Working Group on Bribery in International Business Transactions reviews the implementing legislation of all the countries that have ratified the Convention. In a secondary phase, the Working Group examines the structures in place to ensure that the legislation is effective. The OECD welcomes a greater role for non-governmental organisations (NGOs), such as Transparency International, in the monitoring of the Convention.[3]

17.2 Strengths and weaknesses

The OECD works with a wide range of regional programmes to combat bribery, including the programmes of:

- The Council of Europe's Multidisciplinary Group on Corruption[4]

- The Anti-Corruption Network for Transition Economies[5]

- The Stability Pact Anti-Corruption Initiative for South Eastern Europe[6]

2 Argentina, Brazil and Chile have declared their commitment to the Convention but are not OECD members.
3 On the monitoring of the Convention by NGOs, see TICI 1998.
4 www.coe.int/t/e/legal%5faffairs/legal%5fco%2doperation/combating%5feconomic %5fcrime/corruption/terms_of_reference_gmc.asp
5 www.anticorruptionnet.org
6 www1.oecd.org/daf/SPAIcom

- The Inter-American Convention Against Corruption[7]

- The Asian Development Bank/OECD Anti-Corruption Initiative for Asia–Pacific[8]

Despite this widespread co-operation, the corruption of public officials continues. According to Transparency International's Bribe Payers Index, local firms are more likely to bribe government officials than are multinational companies (Stoddard 2002). The Convention does not address bribery of officials by local business.

The Convention has been criticised for failing to capture the full extent of bribery. For example, it does not cover bribery of private-sector employees. Moreover, it fails to address the bribery of political parties and political candidates. The Convention provides no protection for whistle-blowers who uncover corruption, which can lead to reluctance to disclose incidents of bribery.

17.3 Companies to which the OECD Convention on Combating Bribery of Foreign Public Officials in International Business Transactions applies

The OECD Convention applies to all companies.

17.4 Questions posed and answered

The Convention poses and answers the following questions:

- How can bribery be defined?

- Despite differing legal systems, how can governments criminalise the bribery of foreign officials?

- How can adherence to the Convention be monitored?

17.5 The promise and the challenge

See Section 17.2. The OECD Convention applies only to bribery involving government officials, not to bribery of company staff.

7 www.oas.org/juridico/english/treaties/b-58.html
8 www1.oecd.org/daf/ASIAcom

References

IMF (International Monetary Fund) (2001) *OECD Convention on Combating Bribery of Foreign Public Officials in International Business Transactions* (prepared by the Policy Development and Review Department; approved by J. Boorman; Washington, DC: IMF, 18 September 2001).

Stoddard, A. (2002) 'World: Corporate Bribery on the Rise Says Survey', Inter Press Service, 15 May 2002.

TICI (Transparency International Canada Inc.) (1998) 'The Coalition against Corruption in International Business Transactions: Checklist for Monitoring Implementation of OECD Convention', www.transparency.ca/Readings/TI-F09.htm.

Additional resources

Websites

Organisation for Economic Co-operation and Development: www.oecd.org

OECD Convention on Combating Bribery of Foreign Public Officials in International Business Transactions:

www.oecd.org/document/21/0,2340,en_2649_34855_2017813_1_1_1_1,,00.html

Convention on Combating Bribery of Foreign Public Officials in International Business Transactions*

On 21 November 1997, OECD Member countries and five non-member countries, Argentina, Brazil, Bulgaria, Chile and the Slovak Republic, adopted a Convention on Combating Bribery of Foreign Public Officials in International Business Transactions. Signature of the Convention took place in Paris on 17 December 1997.

PREAMBLE

The Parties,

Considering that bribery is a widespread phenomenon in international business transactions, including trade and investment, which raises serious moral and political concerns, undermines good governance and economic development, and distorts international competitive conditions;

Considering that all countries share a responsibility to combat bribery in international business transactions;

Having regard to the Revised Recommendation on Combating Bribery in International Business Transactions, adopted by the Council of the Organisation for Economic Co-operation and Development (OECD) on 23 May 1997, C(97)123/FINAL, which, inter alia, called for effective measures to deter, prevent and combat the bribery of foreign public officials in connection with international business transactions, in particular the prompt criminalisation of such bribery in an effective and co-ordinated manner and in conformity with the agreed common elements set out in that Recommendation and with the jurisdictional and other basic legal principles of each country;

Welcoming other recent developments which further advance international under-standing and co-operation in combating bribery of public officials, including actions of the United Nations, the World Bank, the International Monetary Fund, the World Trade Organisation, the Organisation of American States, the Council of Europe and the European Union;

---

*   The Preamble, 17 Articles and Commentaries reprinted with permission from 'The OECD Convention on Combating Bribery of Foreign Public Officials in International Business Transactions', 17 December 1997. © OECD 1997.

Welcoming the efforts of companies, business organisations and trade unions as well as other non-governmental organisations to combat bribery;

Recognising the role of governments in the prevention of solicitation of bribes from individuals and enterprises in international business transactions;

Recognising that achieving progress in this field requires not only efforts on a national level but also multilateral co-operation, monitoring and follow-up;

Recognising that achieving equivalence among the measures to be taken by the Parties is an essential object and purpose of the Convention, which requires that the Convention be ratified without derogations affecting this equivalence;

Have agreed as follows:

Article 1
The Offence of Bribery of Foreign Public Officials

1. Each Party shall take such measures as may be necessary to establish that it is a criminal offence under its law for any person intentionally to offer, promise or give any undue pecuniary or other advantage, whether directly or through intermediaries, to a foreign public official, for that official or for a third party, in order that the official act or refrain from acting in relation to the performance of official duties, in order to obtain or retain business or other improper advantage in the conduct of international business.

2. Each Party shall take any measures necessary to establish that complicity in, including incitement, aiding and abetting, or authorisation of an act of bribery of a foreign public official shall be a criminal offence. Attempt and conspiracy to bribe a foreign public official shall be criminal offences to the same extent as attempt and conspiracy to bribe a public official of that Party.

3. The offences set out in paragraphs 1 and 2 above are hereinafter referred to as "bribery of a foreign public official".

4. For the purpose of this Convention:

  a. "foreign public official" means any person holding a legislative, administrative or judicial office of a foreign country, whether appointed or elected; any person exercising a public function for a foreign country, including for a public agency or public enterprise; and any official or agent of a public international organisation;

  b. "foreign country" includes all levels and subdivisions of government, from national to local;

  c. "act or refrain from acting in relation to the performance of official duties" includes any use of the public official's position, whether or not within the official's authorised competence.

Article 2
Responsibility of Legal Persons

Each Party shall take such measures as may be necessary, in accordance with its legal principles, to establish the liability of legal persons for the bribery of a foreign public official.

Article 3
Sanctions

1. The bribery of a foreign public official shall be punishable by effective, proportionate and dissuasive criminal penalties. The range of penalties shall be comparable to that applicable to the bribery of the Party's own public officials and shall, in the case of natural persons, include deprivation of liberty sufficient to enable effective mutual legal assistance and extradition.

2. In the event that, under the legal system of a Party, criminal responsibility is not applicable to legal persons, that Party shall ensure that legal persons shall be subject to effective, proportionate and dissuasive non-criminal sanctions, including monetary sanctions, for bribery of foreign public officials.

3. Each Party shall take such measures as may be necessary to provide that the bribe and the proceeds of the bribery of a foreign public official, or property the value of which corresponds to that of such proceeds, are subject to seizure and confiscation or that monetary sanctions of comparable effect are applicable.

4. Each Party shall consider the imposition of additional civil or administrative sanctions upon a person subject to sanctions for the bribery of a foreign public official.

Article 4
Jurisdiction

1. Each Party shall take such measures as may be necessary to establish its jurisdiction over the bribery of a foreign public official when the offence is committed in whole or in part in its territory.

2. Each Party which has jurisdiction to prosecute its nationals for offences committed abroad shall take such measures as may be necessary to establish its jurisdiction to do so in respect of the bribery of a foreign public official, according to the same principles.

3. When more than one Party has jurisdiction over an alleged offence described in this Convention, the Parties involved shall, at the request of one of them, consult with a view to determining the most appropriate jurisdiction for prosecution.

4. Each Party shall review whether its current basis for jurisdiction is effective in the fight against the bribery of foreign public officials and, if it is not, shall take remedial steps.

Article 5
Enforcement

Investigation and prosecution of the bribery of a foreign public official shall be subject to the applicable rules and principles of each Party. They shall not be influenced by considerations of national economic interest, the potential effect upon relations with another State or the identity of the natural or legal persons involved.

Article 6
Statute of Limitations

Any statute of limitations applicable to the offence of bribery of a foreign public official shall allow an adequate period of time for the investigation and prosecution of this offence.

Article 7
Money Laundering

Each Party which has made bribery of its own public official a predicate offence for the purpose of the application of its money laundering legislation shall do so on the same terms for the bribery of a foreign public official, without regard to the place where the bribery occurred.

Article 8
Accounting

1. In order to combat bribery of foreign public officials effectively, each Party shall take such measures as may be necessary, within the framework of its laws and regulations regarding the maintenance of books and records, financial statement disclosures, and accounting and auditing standards, to prohibit the establishment of off-the-books accounts, the making of off-the-books or inadequately identified transactions, the recording of non-existent expenditures, the entry of liabilities with incorrect identification of their object, as well as the use of false documents, by companies subject to those laws and regulations, for the purpose of bribing foreign public officials or of hiding such bribery.

2. Each Party shall provide effective, proportionate and dissuasive civil, administrative or criminal penalties for such omissions and falsifications in respect of the books, records, accounts and financial statements of such companies.

Article 9
Mutual Legal Assistance

1. Each Party shall, to the fullest extent possible under its laws and relevant treaties and arrangements, provide prompt and effective legal assistance to another Party for the purpose of criminal investigations and proceedings brought by a Party concerning offences within the scope of this Convention and for non-criminal proceedings within the scope of this Convention brought by a Party against a legal person. The requested Party shall inform the requesting Party, without delay, of any additional information or documents needed to support the request for assistance and, where requested, of the status and outcome of the request for assistance.

2. Where a Party makes mutual legal assistance conditional upon the existence of dual criminality, dual criminality shall be deemed to exist if the offence for which the assistance is sought is within the scope of this Convention.

3. A Party shall not decline to render mutual legal assistance for criminal matters within the scope of this Convention on the ground of bank secrecy.

Article 10
Extradition

1. Bribery of a foreign public official shall be deemed to be included as an extraditable offence under the laws of the Parties and the extradition treaties between them.

2. If a Party which makes extradition conditional on the existence of an extradition treaty receives a request for extradition from another Party with which it has no extradition treaty, it may consider this Convention to be the legal basis for extradition in respect of the offence of bribery of a foreign public official.

3. Each Party shall take any measures necessary to assure either that it can extradite its nationals or that it can prosecute its nationals for the offence of bribery of a foreign public official. A Party which declines a request to extradite a person for bribery of a foreign public official solely on the ground that the person is its national shall submit the case to its competent authorities for the purpose of prosecution.

4. Extradition for bribery of a foreign public official is subject to the conditions set out in the domestic law and applicable treaties and arrangements of each Party. Where a Party makes extradition conditional upon the existence of dual criminality, that condition shall be deemed to be fulfilled if the offence for which extradition is sought is within the scope of Article 1 of this Convention.

Article 11
Responsible Authorities

For the purposes of Article 4, paragraph 3, on consultation, Article 9, on mutual legal assistance and Article 10, on extradition, each Party shall notify to the Secretary-

General of the OECD an authority or authorities responsible for making and receiving requests, which shall serve as channel of communication for these matters for that Party, without prejudice to other arrangements between Parties.

Article 12
Monitoring and Follow-up

The Parties shall co-operate in carrying out a programme of systematic follow-up to monitor and promote the full implementation of this Convention. Unless otherwise decided by consensus of the Parties, this shall be done in the framework of the OECD Working Group on Bribery in International Business Transactions and according to its terms of reference, or within the framework and terms of reference of any successor to its functions, and Parties shall bear the costs of the programme in accordance with the rules applicable to that body.

Article 13
Signature and Accession

1. Until its entry into force, this Convention shall be open for signature by OECD members and by non-members which have been invited to become full participants in its Working Group on Bribery in International Business Transactions.

2. Subsequent to its entry into force, this Convention shall be open to accession by any non-signatory which is a member of the OECD or has become a full participant in the Working Group on Bribery in International Business Transactions or any successor to its functions. For each such non-signatory, the Convention shall enter into force on the sixtieth day following the date of deposit of its instrument of accession.

Article 14
Ratification and Depositary

1. This Convention is subject to acceptance, approval or ratification by the Signatories, in accordance with their respective laws.

2. Instruments of acceptance, approval, ratification or accession shall be deposited with the Secretary-General of the OECD, who shall serve as Depositary of this Convention.

Article 15
Entry into Force

1. This Convention shall enter into force on the sixtieth day following the date upon which five of the ten countries which have the ten largest export shares, and which represent by themselves at least sixty per cent of the combined total exports of those ten countries, have deposited their instruments of acceptance, approval, or ratification. For each signatory depositing its instrument after such entry into force, the Convention shall enter into force on the sixtieth day after deposit of its instrument.

2. If, after 31 December 1998, the Convention has not entered into force under paragraph 1 above, any signatory which has deposited its instrument of acceptance, approval or ratification may declare in writing to the Depositary its readiness to accept entry into force of this Convention under this paragraph 2. The Convention shall enter into force for such a signatory on the sixtieth day following the date upon which such declarations have been deposited by at least two signatories. For each signatory depositing its declaration after such entry into force, the Convention shall enter into force on the sixtieth day following the date of deposit.

Article 16
Amendment

Any Party may propose the amendment of this Convention. A proposed amendment shall be submitted to the Depositary which shall communicate it to the other Parties at least sixty days before convening a meeting of the Parties to consider the proposed amendment. An amendment adopted by consensus of the Parties, or by such other means as the Parties may determine by consensus, shall enter into force sixty days after the deposit of an instrument of ratification, acceptance or approval by all of the Parties, or in such other circumstances as may be specified by the Parties at the time of adoption of the amendment.

Article 17
Withdrawal

A Party may withdraw from this Convention by submitting written notification to the Depositary. Such withdrawal shall be effective one year after the date of the receipt of the notification. After withdrawal, co-operation shall continue between the Parties and the Party which has withdrawn on all requests for assistance or extradition made before the effective date of withdrawal which remain pending.

Commentaries on the Convention on Combating Bribery of Officials in International Business Transactions

Adopted by the Negotiating Conference on 21 November 1997

General:

1. This Convention deals with what, in the law of some countries, is called "active corruption" or "active bribery", meaning the offence committed by the person who promises or gives the bribe, as contrasted with "passive bribery", the offence committed by the official who receives the bribe. The Convention does not utilise the term "active bribery" simply to avoid it being misread by the non-technical reader as implying that the briber has taken the initiative and the recipient is a passive victim. In fact, in a number of situations, the recipient will have induced or pressured the briber and will have been, in that sense, the more active.

2. This Convention seeks to assure a functional equivalence among the measures taken by the Parties to sanction bribery of foreign public officials, without requiring uniformity or changes in fundamental principles of a Party's legal system.

Article 1. The Offence of Bribery of Foreign Public Officials:

Re paragraph 1:

3. Article 1 establishes a standard to be met by Parties, but does not require them to utilise its precise terms in defining the offence under their domestic laws. A Party may use various approaches to fulfil its obligations, provided that conviction of a person for the offence does not require proof of elements beyond those which would be required to be proved if the offence were defined as in this paragraph. For example, a statute prohibiting the bribery of agents generally which does not specifically address bribery of a foreign public official, and a statute specifically limited to this case, could both comply with this Article. Similarly, a statute which defined the offence in terms of payments "to induce a breach of the official's duty" could meet the standard provided that it was understood that every public official had a duty to exercise judgement or discretion impartially and this was an "autonomous" definition not requiring proof of the law of the particular official's country.

4. It is an offence within the meaning of paragraph 1 to bribe to obtain or retain business or other improper advantage whether or not the company concerned was the best qualified bidder or was otherwise a company which could properly have been awarded the business.

5. "Other improper advantage" refers to something to which the company concerned was not clearly entitled, for example, an operating permit for a factory which fails to meet the statutory requirements.

6. The conduct described in paragraph 1 is an offence whether the offer or promise is made or the pecuniary or other advantage is given on that person's own behalf or on behalf of any other natural person or legal entity.

7. It is also an offence irrespective of, inter alia, the value of the advantage, its results, perceptions of local custom, the tolerance of such payments by local authorities, or the alleged necessity of the payment in order to obtain or retain business or other improper advantage.

8. It is not an offence, however, if the advantage was permitted or required by the written law or regulation of the foreign public official's country, including case law.

9. Small "facilitation" payments do not constitute payments made "to obtain or retain business or other improper advantage" within the meaning of paragraph 1 and, accordingly, are also not an offence. Such payments, which, in some countries, are made to induce public officials to perform their functions, such as issuing licenses or permits, are generally illegal in the foreign country concerned. Other countries can and should address this corrosive phenomenon by such means as support for programmes of good governance. However, criminalisation by other countries does not seem a practical or effective complementary action.

10. Under the legal system of some countries, an advantage promised or given to any person, in anticipation of his or her becoming a foreign public official, falls within the scope of the offences described in Article 1, paragraph 1 or 2. Under the legal system of many countries, it is considered technically distinct from the offences covered by the present Convention. However, there is a commonly shared concern and intent to address this phenomenon through further work.

Re paragraph 2:

11. The offences set out in paragraph 2 are understood in terms of their normal content in national legal systems. Accordingly, if authorisation, incitement, or one of the other listed acts, which does not lead to further action, is not itself punishable under a Party's legal system, then the Party would not be required to make it punishable with respect to bribery of a foreign public official.

Re paragraph 4:

12. "Public function" includes any activity in the public interest, delegated by a foreign country, such as the performance of a task delegated by it in connection with public procurement.

13. A "public agency" is an entity constituted under public law to carry out specific tasks in the public interest.

14. A "public enterprise" is any enterprise, regardless of its legal form, over which a government, or governments, may, directly or indirectly, exercise a dominant influence. This is deemed to be the case, inter alia, when the government or governments hold the majority of the enterprise's subscribed capital, control the majority of votes attaching to shares issued by the enterprise or can appoint a majority of the members of the enterprise's administrative or managerial body or supervisory board.

15. An official of a public enterprise shall be deemed to perform a public function unless the enterprise operates on a normal commercial basis in the relevant market, i.e., on a basis which is substantially equivalent to that of a private enterprise, without preferential subsidies or other privileges.

16. In special circumstances, public authority may in fact be held by persons (e.g., political party officials in single party states) not formally designated as public officials. Such persons, through their *de facto* performance of a public function, may, under the legal principles of some countries, be considered to be foreign public officials.

17. "Public international organisation" includes any international organisation formed by states, governments, or other public international organisations, whatever the form of organisation and scope of competence, including, for example, a regional economic integration organisation such as the European Communities.

18. "Foreign country" is not limited to states, but includes any organised foreign area or entity, such as an autonomous territory or a separate customs territory.

19. One case of bribery which has been contemplated under the definition in paragraph 4.c is where an executive of a company gives a bribe to a senior official of a government, in order that this official use his office—though acting outside his competence—to make another official award a contract to that company.

Article 2. Responsibility of Legal Persons:

20. In the event that, under the legal system of a Party, criminal responsibility is not applicable to legal persons, that Party shall not be required to establish such criminal responsibility.

Article 3. Sanctions:

Re paragraph 3:

21. The "proceeds" of bribery are the profits or other benefits derived by the briber from the transaction or other improper advantage obtained or retained through bribery.

22. The term "confiscation" includes forfeiture where applicable and means the permanent deprivation of property by order of a court or other competent authority. This paragraph is without prejudice to rights of victims.

23. Paragraph 3 does not preclude setting appropriate limits to monetary sanctions.

Re paragraph 4:

24. Among the civil or administrative sanctions, other than non-criminal fines, which might be imposed upon legal persons for an act of bribery of a foreign public official are: exclusion from entitlement to public benefits or aid; temporary or permanent disqualification from participation in public procurement or from the practice of other commercial activities; placing under judicial supervision; and a judicial winding-up order.

Article 4. Jurisdiction:

Re paragraph 1:

25. The territorial basis for jurisdiction should be interpreted broadly so that an extensive physical connection to the bribery act is not required.

Re paragraph 2:

26. Nationality jurisdiction is to be established according to the general principles and conditions in the legal system of each Party. These principles deal with such matters as dual criminality. However, the requirement of dual criminality should be deemed to be met if the act is unlawful where it occurred, even if under a different criminal statute. For countries which apply nationality jurisdiction only to certain types of offences, the reference to "principles" includes the principles upon which such selection is based.

Article 5. Enforcement:

27. Article 5 recognises the fundamental nature of national regimes of prosecutorial discretion. It recognises as well that, in order to protect the independence of prosecution, such discretion is to be exercised on the basis of professional motives and is not to be subject to improper influence by concerns of a political nature. Article 5 is complemented by paragraph 6 of the Annex to the 1997 OECD Revised Recommendation on Combating Bribery in International Business Transactions, C(97)123/FINAL (hereinafter, "1997 OECD Recommendation"), which recommends, inter alia, that complaints of bribery of foreign public officials should be seriously investigated by competent authorities and that adequate resources should be provided by national governments to permit effective prosecution of such bribery. Parties will have accepted this Recommendation, including its monitoring and follow-up arrangements.

Article 7. Money Laundering:

28. In Article 7, "bribery of its own public official" is intended broadly, so that bribery of a foreign public official is to be made a predicate offence for money laundering legislation on the same terms, when a Party has made either active or passive bribery of its own public official such an offence. When a Party has made only passive bribery of its own public officials a predicate offence for money laundering purposes, this article requires that the laundering of the bribe payment be subject to money laundering legislation.

Article 8. Accounting:

29. Article 8 is related to section V of the 1997 OECD Recommendation, which all Parties will have accepted and which is subject to follow-up in the OECD Working Group on Bribery in International Business Transactions. This paragraph contains a series of recommendations concerning accounting requirements, independent external audit and internal company controls the implementation of which will be important to the overall effectiveness of the fight against bribery in international business. However, one immediate consequence of the implementation of this Convention by the Parties will be that companies which are required to issue financial statements disclosing their material contingent liabilities will need to take into account the full potential liabilities under this Convention, in particular its Articles 3 and 8, as well as other losses which might flow from conviction of the company or its agents for bribery. This also has implications for the execution of professional responsibilities of auditors regarding indications of bribery of foreign public officials. In addition, the accounting offences referred to in Article 8 will generally occur in the company's home country, when the bribery offence itself may have been committed in another country, and this can fill gaps in the effective reach of the Convention.

Article 9. Mutual Legal Assistance:

30. Parties will have also accepted, through paragraph 8 of the Agreed Common Elements annexed to the 1997 OECD Recommendation, to explore and undertake means to improve the efficiency of mutual legal assistance.

Re paragraph 1:

31. Within the framework of paragraph 1 of Article 9, Parties should, upon request, facilitate or encourage the presence or availability of persons, including persons in custody, who consent to assist in investigations or participate in proceedings. Parties should take measures to be able, in appropriate cases, to transfer temporarily such a person in custody to a Party requesting it and to credit time in custody in the requesting Party to the transferred person's sentence in the requested Party. The Parties wishing to use this mechanism should also take measures to be able, as a requesting Party, to keep a transferred person in custody and return this person without necessity of extradition proceedings.

Re paragraph 2:

32. Paragraph 2 addresses the issue of identity of norms in the concept of dual criminality. Parties with statutes as diverse as a statute prohibiting the bribery of agents generally and a statute directed specifically at bribery of foreign public officials should be able to co-operate fully regarding cases whose facts fall within the scope of the offences described in this Convention.

Article 10. Extradition:

Re paragraph 2:

33. A Party may consider this Convention to be a legal basis for extradition if, for one or more categories of cases falling within this Convention, it requires an extradition treaty. For example, a country may consider it a basis for extradition of its nationals if it requires an extradition treaty for that category but does not require one for extradition of non-nationals.

Article 12. Monitoring and Follow-up:

34. The current terms of reference of the OECD Working Group on Bribery which are relevant to monitoring and follow-up are set out in Section VIII of the 1997 OECD Recommendation. They provide for:

i) receipt of notifications and other information submitted to it by the [participating] countries;

ii) regular reviews of steps taken by [participating] countries to implement the Recommendation and to make proposals, as appropriate, to assist [participating] countries in its implementation; these reviews will be based on the following complementary systems:
   - a system of self evaluation, where [participating] countries' responses on the basis of a questionnaire will provide a basis for assessing the implementation of the Recommendation;
   - a system of mutual evaluation, where each [participating] country will be examined in turn by the Working Group on Bribery, on the basis of a report which will provide an objective assessment of the progress of the [participating] country in implementing the Recommendation.

iii) examination of specific issues relating to bribery in international business transactions;

. . .

v) provision of regular information to the public on its work and activities and on implementation of the Recommendation.

35. The costs of monitoring and follow-up will, for OECD Members, be handled through the normal OECD budget process. For non-members of the OECD, the current rules create an equivalent system of cost sharing, which is described in the Resolution of the Council Concerning Fees for Regular Observer Countries and Non-Member Full Participants in OECD Subsidiary Bodies, C(96)223/FINAL.

36. The follow-up of any aspect of the Convention which is not also follow-up of the 1997 OECD Recommendation or any other instrument accepted by all the participants in the OECD Working Group on Bribery will be carried out by the Parties to the Convention and, as appropriate, the participants party to another, corresponding instrument.

Article 13. Signature and Accession:

37. The Convention will be open to non-members which become full participants in the OECD Working Group on Bribery in International Business Transactions. Full participation by non-members in this Working Group is encouraged and arranged under simple procedures. Accordingly, the requirement of full participation in the Working Group, which follows from the relationship of the Convention to other aspects of the fight against bribery in international business, should not be seen as an obstacle by countries wishing to participate in that fight. The Council of the OECD has appealed to non-members to adhere to the 1997 OECD Recommendation and to participate in any institutional follow-up or implementation mechanism, i.e., in the Working Group. The current procedures regarding full participation by non-members in the Working Group may be found in the Resolution of the Council concerning the Participation of Non-Member Economies in the Work of Subsidiary Bodies of the Organisation, C(96)64/REV1/FINAL. In addition to accepting the Revised Recommendation of the Council on Combating Bribery, a full participant also accepts the Recommendation on the Tax Deductibility of Bribes of Foreign Public Officials, adopted on 11 April 1996, C(96)27/FINAL.

18
The Business Principles
for Countering Bribery

Corruption has no respect for national boundaries. In an increasingly globalised world, corruption seriously distorts economic activity and denies people at large the benefits of their efforts. The scourge of corruption has to be confronted through increased cross-border co-operation. Focusing on countering bribery in the private sector is an important contribution to this endeavour.

Peter Eigen, Chairman, Transparency International[1]

Type Framework for companies, multi-stakeholder; process- and performance-oriented

Strength Flexibility

Keywords Bribery • Transparency International • Social Accountability International • Multi-stakeholder • Consultation • Non-governmental organisations • Policies • Procedures • Facilitation payments

18.1 Background

Published in December 2002, the Business Principles for Countering Bribery (hereafter referred to as the Principles) were developed through a multi-stakeholder dialogue including trade unions, companies, non-governmental organisations (NGOs) and academics, from many countries. The convenors of the dialogue are Transparency International and Social Accountability International (SAI). Transparency International was founded in 1993 to build coalitions to fight corruption.

1 www.transparency.org/building_coalitions/private_sector/business_principles.html

With some 90 chapters around the world, Transparency International views corruption as a barrier to development and human rights. SAI is an NGO, founded in 1997 to develop and promote workplace standards through multi-stakeholder dialogue. SAI has developed the Social Accountability 8000 (SA8000) standard and a process for accrediting certifiers to audit against SA8000 (see Chapter 9).

Companies are encouraged to apply (rather than adopt) the Principles by initiating their own internal process of setting policies and procedures within the company through consultation with stakeholders.

According to Transparency International and SAI, the Principles are still at an early stage of what promises to be a long-term process. The intent was to develop principles that could guide companies through a difficult terrain rather than to establish a difficult standard that few companies could meet. As such, the Principles are a 'living document' that will evolve as the field changes. For now, the Principles chart a course for companies on what constitutes good practice rather than best practice.

18.2 Strengths and weaknesses

The Principles are based on the OECD Convention on Combating Bribery of Foreign Public Officials in International Business Transactions (see Chapter 17) and the US Foreign Corrupt Practices Act (FCPA 1977). However, they go further than these foundation standards in that they also focus on private-to-private bribery, whereas the foundation standards focus exclusively on bribery of foreign government officials.

Practical, concise and comprehensive, the Principles require companies to comply with legislation. Companies need to create a 'trust-based and inclusive internal culture in which bribery is not tolerated' (see page 290). Companies are given parameters for setting their own anti-bribery systems and procedures.

The Principles set important definitions and systems for companies. They assert that senior managers of companies 'should monitor the Programme and periodically review the Programme's suitability, adequacy and effectiveness and implement improvements as appropriate' (see page 295). The Principles encourage companies to invest ultimate responsibility for anti-bribery programmes with the chief executive officer.

18.3 Companies to which the Business Principles for Countering Bribery apply

The Principles are designed for small, medium-sized and large companies.

18.4 Questions posed and answered

The Principles pose and answer the following question:

- Which parameters are useful for companies seeking to develop their own internal systems for combating corruption?

18.5 The promise and the challenge

Launched at a time of considerable 'code fatigue' (see footnote 2 on page 499), the Principles will need to promote awareness of and provide training on the Principles around the world. As with other 'living documents', the Principles will need to evolve so as to promote accountability.

Reference

FCPA (Foreign Corrupt Practices Act) (1977) Current through Pub.L 105-366 (November 10, 1998) (Washington, DC: US Government Printing Office).

Additional resources

Websites

Business Principles for Countering Bribery:
www.transparency.org/building_coalitions/private_sector/business_principles.html
Social Accountability International (SAI): www.cepaa.org
Transparency International: www.transparency.org

The Business Principles
for Countering Bribery*

1 INTRODUCTION

The Business Principles for Countering Bribery (the "Business Principles") have been developed by a group of private sector interests, non-governmental organisations and trade unions as a tool to assist enterprises to develop effective approaches to countering bribery in all of their activities.

The Business Principles also give practical effect to recent initiatives such as the OECD Convention on Combating Bribery of Foreign Public Officials in International Business Transactions, the ICC Rules of Conduct to Combat Extortion and Bribery and the anti-bribery provisions of the revised OECD Guidelines for Multinationals.

The Business Principles have been designed for use by large, medium and small enterprises. They apply to bribery of public officials and to private-to-private transactions. The purpose of the document is to provide practical guidance for countering bribery, creating a level playing field and providing a long-term business advantage.

2 THE BUSINESS PRINCIPLES

- **The enterprise shall prohibit bribery in any form whether direct or indirect**

- **The enterprise shall commit to implementation of a Programme to counter bribery**

These Business Principles are based on a commitment to fundamental values of integrity, transparency and accountability. Enterprises shall aim to create and maintain a trust-based and inclusive internal culture in which bribery is not tolerated.

The Programme is the entirety of an enterprise's anti-bribery efforts including values, policies, processes, training and guidance.

---

* Reproduced with the permission of Social Accountability International and Transparency International.

3 AIMS

The aims of the Business Principles are to:

- provide a framework for good business practices and risk management strategies for countering bribery.
- assist enterprises to:
  a) eliminate bribery
  b) demonstrate their commitment to countering bribery
  c) make a positive contribution to improving business standards of integrity, transparency and accountability wherever they operate.

4 DEVELOPMENT OF A PROGRAMME FOR COUNTERING BRIBERY

4.1 An enterprise should develop a Programme reflecting its size, business sector, potential risks and locations of operation, which should, clearly and in reasonable detail, articulate values, policies and procedures to be used to prevent bribery from occurring in all activities under its effective control.

4.2 The Programme should be consistent with all laws relevant to countering bribery in all the jurisdictions in which the enterprise operates, particularly laws that are directly relevant to specific business practices.

4.3 The enterprise should develop the Programme in consultation with employees, trade unions or other employee representative bodies.

4.4 The enterprise should ensure that it is informed of all matters material to the effective development of the Programme by communicating with relevant interested parties.

5 SCOPE OF THE PROGRAMME

In developing its Programme for countering bribery, an enterprise should analyse which specific areas pose the greatest risks from bribery.

The Programme should address the most prevalent forms of bribery relevant to the enterprise but at a minimum should cover the following areas:

5.1 Bribes

5.1.1 The enterprise should prohibit the offer, gift, or acceptance of a bribe in any form, including kickbacks, on any portion of a contract payment, or the use of other routes or channels to provide improper benefits to customers, agents, contractors, suppliers or employees of any such party or government officials.

5.1.2 The enterprise should also prohibit an employee from arranging or accepting a bribe or kickback from customers, agents, contractors, suppliers, or employees of any such party or from government officials, for the employee's benefit or that of the employee's family, friends, associates or acquaintances.

5.2 Political contributions

5.2.1 The enterprise, its employees or agents should not make direct or indirect contributions to political parties, organisations or individuals engaged in politics, as a way of obtaining advantage in business transactions.

5.2.2 The enterprise should publicly disclose all its political contributions.

5.3 Charitable contributions and sponsorships

5.3.1 The enterprise should ensure that charitable contributions and sponsorships are not being used as a subterfuge for bribery.

5.3.2 The enterprise should publicly disclose all its charitable contributions or sponsorships.

5.4 Facilitation payments

5.4.1 Recognising that facilitation payments[1] are a form of bribery, the enterprise should identify, minimise and preferably eliminate them.

5.5 Gifts, hospitality and expenses

5.5.1 The enterprise should prohibit the offer or receipt of gifts, hospitality or expenses whenever such arrangements could affect the outcome of business transactions and are not reasonable and bona fide expenditures.

6 PROGRAMME IMPLEMENTATION REQUIREMENTS

The following section sets out the requirements that enterprises should meet, at a minimum, when implementing the Programme.

6.1 Organisation and responsibilities

6.1.1 The Board of Directors or equivalent body should base their policy on the Business Principles and provide leadership, resources and active support for management's implementation of the Programme.

6.1.2 The Chief Executive Officer is responsible for ensuring that the Programme is carried out consistently with clear lines of authority.

6.1.3 The Board of Directors, Chief Executive Officer and senior management should demonstrate visible and active commitment to the implementation of the Business Principles.

6.2 Business relationships

The enterprise should apply its Programme in its dealings with subsidiaries, joint venture partners, agents, contractors and other third parties with whom it has business relationships.

6.2.1 *Subsidiaries and joint ventures*

6.2.1.1 The enterprise should conduct due diligence before entering into a joint venture.

6.2.1.2 The enterprise should ensure that subsidiaries and joint ventures over which it maintains effective control adopt its Programme. Where an enterprise does not have effective control it should make known its Programme and use its best efforts to monitor that the conduct of such subsidiaries and joint ventures is consistent with the Business Principles.

6.2.2 *Agents*

6.2.2.1 The enterprise should not channel improper payments through an agent.

6.2.2.2 The enterprise should undertake due diligence before appointing an agent.

6.2.2.3 Compensation paid to agents should be appropriate and justifiable remuneration for legitimate services rendered.

6.2.2.4 The relationship should be documented.

6.2.2.5 The agent should contractually agree to comply with the enterprise's Programme.

6.2.2.6 The enterprise should monitor the conduct of its agents and should have a right of termination in the event that they pay bribes.

6.2.3 *Contractors and suppliers*

6.2.3.1 The enterprise should conduct its procurement practices in a fair and transparent manner.

6.2.3.2 The enterprise should undertake due diligence in evaluating major prospective contractors and suppliers to ensure that they have effective anti-bribery policies.

6.2.3.3 The enterprise should make known its anti-bribery policies to contractors and suppliers. It should monitor the conduct of major contractors and suppliers and should have a right of termination in the event that they pay bribes.

6.2.3.4 The enterprise should avoid dealing with prospective contractors and suppliers known to be paying bribes.

6.3 Human resources

6.3.1 Recruitment, promotion, training, performance evaluation and recognition should reflect the enterprise's commitment to the Programme.

6.3.2 The human resources policies and practices relevant to the Programme should be developed and undertaken in consultation with employees, trade unions or other employee representative bodies as appropriate.

6.3.3 The enterprise should make it clear that no employee will suffer demotion, penalty, or other adverse consequences for refusing to pay bribes even if it may result in the enterprise losing business.

6.3.4 The enterprise should apply appropriate sanctions for violations of its Programme.

6.4 Training

6.4.1 Managers, employees and agents should receive specific training on the Programme.

6.4.2 Where appropriate, contractors and suppliers should receive training on the Programme.

6.5 Raising concerns and seeking guidance

6.5.1 To be effective, the Programme should rely on employees and others to raise concerns and violations as early as possible. To this end, the enterprise should provide secure and accessible channels through which employees and others should feel able to raise concerns and report violations ("whistle-blowing") in confidence and without risk of reprisal.

6.5.2 These channels should also be available for employees and others to seek advice or suggest improvements to the Programme. To support this process, the enterprise should provide guidance to employees and others with respect to the interpretation of the Programme in individual cases.

6.6 Communication

6.6.1 The enterprise should establish effective internal and external communication of the Programme.

6.6.2 The enterprise should, on request, publicly disclose the management systems it employs in countering bribery.

6.6.3 The enterprise should be open to receiving communications from relevant interested parties with respect to the Programme.

6.7 Internal controls and audit

6.7.1 The enterprise should maintain accurate books and records, available for inspection, which properly and fairly document all financial transactions. The enterprise should not maintain off-the-books accounts.

6.7.2 The enterprise should establish feedback mechanisms and other internal processes supporting the continuous improvement of the Programme.

6.7.3 The enterprise should subject the internal control systems, in particular the accounting and record keeping practices, to regular audits to provide assurance that they are effective in countering bribery.

6.8 Monitoring and review

6.8.1 Senior management of the enterprise should monitor the Programme and periodically review the Programme's suitability, adequacy and effectiveness and implement improvements as appropriate. They should periodically report to the Audit Committee or the Board the results of the Programme review.

6.8.2 The Audit Committee or the Board should make an independent assessment of the adequacy of the Programme and disclose its findings in the Annual Report to shareholders.

Note:

[1] Facilitation payments: Also called "facilitating", "speed" or "grease" payments, these are small payments made to secure or expedite the performance of a routine or necessary action to which the payer of the facilitation payment has legal or other entitlement.

Part 6
Corporate governance

Society sets the ethical framework within which those who run companies have to work out their own codes of conduct. Responsibility for decisions, therefore, runs both ways. Business has to take account of its responsibilities to society in coming to decisions, but society has to accept its responsibilities for setting the standards against which those decisions are made.

Sir Adrian Cadbury, Ethics prize-winner, 1987[1]

The majority of the codes and principles in this book relate to corporate responsibility, but Part 6 discusses corporate governance—a theme that is inherently linked to corporate responsibility, yet a field apart. As corporate responsibility drills deeper into companies, the linkages between corporate governance and corporate responsibility are becoming more pronounced. As managers develop mechanisms for embedding social and environmental issues into the structure and 'DNA' of companies, they will need to interface with issues of corporate governance. To institutionalise corporate responsibility, companies will need to consider issues of corporate governance, including:

- What are the responsibilities of the board of directors in terms of social and environmental issues?

- How can the company develop reporting that makes it more accountable?

1 Cadbury 1987: 73.

Both corporate responsibility and corporate governance share a common vocabulary, with both fields making frequent references to 'accountability', 'transparency' and 'disclosure'. One of the challenges for corporate responsibility is to develop linkages to the field of corporate governance. The Enron and Ahold scandals demonstrate the increased need for this kind of integration. Both companies had well-developed codes of practice in corporate responsibility, but they had poor corporate governance structures, which permitted abuse.[2]

Corporate governance relates to the 'relationship between business and society' (McIntosh *et al.* 1998: 284). Corporate governance involves the relationship between boards of directors, senior management and shareholders, involving the way in which companies are controlled.[3]

According to the International Business Leaders' Forum (IBLF undated), corporate governance poses the following types of questions:

- **Accountability**. To whom are company directors accountable—to shareholders, or to a wider group of stakeholders, including, but not exclusively, shareholders?

- **Responsibility**. For what are company directors responsible or accountable: their financial performance alone, or their wider social, economic and environmental performance?

- **'Globality'**. Where are company directors accountable: in the home or base country of the company, or in all countries where the company operates?

- **Standard-setting**. Who is responsible for setting standards for corporate governance: government legislators, business bodies, non-governmental organisations (NGOs)—and how widely do they apply in terms of issues and geographies covered?

- **Monitoring** and **disclosure**. How is corporate behaviour against these standards monitored and disclosed to the public, and who does the monitoring?

- **Enforcement**. Related to the above points, how are standards for corporate governance most effectively, efficiently and fairly implemented—by regulation, voluntary approaches or some combination of both?'

There are hundreds of voluntary policies and recommendations on corporate governance.[4] Six countries have issued guidelines on corporate governance: Australia, Canada, France, Japan, South Africa and the United Kingdom.[5] According to the OECD Principles of Corporate Governance, 'there is no single model of good

---

2   For an excellent analysis of the Enron debacle and its lessons for corporate responsibility, see Sullivan 2002; for the Ahold scandal, see *Economist* 2003.

3   For more information on corporate governance, see Cheffins 2000; Elkington 1997.

4   For a list of the major corporate governance policies, see: www.iccwbo.org/CorpGov/Best_Practices_And_Codes.asp.

5   For a full list of these frameworks, see www.iblf.org/csr/csrwebassist.nsf/content/a1a2c3d4.html#anchor1.

corporate governance' (OECD 1999: 12). There is a great deal of variation in how companies are run, depending on their location, size and sector and on other factors. Different countries face different regulatory structures, and different sectors face different constraints.

Progress in the field of corporate governance has been achieved through national committees, internationally agreed principles and a series of voluntary standards. Here, some of the work conducted at the national level is first examined.[6] A number of UK committees have addressed corporate governance and have made significant contributions to the field:

- The Cadbury Committee (Committee on the Financial Aspects of Corporate Governance 1992) drafted the Cadbury Report and a Code of Best Practice on corporate governance. The Code makes recommendations about boards, non-executive directors, executives, controls and reporting.

- The Greenbury Committee (1995)[7] in its report focused on the issue of setting executive pay, at the same time acknowledging the importance of shareholder participation.

- The Hampel Committee (1998),[8] charged with reviewing the Cadbury and Greenbury reports, also identified principles of good corporate governance.

The London Stock Exchange then adopted many elements of the Hampel Report by integrating these recommendations into the Combined Code (LSE 1998 [revised 2002][9]), which includes Principles of Good Governance and a Code of Best Practice. Companies listed on the London Stock Exchange must include in their annual reports and accounts a description of how they are applying the OECD Principles of Good Governance.

In South Africa, the King Report made important contributions to the field of corporate governance.[10] It includes The Code of Corporate Practices and Conduct (reproduced at the end of this section, page 301), which encourages all South African companies to adopt a code of ethics and to develop affirmative action programmes.

The Commonwealth Association for Corporate Governance Guidelines (reproduced at the end of this section, page 322) also are among the key guides available to companies.[11] These Guidelines are useful in linking corporate responsibility with corporate governance issues.

The next chapter presents a discussion of key sections of the OECD Principles of Corporate Governance.

---

6 For a full range of national initiatives, see www.calpers-governance.org/principles/international/other.asp#.
7 See www.iia.org.uk/knowledgecentre/keyissues/corporategovernance.cfm?Action=1&Article_ID=108.
8 See www.ecgi.org/codes/country_documents/uk/hampel_index.htm.
9 See www.fsa.gov.uk/pubs/ukla/lr_comcode3.pdf.
10 See www.iodsa.co.za/corpgov.html.
11 For excerpts, see www.cacg-inc.com/pdf/overview-of-activities.pdf.

References

Cadbury, A. (1987) 'Ethical Managers Make Their Own Rules', *Harvard Business Review* (September/October 1987).

Cheffins, B. (2000) 'Current Trends in Corporate Governance: Going from London to Milan via Toronto', *Duke Journal of Comparative and International Law* 10.

Committee on the Financial Aspects of Corporate Governance (1992) *Report with Code of Best Practice* ('The Cadbury Report'; London: Gee Publishing).

Economist (2003) 'Europe's Enron: Ahold's Shocking Accounting', *The Economist*, 1 March 2003.

Elkington, J. (1997) *Cannibals with Forks: The Triple Bottom Line of 21st Century Business* (Oxford, UK: Capstone Publishing).

IBLF (International Business Leaders' Forum) (undated) 'Business Standards and Corporate Governance Framing the Issue', www.iblf.org/csr/csrwebassist.nsf/content/a1a2c3a4.html.

Institute of Directors in Southern Africa (1994) *The King Report on Corporate Governance for South Africa* (Johannesburg: Institute of Directors in Southern Africa).

McIntosh, M., D. Leipziger, K. Jones and G. Coleman (1998) *Corporate Citizenship: Successful Strategies of Responsible Companies* (London: FT Pitman).

OECD (Organisation for Economic Co-operation and Development) (1999) *Principles of Corporate Governance* (Paris: OECD).

Sullivan, R. (2002) 'One Step Forward or Two Steps Back for Effective Self-regulation?', *Journal of Corporate Citizenship* 8 (Winter 2002): 91-104.

The King Report II:
Code of Corporate Practices and Conduct*

1. Application of Code

1.1.   The Code applies to the following business enterprises (hereinafter referred to as "affected companies"):

   1.1.1. All companies with securities listed on the JSE Securities Exchange South Africa.

   1.1.2. Banks, financial and insurance entities as defined in the various legislation regulating the South African financial services sector.

   1.1.3. Public sector enterprises and agencies that fall under the Public Finance Management Act and the Local Government: Municipal Finance Management Bill (still to be promulgated) including any department of State or administration in the national, provincial or local sphere of government or any other functionary or institution:

   - exercising a power or performing a function in terms of the Constitution or a provincial constitution; or

   - exercising a public power or performing a public function in terms of any legislation, but not including a Court or a judicial officer,

   unless otherwise prescribed by legislation.

1.2.   All companies, in addition to those falling within the categories listed above, should give due consideration to the application of this Code insofar as the principles are applicable. Stakeholders interacting with such companies are encouraged to monitor the application by these companies of the principles set out in this Code (to the extent applicable).

1.3.   While it is acknowledged that certain forms of State enterprises may not lend themselves to some of the principles set out in this Code, it is recommended that the principles should be adapted appropriately by such enterprises. To assist entities falling within this category, National Treasury will be issuing

---

* Reprinted with the permission of the Institute of Directors, South Africa, © 2002.

"Good Practice Guides" as official directives in line with the overall framework for financial management for the public sector.

1.4. All references to "company" or "companies" in this Code and the accompanying Report should be taken to refer to "affected companies" as defined in 1.1 above.

1.5. The Code is a set of principles and does not purport to determine the detailed course of conduct of directors on any particular matter. Clearly, companies and their boards will be required to measure the principles set out in this Code against all other statutes, regulations and other authoritative directives regulating their conduct and operation with a view to applying not only the most applicable requirements but also to seek to adhere to the best available practice that may be relevant to the company in its particular circumstances.

1.6. The Code will be effective in respect of affected companies whose financial years commence on or after 1 March 2002. The Code should be seen as a "living document" that may require to be updated from time to time by the King Committee to ensure the currency of its recommended principles of corporate practices and conduct.

2. Boards and Directors

2.1. *The Board*

2.1.1. The board is the focal point of the corporate governance system. It is ultimately accountable and responsible for the performance and affairs of the company. Delegating authority to board committees or management does not in any way mitigate or dissipate the discharge by the board and its directors of their duties and responsibilities.

2.1.2. Given the positive interaction and diversity of views that take place between individuals of different skills, experience and background, the unitary board structure with executive and non-executive directors interacting in a working group remains appropriate for South African companies.

2.1.3. The board must give strategic direction to the company, appoint the chief executive officer and ensure that succession is planned.

2.1.4. The board must retain full and effective control over the company, and monitor management in implementing board plans and strategies.

2.1.5. The board should ensure that the company complies with all relevant laws, regulations and codes of business practice, and that it communicates with its shareowners and relevant stakeholders (internal and external) openly and promptly and with substance prevailing over form.

2.1.6. The board should define levels of materiality, reserving specific power to itself and delegating other matters with the necessary written authority to management. These matters should be monitored and evaluated on a regular basis.

2.1.7. The board should have unrestricted access to all company information, records, documents and property. The information needs of the board should be well defined and regularly monitored.

2.1.8. The board should consider developing a corporate code of conduct that addresses conflicts of interest, particularly relating to directors and management, which should be regularly reviewed and updated as necessary.

2.1.9. The board should have an agreed procedure whereby directors may, if necessary, take independent professional advice at the company's expense.

2.1.10. Every board should consider whether or not its size, diversity and demographics make it effective.

2.1.11. The board must identify key risk areas and key performance indicators of the business enterprise. These should be regularly monitored, with particular attention given to technology and systems.

2.1.12. The board should identify and monitor the non-financial aspects relevant to the business of the company.

2.1.13. The board should record the facts and assumptions on which it relies to conclude that the business will continue as a going concern in the financial year ahead or why it will not, and in that case, what steps the board is taking to remedy the situation.

2.1.14. The board should ensure that each item of special business included in the notice of the annual general meeting, or any other shareowners' meeting, is accompanied by a full explanation of the effects of any proposed resolutions.

2.1.15. The board should encourage shareowners to attend annual general meetings and other company meetings, at which the directors should be present. More particularly, the chairpersons of each of the board's committees, especially the audit and remuneration committees, should be present at the annual general meeting.

2.1.16. A brief CV of each director standing for election or re-election at the annual general meeting should accompany the notice contained in the annual report.

2.1.17. Every board should have a charter setting out its responsibilities, which should be disclosed in its annual report. At a minimum, the charter should confirm the board's responsibility for the adoption of strategic plans, monitoring of operational performance and management, determination of policy and processes to ensure the integrity of the company's risk management and internal controls, communications policy, and director selection, orientation and evaluation.

2.1.18. The board must find the correct balance between conforming with governance constraints and performing in an entrepreneurial way.

2.2. *Board Composition*

2.2.1. Companies should be headed by an effective board that can both lead and control the company. The board should comprise a balance of executive and non-executive directors, preferably with a majority of non-executive directors, of whom sufficient should be independent of management so that shareowner interests (including minority interests) can be protected. An obvious consideration for South African companies would be to consider the demographics in relation to the composition of the board.

2.2.2. Procedures for appointments to the board should be formal and transparent, and a matter for the board as a whole, assisted where appropriate by a nomination committee. This committee should constitute only non-executive directors, of whom the majority should be independent, and be chaired by the board chairperson.

2.2.3. Board continuity, subject to performance and eligibility for re-election, is imperative, and a programme ensuring a staggered rotation of directors should be put in place by the board to the extent that this is not already regulated.

2.3. *Chairperson and Chief Executive Officer*

2.3.1. There should be a clearly accepted division of responsibilities at the head of the company, to ensure a balance of power and authority, such that no one individual has unfettered powers of decision-making.

2.3.2. The chairperson should preferably be an independent non-executive director.

2.3.3. Given the strategic operational role of the chief executive officer, this function should be separate from that of the chairperson.

2.3.4. Where the roles of the chairperson and chief executive officer are combined, there should be either an independent non-executive director serving as deputy chairperson or a strong independent non-executive director element on the board. Any such decision to combine roles should be justified each year in the company's annual report.

2.3.5. The board should appraise performance of the chairperson on an annual or such other basis as the board may determine. If the roles of chairperson and chief executive officer are combined, then the independent deputy chairperson should play a leading part in the evaluation process.

2.3.6. The chairperson, or a sub-committee appointed by the board, should appraise the performance of the chief executive officer. The board should satisfy itself that an appraisal of the chief executive officer is performed at least annually. The results of such appraisal should also be considered by the Remuneration Committee to guide it in its evaluation of the performance and remuneration of the chief executive officer.

2.4. *Directors*

2.4.1. The board should ensure that there is an appropriate balance of power and authority on the board, such that no one individual or block of individuals can dominate the board's decision taking.

2.4.2. Non-executive directors should be individuals of calibre and credibility, and have the necessary skill and experience to bring judgment to bear independent of management, on issues of strategy, performance, resources, transformation, diversity and employment equity, standards of conduct and evaluation of performance.

2.4.3. In the annual report, the capacity of the directors should be categorised as follows:

- Executive director—an individual who is involved in the day-to-day management and/or is in full-time salaried employment of the company and/or any of its subsidiaries.

- Non-executive director—an individual not involved in the day to day management and not a full-time salaried employee of the company or of its subsidiaries. An individual in the full-time employment of the holding company or its subsidiaries, other than the company concerned, would also be considered to be a non-executive director unless such individual by his/her conduct or executive authority could be construed to be directing the day to day management of the company and its subsidiaries.

- Independent director—is a non-executive director who:
  - (i) is not a representative of a shareowner who has the ability to control or significantly influence the ability to control or significantly influence management;
  - (ii) has not been employed by the company or the group of which it currently forms part, in any executive capacity for the preceding three financial years;

(iii) is not a member of the immediate family of an individual who is, or has been in any of the past three financial years, employed by the company or the group in an executive capacity;

(iv) is not a professional advisor to the company or the group, other than in a director capacity;

(v) is not a significant supplier to, or customer of the company or group;

(vi) has no significant contractual relationship with the company or group; and

(vii) is free from any business or other relationship which could be seen to materially interfere with the individual's capacity to act in an independent manner.

2.4.4. A "shadow director" is considered to be a person in accordance with whose directions or instructions (whether they extend over the whole or part of the activities of the company) the directors of the company are accustomed to act. Shadow directors should be discouraged.

2.4.5. Executive directors should be encouraged to hold other non-executive directorships only to the extent that these do not interfere with their immediate management responsibilities. Non-executive directors should carefully consider the number of appointments they take in that capacity so as to ensure that the companies on which they serve enjoy the full benefit of their expertise, experience and knowledge.

2.4.6. The board should establish a formal orientation programme to familiarise incoming directors with the company's operations, senior management and its business environment, and to induct them in their fiduciary duties and responsibilities. Directors should receive further briefings from time to time on relevant new laws and regulations as well as on changing commercial risks.

2.4.7. New directors with no or limited board experience should receive development and education to inform them of their duties, responsibilities, powers and potential liabilities.

2.4.8. Boards should ascertain whether potential new directors are fit and proper and are not disqualified from being directors. Prior to their appointment, their backgrounds should be investigated along the lines of the approach required for listed companies by the JSE and under the Banks Act. The nomination committee would prove useful for this purpose.

2.5. *Remuneration*

2.5.1. Levels of remuneration should be sufficient to attract, retain and motivate executives of the quality required by the board.

2.5.2. Companies should appoint a remuneration committee or such other appropriate board committee, consisting entirely or mainly of independent non-executive directors, to make recommendations to the board within agreed terms of reference on the company's framework of executive remuneration and to determine specific remuneration packages for each of the executive directors. This is, ultimately, the responsibility of the board. This committee must be chaired by an independent non-executive director. In order to obtain his or her input on the remuneration of the other executives the committee should consult the chief executive officer, who may attend meetings by invitation. However, a chief executive should play no part in decisions regarding his/her own remuneration.

2.5.3. Membership of the remuneration committee or board committee that considers executive remuneration, must be disclosed in the annual report and the chairperson of such committee should attend annual general meetings to answer any questions from shareowners.

2.5.4. Companies should provide full disclosure of director remuneration on an individual basis, giving details of earnings, share options, restraint payments and all other benefits.

2.5.5. Performance-related elements of remuneration should constitute a substantial portion of the total remuneration package of executives in order to align their interests with those of the shareowners, and should be designed to provide incentives to perform at the highest operational standards.

2.5.6. Share options may be granted to non-executive directors but must be the subject of prior approval of shareowners (usually at the annual general meeting) having regard also to the specific requirements of the Companies Act. Because of the apparent dilution of independence, in some international markets the view is that non-executive directors should preferably receive shares rather than share options.

2.5.7. In regard to the allocation of share options, boards should be mindful of the following:

- A vesting period in relation to the allocation of share options to non-executive directors should be applied to dissuade short-term decision taking, but should also have regard to the possibility or consequences of the removal or resignation of such directors prior to the vesting period maturing and any perceived impact on their independence.

- Where it is proposed to re-price share options, this should be the subject of prior shareowner approval. Details of the share options of each executive and non-executive director who stands to benefit from any such proposal should be provided and should be subject to shareowner approval individually for each director.

- If share options are to be issued at a discount to the ruling price, shareowners should vote separately on this clause in the trust deed at its inception. Any subsequent amendments proposed to an existing trust deed that would permit allocations of share options at a discount must be subject to the specific approval of shareowners.

2.5.8. The overriding principle of full disclosure by directors, on an individual basis, should apply to all share schemes and any other incentive schemes proposed by management.

2.5.9. It is not considered appropriate that an executive director's fixed-term service contract, if any, should exceed three years. If so, full disclosure of this fact with reasons should be given and the consent of shareowners should be obtained.

2.5.10. Companies should establish a formal and transparent procedure for developing a policy on executive and director remuneration which should be supported by a Statement of Remuneration Philosophy in the annual report.

2.5.11. The remuneration or such other similar board committee should play an integral part in the succession planning, particularly in respect of the chief executive officer and executive management.

2.5.12. The remuneration committee should consider, and recommend to the board the fees to be paid to each non-executive director. The proposed fees, as confirmed by the board, should be submitted to the shareowners in general meeting for approval prior to implementation and payment. The practice of paying non-uniform fees to non-executive directors should also be carefully considered. The level of fees should preferably be determined according to the relative contributions of each non-executive director and their participation in the activities of the board and its committees.

2.6. Board Meetings

2.6.1. The board should meet regularly, at least once a quarter if not more frequently as circumstances require, and should disclose in the annual report the number of board and committee meetings held in the year and the details of attendance of each director (as applicable).

2.6.2. Efficient and timely methods should be determined for informing and briefing board members prior to meetings while each board member is responsible for being satisfied that, objectively, they have been furnished with all the relevant information and facts before making a decision.

2.6.3. Non-executive directors should have access to management and may even meet separately with management, without the attendance of executive directors. This should, however, be agreed collectively by the board usually facilitated by the non-executive chairperson or lead independent non-executive director.

2.6.4. The board should regularly review processes and procedures to ensure the effectiveness of the company's internal systems of control, so that its decision-making capability and the accuracy of its reporting are maintained at a high level at all times.

2.6.5. The board should ensure that it receives relevant non-financial information going beyond assessing the financial and quantitative performance of the company, and should look at other qualitative performance factors that involve broader stakeholder interests.

2.7. *Board Committees*

2.7.1. Board committees are an aid to assist the board and its directors in discharging their duties and responsibilities, and boards cannot shield behind these committees (see 2.1.1).

2.7.2. There should be a formal procedure for certain functions of the board to be delegated, describing the extent of such delegation, to enable the board to properly discharge its duties and responsibilities and to effectively fulfil its decision taking process.

2.7.3. Board committees with formally determined terms of reference, life span, role and function constitute an important element of the process in 2.7.2 and should be established with clearly agreed upon reporting procedures and written scope of authority.

2.7.4. As a general principle, there should be transparency and full disclosure from the board committee to the board, except where the committee has been mandated otherwise by the board.

2.7.5. At a minimum, each board should have an audit and a remuneration committee. Industry and company specific issues will dictate the requirement for other committees.

2.7.6. Non-executive directors must play an important role in board committees.

2.7.7. All board committees should preferably be chaired by an independent non-executive director, whether this is the board chairperson or some other appropriate individual. Exceptions should be a board committee fulfilling an executive function.

2.7.8. Board committees should be free to take independent outside professional advice as and when necessary.

2.7.9. Committee composition, a brief description of its remit, the number of meetings held and other relevant information should be disclosed in the annual report. The chairpersons of the board committees, particularly those in respect of audit, remuneration and nomination, should attend the company's annual general meeting.

2.7.10. Board committees should be subject to regular evaluation by the board to ascertain their performance and effectiveness (see 2.8.1).

2.8. *Board and Director Evaluation*

2.8.1. The board, through its nomination committee or similar board committee, should regularly review its required mix of skills and experience and other qualities such as its demographics and diversity in order to assess the effectiveness of the board. This should be by means of a self-evaluation of the board as a whole, its committees and the contribution of each individual director.

2.8.2. The evaluations in 2.8.1 should be conducted at least annually.

2.9. *Dealings and Securities*

2.9.1. Every listed company should have a practice prohibiting dealing in its securities by directors, officers and other selected employees for a designated period preceding the announcement of its financial results or in any other period considered sensitive, and have regard to the listings requirements of the JSE in respect of dealings of directors.

2.9.2. The practice in 2.9.1 should be determined by way of a formal policy established by the board and implemented by the company secretary.

2.10. *Company Secretary*

2.10.1. The company secretary, through the board, has a pivotal role to play in the corporate governance of a company.

2.10.2. The board should be cognisant of the duties imposed upon the company secretary and should empower the company secretary accordingly to enable him or her to properly fulfil those duties.

2.10.3. In addition to extensive statutory duties, the company secretary must provide the board as a whole and directors individually with detailed guidance as to how their responsibilities should be properly discharged in the best interests of the company.

2.10.4. The company secretary has an important role in the induction of new or inexperienced directors, and in assisting the chairperson and chief executive officer in determining the annual board plan and the administration of other issues of a strategic nature at the board level.

2.10.5. The company secretary should provide a central source of guidance and advice to the board, and within the company, on matters of ethics and good governance.

2.10.6. The Company secretary should be subjected to a fit and proper test in the same manner as is recommended for new director appointments under 2.4.8.

3. Risk Management

3.1. *Responsibility*

3.1.1. The board is responsible for the total process of risk management, as well as for forming its own opinion on the effectiveness of the process. Management is accountable to the board for designing, implementing and monitoring the process of risk management and integrating it into the day-to-day activities of the company.

3.1.2. The board should set the risk strategy policies in liaison with the executive directors and senior management. These policies should be clearly communicated to all employees to ensure that the risk strategy is incorporated into the language and culture of the company.

3.1.3. The board must decide the company's appetite or tolerance for risk—those risks it will take and those it will not take in the pursuit of its goals and objectives. The board has the responsibility to ensure that the company has implemented an effective ongoing process to identify risk, to measure its potential impact against a broad set of assumptions, and then to activate what is necessary to proactively manage these risks.

3.1.4. The board should make use of generally recognised risk management and internal control models and frameworks in order to maintain a sound system of risk management and internal control to provide reasonable assurance regarding the achievement of organisational objectives with respect to:

- effectiveness and efficiency of operations;
- safeguarding of the company's assets (including information);

- compliance with applicable laws, regulations and supervisory requirements;

- supporting business sustainability under normal as well as adverse operating conditions;

- reliability of reporting; and

- behaving responsibly towards all stakeholders.

3.1.5. The board is responsible for ensuring that a systematic, documented assessment of the processes and outcomes surrounding key risks is undertaken, at least annually, for the purpose of making its public statement on risk management. It should, at appropriately considered intervals, receive and review reports on the risk management process in the company. This risk assessment should address the company's exposure to at least the following:

- physical and operational risks;

- human resource risks;

- technology risks;

- business continuity and disaster recovery;

- credit and market risks; and

- compliance risks.

3.1.6. A board committee, either a dedicated committee or one with other responsibilities, should be appointed to assist the board in reviewing the risk management process and the significant risks facing the company.

3.1.7. Risk management and internal control should be practiced throughout the company by all staff, and should be embedded in day-to-day activities.

3.1.8. In addition to the company's other compliance and enforcement activities, the board should consider the need for a confidential reporting process ("whistleblowing") covering fraud and other risks.

3.2. *Application and Reporting*

3.2.1. A comprehensive system of control should be established by the board to ensure that risks are mitigated and that the company's objectives are attained. The control environment should also set the tone of the company and cover ethical values, management's philosophy and the competence of employees.

3.2.2. Risks should be assessed on an on-going basis and control activities should be designed to respond to risks throughout the company.

Pertinent information arising from the risk assessment, and relating to control activities should be identified, captured and communicated in a form and timeframe that enables employees to carry out their responsibilities properly. These controls should be monitored by both line management and assurance providers.

3.2.3. Companies should develop a system of risk management and internal control that builds more robust business operations. The systems should demonstrate that the company's key risks are being managed in a way that enhances shareowners' and relevant stakeholders' interests. The system should incorporate mechanisms to deliver:

- a demonstrable system of dynamic risk identification;

- a commitment by management to the process;

- a demonstrable system of risk mitigation activities;

- a system of documented risk communications;

- a system of documenting the costs of non-compliance and losses;

- a documented system of internal control and risk management;

- an alignment of assurance of efforts to the risk profile; and

- a register of key risks that could affect shareowner and relevant stakeholder interests.

3.2.4. The board must identify key risk areas and key performance indicators of the company, and monitor these factors as part of a regular review of processes and procedures to ensure the effectiveness of its internal systems of control, so that its decision-making and the accuracy of its reporting are maintained at a high level at all times.

3.2.5. Reports from management to the board should provide a balanced assessment of significant risks and the effectiveness of the system of internal control in managing those risks. Any significant control failings or weaknesses identified should be covered in the reports, including the impact that they have had, or may have had, on the company and the actions being taken to rectify them.

3.2.6. The board is responsible for disclosures in relation to risk management and should, at a minimum disclose:

- that it is accountable for the process of risk management and the system of internal control, which is regularly reviewed for effectiveness and for establishing appropriate risk and control policies and communicating these throughout the company;

- that there is an ongoing process for identifying, evaluating and managing the significant risks faced by the company, that has been in place for the year under review and up to the date of approval of the annual report and financial statements;

- that there is an adequate system of internal control in place to mitigate the significant risks faced by the company to an acceptable level. Such a system is designed to manage, rather than eliminate, the risk of failure or maximise opportunities to achieve business objectives. This can only provide reasonable, but not absolute, assurance;

- that there is a documented and tested process in place that will allow the company to continue its critical business processes in the event of a disastrous incident impacting on its activities;

- where material joint ventures and associates have not been dealt with as part of the group for the purposes of applying these recommendations. Alternative sources of risk management and internal control assurance applied to these activities should be disclosed, where these exist;

- that any additional information in the annual report to assist understanding of the company's risk management processes and system of internal control should be provided as appropriate; and

- where the board cannot make any of the disclosures set out above, it should state this fact and provide a suitable explanation.

3.2.7. Risk should not only be viewed from a negative perspective. The review process may identify areas of opportunity, such as where effective risk management can be turned to competitive advantage.

4. Internal Audit

4.1. *Status and Role*

4.1.1. Companies should have an effective internal audit function that has the respect and co-operation of both the board and management. Where the board, in its discretion, decides not to establish an internal audit function, full reasons must be disclosed in the company's annual report, with an explanation as to how assurance of effective internal controls, processes and systems will be obtained.

4.1.2. Consistent with the Institute of Internal Auditors' ("IIA") definition of internal auditing in an internal audit charter approved by the board, the purpose, authority and responsibility of the internal audit activity should be formally defined.

4.1.3. The IIA has succinctly set out the role and function of internal audit in its *Standards for the Professional Practice of Internal Auditing*, including the code of ethics and the definition of internal audit, which is fully endorsed by the King Committee.

4.1.4. Internal audit should report at a level within the company that allows it to fully accomplish its responsibilities. The head of internal audit should report administratively to the chief executive officer, and should have ready and regular access to the chairperson of the company and the chairperson of the audit committee.

4.1.5. Internal audit should report at all audit committee meetings.

4.1.6. The appointment or dismissal of the head of the internal audit should be with the concurrence of the audit committee.

4.1.7. If the external and internal audit functions are carried out by the same accounting firm, the audit committee and the board should satisfy themselves that there is adequate segregation between the two functions in order to ensure that their independence is not impaired (see also 6.1.5).

4.2. *Scope of Internal Audit*

4.2.1. Internal audit is an independent, objective assurance and consulting activity to add value and improve a company's operations. It helps a company accomplish its objectives by bringing a systematic, disciplined approach to evaluate and improve the effectiveness of risk management, control and governance processes.

4.2.2. An effective internal audit function should provide:

- assurance that the management processes are adequate to identify and monitor significant risks;

- confirmation of the effective operation of the established internal control systems;

- credible processes for feedback on risk management and assurance; and

- objective confirmation that the board receives the right quality of assurance and information from management and that this information is reliable.

4.2.3. The internal audit plan should be based on risk assessment as well as on issues highlighted by the audit committee and senior management. The risk assessment process should be of a continuous nature as to identify not only residual or existing but emerging risks and should be conducted formally at least annually, but more often in complex organisations. This risk assessment should be co-ordinated with the board's own assessment of risk.

4.2.4. The audit committee should approve the internal audit work plan.

4.2.5. The internal audit function should co-ordinate with other internal and external providers of assurance to ensure proper coverage of financial, operational and compliance controls and to minimise duplication of effort.

5. Integrated Sustainability Reporting

5.1. *Sustainability Reporting*

5.1.1. Every company should report at least annually on the nature and extent of its social, transformation, ethical, safety, health and environmental management policies and practices. The board must determine what is relevant for disclosure, having regard to the company's particular circumstances.

5.1.2. Stakeholder reporting requires an integrated approach. This would be best achieved gradually as the board and the company develop an understanding of the intricate relationships and issues associated with stakeholder reporting. Companies should categorise issues into the following levels of reporting:

- First level would be disclosures relating to acceptance and adoption of business principles and/or codes of practice that can be verified by reference to documents, board minutes or established policies and standards.

- Second level should address the implementation of practices in keeping with accepted principles involving a review of steps taken to encourage adherence to these principles evidenced by board directors, designated policies and communiqués, supported by appropriate non-financial accounting mechanisms.

- Third level should involve investigation and demonstration of changes and benefits that have resulted from the adoption and implementation of stated business principles and/or codes of practice.

5.1.3. When making such disclosures, boards will be required to consider:

- clarity on the nature of the disclosing entity, the scope of issues subject to disclosure, performance expectations as an integral aspect of the "going concern" concept, the period under review and the extent to which items disclosed are directly attributable to the company's own action or inaction;

- that disclosure of non-financial information is governed by the principles of reliability, relevance, clarity, comparability, timeliness and verifiability (with reference to the Global Reporting Initiative Sustainability Reporting Guidelines on economic, environmental and social performance); and

- that criteria and guidelines for materiality are developed by each company for consistency (having regard for international models and guidelines, as well as national statutory definitions).

5.1.4. Matters requiring specific consideration should include:

- description of practices reflecting a committed effort to reducing workplace accidents, fatalities, and occupational health and safety incidents against stated measurement targets and objectives and a suitable explanation where appropriate. This would cover the nature and extent of the strategy, plan and policies adopted to address and manage the potential impact of HIV/AIDS on the company's activities;

- reporting on environmental corporate governance that must reflect current South African law by the application of the "Best Practicable Environmental Option" standard (defined as that option that has most benefit, or causes the least damage to the environment at a cost acceptable to society);

- policies that define social investment prioritisation and spending, and the extent of initiatives to support black economic empowerment, in particular procurement practices and investment strategies; and

- disclosure of human capital development in areas such as the number of staff (with a particular focus on progress against equity targets, achievement of corporate training and development initiatives, age, employee development and financial investment committed). This should also address issues that create the conditions and opportunities for previously disadvantaged individuals (in particular women) to have an equal opportunity to reach executive levels in the company and to realise their full potential. It should include progress made in this regard, and mechanisms to positively reinforce the richness of diversity and the added value and contribution from this diversity.

5.2. *Organisational Integrity/Code of Ethics*

5.2.1. Every company should engage its stakeholders in determining the company's standards of ethical behaviour. It should demonstrate its commitment to organisational integrity by codifying its standards in a code of ethics.

5.2.2. Each company should demonstrate its commitment to its code of ethics by:

- creating systems and procedures to introduce, monitor and enforce its ethical code;

- assigning high level individuals to oversee compliance to the ethical code;

- assessing the integrity of new appointees in the selection and promotion procedures;

- exercising due care in delegating discretionary authority;

- communicating with, and training, all employees regarding enterprise values, standards and compliance procedures;

- providing, monitoring and auditing safe systems for reporting of unethical or risky behaviour;

- enforcing appropriate discipline with consistency; and

- responding to offences and preventing re-occurrence.

5.2.3. Disclosure should be made of adherence to the company's code of ethics against the above criteria. The disclosure should include a statement as to the extent the directors believe the ethical standards and the above criteria are being met. If this is considered inadequate there should be further disclosure of how the desired end-state will be achieved.

5.2.4. Companies should strongly consider their dealings with individuals or entities not demonstrating its same level of commitment to organisational integrity.

6. Accounting and Auditing

6.1. *Auditing and Non-audit Services*

6.1.1. The audit committee should draw up a recommendation to the board for consideration and acceptance by the shareowners for the appointment of the external auditors.

6.1.2. The auditors should observe the highest level of business and professional ethics and in particular, their independence must not be impaired in any way.

6.1.3. Companies should aim for efficient audit processes using external auditors in combination with the internal audit function.

6.1.4. Management should encourage consultation between external and internal auditors. Co-ordination of efforts involves periodic meetings to discuss matters of mutual interest, the exchange of working papers and management letters and reports, and a common understanding of audit techniques, methods and terminology.

6.1.5. The audit committee should set the principles for recommending using the accounting firm of the external auditors for non-audit services. In addition to the related Companies Act requirement, there should be separate disclosure of the amount paid for non-audit services with a detailed description in the notes to the annual financial statements of the nature thereof together with the amounts paid for each of the services described.

6.2. Reporting of Financial and Non-financial Information

6.2.1. The audit committee should consider whether or not an interim report should be subject to an independent review by the external auditor.

6.2.2. In the case of an independent review, the audit committee's report commenting on an interim report and the auditors' review report, should be tabled at the board meeting held to adopt the interim report. Where an independent review was not conducted, the audit committee should table the reasons at the board meeting.

6.2.3. The board should minute the facts and assumptions used in the assessment of the going concern status of the company at the year end.

6.2.4. At the interim reporting stage, the directors should consider their assessment at the previous year end of the company's ability to continue as a going concern and determine whether or not any of the significant factors in the assessment have changed to such an extent that the appropriateness of the going concern assumption at the interim reporting stage has been affected. The board should minute the conclusion reached by the directors at the interim reporting stage.

6.2.5. Where non-financial aspects of reporting have been subject to external validation, this fact must be stated and details provided in the annual report.

6.2.6. Companies should make every effort to ensure that information is distributed via a broad range of communication channels, including the Internet, having regard for its security and integrity while bearing in mind the need that critical financial information reaches all shareowners simultaneously.

6.3. Audit Committee

6.3.1. The board should appoint an audit committee that has a majority of independent non-executive directors. The majority of the members of the audit committee should be financially literate.

6.3.2. The chairperson should be an independent non-executive director and not the chairperson of the board. The better view is that the board chairperson should not be a member of the audit committee at all, but could be invited to attend meetings as necessary by the chairperson of that committee. The board should consider whether or not it is desirable for the chief executive officer to be a member of the audit committee, or to attend only by invitation.

6.3.3. The audit committee should have written terms of reference that deal adequately with its membership, authority and duties.

6.3.4. Companies should, in their annual report disclose whether or not the audit committee has adopted formal terms of reference and, if so, whether the committee has satisfied its responsibilities for the year, in compliance with its terms of reference.

6.3.5. Membership of the audit committee should be disclosed in the annual report. The chairperson of the committee should be available at the annual general meeting to answer questions about its work.

7. Relations with Shareowners

7.1. Companies should be ready where practicable, to enter into dialogue with institutional investors based on constructive engagement and the mutual understanding of objectives. This should take due regard of statutory, regulatory and other directives regulating the dissemination of information by companies and their directors and officers.

7.2. When evaluating a company's corporate governance arrangements, particularly those relating to board structure and composition, institutional investors should give due weight to all relevant factors drawn to their attention and to any specific arrangements to eliminate unnecessary variations in criteria and measurement of performance.

7.3. Companies should ensure that each item of special business included in the notice of annual general meeting is accompanied by a full explanation of the effects of a proposed resolution. In the course of the annual general meeting, as should be the case with other shareowner meetings, the chairperson should provide a reasonable time for discussion.

7.4. Companies should consider conducting meetings on the basis of a poll in relation to special business, or where contentious issues are under consideration, in order to ensure that all votes of shareowners (whether in person, by proxy or representation) at company meetings are taken into account. The results of all decisions taken at company meetings should be publicly disseminated in the most appropriate form, immediately on conclusion of the meeting to ensure that all shareowners (particularly those who were not in attendance or were unable to attend) are promptly informed or at least have ready access to such information.

8. Communication

8.1. It is the board's duty to present a balanced and understandable assessment of the company's position in reporting to stakeholders. The quality of the information must be based on the principles of openness and substance over form. Reporting should address material matters of significant interest and concern to all stakeholders.

8.2. Reports and communications must be made in the context that society now demands greater transparency and accountability from companies regarding their non-financial matters.

8.3. Reports should present a comprehensive and objective assessment of the activities of the company so that shareowners and relevant stakeholders with a legitimate interest in the company's affairs can obtain a full, fair and honest account of its performance. In communicating with its stakeholders, the board should take into account the circumstances of the communities in which the company operates.

8.4. The directors should report on the following matters in their annual report:

8.4.1. that it is the directors' responsibility to prepare financial statements that fairly present the state of affairs of the company as at the end of the financial year and the profit or loss and cash flows for that period;

8.4.2. that the auditor is responsible for reporting on whether the financial statements are fairly presented;

8.4.3. that adequate accounting records and an effective system of internal controls and risk management have been maintained;

8.4.4. that appropriate accounting policies supported by reasonable and prudent judgments and estimates have been used consistently;

8.4.5. that applicable accounting standards have been adhered to or, if there has been any departure in the interest of fair presentation, this must not only be disclosed and explained but quantified;

8.4.6. that there is no reason to believe the business will not be a going concern in the year ahead or an explanation of any reasons otherwise; and

8.4.7. that the Code of Corporate Practices and Conduct has been adhered to or, if not, where there has not been compliance to give reasons.

9. Implementation of the Code

All boards and individual directors have a duty and responsibility to ensure that the principles set out in this Code are observed.

Encouraging Good Governance: Commonwealth Corporate Governance Principles

The Commonwealth Business Council has published corporate governance principles in association with the Commonwealth Association for Corporate Governance in the publication *Principles for Corporate Governance in the Commonwealth: Towards Global Competitiveness and Economic Accountability*. The Commonwealth corporate governance principles are given below.

COMMONWEALTH CORPORATE GOVERNANCE PRINCIPLES

The board should:

Principle 1: Exercise leadership, enterprise, integrity and judgement in directing the corporation so as to achieve continuing prosperity for the corporation and to act in the best interest of the business enterprise in a manner based on transparency, accountability and responsibility;

Principle 2: Ensure that through a managed and effective process board appointments are made that provide a mix of proficient directors, each of whom is able to add value and to bring independent judgement to bear on the decision-making process;

Principle 3: Determine the corporation's purpose and values, determine the strategy to achieve its purpose and to implement its values in order to ensure that it survives and thrives, and ensure that procedures and practices are in place that protect the corporation's assets and reputation;

Principle 4: Monitor and evaluate the implementation of strategies, policies, management performance criteria and business plans;

Principle 5: Ensure that the corporation complies with all relevant laws, regulations and codes of best business practice;

Principle 6: Ensure that the corporation communicates with shareholders and other stakeholders effectively;

Principle 7: Serve the legitimate interests of the shareholders of the corporation and account to them fully;

Principle 8: Identify the corporation's internal and external stakeholders and agree a policy, or policies, determining how the corporation should relate to them;

Principle 9: Ensure that no one person or block of persons has unfettered power and that there is an appropriate balance of power and authority on the board which is, inter alia, usually reflected by separating the roles of chief executive officer and chairman, and by having a balance between executive and non-executive directors;

Principle 10: Regularly review processes and procedures to ensure the effectiveness of its internal systems of control, so that its decision-making capability and the accuracy of its reporting and financial results are maintained at a high level at all times;

Principle 11: Regularly assess its performance and effectiveness as a whole, and that of the individual directors, including the chief executive officer;

Principle 12: Appoint the chief executive officer and at least participate in the appointment of senior management, ensure the motivation and protection of intellectual capital intrinsic to the corporation, ensure that there is adequate training in the corporation for management and employees, and a succession plan for senior management;

Principle 13: Ensure that all technology and systems used in the corporation are adequate to properly run the business and for it to remain a meaningful competitor;

Principle 14: Identify key risk areas and key performance indicators of the business enterprise and monitor these factors;

Principle 15: Ensure annually that the corporation will continue as a going concern for its next fiscal year.

19
The OECD Principles of Corporate Governance

> Corporate governance can be defined in a dual context. On the one hand it is a set of behavioural relationships through which enterprises are directed and controlled. Organisational know-how, managerial talent and personal incentives are important elements in this web. But it can also be described in terms of the public and private rules that specify the distribution of rights and responsibilities among different participants in an enterprise, such as managers, the board, the shareholders, the employees and other stakeholders. I believe that one of the key advantages of the OECD Principles of Corporate Governance is that they address both the behavioural and regulatory aspects of the corporate governance debate.
>
> *Seiichi Kondo, Deputy Secretary-General of the OECD* [1]

Type Non-binding principles; process- and performance-oriented

Strength Clarity

Keywords Shareholders • Stakeholders • Disclosure • Transparency • Board of directors • Corporate governance

19.1 Background

Endorsed in 1999 by the Organisation for Economic Co-operation and Development (OECD), the Principles of Corporate Governance (hereafter in this chapter

1 'Opening Remarks to the Eurasian Corporate Governance Roundtable', www.gaap.ru/biblio/icar/112000/015e.htm, 2000.

referred to as the Principles) represent the first initiative by an intergovernmental organisation to develop guiding principles in the field of corporate governance. The Principles are directed at a wide audience, including governments, companies, investors, business groups and others. The Principles are accepted by the Financial Stability Forum as one of its 12 key international standards[2] and have also been endorsed by the World Bank and the International Monetary Fund (IMF). Moreover, they have formed the basis for many national principles.

The OECD promotes policies that contribute to economic growth and development. Founded in 1961, the OECD is an organisation of governments from 30 countries (for a full list of member countries, see footnote 3 on page 53). The OECD has also made a significant contribution to corporate responsibility by developing several CR-related principles, including the OECD Guidelines for Multinational Enterprises (see Chapter 2) and the OECD Convention on Combating Bribery of Foreign Public Officials in International Business Transactions (see Chapter 17).

The OECD makes it clear that the Principles represent minimum standards. The Principles address the following issues:

- The rights of shareholders
- The equitable treatment of shareholders
- The role of stakeholders
- Disclosure and transparency
- The responsibility of the board of directors

19.2 Strengths and weaknesses

The Principles were drafted so as to be a clear and accessible reference point for considering corporate governance arrangements. They are drafted in the form of aspirational principles and avoid prescription. They are therefore applicable in countries with widely varying institutions, legal systems and corporate governance traditions. The Principles were agreed following extensive consultation among key stakeholders so that they enjoy widespread support.

19.3 Companies to which the OECD Principles of Corporate Governance apply

The OECD Principles apply to all companies.

---

2   www.fsforum.org/compendium/key_standards_for_sound_financial_system.html

19.4 Questions posed and answered

The OECD Principles address the following questions:

- What are the fundamental rights of shareholders?
- What is the role of stakeholders in the corporate governance framework?
- What constitutes adequate disclosure and transparency standards for companies?
- What are the responsibilities and functions of the board of directors or the supervisory board?

19.5 The promise and the challenge

The G8 and the G22 have asked the OECD and the World Bank to promote corporate governance in emerging markets. To achieve this, the OECD and the World Bank have developed roundtables to discuss corporate governance standards,[3] resulting in white papers setting priorities for each region.[4] The challenge is now for the countries in each region to design, implement and enforce policies to improve their corporate governance arrangements. The work of the roundtables, supported by the OECD, will now shift to monitoring implementation and comparing experiences (www.oecd.org).

The challenge for the OECD Principles (and for corporate governance in general) will be to evolve to deal adequately with new issues arising in the corporate landscape. To this end, the Principles are being reviewed during 2003 and into 2004 through a transparent and open process,[5] with a revised version expected to be agreed in 2004.

Additional resources

Websites

OECD Corporate Governance Principles:
www.oecd.org/department/0,2688,en_2649_34813_1_1_1_1_1,00.html.
OECD Corporate Governance Principles (text):
www.oecd.org/document/62/0,2340,en_2649_34795_1912830_1_1_1_1,00.html

3   www.oecd.org/department/0,2688,en_2649_34813_1_1_1_1_1,00.html
4   *Ibid.*
5   *Ibid.*

OECD Principles of Corporate Governance*

I. THE RIGHTS OF SHAREHOLDERS

The corporate governance framework should protect shareholders' rights.

A. Basic shareholder rights include the right to: 1) secure methods of ownership registration; 2) convey or transfer shares; 3) obtain relevant information on the corporation on a timely and regular basis; 4) participate and vote in general shareholder meetings; 5) elect members of the board; and 6) share in the profits of the corporation.

B. Shareholders have the right to participate in, and to be sufficiently informed on, decisions concerning fundamental corporate changes such as: 1) amendments to the statutes, or articles of incorporation or similar governing documents of the company; 2) the authorisation of additional shares; and 3) extraordinary transactions that in effect result in the sale of the company.

C. Shareholders should have the opportunity to participate effectively and vote in general shareholder meetings and should be informed of the rules, including voting procedures, that govern general shareholder meetings:

1. Shareholders should be furnished with sufficient and timely information concerning the date, location and agenda of general meetings, as well as full and timely information regarding the issues to be decided at the meeting.

2. Opportunity should be provided for shareholders to ask questions of the board and to place items on the agenda at general meetings, subject to reasonable limitations.

3. Shareholders should be able to vote in person or in absentia, and equal effect should be given to votes whether cast in person or in absentia.

D. Capital structures and arrangements that enable certain shareholders to obtain a degree of control disproportionate to their equity ownership should be disclosed.

---

* (1) The rights of shareholders, page 19; (2) The equitable treatment of shareholders, page 32; (3) The role of stakeholders in corporate governance, page 22; (4) Disclosure and transparency, page 23; and (5) The responsibility of the board, page 24 reprinted with permission from 'The OECD Principles of Corporate Governance', 1999 (Part One). © OECD 1999.

E. Markets for corporate control should be allowed to function in an efficient and transparent manner.

   1. The rules and procedures governing the acquisition of corporate control in the capital markets, and extraordinary transactions such as mergers, and sales of substantial portions of corporate assets, should be clearly articulated and disclosed so that investors understand their rights and recourse. Transactions should occur at transparent prices and under fair conditions that protect the rights of all shareholders according to their class.

   2. Anti-take-over devices should not be used to shield management from accountability.

F. Shareholders, including institutional investors, should consider the costs and benefits of exercising their voting rights.

II. THE EQUITABLE TREATMENT OF SHAREHOLDERS

The corporate governance framework should ensure the equitable treatment of all shareholders, including minority and foreign shareholders. All shareholders should have the opportunity to obtain effective redress for violation of their rights.

A. All shareholders of the same class should be treated equally.

   1. Within any class, all shareholders should have the same voting rights. All investors should be able to obtain information about the voting rights attached to all classes of shares before they purchase. Any changes in voting rights should be subject to shareholder vote.

   2. Votes should be cast by custodians or nominees in a manner agreed upon with the beneficial owner of the shares.

   3. Processes and procedures for general shareholder meetings should allow for equitable treatment of all shareholders. Company procedures should not make it unduly difficult or expensive to cast votes.

B. Insider trading and abusive self-dealing should be prohibited.

C. Members of the board and managers should be required to disclose any material interests in transactions or matters affecting the corporation.

III. THE ROLE OF STAKEHOLDERS IN CORPORATE GOVERNANCE

The corporate governance framework should recognise the rights of stakeholders as established by law and encourage active co-operation between corporations and stakeholders in creating wealth, jobs, and the sustainability of financially sound enterprises.

A. The corporate governance framework should assure that the rights of stake-holders that are protected by law are respected.

B. Where stakeholder interests are protected by law, stakeholders should have the opportunity to obtain effective redress for violation of their rights.

C. The corporate governance framework should permit performance-enhancing mechanisms for stakeholder participation.

D. Where stakeholders participate in the corporate governance process, they should have access to relevant information.

IV. DISCLOSURE AND TRANSPARENCY

The corporate governance framework should ensure that timely and accurate disclosure is made on all material matters regarding the corporation, including the financial situation, performance, ownership, and governance of the company.

A. Disclosure should include, but not be limited to, material information on:

1. The financial and operating results of the company.

2. Company objectives.

3. Major share ownership and voting rights.

4. Members of the board and key executives, and their remuneration.

5. Material foreseeable risk factors.

6. Material issues regarding employees and other stakeholders.

7. Governance structures and policies.

B. Information should be prepared, audited, and disclosed in accordance with high quality standards of accounting, financial and non-financial disclosure, and audit.

C. An annual audit should be conducted by an independent auditor in order to provide an external and objective assurance on the way in which financial statements have been prepared and presented.

D. Channels for disseminating information should provide for fair, timely and cost-efficient access to relevant information by users.

V. THE RESPONSIBILITIES OF THE BOARD

The corporate governance framework should ensure the strategic guidance of the company, the effective monitoring of management by the board, and the board's accountability to the company and the shareholders.

A. Board members should act on a fully informed basis, in good faith, with due diligence and care, and in the best interest of the company and the shareholders.

B. Where board decisions may affect different shareholder groups differently, the board should treat all shareholders fairly.

C. The board should ensure compliance with applicable law and take into account the interests of stakeholders.

D. The board should fulfil certain key functions, including:

1. Reviewing and guiding corporate strategy, major plans of action, risk policy, annual budgets and business plans; setting performance objectives; monitoring implementation and corporate performance; and overseeing major capital expenditures, acquisitions and divestitures.

2. Selecting, compensating, monitoring and, when necessary, replacing key executives and overseeing succession planning.

3. Reviewing key executive and board remuneration, and ensuring a formal and transparent board nomination process.

4. Monitoring and managing potential conflicts of interest of management, board members and shareholders, including misuse of corporate assets and abuse in related party transactions.

5. Ensuring the integrity of the corporation's accounting and financial reporting systems, including the independent audit, and that appropriate systems of control are in place, in particular, systems for monitoring risk, financial control, and compliance with the law.

6. Monitoring the effectiveness of the governance practices under which it operates and making changes as needed.

7. Overseeing the process of disclosure and communications.

E. The board should be able to exercise objective judgement on corporate affairs independent, in particular, from management.

1. Boards should consider assigning a sufficient number of non-executive board members capable of exercising independent judgement to tasks where there is a potential for conflict of interest. Examples of such key responsibilities are financial reporting, nomination and executive and board remuneration.

2. Board members should devote sufficient time to their responsibilities.

F. In order to fulfil their responsibilities, board members should have access to accurate, relevant and timely information.

Part 7
Company codes of conduct

Company codes or unilaterally declared codes of conduct vary greatly in the degree to which they are embedded in the organisation. Although some statements are afterthoughts, some are becoming integrated into day-to-day decision-making. These statements also vary greatly in length, scope, audience, auditability and accessibility. Another important criterion is the degree to which they do or do not reference key foundation standards, such as the Universal Declaration of Human Rights (Chapter 5).

Company codes vary greatly by sector. Companies in the retail and/or clothing sector have codes of conduct for suppliers, whereas petroleum companies are more likely to have codes addressing human rights. Regardless of the sector, companies with unilaterally declared codes benefit greatly from the process standards and tools described in Part 9, such as the AccountAbility 1000 Framework (AA1000; Chapter 24, the 'Sustainability: Integrated Guidelines for Management' (SIGMA) project (Chapter 28) and the Global Reporting Initiative (GRI; Chapter 26).

The Human Rights Library of the University of Minnesota lists company codes of conduct,[1] all of which are accessible through the websites of these companies (see Table vii.1). It is an irony that the list begins with Ahold, considering the recent allegations that Ahold's operations in the USA have behaved unethically (see also page 298).

---

1 See the Library's web page at www1.umn.edu/humanrts/links/sicc.html; see also www.shell.com → About Shell → How We Work → Business Principles.

Company	Code or tool	Web address
Ahold	Mission, Vision and Common Values	ahold.com
The Body Shop	'Our Values'	thebodyshop.com
Boeing Company	Ethics and Business Conduct	boeing.com
BP Amoco	On the Side of Human Rights	bpamoco.com
Dillard Department Stores	Business Policy	dillards.com
The Dress Barn Inc. and its subsidiaries	Standards of Engagement	dressbarn.com
ExxonMobil	Corporate Guiding Principles	exxonmobil.com
Exxon	Environment, Health and Safety Policies, 1999	
Federated Department Stores	Statement of Corporate Policy	federated-fds.com
Fruit of the Loom	Contractor Code of Conduct	fruit.com
Gap Inc.	Code of Vendor Conduct	gap.com
Georgia-Pacific	Corporate Principles	gp.com
Halliburton Company and its subsidiaries	Code of Business Conduct	halliburton.com
Hartmarx*	Corporation Policy: Statement of Responsibility	hartmarx.com
Hennes & Mauritz (H&M)	Code of Conduct	hm.com
ITT Industries	Corporate Code of Conduct: Basic Principles	itt.com
JC Penney	Foreign Sourcing Requirements	jcpenney.com
Jones Apparel Group Inc.	Business Partner Standards, May 1996	jny.com
Kellwood	Policy on Business Conduct	kellwood.com
Kmart Corporation	Vendor Agreement, 13 June 1996	kmartcorp.com
Lands' End, Inc.	Standards of Business Conduct	landsend.com
Levi Strauss & Co.	Code of Conduct Global Sourcing and Operating Guidelines	levi.com
Liz Claiborne	Workplace Code of Conduct	lizclaiborne.com

* Hartmarx's policy is that of the American Apparel Manufacturers' Association (AAMA; americanapparel.com).

Table vii.1 Examples of self-imposed company codes of conduct (continued opposite)

Source: adapted from Human Rights Library, University of Minnesota, Minneapolis, MN, www1.umn.edu/humanrts/links/sicc.html

Company	Code or tool	Web address
Lockheed Martin	Corporation Code of Ethics and Business Conduct	lockheedmartin.com
Mobil	Environment, Health and Safety Statement, 1998	mobil.com
Oxford Industries Inc.	Contractor Sourcing Policy	oxfordinc.com
Reebok International Ltd	Human Rights Production Standards	reebok.com
Royal Dutch/Shell	Statement of General Business Principles Use-of-force Guidelines	shell.com
Russell Corporation	Vendor Policy	rusellcorp.com
Sara Lee Corporation	Supplier Selection Guidelines	saralee.com
Sears, Roebuck & Co.	Import Buying Policy and Procedures	sears.com
South African Beers (SAB)	Corporate Code of Conduct	sabmiller.com
Spiegel	Standards for Business Partnerships	spiegel.com
TotalFina	Health, Safety and Environment Charter	
Total	General Policy Regarding the Management of Human Resources	totalfinaelf.com
Total Myanmar Exploration and Production	Code of Conduct	totalfinaelf.com/us/html/de/ya/de ya4-1c.htm
Unocal	Statement of Principles	unocal.com
VF Corporation	Contractor Terms of Engagement, 8 July 1996	vfc.com
Wal-Mart Stores Inc.	Standards for Vendor Partners	walmart.com
WARNACO	Business Partner Terms of Engagement and Guidelines for Country Selection	warnaco.com
WMC	Code of Conduct Indigenous Peoples Policy	wmc.com
Woolworth Corporation	Contractor Certificate	woolworths.co.uk

Table vii.1 (continued)

20
Shell's Business Principles

What is remarkable about Shell's Business Principles is the degree to which Shell staff around the world are aware of the Principles and the values of the company. This is quite unusual.

Gemma Crijns, Nyenrode University and Amnesty International Business Group[1]

Type   Principles, company-specific; performance-oriented

Strength   Clarity

Keywords   Economic principles • Business integrity • Political activities • Health, safety and environment • Community • Competition • Stakeholders

20.1 Background

First published in 1976, Shell's Business Principles constitute a living document that has evolved over time. The Principles are derived from values of honesty, integrity and respect for people. One of the most significant aspects of the Principles is the section on 'responsibilities', in which Shell identifies its five key stakeholders: shareholders, customers, employees, those with whom Shell does business, and society.

The Principles cover a very wide range of issues, including economic principles, business integrity, political activities, health, safety, environment, community and competition. According to Mark Wade of Shell:

---

1 Personal communication with the author by Gemma Crijns, Nyenrode University, Breukelen, The Netherlands, 22 May 2003.

the Principles represent the magnetic north of the company, giving the employees a benchmark on what the company stands for and making clear the behaviour expected of all Shell employees in their business dealings large or small wherever Shell operates around the world).[2]

With operations in 140 countries, Shell has to ensure its Principles resonate with staff worldwide, with wide-ranging cultural and religious differences.

The Principles have broken new ground in several respects. According to Geoffrey Chandler, a key force behind the Principles:

We were pioneers among transnational companies in doing this. It took a year's discussion. The process of involving both the centre and the operating companies in that discussion was as important as the eventual product.[3]

20.2 Strengths and weaknesses

The Principles are a living document in that they continue to change over time. They have been through six revisions. Shell's Principles are grounded in management systems. For example, on health and safety and the environment, the Principles state that 'Shell companies have a systematic approach to health, safety and environmental management in order to achieve continuous performance improvement' (Principle #6; see page 339).

Shell is active in an array of corporate responsibility (CR) initiatives (see Fig. 20.1) and organisations, including, among others, the UN Global Compact (see Chapter 4) the World Business Council for Sustainable Development (WBCSD, www.wbcsd. org), the Voluntary Principles on Security and Human Rights (see Chapter 6) and the Business Principles for Countering Bribery (see Chapter 18).

It would be helpful to stakeholders if the Principles were to list commitments to other codes and standards, or to provide information on this in a document attached to the Principles. (Note, however, that Shell does list the main codes and standards that it supports in its *Shell Report*.) It is unfortunate that Shell's Principles do not reference the Universal Declaration of Human Rights (Chapter 5).

Additional resource

Website

Royal Dutch/Shell: www.shell.com.

---

2 Interview with Mark Wade, Shell Learning–Leadership Development, London, 11 April 2003.
3 E-mail to author from Sir Geoffrey Chandler, formerly of Shell and Amnesty International's Business Group, 18 April 2003.

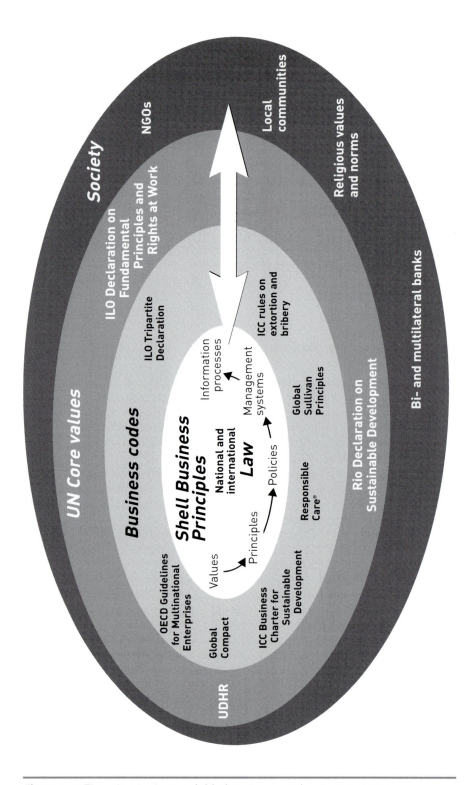

Figure 20.1 The role of voluntary initiatives for operational performance

Shell's Statement of
General Business Principles*

1. Objectives

The objectives of Shell companies are to engage efficiently, responsibly and profitably in the oil, gas, chemicals and other selected businesses and to participate in the search for and development of other sources of energy. Shell companies seek a high standard of performance and aim to maintain a long-term position in their respective competitive environments.

2. Responsibilities

Shell companies recognise five areas of responsibility:

a. To shareholders

To protect shareholders' investment, and provide an acceptable return.

b. To customers

To win and maintain customers by developing and providing products and services which offer value in terms of price, quality, safety and environmental impact, which are supported by the requisite technological, environmental and commercial expertise.

c. To employees

To respect the human rights of their employees, to provide their employees with good and safe conditions of work, and good and competitive terms and conditions of service, to promote the development and best use of human talent and equal opportunity employment, and to encourage the involvement of employees in the planning and direction of their work, and in the application of these principles within their

---

*   Reprinted with the permission of Royal Dutch/Shell.

company. It is recognised that commercial success depends on the full commitment of all employees.

d. To those with whom they do business

To seek mutually beneficial relationships with contractors, suppliers and in joint ventures and to promote the application of these principles in so doing. The ability to promote these principles effectively will be an important factor in the decision to enter into or remain in such relationships.

e. To society

To conduct business as responsible corporate members of society, to observe the laws of the countries in which they operate, to express support for fundamental human rights in line with the legitimate role of business and to give proper regard to health, safety and the environment consistent with their commitment to contribute to sustainable development.

These five areas of responsibility are seen as inseparable. Therefore it is the duty of management continuously to assess the priorities and discharge its responsibilities as best it can on the basis of that assessment.

3. Economic Principles

Profitability is essential to discharging these responsibilities and staying in business. It is a measure both of efficiency and of the value that customers place on Shell products and services. It is essential to the allocation of the necessary corporate resources and to support the continuing investment required to develop and produce future energy supplies to meet consumer needs. Without profits and a strong financial foundation it would not be possible to fulfil the responsibilities outlined above.

Shell companies work in a wide variety of changing social, political and economic environments, but in general they believe that the interests of the community can be served most efficiently by a market economy.

Criteria for investment decisions are not exclusively economic in nature but also take into account social and environmental considerations and an appraisal of the security of the investment.

4. Business Integrity

Shell companies insist on honesty, integrity and fairness in all aspects of their business and expect the same in their relationships with all those with whom they do business. The direct or indirect offer, payment, soliciting and acceptance of bribes in any form are unacceptable practices. Employees must avoid conflicts of interest between their private financial activities and their part in the conduct of company business. All business transactions on behalf of a Shell company must be reflected accurately and fairly in the accounts of the company in accordance with established procedures and be subject to audit.

5. Political Activities

a. Of companies

Shell companies act in a socially responsible manner within the laws of the countries in which they operate in pursuit of their legitimate commercial objectives.

Shell companies do not make payments to political parties, organisations or their representatives or take any part in party politics. However, when dealing with governments, Shell companies have the right and the responsibility to make their position known on any matter which affects themselves, their employees, their customers, or their shareholders. They also have the right to make their position known on matters affecting the community, where they have a contribution to make.

b. Of employees

Where individuals wish to engage in activities in the community, including standing for election to public office, they will be given the opportunity to do so where this is appropriate in the light of local circumstances.

6. Health, Safety and the Environment

Consistent with their commitment to contribute to sustainable development, Shell companies have a systematic approach to health, safety and environmental management in order to achieve continuous performance improvement.

To this end, Shell companies manage these matters as any other critical business activity, set targets for improvement, and measure, appraise and report performance.

7. The Community

The most important contribution that companies can make to the social and material progress of the countries in which they operate is in performing their basic activities as effectively as possible. In addition Shell companies take a constructive interest in societal matters which may not be directly related to the business. Opportunities for involvement—for example through community, educational or donations programmes—will vary depending upon the size of the company concerned, the nature of the local society, and the scope for useful private initiatives.

8. Competition

Shell companies support free enterprise. They seek to compete fairly and ethically and within the framework of applicable competition laws; they will not prevent others from competing freely with them.

9. Communication

Shell companies recognise that in view of the importance of the activities in which they are engaged and their impact on national economies and individuals, open communication is essential. To this end, Shell companies have comprehensive corporate information programmes and provide full relevant information about their activities to legitimately interested parties, subject to any overriding considerations of business confidentiality and cost.

21
Johnson & Johnson's 'Credo'

The Credo has become a trust mark. The public trusts the company to operate ethically and to create products that will help them live longer and more healthily. Similarly, potential recruits and existing staff have faith in the organisation to provide gainful employment and shareholders understand that taking care of people and the planet can lead to profits.

Ralph S. Larsen, Former Chairman, Johnson & Johnson[1]

Type Principles, company-specific, aspirational

Strength Stakeholder focus

Keywords Values • Responsibilities • Stakeholders

21.1 Background

At Johnson & Johnson there is no mission statement that hangs on the wall. Instead, for more than 50 years, a simple, one-page document—'Our Credo'—has guided the company's actions in fulfilling its responsibilities to customers, employees, the community and stockholders.

General Robert Wood Johnson, who guided Johnson & Johnson from a small, family-owned business to a worldwide enterprise, had a very perceptive view of a corporation's responsibilities beyond the manufacturing and marketing of products.

As early as 1935, in a pamphlet titled 'Try Reality', he urged his fellow industrialists to embrace what he termed 'a new industrial philosophy'. Johnson defined

1 www.jjeurope-csr.com/credo.htm

this as the corporation's responsibility to customers, employees, the community and stockholders.

But it was not until eight years later, in 1943, that Johnson wrote and first published the Johnson & Johnson Credo, a one-page document outlining these responsibilities in greater detail. Johnson ensured that the Credo was embraced by his company, and he urged his management to apply it as part of their everyday business philosophy.

The Credo, seen by business leaders and the media as being far-sighted, received wide public attention and acclaim. Putting customers first, and stockholders last, was a refreshing approach to the management of a business. But it should be noted that Johnson was a practical-minded businessman. He believed that by putting the customer first the business would be well served, and it was.

The corporation has drawn heavily on the strength of the Credo for guidance through the years, and at no time was this more evident than during the Tylenol® crises of 1982 and 1986, when the McNeil Consumer & Specialty Pharmaceuticals product (the number-one over-the-counter analgesic in the US market) was adulterated with cyanide by an extortioner and used as a murder weapon. With Johnson & Johnson's good name and reputation at stake, company managers and employees made countless decisions that were inspired by the philosophy embodied in the Credo. Company managers alerted consumers via the media not to purchase any type of Tylenol product until the extent of the tampering was known and withdrew 31 million bottles of the product with a retail value of more than US$100 million from the market. The company's reputation was preserved and the Tylenol acetaminophen business was regained.

Today the Credo lives on in Johnson & Johnson stronger than ever. Company employees now participate in a periodic survey and evaluation of how well the company performs its Credo responsibilities. These assessments are then fed back to the senior management, and, where there are shortcomings, corrective action is promptly taken.

Over the years, some of the language of the Credo has been updated and new areas recognising the environment and the balance between work and family have been added. But the spirit of the document remains the same today as when it was first written.

The Johnson & Johnson Credo is available in 36 languages spreading across Africa, Asia–Pacific, Eastern Europe, Europe, Latin America, Middle East and North America.

21.2 Strengths and weaknesses

Managers at Johnson & Johnson believe that the Credo:[2]

- Helps to unify the management team and the company's employees in achieving the corporate objectives

2   See www.jjeurope-csr.com/credo.htm.

- Provides a common set of values
- Serves as a constant reminder of the company's responsibilities to its customers, employees, communities and shareowners

The company's stock is included in the Dow Jones Sustainability Index (DJSI).

Additional resource

Website
Johnson & Johnson, 'Social responsibility': www.jnj.com/community/index.htm

Our Credo*

We believe our first responsibility is to the doctors, nurses and patients,
to mothers and fathers and all others who use our products and services.
In meeting their needs everything we do must be of high quality.
We must constantly strive to reduce our costs
in order to maintain reasonable prices.
Customers' orders must be serviced promptly and accurately.
Our suppliers and distributors must have an opportunity
to make a fair profit.

We are responsible to our employees,
the men and women who work with us throughout the world.
Everyone must be considered as an individual.
We must respect their dignity and recognize their merit.
They must have a sense of security in their jobs.
Compensation must be fair and adequate,
and working conditions clean, orderly and safe.
We must be mindful of ways to help our employees fulfill
their family responsibilities.
Employees must feel free to make suggestions and complaints.
There must be equal opportunity for employment, development
and advancement for those qualified.
We must provide competent management,
and their actions must be just and ethical.

We are responsible to the communities in which we live and work
and to the world community as well.
We must be good citizens—support good works and charities
and bear our fair share of taxes.
We must encourage civic improvements and better health and education.
We must maintain in good order
the property we are privileged to use,
protecting the environment and natural resources.

---

*   Reprinted with the permission of Johnson & Johnson.

Our final responsibility is to our stockholders.
Business must make a sound profit.
We must experiment with new ideas.
Research must be carried on, innovative programs developed
and mistakes paid for.
New equipment must be purchased, new facilities provided
and new products launched.
Reserves must be created to provide for adverse times.
When we operate according to these principles,
the stockholders should realize a fair return.

Part 8
Framework, sectoral and regional agreements

Codes of conduct require new social alliances.

Ingeborg Wick[1]

Part 8 will focus on:

- Framework agreements

- Sectoral and regional agreements

In the following chapters, a general discussion of such agreements will be provided, followed by case-study examples.

Framework agreements, like sectoral and regional agreements, are forming new social alliances between stakeholders. These social alliances serve to foster trust and promote enhanced and more regular communication between a diverse range of actors. If well formulated, these new partnerships will succeed in preventing conflicts before they arise.

---

1   *Workers' Tool or PR Ploy? A Guide to Codes of International Labour Practice* (Bonn/Siegburg: Friedrich Ebert Foundation and Südwind Institut für Ökonomie und Ökumene, 3rd rev. edn, 2003, www.fes.de): 24.

22
Framework agreements

[Framework] agreements provide the basis for future global dialogue and a framework for tackling individual problems as they crop up. They are the way forward in democratising the multi-nationals.

Philip Jennings, General Secretary,
Union Network International[1]

Type   Negotiated agreement, performance-oriented

Strength Institutionalises consultation and builds trust

Keywords Labour • Trade unions • ILO conventions

22.1 Background

Global framework agreements are bilateral agreements between a multinational company (MNC) and the international trade union, or global union federation (GUF), that represents workers within the company. In a number of cases, the agreement also involves as a signatory the national union within the country in which the MNC has its home base. Since 1988, 20 companies have signed framework agreements, and they are becoming more common (see Table 22.1).

These agreements are based on conventions of the International Labour Organisation (ILO) and seek to establish a 'continual working relationship and dialogue' (IFBWW 2003: 2) between the trade union and the MNC. According to the International Federation of Building and Wood Workers (IFBWW), which accounts for a quarter of all such agreements (see Table 22.1):

---

1 Quoted in Graham and Bibby 2002.

Company	Country	Sector	Global union federation	Year
Danone	France	Food processing	IUF	1988
Accor	France	Hotels	IUF	1995
Ikea	Sweden	Furniture	IFBWW	1998
Statoil	Norway	Oil	ICEM	1998
Faber-Castell	Germany	Office materials	IFBWW	1999
Freudenberg	Germany	Chemicals	ICEM	2000
Hochtief	Germany	Construction	IFBWW	2000
Carrefour	France	Retailing	UNI	2001
Chiquita	USA	Agriculture	IUF	2001
OTE Telecom	Greece	Telecommunications	UNI	2001
Skanska	Sweden	Construction	IFBWW	2001
Telefonica	Spain	Telecommunications	UNI	2001
Merloni	Italy	Metals	IMF	2002
Endesa	Spain	Power	ICEM	2002
Ballast-Nedam	Netherlands	Construction	IFBWW	2002
Fonterra	New Zealand	Dairy	IUF	2002
Volkswagen	Germany	Automobiles	IMF	2002
Norske Skog	Norway	Paper	ICEM	2002
AngloGold	South Africa	Mining	ICEM	2002
DaimlerChrysler	Germany	Automobiles	IMF	2002
Eni	Italy	Energy	ICEM	2002

ICEM   International Federation of Chemical, Energy, Mine and General Workers' Unions
IFBWW   International Federation of Building and Wood Workers
IMF   International Metalworkers' Federation
IUF   International Union of Food, Agricultural, Hotel, Restaurant, Catering, Tobacco and Allied Workers'
        Associations
UNI   Union Network International

Table 22.1 Framework agreements: chronological list, as up to the end of 2002

Sources: Briefing by the International Federation of Building and Wood Workers on framework agreements
(www.ifbww.org); correspondence with the International Federation of Chemical, Energy, Mine and
General Workers' Unions

framework agreements are not intended to substitute for national
law or collective bargaining; they are intended to create a framework
within which all workers are guaranteed established international
minimum standards for work (IFBWW 2003: 2).

Framework agreements generally commit the company to comply with national
legislation and ILO conventions and recommendations that relate to the company's work. Such agreements usually acknowledge that the MNC bears respon-

sibility for the conditions under which its products are made, even if the company outsources a majority of its products.

Framework agreements can include provisions on monitoring. For example, the agreement between Ikea and the IFBWW establishes a monitoring group composed of Ikea and trade-union employees, who conduct site visits to Ikea suppliers. With 287 affiliates in 124 countries, the IFBWW has a strong network to assist in monitoring (see www.ifbww.org). These monitoring arrangements serve to prevent conflict; when problems arise, the framework agreement allows for resolution without leading to damaging exposure. Secretary-General of the IFBWW, Anita Normark, says that most problems are resolved internally, between the partners, of the agreement.[2]

22.2 Strengths and weaknesses

Framework agreements complement company codes of conduct and other standards by providing mechanisms for monitoring and institutionalising dialogue. The relationship between Accor and the International Union of Food, Agricultural, Hotel, Restaurant, Catering, Tobacco and Allied Workers Associations (IUF) helped to reduce the anti-trade union nature of the company's operations in the USA and Australia (Wick 2003: 20).

22.3 Companies to which framework agreements apply

It is interesting to note that the majority of the framework agreements are signed by Scandinavian and Northern European companies with a strong tradition of social dialogue. Also, the companies signing such agreements tend to have strong trade unions, whereas sectors where trade unions are weak tend to rely more on codes of conduct than on framework agreements. The forestry sector has been successful in developing framework agreements because it is building on the success of the sustainable forestry movement, which has already fostered awareness about social and environmental issues.

---

2 Interview with Anita Normark, Secretary-General, International Federation of Building and Wood Workers, 14 March 2003.

22.4 Questions posed and answered

Framework agreements pose the following question:

- What are the key areas of agreement between a multinational company and its global union federation?

22.5 The promise and the challenge

The challenge for framework agreements will be to gain visibility and recognition. They are not well known or well understood, despite their effectiveness. When successful, such agreements can serve as confidence-building measures.

22.6 Case study: agreement between the Norwegian Oil and Petrochemical Workers' Union, of the International Federation of Chemical, Energy, Mine and General Workers' Unions, and Statoil

With 16,000 employees in 21 countries (Westgaard 2001: 25), Statoil is a Norwegian company. According to its website (www.statoil.com), Statoil is one of the world's largest net sellers of crude oil and is also a key supplier of natural gas within the European market. Statoil has a policy of 'zero harm to the people or the environment [and] zero accidents or losses'.[3]

In 1998, Statoil signed an agreement with the International Federation of Chemical, Energy, Mine and General Workers' Unions (ICEM). The agreement covers labour, human rights and the environment.[4] The goal of the agreement is to:

> create an open channel of information between ICEM and Statoil management about industrial relations issues in order to continuously improve and develop good work practice in Statoil's worldwide operations (Statoil undated: 5).

The agreement was revised in 2001 in order to comply with the Global Compact (Chapter 4).

---

3 See the 'Our Values' health, safety and the environment poster, at www.statoil.com → Our values → Health, safety and the environment → About HSE → Our objectives.

4 On page 1 of the guiding questions of the Global Compact Learning Forum (www.unglobalcompact.org), the agreement is referred to as the Statoil–ICEM Agreement.

The most significant aspect of the agreement is that it sets a global policy to guide and empower decisions at the local level. Labour issues need to be resolved as close as possible to the plant or worksite—but local practice is varied. With an agreement in place, each operation knows the company's policy and can make decisions and negotiate with a consistent message.

The GUF concerned, ICEM, represents 20 million workers in 110 countries.[5] The agreement was negotiated between the Norwegian Oil and Petrochemical Workers' Union (NOPEF), the central union in Norway and a part of ICEM.

Through the agreement, Statoil provides assurances that it will:

1. Protect the rights of workers to be represented by a trade union of their own choice and to bargain collectively (Principle 3 of the Global Compact [see page 80], and ILO Conventions 87 and 98)

2. Avoid use of forced labour or bonded labour (Principle 4 of the Global Compact, and ILO Conventions 29 and 105)

3. Avoid use of child labour (Principle 5 of the Global Compact, and ILO Convention 138)

4. Promote diversity and avoid discrimination (Principle 6 of the Global Compact, and ILO Conventions 100 and 111)

5. Commit to paying fair wages and benefits according to good industry standards in each country

6. Provide a safe and healthy work environment

7. Support a precautionary approach to environmental challenges (Principle 7 of the Global Compact)

8. Undertake initiatives to promote greater environmental responsibility (Principle 8 of the Global Compact)

9. Encourage the development and diffusion of environmentally friendly technologies (Principle 9 of the Global Compact)

The agreement includes provisions for effective management and oversight. These include:

● Annual meetings at a senior level of the parties to the agreement

● Training programmes in health, safety and environment for trade-union representatives, and management training

● A commitment to notify subcontractors and licensees of the agreement and to seek their compliance

The business benefits of such an agreement are significant. According to Geir Westgaard, Vice-President of Statoil, the agreement helps the company to manage complexity (Westgaard 2001). For a global company, such an agreement makes it easier to deal with local challenges by developing a global approach. Other bene-

5   www.icem.org/uniteen.html

fits include decreasing risk and thereby increasing protection of the Statoil reputation and licence to operate (Westgaard 2001: 25). By securing good industrial relations, Statoil has faced few conflicts and has increased its retention of employees and job satisfaction (Statoil undated: 5).

Reg Green, responsible for health, safety and environmental affairs at ICEM, believes that global agreements highlight the importance of—and the need for agreements to be based on—genuine transparency, honesty, co-operation, participation and conflict identification and resolution, vital elements of any corporate social responsibility commitment. Signatories to such agreements recognise that there are two sides to such agreements: the commitments and obligations of the company on the one hand, and those of the relevant GUF on the other. According to Reg Green, for any framework agreement to be effective, it is a *sine qua non* that both sides to the agreement derive benefit from it.[6]

References

Graham, I., and A. Bibby (2000) 'Global Labour Agreements: A Framework for Rights', *World of Work* 45 (December 2002, www-ilo-mirror.cornell.edu/public/english/bureau/inf/magazine/45/rights.htm).

IFBWW (International Federation of Building and Wood Workers) (2003) IFBWW *Strategy on Multinational Corporations (MNC): A Co-ordinated Approach to Framework Agreements and Company Codes of Conduct, Corporate Campaigns and European Works Councils* (Carouge, Switzerland: IFBWW, www.ifbww.org/files/startegy-mnc-en.pdf [*sic*]).

Statoil (undated) *The Exchange of Information and the Development of Good Working Practice within Statoil Worldwide Operations* (submission to the Global Compact Learning Forum; Stavanger, Norway: Statoil).

Westgaard, G. (2001) 'Charting the Way Forward', presentation at the meeting of the Global Compact Learning Forum, Denham, UK, 29–30 October 2001.

Wick, I. (2003) *Workers' Tool or PR Ploy? A Guide to Codes of International Labour Practice* (Bonn/Siegburg: Friedrich Ebert Foundation and Südwind Institut für Ökonomie und Ökumene, 3rd rev. edn, www.fes.de).

6 Personal communication with the author.

Agreement between NOPEF/ICEM and Statoil on the Exchange of Information and the Development of Good Working Practice within Statoil Worldwide Operations*

1 PREAMBLE

This agreement is set up by NOPEF (Norsk Olje og Petrokjemisk Fagforbund), as the central bargaining union for Statoil operations in Norway and NOPEF on behalf of ICEM (International Federation of Chemical, Energy, Mine and General Workers' Unions) which represents trade unions organising Statoil employees in the Company worldwide, and Statoil.

The purpose of the agreement is to create an open channel of information between NOPEF/ICEM and Statoil Management about industrial relations issues in order to continuously improve and develop good work practices in Statoil's worldwide operations.

This agreement covers all activities where Statoil has direct control. Where Statoil does not have overall control, it will exercise its best efforts in order to secure compliance with the standards set out in this agreement. Statoil will notify its subcontractors and licensees of this agreement and encourage compliance with the standards.

Based on the Parties' common recognition of fundamental human rights and Statoil's own values, the purpose is to monitor the practical application of the agreed principles and to discuss any improvements in the working practices or any positive contribution the Parties may make to the eradication of poverty through economic and social progress.

---

* Reprinted with the permission of ICEM.

2 HUMAN RIGHTS, INDUSTRIAL RELATIONS AND HSE ISSUES

Statoil and NOPEF/ICEM affirm their support for fundamental human rights in the community and in the place of work. Furthermore, the Parties recognise the importance of protecting safety, health and well-being at work, and share the concern about the impact of exploitation that production, use and disposal may have upon the natural and human environment. This agreement is intended to ensure the best possible standards of protection for those employed in our business.

The respect of human rights includes:

- the right of every employee to be represented by a union of his or her own choice and the basic trade union rights as defined by ILO Convention 87 and 98 covering freedom of association and the right to organise, as well as the right to engage in collective bargaining. Statoil therefore agrees not to oppose efforts to unionise its employees

- a commitment not to employ forced or bonded labour as proscribed in the ILO Conventions 29 and 105 or otherwise

- a commitment to employ no child labour as proscribed by ILO Convention 138

- a commitment to exercise equality of opportunity and treatment in employment, including equal remuneration for men and women for work of equal value, and the prevention of discrimination* in respect of employment and occupation as required by ILO Conventions 100 and 111 respectively

- a commitment to pay fair wages and benefits according to good industry standards in the country concerned

- a commitment to provide a safe and healthy work environment, deploying common "best practice" standards.

3 ENVIRONMENTAL ISSUES

Statoil and NOPEF/ICEM will cooperate to ensure that Statoil activities are carried out with the fullest possible regard for the environment. In particular this will include:

- supporting a precautionary approach to environmental challenges
- undertaking initiatives to promote greater environmental responsibility
- encouraging the development and diffusion of environmentally friendly technologies.

4 IMPLEMENTATION

4.1 Annual Meeting

Statoil and NOPEF/ICEM will meet annually to review practice in the area of the agreed principles and follow up this Agreement. The purpose shall be to discuss the issues covered by this agreement with a view to jointly agreeing actions that will further develop good working practices. In addition to the general industrial issues and HSE matters, the following topics may be addressed:

- general corporate policy on employment, occupational health, safety and environmental issues affecting those within the company and, as appropriate, between the company and its related companies including suppliers and subcontractors

- the economic and financial position of the company and the development of its business and related activities

- training matters

- issues affecting the exercise of trade union rights

- any other issues mutually agreed upon.

Participants at these annual meetings will normally be 4-5 senior officials from NOPEF/ICEM and relevant managers from Statoil.

4.2 Local Industrial Relations Practice

The agreement between the Parties shall be applied consistently throughout Statoil operations but is not intended to replace or interfere with local industrial relations practice related to information, problem-solving and negotiations. The Parties to the agreement respect the principle that industrial relations issues are best resolved as close as possible to the place of work.

4.3 Training Programmes

NOPEF/ICEM and Statoil will cooperate in developing joint training arrangements covering those issues—and their implementation—dealt with in this agreement. This will include appropriate training in health, safety and environmental best practice for union delegates from countries where Statoil is the operator. It will also include Management training programmes within Statoil. The cost of NOPEF/ICEM involvement in Statoil training programmes may be covered by Statoil, subject to agreement.

4.4 Union Delegates

Statoil will refrain from dismissing or otherwise discriminating against union delegates, identified as such by the Parties, or employees providing information relevant to the observance and implementation of this Agreement. All union delegates must agree to respect the commercial confidentiality of information disclosed in the exercise of their duties.

Statoil will assist union delegates in the performance of their functions by making available relevant information and other agreed facilities. When it is necessary to take time off from work to perform these functions this will be agreed upon locally and may be given as paid time off within the framework of local agreements.

Statoil may also facilitate the opportunity for union representatives from Statoil operations to meet as necessary to discuss the application and future development of this agreement.

4.5 Information

NOPEF/ICEM will distribute copies of this Agreement to all its member unions that organise employees in Statoil companies around the world, and will broadly publicise the existence of the Agreement and explain its implications to its unions in the Company.

Statoil will in the same manner distribute copies of this Agreement to all Statoil offices in local languages of the countries concerned and will inform local management of the existence and contents of this Agreement.

Any external information about this Agreement shall be mutually agreed by the Parties.

4.6 Administration

The President of NOPEF on behalf of ICEM and the Vice President Labour Relations in Statoil are responsible for the administration of this Agreement.

5 DURATION AND EVALUATION

The duration of this agreement is two years, after which this Agreement will be evaluated and may be prolonged for a new period.

Signed in Stavanger on 15th March 2001

Lars Myhre	Jostein Gaasemyr	Fred Higgs
NOPEF	**STATOIL**	**ICEM**

Note:

* Discrimination is defined as any distinction, exclusion, or preference made on the basis of race, colour, sex, religion, political opinion, national extraction or social origin, which has the effect of nullifying or impairing equality of opportunity or treatment.

23
Sectoral and regional agreements

Corporate responsibility will live or die based on the ability of
codes and standards to address industry-specific concerns. To
date, much work has been done to build global initiatives within a
general context, but more work is needed to build expertise on
sectoral and regional dimensions of corporate responsibility.

Deborah Leipziger[1]

Type   Generally performance-oriented, with commitments to take joint action

Strength Foster dialogue and alliances

23.1 Background

Of all of the types of initiatives profiled in this book, sectoral and regional agreements are the most difficult to track from outside the industry and/or region
involved. Sectoral agreements often develop as a result of intense media pressure.
A useful example is the case of the cocoa industry developing a joint project to
address forced child labour in West Africa for the harvesting of cocoa (see Section
23.6.1).

23.2 Strengths and weaknesses

Sectoral and regional agreements are able to forge partnerships and networks that
can build trust and awareness. Such agreements can serve to deepen the under-

---

1 Leipziger 2003.

standing of how particular issues in corporate responsibility affect a specific group of companies. Sectoral agreements can spawn organisations, such as the Marine Stewardship Council in the fisheries sector and the Forest Stewardship Council in the timber industry, described in Sections 23.6.3 and 23.6.4, respectively. Industry standards, such as Responsible Care® (Section 23.6.2), which is focused on the chemical industry, can be effective tools for industry associations for use in membership criteria.

Because of their specificity, sectoral tools can achieve a greater depth than can the more aspirational standards and can achieve a greater sense of cohesion and common purpose. At their worst, sectoral codes may serve the lowest common denominator within an industry body.

According to Jane Nelson of the John F. Kennedy School at Harvard University, sectoral codes are becoming more and more significant.[2] Because they cover a more narrowly defined group, regional and sectoral initiatives can develop common protocols, accreditation and certification systems, product labels and cases of best practice. The specificity of sectoral agreements can lead to standards that are prescriptive and specific.

23.3 Companies to which sectoral and regional agreements apply

Sectoral and regional agreements can be forged in any industry and within any region.

23.4 Questions posed and answered

Are there measures the industry or region can take to promote corporate responsibility (CR)? What types of mechanisms can institutionalise these measures (e.g. reporting, pilots, new organisations)?

23.5 The promise and the challenge

Global principles and guidelines will require more specific guidelines along sectoral lines. For example, the Global Reporting Initiative (Chapter 26) and Social

2 Interview with Jane Nelson, John F. Kennedy School, Harvard University, Cambridge, MA, 9 April 2003; at the time of the interview Jane Nelson was still working with the International Business Leaders' Forum.

Accountability 8000 (SA8000, Chapter 9) are among the many global and multi-sectoral initiatives that are developing sectoral supplements. Another challenge is communication between the industry and the public. Sectoral agreements may be less transparent than tools developed by non-governmental organisations (NGOs) or multilateral organisations.

23.6 Sectoral agreements: case studies

Sectoral agreements include:

- Those of the Fair Labor Association for the apparel and retail sectors (on the Fair Labor Association, see Chapter 10)
- Those of the Clean Clothes Campaign (see Chapter 12)
- Voluntary Principles on Human Rights and Security (see Chapter 6)
- That of the cocoa industry (see Section 23.6.1)
- Responsible Care® (see Section 23.6.2)
- That of the Marine Stewardship Council (see Section 23.6.3)
- That of the Forest Stewardship Council (see Section 23.6.4)
- Industry Model Code of the World Federation of Sporting Goods[3]

23.6.1 The International Cocoa Initiative: Working towards Responsible Labour Standards for Cocoa Growing

For a brief interval in April 2001, the world's attention focused on a boat thought to be carrying between 180 and 250 child slaves. Afloat in the Bight of Benin, the boat *MV Etireno* had left Cotonou, the capital of Benin, and had gone missing. When the boat was eventually located, there were only 43 children on board. Aid workers from Terre des Hommes interviewed some of the children on board and reported that the children were being sent to work in Gabon (ASI 2001). Although much about this case remains a mystery, the incident did serve to focus attention on forced child labour in West Africa.

According to the US State Department, 15,000 children between the ages of 9 and 12 have been sold into forced labour to harvest cocoa, cotton and coffee in the northern Ivory Coast in the past few years (Raghavan and Chatterjee 2001). Anti-Slavery International believes that there are tens of thousands of children being trafficked in West Africa, working in a range of industries, including cocoa, quarries and fishing (ASI 2001).

The linkage between what occurs at the global and national level and its impact at the rural level is critical for understanding that the situation will require part-

3 www.wfsgi.org/_wfsgi/new_site/about_us/codes/code_conduct.htm

The following organisations brokered the International Cocoa Initiative in July 2002:

- From the cocoa and chocolate industry:
  - The Association of the Chocolate, Biscuit and Confectionery Industries of the European Union
  - The Chocolate Manufacturers' Association of the USA and the National Confectioners' Association
  - The World Cocoa Foundation
  - The European Cocoa Association and others
  - The International Confectionery Association
  - The International Office of Cocoa, Chocolate and Confectionery
  - The Federation for Cocoa Commerce, London
  - The Cocoa Association of London
  - The Cocoa Merchants' Association of America
  - The Confectionery Manufacturers' Association of Canada

- From trade unions, international organisations and non-governmental organisations (NGOs):
  - The International Labour Organisation (ILO)
  - Free the Slaves
  - The Child Labour Coalition
  - The National Consumers League
  - Global March against Child Labour
  - The International Union of Food, Agricultural, Hotel, Restaurant, Catering, Tobacco and Allied Workers' Associations

The organisations listed above have developed a plan to address working conditions in the cocoa industry in West Africa, to include (Candy USA 2001):

- A study on working conditions
- An advisory group for that study
- A consultative group and the signing of a joint statement
- Pilot programmes in West Africa
- Enforcement, monitoring and public reporting
- A joint foundation
- A public certification system

Box 23.1 Organisations involved in the International Cocoa Initiative

nerships across countries and sectors. The cocoa industry mobilised a response to the crisis that can serve as an example to other industries on how to deal with complex social issues. Often, the greatest difficulty is access to accurate information on what is happening. The cocoa industry responded by assuring the world community[4] of its commitment to ILO Convention 182 concerning the Prohibition and Immediate Action for the Elimination of the Worst Forms of Child Labour,[5] by formulating a plan for surveying what is happening and by developing a credible certification system to ensure that cocoa is harvested without forced or child labour by 2005.

In many ways, the cocoa industry is breaking new ground:

> There has never been a comprehensive investigation of working conditions on West African cocoa farms, but there must be a scientifically valid and accurate picture of the situation in order to develop the most effective solutions (Candy USA 2001).

The study of working conditions will be conducted on 3,000 farms by the International Institute for Tropical Agriculture, with support from the US Agency for International Development (USAID). The initiative takes advantage of research work already under way. Based on the findings of the study, the initiative will change course if necessary.

The Advisory Group responsible for the survey includes representatives from the various governments involved, including Cote d'Ivoire, Nigeria, Ghana and Cameroon, along with representatives from the ILO, UNICEF, the World Bank, USAID and NGOs such as Free the Slaves. In addition to this group, a broader, consultative, group (see Box 23.1) will oversee the implementation of a plan of action and sign a joint statement. Based on the results of the survey, pilot programmes will be set up to develop responsible cocoa production. The group has an ambitious agenda: an enforcement, monitoring and public reporting system. The chocolate industry will provide funding for a foundation to assess best practice. By July 2005, the industry plans to have a system for public certification.

The cocoa industry partnership model offers several important lessons on how to respond in a crisis:

- Work within a multi-stakeholder framework, involving NGOs, industry, government and so on

- Refer to ILO conventions

- Take immediate action and set a timetable for action

23.6.2 Responsible Care®

Responsible Care was first conceived in Canada in 1985 to address public concern about the manufacture, distribution and use of chemicals. In 1988, the American Chemistry Council launched Responsible Care in the US. The focus of Responsible

---

4 See www.candyusa.org/Press/New/cl_summary.shtml.
5 www.ilo.org/public/english/standards/ipec/ratification/convention/text.htm

Care is to minimise risk by addressing environment, health and safety issues in an industry characterised as high-risk from a social and environmental perspective. A voluntary programme, Responsible Care includes: Guiding Principles, a management system, an independent third-party verification system, and performance indicators. Companies certified to the Responsible Care system can use the logo. In 2003, Responsible Care has been adopted in 47 countries.

Responsible Care®
Good Chemistry at Work

Responsible Care has become *de rigueur* for the chemical industry. While the initiative is 'voluntary', it has become the industry norm. This is due to the fact that, in order to join the American Chemistry Council, companies must adhere to Responsible Care. The programme also requires significant community outreach through the development of Community Advisory Panels. Companies benefit from sharing best practices (www.americanchemistry.com).

23.6.3 The Marine Stewardship Council's Principles and Criteria for Sustainable Fishing

Founded in 1997 by Unilever and WWF, the Marine Stewardship Council (MSC, www.msc.org) became an independent organisation in 1999. The MSC is a multi-stakeholder organisation that is 'seeking to harness consumer purchasing power to generate change and promote environmentally responsible stewardship of the world's most important renewable food source'.[6] Certification bodies accredited by the MSC undertake independent assessments of fisheries to its environmental standard for sustainable fishing. Products from fisheries that

Customer Licence Code MSCI0187
www.msc.org

pass this assessment can display the MSC's logo once the company wishing to do so has had undertaken a chain of custody certification to ensure traceability of the product from the fishery to the consumer .

The MSC has developed principles and criteria for sustainable fishing,[7] which are reproduced on page 367.

23.6.4 Forest Stewardship Council

As a multi-stakeholder organisation, the Forest Stewardship Council (FSC, www.fscoax.org) includes a wide range of views, from the timber trade to NGOs representing environmental and social concerns, indigenous peoples and certifiers. Founded in 1993, the FSC promotes sustainable forestry by accrediting certifiers that audit wood producers to assure that those producers pass the FSC Principles and Criteria.[8] Certified companies can display the FSC logo on their products and in their promotional materials.

6 See www.msc.org/html/ni_33.htm
7 www.msc.org/assets/docs/fishery%20certification?MSCprinciples&criteria.doc
8 www.fscoax.org/html/1-2.html

23.7 Regional agreements: case study

23.7.1 Asia–Pacific Economic Co-operation (APEC) Code of Business Conduct

The Asia–Pacific Economic Co-operation (APEC, www.apecsec.org.sg) seeks to promote open trade and co-operation in the Asia–Pacific region. With 21 members in Asia and the Americas, APEC countries account for 43.85% of global trade.

In 1999, a group of Asian business leaders issued a draft of the APEC Code of Business Conduct. This initiative is intended to serve as a model or aspirational code, but it also includes recommendations for concrete steps that companies can take to adopt the code and focuses on the area of corruption, referencing the Rules of Conduct to Combat Extortion and Bribery of the International Chamber of Commerce[9], the Caux Round Table 'Principles for Business'[10] and the OECD's Principles of Corporate Governance (see Chapter 19). The APEC Code articulates seven standards for corporate conduct:

1. **International and local communities.** A company must recognise its responsibilities toward the international and local communities within which it operates and the individuals that make up those communities.

2. **Respect for laws.** A company must respect international and domestic rules and recognise that some behaviour, although legal, may still have adverse consequences.

3. **Stakeholder responsibility.** A company must recognise the rights of stakeholders as established by laws and encourage active co-operation between companies and stakeholders in creating wealth, jobs, and the sustainability of financially sound enterprises.

4. **Responsibility for the environment.** A company must protect and, where possible, improve the environment within which it operates, promote sustainable development and prevent the wasteful use of natural resources.

5. **Free and fair competition.** A company must support free and fair competition in our industries and avoid anti-competitive actions.

6. **Company governance.** A company should implement a company governance framework that ensures timely and accurate disclosure on all material matters regarding the company.

7. **Illicit actions.** A company must not participate in or condone extortion, bribery, money laundering, or other corrupt practices.

9 www.iccwbo.org/home/extortion_bribery/rules.asp
10 www.cauxroundtable.org

While intended to supplement company codes of conduct, 'it is expected that the CEO of any enterprise using the APEC Business Code would sign the Code and formally agree to uphold the moral obligations it expresses'. The APEC code also includes policy recommendations for governments.

The APEC Code is limited in the area of accountability. It does not require companies to report to anyone but shareholders, nor does it include verification or monitoring of any kind.

The Code is very general about human rights and does not address child or forced labour. APEC is not a particularly transparent organisation—accessing information about the APEC Code, its signatories and content is not easy, but information may become available online at www.apecsec.org.sg.

References

ASI (Anti-Slavery International) (2001) 'Trafficked Children were on Benin "Slave Ship" ', 1 May 2001, available at www.antislavery.org/homepage/news/beninship010501.htm.

Candy USA (2001) 'Global Chocolate Industry Plan to Combat Abusive Child Labour', 1 October 2001, www.candyusa.org/Press/labour/labor_issue.shtml, updated 1 December 2001.

Leipziger, D. (2003) *Sustainable Futures* (draft; London: Morley Fund Management, Winter 2003, forthcoming).

Raghavan, S., and S. Chatterjee (2001) 'A Slave Labour Force of Youths', *Philadelphia Inquirer*, 24 June 2001.

Additional resources

Websites

Forest Stewardship Council: www.fscoax.org
Marine Stewardship Council: www.msc.org
Responsible Care®: www.icca-chem.org

Statement on Responsible Care®
of the International Council of Chemical Associations*

Responsible Care is the voluntary initiative of the global chemical industry in which companies, through their national associations, commit to work together to:

- continuously improve their company's and the chemical industry's performance in protecting people and the environment throughout the life cycle of their products and processes;

- contribute to the sustainable development of local communities and of society as a whole;

- inform their publics of the risks and benefits of what they make and do, and about their performance, achievements and challenges;

- dialogue and work with their stakeholders at the local, national and international level to understand and address their concerns and aspirations;

- cooperate with governments and organizations at all levels in the development and implementation of effective regulations and standards, and to meet or exceed those requirements;

- extend Responsible Care to all those who manage chemicals.

* Reprinted with the permission of the International Council of Chemical Associations.

MSC Principles and Criteria
for Sustainable Fishing*

At the centre of the MSC is a set of *Principles and Criteria for Sustainable Fishing* which are used as a standard in a third party, independent and voluntary certification programme. These were developed by means of an extensive, international consultative process through which the views of stakeholders in fisheries were gathered.

These Principles reflect a recognition that a sustainable fishery should be based upon:

- The maintenance and re-establishment of healthy populations of targeted species;

- The maintenance of the integrity of ecosystems;

- The development and maintenance of effective fisheries management systems, taking into account all relevant biological, technological, economic, social, environmental and commercial aspects; and

- Compliance with relevant local and national local laws and standards and international understandings and agreements

The Principles and Criteria are further designed to recognise and emphasise that management efforts are most likely to be successful in accomplishing the goals of conservation and sustainable use of marine resources when there is full co-operation among the full range of fisheries stakeholders, including those who are dependent on fishing for their food and livelihood.

On a voluntary basis, fisheries which conform to these Principles and Criteria will be eligible for certification by independent MSC-accredited certifiers. Fish processors, traders and retailers will be encouraged to make public commitments to purchase fish products only from certified sources. This will allow consumers to select fish products with the confidence that they come from sustainable, well managed sources. It will also benefit the fishers and the fishing industry who depend on the abundance of fish stocks, by providing market incentives to work towards sustainable practices. Fish processors, traders and retailers who buy from certified sustainable sources will in turn benefit from the assurance of continuity of future supply and hence sustainability of their own businesses.

The MSC promotes equal access to its certification programme irrespective of the scale of the fishing operation. The implications of the size, scale, type, location and

---

* Reprinted with the permission of the Marine Stewardship Council.

intensity of the fishery, the uniqueness of the resources and the effects on other ecosystems will be considered in every certification.

The MSC further recognises the need to observe and respect the long-term interests of people dependent on fishing for food and livelihood to the extent that it is consistent with ecological sustainability, and also the importance of fisheries management and operations being conducted in a manner consistent with established local, national, and international rules and standards as well as in compliance with the MSC Principles and Criteria.

Preamble

The following Principles and Criteria are intended to guide the efforts of the Marine Stewardship Council towards the development of sustainable fisheries on a global basis. They were developed assuming that a sustainable fishery is defined, for the purposes of MSC certification, as one that is conducted in such a way that:

- it can be continued indefinitely at a reasonable level;
- it maintains and seeks to maximise, ecological health and abundance;
- it maintains the diversity, structure and function of the ecosystem on which it depends as well as the quality of its habitat, minimising the adverse effects that it causes;
- it is managed and operated in a responsible manner, in conformity with local, national and international laws and regulations;
- it maintains present and future economic and social options and benefits;
- it is conducted in a socially and economically fair and responsible manner.

The Principles represent the overarching philosophical basis for this initiative in stewardship of marine resources: the use of market forces to promote behaviour which helps achieve the goal of sustainable fisheries. They form the basis for detailed Criteria which will be used to evaluate each fishery seeking certification under the MSC programme. Although the primary focus is the ecological integrity of world fisheries, the principles also embrace the human and social elements of fisheries. Their successful implementation depends upon a system which is open, fair, based upon the best information available and which incorporates all relevant legal obligations. The certification programme in which these principles will be applied is intended to give any fishery the opportunity to demonstrate its commitment to sustainable fishing and ultimately benefit from this commitment in the market place.

Scope

The scope of the MSC Principles and Criteria relates to marine fisheries activities up to but not beyond the point at which the fish are landed. However, MSC-accredited certifiers may be informed of serious concerns associated with post-landing practices.[1]

The MSC Principles and Criteria apply at this stage only to wildcapture fisheries (including, but not limited to shellfish, crustaceans and cephalopods). Aquaculture and the harvest of other species are not currently included.

Issues involving allocation of quotas and access to marine resources are considered to be beyond the scope of these Principles and Criteria.

PRINCIPLE 1:

A fishery must be conducted in a manner that does not lead to over-fishing or depletion of the exploited populations and, for those populations that are depleted, the fishery must be conducted in a manner that demonstrably leads to their recovery[2]:

Intent:

The intent of this principle is to ensure that the productive capacities of resources are maintained at high levels and are not sacrificed in favour of short-term interests. Thus, exploited populations would be maintained at high levels of abundance designed to retain their productivity, provide margins of safety for error and uncertainty, and restore and retain their capacities for yields over the long term.

Criteria:

1. The fishery shall be conducted at catch levels that continually maintain the high productivity of the target population(s) and associated ecological community relative to its potential productivity.

2. Where the exploited populations are depleted, the fishery will be executed such that recovery and rebuilding is allowed to occur to a specified level consistent with the precautionary approach and the ability of the populations to produce long-term potential yields within a specified time frame.

3. Fishing is conducted in a manner that does not alter the age or genetic structure or sex composition to a degree that impairs reproductive capacity.

PRINCIPLE 2:

Fishing operations should allow for the maintenance of the structure, productivity, function and diversity of the ecosystem (including habitat and associated dependent and ecologically related species) on which the fishery depends.

Intent:

The intent of this principle is to encourage the management of fisheries from an ecosystem perspective under a system designed to assess and restrain the impacts of the fishery on the ecosystem.

Criteria:

1. The fishery is conducted in a way that maintains natural functional relationships among species and should not lead to trophic cascades or ecosystem state changes.

2. The fishery is conducted in a manner that does not threaten biological diversity at the genetic, species or population levels and avoids or minimises mortality of, or injuries to endangered, threatened or protected species.

3. Where exploited populations are depleted, the fishery will be executed such that recovery and rebuilding is allowed to occur to a specified level within specified time frames, consistent with the precautionary approach and considering the ability of the population to produce long-term potential yields.

PRINCIPLE 3:

The fishery is subject to an effective management system that respects local, national and international laws and standards and incorporates institutional and operational frameworks that require use of the resource to be responsible and sustainable.

Intent:

The intent of this principle is to ensure that there is an institutional and operational framework for implementing Principles 1 and 2, appropriate to the size and scale of the fishery.

A. *Management System Criteria:*

1. The fishery shall not be conducted under a controversial unilateral exemption to an international agreement.

The management system shall:

2. demonstrate clear long-term objectives consistent with MSC Principles and Criteria and contain a consultative process that is transparent and involves all interested and affected parties so as to consider all relevant information, including local knowledge. The impact of fishery management decisions on all those who depend on the fishery for their livelihoods, including, but not confined to subsistence, artisanal, and fishing-dependent communities shall be addressed as part of this process;

3. be appropriate to the cultural context, scale and intensity of the fishery—reflecting specific objectives, incorporating operational criteria, containing procedures for implementation and a process for monitoring and evaluating performance and acting on findings;

4. observe the legal and customary rights and long term interests of people dependent on fishing for food and livelihood, in a manner consistent with ecological sustainability;

5. incorporates an appropriate mechanism for the resolution of disputes arising within the system[3];

6. provide economic and social incentives that contribute to sustainable fishing and shall not operate with subsidies that contribute to unsustainable fishing;

7. act in a timely and adaptive fashion on the basis of the best available information using a precautionary approach particularly when dealing with scientific uncertainty;

8. incorporate a research plan—appropriate to the scale and intensity of the fishery—that addresses the information needs of management and provides for the dissemination of research results to all interested parties in a timely fashion;

9. require that assessments of the biological status of the resource and impacts of the fishery have been and are periodically conducted;

10. specify measures and strategies that demonstrably control the degree of exploitation of the resource, including, but not limited to:

    a) setting catch levels that will maintain the target population and ecological community's high productivity relative to its potential productivity, and account for the non-target species (or size, age, sex) captured and landed in association with, or as a consequence of, fishing for target species;

    b) identifying appropriate fishing methods that minimise adverse impacts on habitat, especially in critical or sensitive zones such as spawning and nursery areas;

    c) providing for the recovery and rebuilding of depleted fish populations to specified levels within specified time frames;

    d) mechanisms in place to limit or close fisheries when designated catch limits are reached;

    e) establishing no-take zones where appropriate;

11. contains appropriate procedures for effective compliance, monitoring, control, surveillance and enforcement which ensure that established limits to exploitation are not exceeded and specifies corrective actions to be taken in the event that they are.

B. *Operational Criteria:*

Fishing operation shall:

12. make use of fishing gear and practices designed to avoid the capture of non-target species (and non-target size, age, and/or sex of the target species); minimise mortality of this catch where it cannot be avoided, and reduce discards of what cannot be released alive;

13. implement appropriate fishing methods designed to minimise adverse impacts on habitat, especially in critical or sensitive zones such as spawning and nursery areas;

14. not use destructive fishing practices such as fishing with poisons or explosives;

15. minimise operational waste such as lost fishing gear, oil spills, on-board spoilage of catch, etc.;

16. be conducted in compliance with the fishery management system and all legal and administrative requirements; and

17. assist and co-operate with management authorities in the collection of catch, discard, and other information of importance to effective management of the resources and the fishery.

Notes:

[1] Other complementary certification programmes (e.g., ISO 14000) provide opportunities for documenting and evaluating impacts of post-landing activities related to fisheries products certified to MSC standards. Constructive solutions to address these concerns through appropriate measures should be sought through dialogue with certification organisations and other relevant bodies.

[2] The sequence in which the Principles and Criteria appear does not represent a ranking of their significance, but is rather intended to provide a logical guide to certifiers when assessing a fishery. The criteria by which the MSC Principles will be implemented will be reviewed and revised as appropriate in light of relevant new information, technologies and additional consultations.

[3] Outstanding disputes of substantial magnitude involving a significant number of interests will normally disqualify a fishery from certification.

Part 9
Implementation

Parts 1–8 of this book have addressed performance standards, defining acceptable norms for companies. Part 9 addresses process standards and guidelines that can assist companies in the implementation of corporate responsibility.

Part 9 will be looking at the 'how-to' side of corporate responsibility, covering:

- Stakeholder engagement
- Reporting
- Environmental management systems
- Assurance
- Professional qualifications

This part contains, in order of presentation, the following process standards and guidelines:

- AccountAbility 1000 (AA1000) Framework
- AA1000 Assurance Standard
- Global Reporting Initiative
- ISO 14001
- SIGMA ('Sustainability: Integrated Guidelines for Management') project

24
AccountAbility 1000 Framework

The AA1000 Framework provides the requisite flexibility that is essential to achieve innovation and continuous improvement.

Judith M. Mullins, Director of Emerging Issues and Process Integration, General Motors[1]

The biggest challenge for the assurance professionals in responding to the increasing demands of corporate accountability and transparency, whether from a financial, environmental or other audit background, is to take an open and flexible approach and to dare to experiment. The AccountAbility 1000 Framework provides an excellent structure for this experimentation by bringing together a multistakeholder view on what constitutes current best practice—both in terms of the principles and the processes our experimentation should be guided by and aspire to . . . Auditors must be prepared to work in new alliances and dialogue with our stakeholders.

David Coles, Partner, KPMG, Sustainability Advisory Services[2]

Type   Process standard, foundation standard

Strength   It provides an overarching framework for corporate responsibility

Keywords Social accounting • Ethical accounting • Auditing • Reporting • Stakeholder engagement

---

1 'Launch of AccountAbility 1000: Endorsement Quotes', in *Notes for AccountAbility's Council Meeting in Copenhagen, 14 November, 1999.*
2 *Ibid.*

24.1 Background

The AccountAbility 1000 (AA1000) Framework defines best practice in social and ethical auditing, accounting and reporting. Stakeholder engagement is an integral aspect of the AA1000 Framework. Launched in 1999, the AA1000 Framework is designed to assist companies, stakeholders, auditors, consultants and standard-setting bodies. The AA1000 Framework can be used in two ways: on its own, or in conjunction with other corporate responsibility (CR) standards. It provides a road-map for companies on key CR issues, explaining points of divergence and convergence with other major standards.

Founded in 1996, the Institute for Social and Ethical AccountAbility (Account-Ability) is a professional membership organisation committed to promoting accountability as a means to achieving sustainable development.

The AA1000 Framework contains processes as well as principles for reporting, accounting and auditing. The implementation of its processes has five phases:

- **Phase 1: planning.** The company commits itself to social and ethical accounting, auditing and reporting, with stakeholders playing a key role. Stakeholders are identified and the company describes its relationship with each stakeholder group. Managers define and review the mission and values of the organisation.

- **Phase 2: accounting.** Through stakeholder consultation, the company identifies issues relating to social and ethical performance. The scope of the audit is defined, as are indicators. Information is collected and analysed.

- **Phase 3: auditing and reporting.** The company prepares the report. An external group audits the report. The company communicates the report and gathers feedback.

- **Phase 4: embedding.** The company embeds the systems.

- **Phase 5: stakeholder engagement.** This underpins all of the four previous phases.

One of the most important contributions of the AA1000 Framework is that it provides definitions for key terms (AccountAbility 1999a: 18; see Box 24.1). The definitions and processes delineated by AA1000 will underpin the field of corporate responsibility and thus are relevant to all standards for which assurance will be sought.

This chapter includes the following text of the AA1000 Framework:

- Executive summary

- Processes

- Stakeholder engagement

- First Steps

> ● **To account:** to explain or justify the acts, omissions, risks and dependencies for which one is responsible to people with a legitimate interest.
>
> ● **Independent social and ethical auditor:** a person or an organisation who [or that] is and can be seen to be independent of the organisation being audited and is in a position to challenge and question the organisation's approach ... the organisation selects an auditor that possess legitimacy with its stakeholders.

Box 24.1 Definitions

Source: AccountAbility 1999a: 18, 48

Owing to space constraints, the following sections are not included:

● Principles

● Auditing and quality assurance

● Integrating AA1000

● Professional qualifications

● Glossary

24.2 Strengths and weaknesses

The AA1000 Framework emphasises innovation over compliance, allowing companies to chart their own course. Although such a model can lead to breakthrough approaches, it places a significant amount of responsibility onto companies, many of which are looking for simplicity. The AA1000 Framework has been criticised for being too complex. The five stages inherent in its system, from planning to embedding, require a significant commitment of resources. According to an independent study commissioned by the Institute for Business Ethics, the external stakeholder engagement can be seen as 'daunting and expensive' (Smith 2002: 35).

In a post-Enron world, the AA1000 Framework includes a valuable series of first steps for companies interested in becoming more accountable (see page 408). Companies can use the first steps to make preliminary forays into corporate responsibility. However, according to Deborah Smith:

> [the] time-scale for completion of first social reporting cycle can be long, [with a] delayed reputational payback. [The] iterative process based on a long-term commitment to engagement and reporting may damage reputation if terminated (Smith 2002: 35).

AccountAbility is building capacity by conducting training on the AA1000 Framework and by setting professional qualifications for individuals seeking to become service providers in the field of corporate responsibility. According to

Simon Zadek, chief executive officer of AccountAbility, the AA1000 Framework 'gives internal and external stakeholders reassurance that there is real substance behind an organisation's actions—that it's more than PR' (quoted in Account-Ability 1999b).

24.3 Companies to which the AccountAbility 1000 Framework applies

The AA1000 Framework is designed for organisations of all sizes in any country or sector. It can be used in conjunction with the Global Reporting Initiative (GRI, Chapter 26), ISO standards (on ISO 14001, see Chapter 27) and Social Accountability (SA8000, Chapter 9), among others.

24.4 Questions posed and answered

Given the complexity and breadth of issues covered, the AA1000 Framework poses and answers many questions. Among the key questions addressed are:

- What constitutes high quality in social and ethical accounting, auditing and reporting?
- What is accountability? What is transparency?
- What are the principles that underpin accountability?
- How can an organisation define values, issues and targets that represent its stakeholders?
- How can a company assess the needs of stakeholders and integrate their information needs into its reporting?
- What processes does a social and ethical auditor need to follow to provide assurance?

24.5 The promise and the challenge

The AA1000 Framework is the basis for a continuing evolution of documents known as the AA1000 Series. The AA1000 Assurance Standard (Chapter 25), which was launched on 25 March 2003, represents the first such document in the AA1000 Series. AA1000 Assurance Standard Guidance and Practitioner Notes, as well as other documents, are being developed in an ongoing process.

24.5.1 The AA1000 principles

The AA1000 principles are:

- **Principle 1:** Materiality
- **Principle 2:** Completeness
- **Principle 3:** Responsiveness

These principles are common across all aspects of the AA1000 Series, including the AA1000 Framework (1999), AA1000 Assurance Standard (2003), as well as related Guidance and Practitioner Notes. These principles and their definitions as described in the AA1000 Assurance Standard supersede those of the AA1000 Framework.

References

AccountAbility (Institute for Social and Ethical AccountAbility) (1999a) *AA1000 Framework* (exposure draft; London: AccountAbility).

—— (1999b) 'First Standard for Building Corporate Accountability and Trust', press release, 15 November 1999.

Smith, D. (2002) *Demonstrating Corporate Values: Which standard for your company?* (London: Institute for Business Ethics).

Additional resource

Website

AccountAbility (Institute for Social and Ethical AccountAbility): www.accountability.org.uk

AccountAbility 1000 (AA1000) Framework

1 Executive Summary

1.1 AccountAbility 1000—The foundation standard

Introduction

AccountAbility 1000 (AA1000) is an **accountability** standard, focused on securing the quality of **social and ethical** accounting, auditing and reporting.

It is a **foundation** standard, and as such can be used in two ways:

a) As a common currency to underpin the quality of specialised accountability standards, existing and emergent.

b) As a stand-alone system and process for managing and communicating social and ethical accountability and performance.

Accountability standards and guidelines

Recent years have witnessed a proliferation of standards and guidelines to support and measure accountability and performance. These include process standards and substantive performance standards, standards focused on a single-issue or encompassing a variety of issues, and mandatory and voluntary standards.

The processes and issues covered by these standards include stakeholder dialogue and social and ethical reporting, organisational culture, fair trade and ethical trade, working conditions, human resource management and training, environmental and animal protection, community development and human rights. Some of the more notable examples are the:

Australian Criminal Code Act, Caux Round Table Principles for Business, CERES Principles, EMAS, Ethical Trading Initiative, Forest Stewardship Council, Global Reporting Initiative, Global Sullivan Principles, Humane Cosmetics Standard, ICFTU Basic Code of Labour Practice, Investors in People, ICC Business Charter for Sustainable Development, ISO 14001, OHSAS18001, PERI Reporting Guidelines, Social Accountability 8000 (SA8000), South African Government Employment Equity Act, Sunshine Corporate Reporting, and the US Government Federal Sentencing Guidelines.

AA1000 comprises **principles** (the characteristics of a quality process) and a set of **process standards**. The process standards cover the following stages:

---

a) Planning.

b) Accounting.

c) Auditing and reporting.

d) Embedding.

e) Stakeholder engagement.

The principles and process standards are underpinned by the principle of accountability to stakeholders.

Accountability and performance

The AA1000 process standards link the definition and embedding of an organisation's values to the development of performance targets and to the assessment and communication of organisational performance. By this process, focused around the organisation's engagement with stakeholders, AA1000 ties social and ethical issues into the organisation's strategic management and operations.

AA1000 aims to **support organisational learning and overall performance—social and ethical, environmental and economic—and hence organisations' contribution towards a path of sustainable development.**

It seeks to achieve its aim through **improving the quality of social and ethical accounting, auditing and reporting.**

What is social and ethical?

The terms ethical and social have a number of theoretical and practical traditions in organisational accountability. For some, ethical (or ethics) refers to an organisation's systems and the behaviour of individuals within the organisation, whereas social refers to the impacts of the organisation's behaviour on its stakeholders, both internal and external. For others, ethical embraces both the systems and individual behaviour within an organisation, and the impacts of the systems and behaviour—on stakeholders, on the environment, on the economy, etc.

AA1000 recognises these different traditions. It combines the terms **social and ethical** to refer to the systems and individual behaviour within an organisation **and** to the **direct and indirect** impact of an organisation's activities on stakeholders.

Social and ethical issues (relating to systems, behaviour and impacts) are defined by an organisation's values and aims, through the influence of the interests and expectations of its stakeholders, and by societal norms and expectations.

Building performance not compliance

The Institute recognises and advocates the need for experimentation and innovation in embedding the management of (and accountability for) social and ethical issues in organisations' strategies and operations. It furthermore recognises that any useful standard at this stage must stimulate innovation above an agreed quality floor, rather than encouraging the development of a more rigid compliance-oriented culture.

Therefore in the first instance, the Institute has taken the decision not to position AA1000 as a certifiable standard. Rather, its design is intended to encourage innovation around key quality principles, which at this stage it considers a more effective approach in taking forward individual adopting organisations and the field as a whole.

AA1000 does, however, incorporate an auditing standard through which organisations will provide assurance to stakeholders as to the quality of their social and ethical accounting, auditing and reporting. This assurance is one basis of effective engagement between organisations and stakeholders, and hence supports organisations' strategic management and operations.

Stakeholders: leadership and engagement

An organisation's stakeholders are **those groups who affect and/or are affected by the organisation and its activities**.

These may include, but are not limited to: owners, trustees, employees and trade unions, customers, members, business partners, suppliers, competitors, government and regulators, the electorate, non-governmental-organisations (NGOs)/not-for-profit organisations, pressure groups and influencers, and local and international communities.

There is growing recognition by organisations that some stakeholders possess significant influence over them:

a) More information is publicly available on the activity of organisations and the impact of these activities on employees, shareholders, society, the environment and the economy.

b) Stakeholders demand higher standards of behaviour from organisations.

c) The legitimacy of these demands is more widely recognised by government, regulators and civil society.

At the same time, organisations recognise the conflicts of interest they have with stakeholders, and the lack of consensus between and within stakeholder groups.

This is a dilemma that AA1000 seeks to address. It does not provide a prescriptive framework for the resolution of conflicts, but it does provide a process for organisations to begin to address them through engaging with stakeholders to find common ground and build trust.

This process of engagement with stakeholders is at the heart of AA1000. Engagement is not about organisations abdicating responsibilities for their activities, but rather **using leadership to build relationships with stakeholders**, and hence improving their overall performance.

2.3 Process standards

Introduction

2.3.1 AA1000 is a process standard, not a substantive performance standard. That is, it specifies processes that an organisation should follow to account for its performance, and not the levels of performance the organisation should achieve.

2.3.2 It is a dynamic model for a process of continuous improvement, each cycle of which has five main categories of action. The process model is broadly linear, but stages frequently operate in parallel, and earlier stages may have to be repeated. The stages are described below and illustrated in figure 4. Throughout the AA1000 standard, **'the process'** refers to an organisation's process of social and ethical accounting, auditing and reporting.

a) The organisation commits to the process, and defines and reviews its values and social and ethical objectives and targets (*Planning*).

b) The scope of the process is defined, information is collated and analysed, and performance targets and improvement plans are developed (*Accounting*).

c) A report(s) **(written or verbal communication)** on the organisation's systems and performance is prepared, the process (including the social and ethical reporting) is externally audited, the report(s) is made accessible to stakeholders, and stakeholder feedback is obtained (*Auditing and Reporting*).

d) To support each of these stages, structures and systems are developed to strengthen the accounting, auditing and reporting process and to integrate it into the organisation's activities (*Embedding*).

e) Each process stage (from a) to d)) is permeated by the organisation's engagement with its stakeholders (*Stakeholder engagement*).

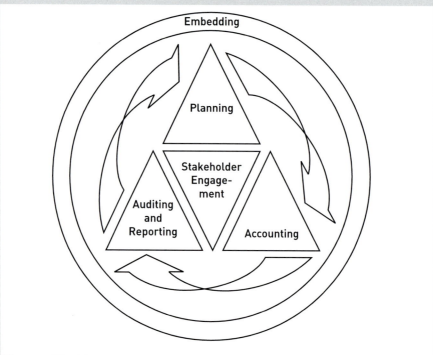

Figure 4: The AA1000 Process Model

2.3.3 During these stages, the organisation begins planning for the next cycle of the process incorporating the experience from previous cycles.

2.3.4 Within this broad process model, the Institute's process standards identify a set of steps that an organisation should follow to help satisfy the AA1000 quality principles. The process steps are summarised in table 1.

Status of the standards

2.3.5 The AA1000 process standards are set out together with guidance that assists in their interpretation. This guidance also identifies the relationship between the standards and the underlying social and ethical accounting, auditing and reporting principles.

2.3.6 The Institute recognises that organisations may adopt a stepped approach to building accountability, and will use AA1000 as **a model to aspire to** over time.

2.3.7 It is recognised that a variety of different approaches to the AA1000 processes, for example towards stakeholder engagement, will address the quality requirements identified by the process standards, and that **different approaches will be more appropriate in different organisation types and geographies**.

2.3.8 Where there is a potential conflict between alternative process steps, an organisation should refer to the principles to resolve the conflict. Where there appears to be or there is a conflict of principles, the organisation should make its decision to support a long-term goal of accountability, and disclose this in its social and ethical report(s).

The AA1000 Process Model

Planning

(P)rocess1 **Establish commitment and governance procedures**

The organisation commits itself to the process of social and ethical accounting, auditing and reporting, and to the role of stakeholders within this process. It defines governance procedures to ensure the inclusion of stakeholders in the process.

P2 **Identify stakeholders**

The organisation identifies its stakeholders and characterises its relationship with each group of them.

P3 **Define/review values**

The organisation defines or reviews its current mission and values.

Table 1: The AA1000 Process Model (continued over)

Accounting

P4 **Identify issues**

The organisation identifies issues through engagement with its stakeholders regarding its activities and social and ethical performance.

P5 **Determine process scope**

The organisation determines, based on engagement with its stakeholders, the scope of the current process in terms of the stakeholders, geographical locations, operating units and issues to be included, and identifies how it plans to account for the excluded stakeholders, operations, locations or issues in future cycles. It identifies the timing of the current cycle. The organisation also identifies the audit method(s), the audit scope, and the auditor(s) to provide a high level of quality assurance to all its stakeholders.

P6 **Identify indicators**

The organisation identifies social and ethical indicators through engagement with its stakeholders. The indicators reflect the organisation's performance in relation to: its values and objectives; the values and aspirations of its stakeholders, as determined through a process of consultation with each group of them; and wider societal norms and expectations.

P7 **Collect information**

The organisation collects information about its performance in respect of the identified indicators. The organisation engages with stakeholders in the design of the collection methods, which allow stakeholders to accurately and fully express their aspirations and needs.

P8 **Analyse information, set targets and develop improvement plan**

From the information collected, the organisation:
  a) Evaluates its performance against values, objectives and targets previously set.
  b) Uses this evaluation and engagement with stakeholders to develop or revise objectives and targets for the future, with a focus on improving performance.

Auditing and reporting

P9 **Prepare report(s)**

The organisation prepares a social and ethical report (written or verbal communication) or reports relating to the process undertaken in a specified period. The report(s) clearly and without bias explains the process and demonstrates how the organisation's performance relates to its values, objectives and targets. It includes information about its performance measured against its key social and ethical performance targets. The organisation provides comparative information for previous period(s) to help stakeholders understand the current performance in the context of prior period trends and in the context of external benchmarks, if available.

P10 **Audit report(s)**

The organisation arranges and supports the external audit of the process, including the social and ethical report(s). Support is provided to the auditor throughout the planning and accounting processes as appropriate.

Table 1 (from previous page; continued opposite)

P11 **Communicate report(s) and obtain feedback**

The organisation communicates information on the process and the social and ethical performance of the organisation to all stakeholder groups. This includes making accessible to all stakeholder groups the social and ethical report(s) together with the independent audit opinion(s). The organisation actively seeks feedback from its stakeholder groups in order to further develop its process.

Embedding

P12 **Establish and embed systems**

The organisation establishes systems to support the process, and the on-going achievement of its objectives and targets in line with its values. Systems include those to implement and maintain values, to manage the collection and documentation of information and to perform the internal audit/review of the process.

Table 1 (continued)

AA1000—The process standards

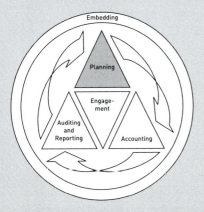

Establish commitment and governance procedures

P1 **The organisation commits itself to the process of social and ethical accounting, auditing and reporting, and to the role of stakeholders within this process. It defines governance procedures to ensure the inclusion of stakeholders in the social and ethical accounting, auditing and reporting process.**

P1.1 The organisation is guided in its commitment to the process and its choice of governance structure by the principle of inclusivity, and hence it reflects the aspirations and needs of all stakeholder groups through the entire process.

P1.2 The 'organisation' refers to the legal entity that assumes responsibility for the process.

P1.3   Stakeholders are defined as those individuals or groups of individuals who affect and/or are affected by an organisation or its activities.

P1.4   The governing body of the organisation (e.g. its board) is ultimately responsible for the conduct of the process. The individual processes may, however, be performed by a variety of members of the organisation (including trustees, board, management and employees) and by external advisers and auditors.

P1.5   The governing body of the organisation makes a commitment to involving stakeholders in the process. The role of stakeholders in the process (and the relationship of this role to the overall process, including the organisation's decision-making processes) is clearly communicated to them.

P1.6   The inclusion of stakeholder interests in the process may be addressed in a variety of ways. These may include, but are not limited to:

a) Engagement with stakeholders (see all AA1000 process standards, but especially 7.2-7.6).

b) Formal inclusion of representatives of stakeholders on the governing body or a governing committee responsible for, inter alia, the process.

c) Formal representation of stakeholder groups on an audit panel (see AA1000 process standard 10). An audit panel refers to a panel of advisors who are publicly recognised as either representatives of key stakeholders or experts in the field of social and ethical accountability more generally.

d) Stakeholders employed as auditors of the process, including the social and ethical report(s) (see AA1000 process standard 10).

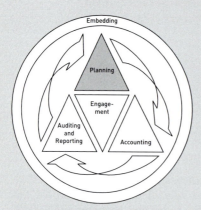

Identify stakeholders

P2   **The organisation identifies its stakeholders and characterises its relationship with each group of them.**

P2.1   The identification of all stakeholder groups is a key part of ensuring the inclusivity of the process of social and ethical accounting, auditing and reporting.

P2.2   The organisation's stakeholder groups may include, but are not limited to: owners, trustees, employees (e.g. managers, staff and trade unions), customers, members (e.g. of cooperative, mutual or friendly societies), suppliers and other partners, competitors, government and regulators, the electorate (e.g. for public sector bodies), NGO /not for profit organisations, pressure groups and influencers, and local and international communities.

P2.3 The organisation may categorise its stakeholder groups in various ways, for example, internal and external, primary and secondary, direct, representative and intermediary, or local and international.

P2.4 Whichever categorisation (if any) is used, the organisation prepares a complete list of its stakeholder groups.

P2.5 For each stakeholder group, the organization describes its relationship with the group, and its aims and policies regarding the relationship. The dimensions of the relationships will differ for each stakeholder group, and may vary over time. They may include, but are not limited to the:

a) Length of relationship.

b) Nature of relationship.

   i) Type of organisation (e.g. supplier, customer).

   ii) Number/size of members of stakeholder groups.

   iii) Frequency of contact.

c) Key events/history of relationship.

d) Organisation's perceptions of relationship and expectations from it.

e) Stakeholders' perceptions of relationship and expectations from it.

P2.6 The on-going process of stakeholder engagement will assist the organisation in the examination and/or revision of its stated relationship with each stakeholder group.

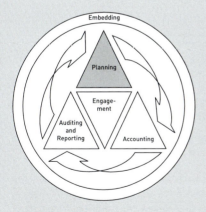

Define/review values

P3 **The organisation defines or reviews its current mission and values.**

P3.1 The organisation examines and develops its values on an on-going (regular and timely) basis. The process of inclusive stakeholder engagement (throughout the process) is central to the development of the organisation's values.

P3.2 The organisation's current mission and values provide a framework for the process. They are a basis for understanding the aims and activities of the organisation, and provide a base against which the organisation's performance is assessed.

P3.3 The organisation reviews its current mission and values, and formalises them in a statement or statements available to all stakeholders.

P3.4 The techniques adopted to engage with stakeholders vary depending on the organisation and the scope of the engagement (see AA1000 process standards 7.2-7.6).

P3.5 In a first cycle of the process, the organization reviews its existing objectives and targets for social and ethical performance, and examines the consistency of its targets with its mission and values. In all cycles the organisation's objectives and targets are reviewed as part of the accounting and reporting stages of the process (see AA1000 process standards 8 and 11).

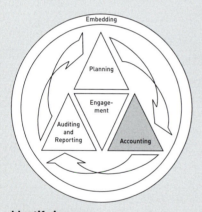

Identify issues

P4 **The organisation identifies issues through engagement with its stakeholders regarding its activities and social and ethical performance.**

P4.1 The organisation is guided by the principles of inclusivity, completeness and materiality in identifying issues.

P4.2 The identification of issues relevant to each stakeholder group assists the analysis and understanding of the organisation's activities and performance. The organisation identifies issues and case studies that address aspects of selected issues.

P4.3 The issues may reflect broad themes important to the organisation and its stakeholders, or may be narrowly defined. They may be drawn from the following categories, but are not limited to them: the organisation's values and governance, regulation and controls, the organisation's operational practices including its marketing, its accountability, human rights issues, labour and working conditions, the organisation's supply chain, its product, service and investment impact, its impacts on other species and its impact on the environment.

P4.4 The issues are examined to assess the likely impact of the organisation's activities on the organisation and its stakeholders. This assessment includes a process of engagement with stakeholders. The engagement accurately and fully obtains stakeholder views in an atmosphere without fear or restriction (see AA1000 process standards 7.2-7.6).

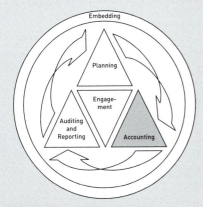

Determine process scope

P5 **The organisation determines, based on engagement with its stakeholders, the scope of the current process in terms of the stakeholders, geographical locations, operating units and issues to be included, and identifies how it plans to account for any excluded stakeholders, operations, locations or Issues in future cycles. It identifies the timing of the current cycle. The organisation also identifies the audit method(s), the audit scope and the auditor(s) to provide a high level of quality assurance to all its stakeholders.**

P5.1 The organisation is guided by the principles of inclusivity, completeness and materiality in determining the scope of the process.

Stakeholders, locations and operations scope

P5.2 The organisation is accountable to all its stakeholder groups, and for its activities in all geographic locations and operating units. However, for reasons of time or financial constraints, the organisation may choose not to include all stakeholders, locations or operations in any cycle of the process. If a shortlist of stakeholder groups, locations or operations is identified for a cycle, the selection criteria are documented, and communicated together with a list of excluded stakeholders, locations and units, and plans for future inclusion in the process.

P5.3 If the exclusion of a particular location or operation is likely to have a material impact on the understanding of the operations and locations included, the relationship between the information included and excluded is documented and communicated in the social and ethical report(s).

P5.4 If the organisation has subsidiaries or joint ventures outside the accounting entity the exclusion of which would have a material impact on the understanding of the organisation's overall activities, it documents these and communicates them in the social and ethical report(s).

Issues scope

P5.5 In order to provide a complete and inclusive account it is necessary to account for all issues that are likely to have a material impact on the organisation's stakeholders.

P5.6 The rationale and processes of selecting issues for the process, and the relevance of the issues to particular stakeholder groups are documented to allow internal and external auditing. In addition, to demonstrate inclusivity and the completeness of issues identified, the social and ethical report(s) may include stakeholder comments on the selection of issues (see AA1000 process standard 9).

P5.7 The organisation identifies any changes to the scope from any previous cycle. Such changes are documented as part of the accounting process and communicated in the social and ethical report(s).

Audit scope

P5.8 The social and ethical audit provides quality assurance to stakeholders concerning the process (including social and ethical reporting). The organisation selects the audit method, the audit scope and the auditor(s) to provide an overall high level of assurance to all of its stakeholders (see AA1000 process standard 10).

P5.9 The scope of the audit may include the accuracy/validity of data and supporting systems, compliance to the requirements of social and ethical standards and guidelines, and the completeness and inclusivity of the process, including the social and ethical report(s). It may also include suggestions to the organisation regarding areas for improvement in the process and social and ethical performance (see AA1000 process standard 10).

P5.10 The scope of the audit is documented by the organisation. A description of this scope forms part of the audit report of the social and ethical auditor.

Timing

P5.11 Each cycle of the process should be completed on a regular and timely basis. It is recognised that the accounting, auditing cycle may not match other reporting cycles, but the rationale for the time period chosen is documented to allow internal and external auditing.

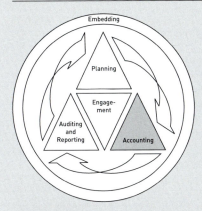

Identify indicators

P6 **The organisation identifies social and ethical indicators through engagement with its stakeholders. The indicators reflect the organisation's performance in relation to: its values and objectives; the values and aspirations of its stakeholders, as determined through a process of consultation with each group of them; and wider societal norms and expectations.**

P6.1 The organisation's choice of indicators to measure its social and ethical perfor- mance is based on the principles of inclusivity, completeness, materiality and information quality (comparability, reliability, relevance and understandability).

P6.2 Indicators are pieces of qualitative or quantitative data that provide information on the performance of the organisation.

P6.3 The organisation's choice of indicators reflects a three-tier approach covering its values, the values of its stakeholders and wider societal values.

a) The first tier of values to be reflected in the indicators is based on the organ- isation's statement of mission and values, and the standards, codes and guidelines to which the organisation subscribes.

b) The choice of indicators also reflects stakeholders' views of the organisa- tion's performance against its values and in respect of the specific needs and aspirations of stakeholders. Stakeholder views are obtained through an inclusive process of stakeholder engagement (see AA1000 process standards 7.2-7.6). Following the initial definition of indicators, the organisation will refine these and reconcile conflicting opinions through further engagement with stakeholders.

c) The third tier of values reflected in the indicators is based on benchmarks established in societies that are part of the process scope. These may be evident in legal statute or from the evidence of stakeholders. The organisation includes indicators for its performance against its legal requirements for performance and disclosure.

P6.4 Within these tiers, the organisation selects indicators that reflect both its pro- cesses and the outcomes of its activities. Outcomes may include the output of an activity, and/or its impact.

P6.5 Indicators selected are sufficient to provide coverage of the defined scope of the process including stakeholders, geographies, operations and issues.

P6.6 For the second and third tiers of values, the organisation may choose not to pursue the measurement of all the indicators identified by stakeholders. Indicators may be suggested for issues outside the direct or indirect power or influence of the organisation; the number and nature of the indicators may exceed resource boundaries; and the number of indicators may weaken the clarity of communication. Where the organisation limits the number of indicators suggested by stakeholders, it engages stakeholders in a process of prioritisation.

P6.7 Indicators may be selected individually or as a group to address a specific issue.

P6.8 The rationale and processes of identifying indicators are documented to support internal and external auditing.

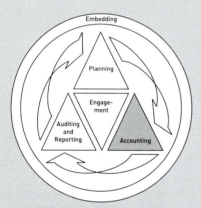

Collect information

P7 **The organisation collects information about its performance in respect of the identified indicators. The organisation engages with stakeholders in the design of the collection methods, which allow stakeholders to accurately and fully express their aspirations and needs.**

P7.1 Information about the organisation's performance is available from both:

a) The organisation's management information systems, which are embedded in the organisation (see AA1000 process standards 12.8-12.11).

b) Engagement with stakeholders. The role of stakeholders in the collection of information reflects the AA1000 principles, including completeness, inclusivity and materiality.

P7.2 A variety of methods of engagement may be used by organisations. These may include, but are not limited to:

a) One-to-one interviews, face-to-face and distance.

   b) Group interviews.

   c) Focus groups.

   d) Workshops and seminars.

   e) Public meetings.

   f) Questionnaires—face-to-face, by letter, telephone, internet, or other techniques.

P7.3 The methods adopted to engage with stakeholders vary depending on the nature and size of the organisation and the scope of the engagement—the stakeholders included, the complexity and nature of the issues covered and the geographic location.

P7.4 The choice of method will also be affected by the capacity of the organisation—in terms of financial resources, staff resources and management systems—and by the capacity of its stakeholders.

P7.5 The organisation may use sampling techniques for its data collection processes. The samples are robust, and ensure that a representative spread of each stakeholder category within the process scope is included. In defining samples, the organisation is aware of key diversity issues, which may include but are not limited to: the gender, race, age, disabilities and culture of the samples.

P7.6 Regardless of the method chosen, the stakeholders are encouraged and helped to understand the process (see AA1000 process standard 1.5) and to provide information. The organisation also involves stakeholders in the design of the questions to be addressed in the processes of information gathering.

P7.7 The rationale and processes of data collection are documented to enable internal and external auditing of their appropriateness. For the audit of stakeholder engagement processes, the organisation allows the auditor to examine documentation and to attend dialogues, unless this raises conflict with other principles of accountability or issues of sensitivity for stakeholders. These conflicts are discussed with the auditor.

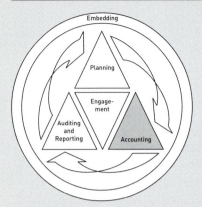

Analyse information, set targets and develop improvement Plan

P8   From the information collected, the organisation:

a) Evaluates its performance against values, objectives and targets previously set.

b) Uses this evaluation and engagement with stakeholders to develop or revise objectives and targets for the future, with a focus on improving performance.

P8.1 To interpret the information collected and evaluate performance, the social and ethical accounting approach links the organisation's performance to its stated values, objectives and targets, incorporating an analysis of the organisation's activities and the key issues identified by stakeholders.

P8.2 The emphasis and weighting given to particular findings in the evaluation of the social and ethical performance is a matter of judgement. In making judgements the organisation seeks to ensure that a balanced, unbiased view of the organisation's performance is made and that it reflects the principles of inclusivity and completeness.

P8.3 The organisation identifies changes to improve its social and ethical performance in the future. It develops a plan for the implementation of these changes including objectives, targets and prioritised actions. The organisation may also reflect on the need for changes to its values and its methods of embedding these within the organisation, including its processes of social and ethical accounting, auditing and reporting.

P8.4 In defining or reviewing its objectives and targets, the organisation considers the legal requirements it faces concerning social and ethical issues. It develops its targets to be consistent with its mission and values.

P8.5 The organisation's objectives and targets reflect the issues and activities over which the organisation has control or can expect to have an influence.

P8.6 The targets reflect the principle of continuous improvement in performance vis-à-vis its social and ethical mission, values and objectives. Where possible, the organisation's targets are measurable.

P8.7 The organisation's development of targets includes the consideration of any comments of the external auditor regarding future performance targets (see AA1000 process standard 10).

P8.8 Where possible, the organisation consults stakeholders on the development of targets and priorities prior to the preparation and publication of the social and ethical report(s). Where consultation does not take place prior to publication, the organisation revises its objectives and targets on the basis of engagement with all stakeholder groups after publication (see AA1000 process standard 11).

P8.9 The engagement with stakeholders includes consideration of the issues covered by the organisation's objectives and targets, the indicators used to measure performance, and the selection of the objectives and targets.

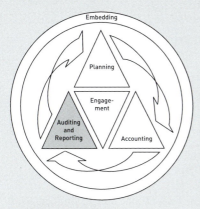

Prepare report(s)

P9 **The organisation prepares a social and ethical report (written or verbal communication) or reports relating to the process undertaken in a specified period. The report(s) clearly and minimising bias, explains the process and demonstrates how the organisation's performance relates to its values, objectives and targets. It includes information about its performance measured against its key social and ethical performance targets. The organisation provides comparative information for previous period(s) to help stakeholders understand the current performance in the context of prior period trends and in the context of external benchmarks, if available.**

P9.1 The content of the report reflects the AA1000 principles, and is inclusive, complete, material, comparable, reliable, relevant and understandable. In defining the structure of the social and ethical report the organisation is guided by the principles of information quality.

P9.2 A social and ethical report is a written document or other communication prepared to reflect the social and ethical performance of the organisation relating to its values, objectives and targets.

P9.3 The format of the report will reflect the information requirements of the organisation's stakeholders (see also AA1000 process standard 11).

P9.4 The organisation may produce more than one social and ethical report (in any accounting period) to address the information needs of different stakeholder groups. Where more than one social and ethical report is produced, each report should clearly indicate its relationship to the other social and ethical reports produced by the organisation for relevant accounting period(s).

P9.5 The social and ethical report(s) should indicate the accounting entity(s) covered by the report(s) and any significant variations from entities covered in the previous period. It includes information relating to the relevant period as well as material developments, if any, that may have occurred from the end of the period to the date of issue of the statement.

P9.6 The report(s) also includes:

a) **Descriptive information**, including a statement of the organisation's:

i) Mission and values.

ii) Governance procedures including the role of stakeholders.

iii) Structures and processes for dealing with social and ethical issues.

iv) Methodology adopted for process, including the scope of the exercise and the reasons for the exclusion of any activities, locations, stakeholders or issues from the process cycle.

v) Plans for future cycles of the process.

b) **Performance information**, which includes information on the organisation's performance against the three tiers of indicators identified. This includes:

i) Information on the organisation's performance against its mission and values, and information on its performance against standards, codes and guidelines to which it subscribes.

ii) Information on stakeholder identified indicators (including stakeholder commentary on the organisation's performance in relation to stakeholder values) for the current cycle and also comparative data for previous periods of account, if appropriate.

iii) Information reflecting societal benchmarks—these include indicators for the organisation's performance against legal requirements for performance and disclosure.

P9.7 To reflect the principles of information quality, the report(s) may be segmented by the organisation's values and objectives, by its issues, by its indicator categories, by key themes, by its stakeholders, or by other appropriate methods.

P9.8 If the organisation has completed a cycle of the process previously, including a social and ethical report(s), it engages with its stakeholders on the structure, format and content of the social and ethical report(s) being written.

P9.9 The social and ethical report(s) make clear where issues and indicators are outside the power of influence of the organisation, or where the organisation is operating in partnership to affect the indicators.

P9.10 The social and ethical report(s) may also include:

a) Stakeholder commentary on the organisation's selection of issues, indicators and social and ethical auditor(s).

b) Commentary attributed to specific stakeholders on the organisation's performance against its values and on salient issues relating to the interplay between the organisation and the stakeholder group.

c) An indication of any links with financial and environmental information. The statement should seek, where possible, to integrate information on social and ethical performance with environmental and financial performance data where this enables a better understanding of the particular issues or the organisation's decision-making processes.

P9.11 Depending on the information being reported, it may be appropriate for the organisation to provide comparative information for more than one previous period, so that its performance over time can be judged. Where comparative information is not available, the reasons for this are clearly explained in the report.

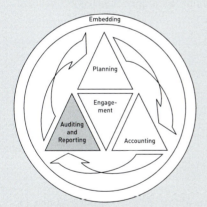

Audit report(s)

P10 **The organisation arranges and supports the independent external audit of the process, including the social and ethical report(s). Support is provided to the auditor(s) throughout the planning and accounting processes as appropriate.**

Audit responsibilities and audit opinion

P10.1 Social and ethical auditing encompasses a variety of methods through which an organisation develops understanding of its processes and performance, builds credibility in its reporting, and hence provides quality assurance to itself and its stakeholders. This credibility is the basis of effective engagement with stakeholders.

P10.2 An independent social and ethical auditor is a person or an organisation who is and can be seen to be independent of the organisation being audited and is in a position to challenge and question the organisation's approach. (See section 3 for guidelines for the ethical behaviour of the social and ethical auditor, and for the conduct and output of the audit.)

P10.3 The organisation appoints an independent external auditor or auditors to audit the process (including the social and ethical report(s)) according to the scope of the audit defined by the organisation (see AA1000 process standard 5.8-5.9) and to provide assurance as to the quality of the process. The organisation selects an auditor(s) that possesses legitimacy with its stakeholders. The auditor(s) liaise with the organisation to refine the audit method and scope to address the level of assurance identified by the organisation.

P10.4 The independent social and ethical auditor(s) is appointed from the outset of the scoping process, so that they can observe the planning of the accounting, auditing and reporting process and its execution.

P10.5 The auditor(s) is responsible for the conduct of the social and ethical audit and the production of a social and ethical audit report, including audit opinion. The audit does not relieve the governing body of the organisation of its responsibilities for the overall process.

P10.6 The auditor alone is responsible for writing the social and ethical audit report. Where the organisation has sought advice, either from a panel or other experts, the auditor remains responsible for the social and ethical audit report.

P10.7 The nature of the audit report will reflect the method and scope of the audit and the auditor(s) degree of confidence in their opinion based on the quality of available information.

P10.8 The audit report(s) includes commentary that enables the organisation and its stakeholders to understand:
a) The scope of the audit.
b) The relevant professional qualifications of the social and ethical auditor(s).
c) The opinion of the auditor(s) regarding the quality of the process and report(s), and the assurance that these provide. The opinion may include different levels of assurance for different parts of the process and report(s).

P10.9 The overall judgement of the external auditor(s) may be expressed in a variety of forms of audit opinion. For some audits, the assurance given by the audit opinion may be 'absolute' in terms of the absence/presence or correctness/ incorrectness of a piece of information; for other methods the assurance may be qualitative, indicating high, medium or low performance, areas for improvement, and/or predicted future progress.

P10.10 The audit report(s) may also include suggestions to the organisation regarding areas for improvement in its process and social and ethical performance.

P10.11 The auditor(s) sign and date the audit report(s) following approval by the governing body of the organisation. The audit opinion includes assessment of events occurring up to the date that the opinion is expressed. The audit report is addressed to the governing body of the organisation.

Audit process and quality assurance

P10.12 The external audit methods aim to provide an overall high level of quality assurance to the organisation and its stakeholders (see process standard 5.8). This assurance encompasses:

a) The **external auditor's assurance**, based on confidence in the sufficiency and appropriateness of information audited (see AA1000 process standards 10.13-10.18).

b) The **assurance provided to stakeholders**, based on the external auditor's assurance (as above), on the scope of the social and ethical audit, and on the legitimacy of the auditors(s) to each stakeholder group (see AA1000 process standards 10.19-10.20).

P10.13 'Sufficiency' is the measure of the quantity of audit evidence and refers to the extent of the audit procedures performed. 'Appropriateness' is the measure of quality or reliability of audit evidence and refers to the nature and timing of the audit procedures performed and the accounting, auditing and reporting process.

P10.14 The sufficiency and appropriateness of information is dependent on the subject matter/scope of the audit, the audit method(s), and the nature of the process.

P10.15 The **subject matter** of the audit may include quantitative and qualitative descriptive and performance information, information systems, and the processes of social and ethical accounting and reporting. In particular, the external audit addresses the AA1000 principles by assessing the following scope (see points 10.15 a to d). The auditor may derive different levels of confidence from each aspect of the scope:

a) Accuracy/validity of data and supporting information systems.

b) Compliance to the requirements of social and ethical standards and guidelines.

c) Inclusivity of the process and social and ethical report(s).

d) Completeness of the process, including the social and ethical report(s). A 'completeness' audit may consider the completeness of a report within a limited scope (e.g. one region of the organisation's operations), or may cover a full scope (i.e. all the organisation's values, issues, stakeholders, geographies and operations).

P10.16 The external **audit methods** used to address the subject matter/scope may include, but are not limited to:

a) 'Traditional' financial audit methods.

b) Surveys of stakeholder opinion.

c) 'Expert' commentary/review.

d) Stakeholder panels (to advise the organisation or the lead auditor).

The auditor may derive different levels of confidence from each audit method.

P10.17 For each audit method, the external auditor(s) may be supported by the work of the organisation's internal review/audit (see AA1000 process standard 12), and by other audit processes, such as the external certification of social and ethical performance and/or management systems (e.g. ISO standards, SA8000).

P10.18 The auditor(s) level of confidence will also be affected by the **nature of the process**. Factors that may be relevant include, but are not limited to:

a) The experience gained by the auditor during previous audits and the auditor's knowledge of the organisation's sector of operations.

b) The nature of the process adopted by the organisation, and the extent to which it is embedded in the management information systems, in particular.

c) The values of the organisation and their embeddedness in the organisation's systems.

P10.19 In addition to the auditor's assurance, quality assurance to stakeholders is supported by the scope of the audit and the legitimacy of the auditor(s) to each stakeholder group. Quality assurance will be increased the greater the scope (see AA1000 process standard 10.16) of the audit process.

P10.20 The legitimacy of an auditor will vary by stakeholder group, and will depend, in part, on the audit scope addressed by the auditor. The following factors will also be relevant in determining the legitimacy of the social and ethical auditor:

a) The qualifications of the auditor—see section 3 (audit guidelines) and section 8 (professional qualification).

b) The ethical principles associated with the audit qualification—see section 3 (audit guidelines).

c) The nature of the auditing organisation—size, type of organisation, experience, geographic focus, etc.

P10.21 The organisation may choose to use more than one auditor in order to build the credibility of its process. The organisation's choice reflects the legitimacy and expertise that different auditors possess with regard to different geographies, stakeholders or issues. Where the organisation's audit method includes the use of more than one social and ethical auditor, the role of each auditor is clearly documented and identified to each auditor.

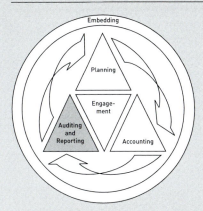

Communicate report(s) and obtain feedback

P11 **The organisation communicates information on the process and social and ethical performance of the organisation to all stakeholder groups. This includes making accessible to all stakeholder groups the social and ethical report(s) together with the independent audit opinion(s). The organisation actively seeks feedback from its stakeholder groups in order to further develop its process.**

P11.1 The manner in which the social and ethical report(s) (including the social and ethical audit report) and other information on the organisation's process and social and ethical performance is communicated is important to meet the principles of accessibility and information quality.

P11.2 The report(s) also form part of the inclusive engagement process with stakeholders. Stakeholder feedback on the report(s) is facilitated by the organisation. To address the principle of continuous improvement, the feedback includes consideration of methods to improve the organisation's process as well as its social and ethical performance.

P11.3 The organisation makes a commitment to stakeholders to report upon the stakeholder feedback in future reporting periods, and to address the comments in future cycles of the process.

P11.4 The main audience for the report(s) are the organisation's stakeholders, although other parties may be interested. The document is accessible to all stakeholders. Accessibility is concerned with the media through which the report(s) are distributed and the cost of accessing the report(s).

P11.5 The report(s) and other communications should be logically structured and written and/or presented in a manner understandable to all stakeholder groups, although individual communications may be targeted to specific stakeholder groups. Understandability includes issues of language, style and format. Technical and scientific terms are explained within the report.

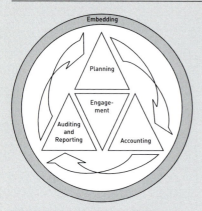

Establish and embed systems

P12 **The organisation establishes systems to support the process, and the on-going achievement of its objectives and targets in line with its values. Systems include those to implement and maintain values, to manage the collection and documentation of information and to perform the internal audit/review of the process.**

P12.1 The process, in current and future cycles, is supported through the development of systems to embed it in the organisation. These systems address the implementation of values, the collection of data and documentation, and internal review/audit. Together, the systems support the continuous improvement of the process and the organisation's social and ethical performance.

Implement and maintain values

P12.2 The organisation establishes systems to implement the organisation's values, and to ensure its activities are aligned with these values.

P12.3 The organisation's mission and values statement(s) are made available to all stakeholders (see AA1000 process standard 3.3), and the role of stakeholders in the process is clearly communicated to them (see AA1000 process standard 1.5).

P12.4 The organisation demonstrates a commitment to its values:

a) The roles and responsibilities of the board for social and ethical issues are clearly defined. These include the responsibility to ensure the implementation of the values throughout the organisation.

b) Core operating processes incorporate consideration of the organisation's values, objectives and targets. These may include, but are not limited to, the organisation's strategic planning, budgeting and investment planning processes.

c) The organisation may incorporate best practice in a code of conduct.

P12.5 The organisation supports adherence to its values. This may be achieved through the following (and other) methods:

a) Incorporating the organisation's values in employee hiring, job descriptions and reviews.

b) Training programmes including continuous learning.

c) Reward and sanction procedures related to social and ethical behaviour and performance.

d) Mechanisms to allow employees to address conflicts of interest or ethical dilemmas.

e) Recourse mechanisms for employees and partners such as confidential help-lines and other whistle-blowing mechanisms.

f) Ensuring employees and other relevant stakeholders are aware of and understand the programmes, procedures, etc, listed in points 12.5 b) to e).

P12.6 The organisation makes its employees aware of mechanisms that address ethical dilemmas and that offer recourse to sanctions. It makes access to these facilities easily and freely available.

P12.7 The organisation develops other systems/controls as required to enhance the likelihood that its objectives and targets will be achieved. These may include systems that are:

a) Directive—to cause or encourage a desirable event to occur.

b) Detective—to detect and correct undesirable events that have occurred.

c) Preventive—to monitor, predict and deter undesirable events from occurring.

Establish data collection and documentation systems

P12.8 The organisation develops systems for information collection and documentation to facilitate the continual monitoring of the organisation's social and ethical performance. This includes the management of the organisation's engagement with stakeholders throughout the process.

P12.9 The systems are developed to incorporate the geographic locations, operating units, issues and indicators identified as part of the process scope (see AA1000 process standards 4 and 5).

P12.10 Information on the process and social and ethical performance is documented efficiently to allow easy examination by internal and external auditors. The documentation includes, but is not limited to:

a) Information on the organisation's mission, values, objectives, targets and social and ethical performance.

b) Processes to identify stakeholders, and examine the organisation's relationship with them.

c) Processes to define and implement the organisation's values.

d) Processes to identify the scope of the process including stakeholders, geographical locations and business units.

e) Processes to identify social and ethical issues and indicators.

f) Processes to collect and analyse social and ethical information.

P12.11 Where possible the organisation seeks to integrate management information systems for social and ethical performance with its systems for financial and environmental performance (and with other operating systems in all functions) so that each area and the linkages between each area can be considered simultaneously.

Establish internal review/audit process

P12.12 The organisation develops an internal review/audit system to examine the adequacy of systems to provide reasonable assurance that:

a) The organisation's objectives and targets are met efficiently and effectively, and where targets are not met that the reasons for this are examined.

b) The objectives and targets reflect the values of the organisation.

c) The process is developed for future cycles.

P12.13 The internal review/audit process considers:

a) Systems to implement and maintain values.

b) Systems to collect and document information.

P12.14 The internal review/audit process may also consider:

a) The reliability of information.

b) Compliance with laws, standards and guidelines.

c) The inclusivity and completeness of the process.

d) The achievement of objectives and targets.

e) The economy and efficiency of the use of resources.

5 Stakeholder engagement

5.1 Introduction

There is growing recognition by organisations that some stakeholders possess significant influence over them:

a) More information is publicly available on the activity of organisations and the impact of these activities on employees, shareholders, society, the environment and the economy.

b) Stakeholders demand higher standards of behaviour from organisations.

c) The legitimacy of these demands is more widely recognised by government, regulators and civil society.

At the same time, organisations recognise the conflicts of interest they have with stakeholders, and the lack of consensus between and within stakeholder groups.

This is a dilemma that AA1000 seeks to address. It does not provide a prescriptive framework for the resolution of these dilemmas. However, it does provide a process for the organisation to begin to address them through engaging with stakeholders to find common ground and build trust.

This process of engagement with stakeholders is at the heart of AA1000. Engagement is not about an organization abdicating responsibilities for its activities, but rather using leadership to build relationships with stakeholders, and hence improving the organisation's accountability and performance.

But how can organisations and stakeholders ensure quality in the consultation and dialogue that takes place between them? The guidelines begin to answer this question by outlining good practice in engagement.

The guidelines have three elements. They:

a) Define the aims of stakeholder engagement in the context of AA1000.

b) Describe a number of methods of stakeholder engagement.

c) Describe techniques and provide advice to support the good practice of the methods defined above.

5.2 Development of the guidelines

The stakeholder engagement guidelines are designed for all main user groups of AA1000. Adopting organisations, stakeholders and service providers can each use the guidelines to understand the aims of engagement, and to examine the methods and techniques that may be used to support these aims. Standards developers can also use the guidelines as the basis for their own specialized engagement guidelines. These may include, for example, guidelines for:

a) Engagement on different issues, e.g. environmental and social issues.

b) Engagement in different countries and cultures, and with different genders and races.

c) Engagement in crisis situations.

d) Engagement with internal and external stakeholders.

e) Engagement by different organisation types, e.g. large and small, public, private and non-profit, and in different sectors of operation.

f) Audit of engagement processes.

5.3 Aims of stakeholder engagement

As part of the AA1000 process, stakeholder engagement is focused on improving the accountability and performance of the organisation.

The AA1000 definition of accountability is an accountability of organisations to their stakeholders. The nature of this accountability is defined by the organisation's engagement with its stakeholders.

Stakeholder engagement can also be at the heart of a virtuous circle of performance improvement. Meaningful engagement with stakeholders can:

a) **Anticipate and manage conflicts**.

b) Improve **decision-making** from management, employees, investors and other external stakeholders.

c) Build **consensus** amongst diverse views.

d) Create stakeholder **identification** with the outcomes of the organisation's activities.

e) Build **trust** in the organisation.

These five factors are key to improving financial performance, for example, through the improved recruitment and retention of employees, or the increased sophistication of risk management systems. They are also key to improving the organisation's performance on other measures in a manner that satisfies the aspirations of the organisation's stakeholders. If the engagement improves stakeholder satisfaction, this will also play a role in supporting the long-term financial performance of the organisation.

But what does it mean to have meaningful engagement? At a high level, it requires that the organisation is **accountable** (transparent, responsive and compliant), and in particular that its leadership makes decisions based on an **accurate and full understanding** of stakeholder aspirations and needs. To achieve this, engagement needs to:

a) Allow stakeholders to assist in the identification of other stakeholders.

b) Ensure that stakeholders trust the social and ethical accountant (internal or external) that is collecting and processing the findings of the engagement.

c) Be a dialogue, not a one-way information feed.

d) Be between parties with sufficient preparation and briefing to make well-informed decisions.

e) Involve stakeholders in defining the terms of the engagement. The terms will include, but are not limited to the issues covered, the methods and techniques of engagement used, the questions asked, the means of analysing responses to questions and the stakeholder feedback process.

f) Allow stakeholders to voice their views without restriction and without fear of penalty or discipline. However, stakeholders must be aware that if their opinions are taken seriously and acted upon, this will have consequences upon them and other stakeholder groups.

g) Include a public disclosure and feedback process that offers other stakeholders information that is valuable in assessing the engagement and allows them to comment upon it.

5.4 Methods of stakeholder engagement

A variety of methods of engagement can be used by organisations. These include, but are not limited to (see AA1000 process standard 7.2):

a) One-to-one interviews, face-to-face and distance.

b) Group interviews.

c) Focus groups.

d) Workshops and seminars.

e) Public meetings.

f) Questionnaires—face-to-face, by letter, telephone, internet or other techniques.

The appropriate method for each process of stakeholder engagement will depend on the nature and size of the organisation and the scope of the engagement—the stakeholders included, the complexity and nature of the issues covered and the geographic location.

The choice of method will also be affected by the capacity of the organisation—in terms of financial resources, staff resources and management systems—and by the capacity of its stakeholders. **A key element of stakeholder engagement therefore lies in the organisation's definition and building of its own capacities and the capacities of its stakeholders.**

5.5 Techniques of stakeholder engagement

The techniques of stakeholder engagement are designed and implemented to support the aim of the engagement process—accountability, including the accurate and full understanding of stakeholder aspirations and needs.

Accountability

a) The organisation may use **sampling** techniques for engagement with stakeholders. Samples are statistically robust, and ensure that a representative spread of each stakeholder group within the accounting, auditing and reporting scope is included. In defining samples, the organisation is aware of key diversity issues, which may include but are not limited to: the gender, race, age, disabilities and culture of the samples (see AA1000 process standard 7.5).

b) The organisation should ensure the independence and objectivity of the social and ethical accountant (internal or external) that is collecting and processing the results of the engagement.

c) The rationale and processes of stakeholder engagement are documented to facilitate internal and external audit. The auditor may examine documentation or attend dialogues, unless this raises conflict with other AA1000 principles or issues of sensitivity for stakeholders (see AA1000 process standard 7.7).

d) Stakeholders are encouraged to comment upon engagement processes and to recommend improvements.

Accurate and full expression of aspirations and needs

e) Stakeholders are encouraged to understand the context of stakeholder engagement in the overall social and ethical accounting, auditing and reporting process (see AA1000 process standard 1.5).

f) Stakeholders are involved in the design of questions to be addressed in the stakeholder engagement process (see AA1000 process standard 7.6) and the format of the engagement.

g) Genuine differences between stakeholders and the organisation and between stakeholder groups are acknowledged. Stakeholder views are listened to and noted. Points may be challenged, but are not dismissed.

h) Confidentiality is ensured where it is desired by stakeholders.

i) Stakeholders are briefed by the organisation to ensure that opinions and decisions are well-informed.

j) Questionnaires are designed to be understandable and easy to complete. Space is provided to allow the free expression of views. For employee surveys, employees should be allowed sufficient official time to complete responses.

k) Communication tools are used that address issues of cultural, racial, gender or educational bias.

l) Quieter stakeholders are drawn out and allowed time to express their views.

m) Leading questions are avoided.

n) Avoid stakeholder fatigue through innovative methods of engagement.

7 First steps

7.1 Introduction

Organisations have adopted **a variety of approaches to social and ethical accounting, auditing and reporting.** Each approach has a different balance in terms of the issues on which it is focused, and the processes by which the organisation measures, communicates and develops its values, processes, objectives and targets. These methods include:

a) Developing internal codes of conduct and auditing compliance with codes.

b) Reporting costs and benefits of activities to key constituencies and stakeholders.

c) Measuring the financial costs and benefits of 'social and ethical' activities.

d) External and internal rating of performance against benchmarks and indicators.

e) Stakeholder-based valuation, linked to the valuation of intangible assets.

f) Reporting compliance to legislation and other standards and guidelines to which the organisation has committed itself.

g) Assessing systems and processes to implement and develop the organisation's values.

h) Accounting, auditing and reporting the behaviour of individuals within the organisation, and the impacts of the organisation's activities (social and ethical, environmental and/or economic) on stakeholders.

i) Developing and assessing the organisation's dialogue with stakeholders.

The alternative methods (and the extent to which they have been pursued) reflect **a number of dimensions of organisations' identities**. Among the more important dimensions include:

a) The nature of the organisation:

  i) Public, private or non-profit.

  ii) Large or small.

  iii) National or international.

  iv) Nature of mission and values.

b) The driver of the organisation's adoption of social and ethical accounting, auditing and reporting:

  i) Aim to explain aims and performance of the organisation, and to discharge accountability to stakeholders.

  ii) Aim to develop competitive advantage through defined social and ethical stance.

  iii) Response to public pressures—actual or potential.

  iv) Aim to realise and develop the values of the organisation.

  v) Aim to improve management of organisation through developed understanding of values and intentions of internal and external stakeholders.

c) The legal requirements and societal norms of the regions within which the organisation operates.

d) The level of development of existing environmental accounting and reporting systems.

e) The existence of other programmes (mandatory or voluntary) regarding the management of social and ethical issues (e.g. Best Value in UK local government).

f) Key stakeholders in the organisation, and their demands.

  i) Levels of trust in the organisation.

  ii) Legitimacy of the auditors.

g) Cost pressures.

h) Uncertainty about costs and benefits of the process.

The AA1000 foundation standard recognises that organisations may adopt a stepped approach to building accountability, and will use AA1000 as a model to aspire to over time.

Within the context of the AA1000 standards, these 'first step' guidelines

a) Briefly discuss how different approaches to social and ethical accounting, auditing and reporting can be understood in terms of **a model of development towards accountability**.

b) Suggest a set of first steps (and considerations at each step) towards starting a social and ethical accounting, auditing and reporting process.

7.2 Development of the guidelines

The first step guidelines will be developed to incorporate experience from those organisations addressing social and ethical accounting, auditing and reporting for the first time, in particular those addressing it through the perspective of AA1000.

7.3 Developing accountability

Three aspects of any approach to social and ethical accounting, auditing and reporting can be examined to understand its level of development. The higher the level of stakeholder involvement, the greater the scope and regularity of the process, and the more complete the stages of AA1000 completed, the further the organisation progresses towards discharging its accountability. The approaches identified in the introduction can be assessed against this simple matrix. To develop its accountability, an organisation may address both the quantity and sophistication of methods used on each dimension.

7.4 First steps

An organisation considering a process of social and ethical accounting, auditing and reporting may address the following steps (see figure 22):

a) Formalise its reasons for (and against) beginning the process ('Defining Aims').

b) Understand its capability to achieve aims ('Defining Capacity').

If it chooses to proceed the organisation may:

c) Outline the nature of the process to be adopted, including the processes to be followed and issues covered ('Outlining Scope').

d) Build its resources to match the aims of the project ('Building Capacity').

This final stage of **building capacity is central to the success of the process**.

These stages begin to cover some aspects of the 'Planning' and 'Embedding' stages of the AA1000 process. Some organisations have used these first steps as a scoping exercise in which the aims of the project, etc, are clarified before investing significant resources in a full process. Others, however, have incorporated these first steps within the full accounting, auditing and reporting process.

In this section, **'the process'** refers to an organisation's process of social and ethical accounting, auditing and reporting.

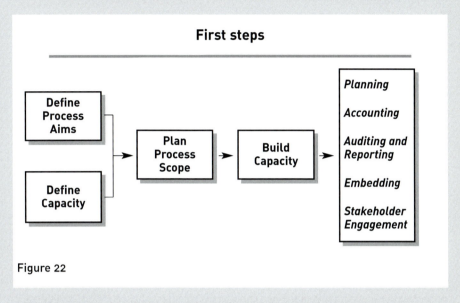

First steps

Figure 22

a) Defining aims

An organisation may address the following considerations (amongst others) in defining its aims from the social and ethical accounting, auditing and reporting process.

a) To address specific stakeholder concerns.

b) To pre-empt stakeholder or public criticism.

c) To discharge accountability.

d) To help build a sustainable organisation.

e) To better understand stakeholder aspirations and needs from their relationship with the organisation.

f) To build a common understanding with stakeholders of the aims and values of the organisation.

g) To improve long-term financial performance.

h) To build relationships with specific stakeholder groups.

An organisation's aims are likely to be complex, and understanding the relative balance of each factor will help define the accountability processes the organisation will choose, as well as the scope of the process (see point c—Outlining scope).

b) Defining capacity

In measuring its capacity to achieve its aims, the organisation may consider, inter alia, its:

a) Financial resources.

b) Staff resources:

    i) Numbers.

    ii) Experience in relevant fields, e.g. environmental accounting, stakeholder engagement.

c) Stakeholder resources and capabilities.

d) Existing management systems, including strategic tools, measurement systems and data collection systems.

e) Applicability of existing systems, (e.g. management scorecards), to the social and ethical accounting, auditing and reporting process.

f) Leadership capabilities.

g) Relationships with each stakeholder group (see AA1000 process standard 2.6).

c) Outlining scope

With an understanding of its aims and capacity, an organisation may consider the relationship between these aims and the options of different accounting, auditing and reporting processes. These options (suggested by the list below) include different alternatives for the process steps and the scope of the process.

a) Will the process include a social and ethical audit(s)?

b) If so, what sort of audit process(es)?

    i) What is the scope of the audit?

    ii) Who is the auditor(s)?

c) Will the process include a social and ethical report(s)?

d) If so, what sort of report?

    i) What is the audience of the report?

    ii) What reporting media are used?

    iii) What is the scope of the report?

e) What is the scope of the accounting process?

    i) Stakeholders.

    ii) Geographies.

    iii) Operating units.

    iv) Issues.

f) What are the key areas in this scope to focus on in the process?

g) What sort of indicators will we use for measurement?

   i) Input, output and outcome

   ii) Qualitative and quantitative.

h) What methods and techniques of stakeholder engagement will be used?

i) What will be the role of other standards and guidelines?

   i) Defining/implementing values.

   ii) Developing systems.

   iii) Defining issues/indicators.

   iv) Defining reporting formats/content.

   v) Certifying processes and performance.

j) What internal systems are required for the process?

k) What is the timetable for the process?

   i) Start date.

   ii) Key stages.

   iii) Key outputs.

l) What are the plans for future cycles of the process?

d) Building capacity

In order to build capacity the organisation will reflect on the definition of the process. It should consider, inter alia, the following requirements:

a) Building commitment amongst governing body for the process.

b) Definition of roles and responsibilities for management of the process.

c) Creation of project champions.

d) Identification of gaps in skills.

e) Where gaps exist, identification and hire of external support for key steps of the process.

f) Building and implementation of training programmes for its employees.

g) Building knowledge and capabilities of stakeholders.

25
AccountAbility 1000 Assurance Standard

> The AA1000 Assurance Standard offers a unique opportunity to resurrect assurance, phoenix-like, from the ashes of Enron, WorldCom and other trust-eroding corporate disasters.
>
> *John Elkington, Chairperson, SustainAbility Ltd* [1]

Type   Process standard

Strength   It promotes the development of professional qualifications

Keywords   Assurance • Assurance providers • AccountAbility • Principles • Quality

25.1 Background

In an age of cynicism, one of the key challenges for corporate responsibility is the need to demonstrate that social and environmental programmes are making a difference. Consumers and investors are less inclined to trust companies after the scandals of WorldCom, Enron (Fox 2002; Sullivan 2002) and Ahold (*Economist* 2003). The assurance of corporate responsibility (CR) initiatives plays a key role in building the trust necessary to sustain these programmes. According to Account-Ability:

> The concern that more data does not always equate to accurate or useful information is damaging the credibility and effectiveness of today's progressive drive to increase social and sustainability accounting and reporting (AccountAbility 2002).

---

1 Speaking at the launch of the AA1000 Assurance Standard, London, 25 March 2003 (see www.accountability.org.uk/aa1000/default.asp?pageid=95#je.

AccountAbility has turned the field of corporate responsibility into a discipline, setting out professional qualifications, providing training and developing methodologies—'the how'—of corporate responsibility.

According to the AA1000 Assurance Standard:

> Assurance is an evaluation method that uses a specified set of principles and standards to assess the quality of a Reporting Organisation's subject matter, such as reports, and the organisation's underlying systems, processes and competences that underpin its performance. Assurance includes the communication of the results of this evaluation to provide credibility to the subject matter for its users (AccountAbility 2003: 5).

The AA1000 Assurance Standard includes four elements:

- Core assurance principles

- Practice and quality standards and guidelines

- Guidelines for organisations

- Qualifications of assurance providers

As for the AccountAbility 1000 Framework, owing to space constraints only some sections of the AA1000 Assurance Standard are included—covering the principles and annexes on assurance aspects (Glossary) and the AA1000 Series.

25.2 Strengths and weaknesses

The AA1000 Assurance Standard is designed to cover assurance processes across the spectrum of sustainability issues. It is compatible with the Global Reporting Initiative (GRI, Chapter 26) in that it provides guidance to global reporters using the GRI guidelines. Furthermore, the AA1000 Assurance Standard is compatible with the SIGMA ('Sustainability: Integrated Guidelines for Management') framework (Chapter 28). The AA1000 Assurance Standard can also be used with audits of factory compliance with labour standards and carbon emissions.

The AA1000 Assurance Standard is accessible online at no cost. This accessibility of the standard is important, as it facilitates consultation with stakeholders. The consultation process for the AA1000 Assurance Standard has been thorough, benefiting from input from a wide range of organisations.

The AA1000 Assurance Standard is based on continuous improvement. Companies commit themselves to increasing levels of assurance over time. This gradual approach will be an important factor in building the field of assurance. Another strength of the standard is that it is oriented towards the future. Hence, it 'indicates how able an organisation is to carry out stated policies and goals, as well as to meet future standards and expectations' (AccountAbility 2003: 6). As it is one of the newest standards, it is still too early to assess its full impact.

25.3 Organisations to which the AA1000 Assurance Standard applies

The AA1000 Assurance Standard is designed for organisations of all sizes and sectors, as well as for assurance providers.

25.4 Questions posed and answered

The AA1000 Assurance Standard asks:

- What are the criteria by which one can assess the quality of the assurance processes?
- What constitutes a credible assurance statement?
- What constitutes a credible assurance provider?

25.5 The challenge and the promise

As more and more companies and assurance providers are guided by the AA1000 Assurance Standard, the credibility of corporate responsibility will increase, with a corresponding decrease in apathy. Reporting should become more focused, credible and, most importantly, useful to stakeholders. The AA1000 Assurance Standard should limit conflicts of interest between service providers and the organisations to which they provide assurance. These benefits will also promote the field of socially responsible investment (SRI), making the decision-making process within the SRI community more likely to be based on credible and accurate information. Furthermore, the AA1000 Assurance Standard, if implemented broadly, will promote the comparability of reports across different sectors.

A major challenge facing the field of assurance will be to build capacity among assurance providers. The AA1000 Assurance Standard provides useful guidance in this emerging field.

References

AccountAbility (Institute for Social and Ethical AccountAbility) (2002) 'Closing the Assurance Gap: The AA1000 Series Quality Assurance Framework' (London: AccountAbility, April 2002).
—— (2003) *AccountAbility 1000 Assurance Standard* (London: AccountAbility).

Economist (2003) 'Europe's Enron: Ahold's Shocking Accounting', *The Economist*, 1 March 2003.

Fox, L. (2002) *Enron: The Rise and Fall* (New York; John Wiley).

Sullivan, R. (2002) 'One Step Forward or Two Steps Back for Effective Self-regulation?', *Journal of Corporate Citizenship* 8 (Winter 2002): 91-104.

Additional resource

Website

Institute for Social and Ethical AccountAbility (AccountAbility): www.accountability.org.uk.

AA1000 Assurance Standard[*]

Organisations adopting any part of the AA1000 Series, including the *AA1000 Assurance Standard*, commit themselves to the practice of *'inclusivity'*, by which is meant an organisation's:

- Commitment to *identify and understand* its social, environmental and economic performance and impact, and the associated views of its Stakeholders.

- Commitment to *consider* and *coherently respond* (whether negatively or positively) to the aspirations and needs of its Stakeholders in its policies and practices, and

- Commitment to *provide an account* to its Stakeholders for its decisions, actions and impacts.

The principles set out below are the basis on which the credibility of an organisation's fulfilment of this over-arching Accountability Commitment can be assured.[11] Annex B provides further details on the AA1000 Series.

The AA1000 Principles

The following principles must be applied in an Assurance process undertaken using the *AA1000 Assurance Standard*:

Principle 1. (P.1) Materiality

Principle 2. (P.2) Completeness

Principle 3. (P.3) Responsiveness

These principles are common across all aspects of the AA1000 Series, but are set out below as they relate to an Assurance process.

4.1 Application of Principles and Levels of Assurance

All 'AA1000 principles' must be applied in any Assurance assignment. The manner in which they are applied depends on the level of Assurance pursued.

---

[*] The AA1000 Assurance Standard Principles and Appendices are reprinted with the permission of The Institute for Social and Ethical AccountAbility (AccountAbility). © 2003 AccountAbility.

Assurance levels may depend on the extent and quality of the following:[12]

- *Information available.*

- *Sufficiency of evidence.*

- Underlying *systems and processes.*

- *Internal* Assurance systems.

- *Existing Assurance* for specific aspects of performance Reporting

- *Resources allocated* for Assurance by the Reporting Organisation.

- Legal or commercial *constraints.*

- *Competencies* of the Assurance Provider.

The level of Assurance is expected, although not required, to increase over time as information and underlying systems and processes for accounting for Sustainability Performance improve.

The Assurance Provider must convey in the Report how the application of the AA1000 principles may vary across different aspects of performance and, consequently, the Report, within a single assignment. The Assurance Provider and Reporting Organisation should together plan and agree on the level of Assurance to be pursued. The level of Assurance may change as the Assurance Provider carries out its work; this should then be communicated to Stakeholders to enable them to understand the degree of credibility they should attach to the Assurance.

4.2 Materiality (P.1)

The AA1000 *Materiality Principle* requires that the Assurance Provider states whether the Reporting Organisation has included in the Report the information about its Sustainability Performance required by its Stakeholders for them to be able to make informed judgements, decisions and actions.

Information is material if its omission or misrepresentation in the Report could influence the decisions and actions of the Reporting Organisation's Stakeholders.

Guidance on the interpretation of a Stakeholder-based approach to materiality will in practice evolve over time, and be covered in both Guidance and Practitioner Notes. Given the centrality of this definition and its interpretation, however, an indication of the parameters that might be taken into account is provided below.

(a) *Compliance performance.* The materiality test must consider those aspects of non-financial performance where a significant legal, regulatory or direct financial impact exists.

(b) *Policy-related performance.* The materiality test should identify those aspects of performance linked to agreed policy positions, irrespective of financial consequences.

(c) *Peer-based norms.* Aspects of performance could be material where a company's peers and competitors take it as being so in their own case, irrespective of whether the company itself has a related policy or whether financial consequences can be demonstrated.

(d) Stakeholder-based materiality, which can include:

i. *Stakeholder behaviour impact.* Materiality should take into account concerns of Stakeholders where disclosure of related information could impact on their decisions and behaviour, both towards the company and in other situations.

ii. *Stakeholder views and perceptions.* Materiality should include aspects of performance demonstrably relevant to the views and perceptions of Stakeholders where these are considered relevant to their future decisions and behaviour.

On the basis of parameters such as those set out above, criteria will be agreed upon between the Assurance Provider and Reporting Organisation that enable the Provider to undertake the Assurance assignment.

The Assurance Provider needs to determine whether what is in the Report is material for the:

- Reporting Organisation, e.g. whether indicators and targets included in the Report can be, and are, used in strategic and operational decision-making tools and processes.

- Reporting Organisation's Stakeholders, to enable them to interpret the information in ways that are relevant to their specific decision-making needs; e.g. ensuring Reporting comparability over time with other organisations and against relevant standards.[13]

Based on the evidence, the Assurance Provider should form an opinion as to the materiality of possible omissions and misrepresentations in the Report. The Assurance Provider should discuss material omissions and misrepresentations with the Reporting Organisation and encourage it to amend the Report. If these material omissions and misrepresentations are not included in the Report the Assurance Provider should include them in its Assurance Statement.

The application of this principle by the Assurance Provider will be conditioned by the level of Assurance (see 4.1).

4.3 Completeness (P.2)

The AA1000 *Completeness Principle* requires that the Assurance Provider evaluate the extent to which the Reporting Organisation can identify and understand material aspects (see P.1) of its Sustainability Performance.

The Completeness Principle requires that the Assurance process evaluate the extent to which the Reporting Organisation can identify and understand its Sustainability Performance associated with activities, products, services, sites and subsidiaries, for which it has management and legal responsibility.[14] Such aspects, which are material to the Reporting Organisation or its Stakeholders, can extend beyond what would normally be included in these boundaries. These aspects of Sustainability Performance relate to the Completeness Principle where the Reporting Organisation has the ability to influence such performance, e.g. effects of product use.

The Assurance Provider should identify material shortfalls in the Reporting Organisation's understanding of its own performance. The Assurance Provider should also discuss shortcomings of completeness with the Reporting Organisation, which should be encouraged to address them or else reflect the shortcoming in their Report. Failing these options, the Assurance Provider should refer to them in its Assurance Statement.

The application of this principle by the Assurance Provider will be conditioned by the level of Assurance (see 4.1).

4.4 Responsiveness (P.3)

The AA1000 *Responsiveness Principle* requires that the Assurance Provider evaluate whether the Reporting Organisation has responded to Stakeholder concerns, policies and relevant standards, and adequately communicated these responses in its Report.

The Responsiveness Principle requires that the Reporting Organisation demonstrate in its Report what it has decided to do in response to specified Stakeholder concerns and interests, and also provide adequate indicators of associated changes in Sustainability Performance. This principle does not require that the Reporting Organisation agrees or complies with Stakeholders' concerns and interests, but that it has responded coherently and consistently to them.

Assurance Providers must evaluate whether the Reporting Organisation has:

- Decided how it intends to respond to *Stakeholder concerns and interests*.

- Established associated *policies, targets and indicators*.

- Demonstrated that it has allocated *adequate resources* to enable it to implement associated policies and commitments.

- Communicated the above in its Report in a manner that is both *timely and accessible* to Stakeholders.

The Assurance Provider must form an opinion based on the available evidence. Information concerning evidence is supplied by the Reporting Organisation, in addition to other information concerning the views of Stakeholders, as well as industry and other benchmarks.

The application of this principle by the Assurance Provider will be conditioned by the level of Assurance (see 4.1).

Annex A. Assurance Aspects—Glossary

A.1 Reporting Organisation

The Reporting Organisation may be one or more legal organisations, a partnership or network, or a well-defined project or programme.

A.2 Who Is Assurance For?

Assurance should provide confidence in the Report's underlying information to the Reporting Organisation's Stakeholders, particularly the direct users of the Report.

A.3 Sustainability Performance

Sustainability Performance refers to an organisation's total performance, which might include its policies, decisions, and actions that create social, environmental and/or economic (including financial) outcomes.

A.4 Stakeholders

Stakeholders are those individuals and groups that affect and/or are affected by the organisation and its activities.

The *operational* definition of Stakeholders used here does not, therefore, include all people who may have knowledge or views about the organisation. Organisations will, nevertheless, have many Stakeholders, each with distinct types and levels of involvement, and often with diverse and sometimes conflicting interests and concerns. This is why organisations need systematic processes for managing this complexity in ways that build accountability to Stakeholders and overall performance.[18]

A.5 The Report

The Report is a set of information prepared by the Reporting Organisation about its Sustainability Performance, whether for general publication, targeted external distribution or internal use. This will generally refer to information contained within a specific Report prepared periodically to inform Stakeholders about the organisation's Sustainability Performance. The Assurance Provider may, however, choose to take a wider range of information into account when, for example, the main Report forms part of a broader set of communications on issues and aspects of performance they are assuring.

A.6 The Accounting Period

Assurance covers an agreed Accounting Period established within two clearly defined historical dates. This is typically one year,[19] although the increased use of internet-based Reporting may result in shorter Accounting Periods in the future, and indeed Accounting Periods that may vary for different types of information.

A.7. The Assurance Provider

The Assurance Provider is one or more individuals, or an organisation, contracted by the Reporting Organisation to provide Assurance of their Report.

Annex B. The AA1000 Series

B.1 The AA1000 Series

The AA1000 Series, which includes the AA1000 Assurance Standard, guides organisations in establishing systematic accountability processes that involve Stakeholders in the generation of strategies, policies and programmes as well as associated indicators, targets and communication systems, which effectively guide decisions, activities and overall organisational performance.

B.2 Defining Accountability

The AA1000 Series defines 'accountability' as being made up of:[20]

- Transparency: to account to its Stakeholders.

- Responsiveness: to respond to Stakeholder concerns.

- Compliance: to comply with standards to which it is voluntarily committed, and rules and regulations that it must comply with for statutory reasons.

These aspects of accountability may in practice have very different drivers, including legal compliance, stated policy commitments, reputation and risk management, and the company's sense of moral and ethical duty.

B.3 Assurance and the AA1000 Series

The AA1000 Assurance Standard is a stand-alone approach to Assurance, and is also an element of the AA1000 Series, and so:

- Provides the basis for assuring a Report and underlying processes, systems and competencies against the AA1000 Series definition of accountability and associated principles.

- The core Assurance principles are equivalent to the revised accountability principles underpinning the overall AA1000 Series.[21]

B.4 AA1000 Assurance Standard Guidance Notes

The *AA1000 Assurance Standard Guidance Notes* are intended to provide detailed guidance in the implementation and use of the AA1000 Assurance Standard. A growing number of Guidance Notes are expected, and each set is likely to go through revisions based on practitioner experience and other developments (e.g. regulatory).

Notes:

[11] The original accountability principles are described in the Exposure Draft: AccountAbility (1999) *AA1000 AccountAbility Framework: Standards, Guidelines and Professional Qualifications—Exposure Draft*, AccountAbility, London (www.accountability.org.uk).

[12] The list is not intended to signify a hierarchy of levels of Assurance.

[13] The GRI Guidelines also highlight the importance of an 'inclusive' process of developing indicators and public Reporting to increase the relevance to Stakeholders.

[14] Equivalent to what the GRI calls 'full-scope' Reporting.

[18] The *AA1000 Accountability Framework* details how an organisation can map its Stakeholders, and build a systematic process of Stakeholder engagement.

[19] As advocated for example by the GRI Guidelines.

[20] AccountAbility (1999): 8.

[21] For existing users of the original AA1000 Framework, the revised accountability/Assurance principles are a consolidation of the original accountability principles, and do not therefore involve any substantive change in direction or meaning.

26
The Global Reporting Initiative

GRI may well become the Securities and Exchange Commission for worldwide economic, environmental and social sustainability reporting.

Peter Downing, The Corporate Board[1]

The GRI Guidelines have been a great help for us in understanding and translating the changing global agenda into topics and issues that Novo Nordisk should report on to the public.

Lise Kingo, Senior Vice President,
Stakeholder Relations, Novo Nordisk[2]

Type   Process-oriented tool, multi-stakeholder tool

Strength   Its comprehensive and standardised reporting framework

Keywords Sustainability • Guidelines • Reporting • Social reports • Environment • Framework • Indicators • Multi-stakeholder

26.1 Background

The Global Reporting Initiative (GRI) has pioneered sustainability reporting, providing guidelines that serve as a framework for economic, social and environmental reporting. The mission of GRI is 'to elevate the quality of reporting to a higher level of comparability, consistency and utility' (GRI 2002a: 9).

---

1   Quoted on GRI website, www.globalreporting.org → What others say → Comments about GRI from others.
2   GRI 2002b: 3.

In 1997, the Coalition for Environmentally Responsible Economies (CERES) (see Chapter 15), in collaboration with the Tellus Institute, convened the GRI. The UN Environment Programme (UNEP) has also played an important role in the formation of the GRI. The Guidelines are the product of an intensive, multi-stakeholder, consultation process, involving thousands of non-governmental organisations (NGOs), companies, business groups, trade unions and accountancy organisations (United Nations 2002).

In June 2000, GRI launched the Sustainability Reporting Guidelines, and a fully revised and updated version was released in September 2002 during the World Summit on Sustainable Development. There are 313 companies in 31 countries that issue GRI reports, earning them the title 'GRI Reporters'. The majority of the reporters are in Europe (Downing 2003: 32), but the Guidelines are becoming well known throughout the world.

Although the GRI Guidelines are not a code of conduct, a management system or a standard, they are extremely useful to companies working on code implementation. The Guidelines promote the communication of (GRI 2002a: 11):

- Actions taken to improve economic, environmental and social performance

- The outcomes of such actions

- Future strategies for improvement

The Guidelines are structured in five parts. First, an Introduction explains the trends driving sustainability reporting and the benefits of reporting; second (in Part A), general guidance is given on using the Guidelines; third (in Part B), the principles and practices that promote rigorous reporting and underlie the application of the Guidelines are set out; fourth (in Part C), the content and compilation of a report is considered; and finally a glossary and a series of annexes provide additional guidance and resources.

Due to space limitations, only the following excerpts from the Guidelines are included in this book: 'Reporting Expectations and Design' from Part A: 'Using the Guidelines'); all of Part B: 'Reporting Principles'; and all of Part C: 'Report Content'.[3]

The Guidelines set a framework for GRI reporters. Reporting organisations can strive to have their reports be 'in accordance' with the Guidelines or simply use the Guidelines informally. If companies select the former approach, they must meet certain set criteria. There is no formal verification by GRI to ensure that these criteria have been met.

---

3 In the reproduced Global Reporting Initiative text, there are several references to the annexes to the Guidelines; however, there was insufficient space in this book to include these. Please refer to www.globalreporting.org.

26.2 Strengths and weaknesses

The GRI has strong support from companies and NGOs around the world. One of the factors that has led to its strong position as a brand leader among corporate responsibility (CR) initiatives, among all sectors, is the degree to which GRI has been very inclusive of its many stakeholder groups. In the first three years of its existence, GRI engaged with 10,000 stakeholders from more than 50 countries (United Nations 2002: 5). The 2000 version of the Guidelines was distributed to 12,000 people in eight different languages (United Nations 2002: 5). This unprecedented degree of outreach is one of the greatest achievements of the GRI. This level of engagement sets an important standard for consultation for new initiatives.

The GRI encourages companies to set targets and then to report on whether or not those targets have been met. If the company has not met its targets, it should give reasons. By encouraging companies to set and report on targets, stakeholders have 'standards' to which they can hold the company accountable. The GRI also encourages organisations to engage with stakeholders and to select organisation-specific performance indicators most relevant both to the reporting organisation and to its key stakeholders.

Many companies find the large number of indicators within the GRI framework daunting. Reporting can also be expensive, especially for large organisations. For Rio Tinto, the cost of reporting in 2001 was more than US$1 million (Downing 2003: 32). For Agilent Technologies the costs were approximately US$240,000, and for Ford Motor Company, they were US$350,000 (Downing 2003: 33). These costs do not include data collection and verification.

The GRI is a very valuable tool—it serves as an 'internal tool for evaluating the consistency between corporate sustainability policy and strategy on the one hand, and actual performance on the other' (GRI 1999: 5). Research is needed to demonstrate the link between reporting and improved social and environmental performance.

26.3 Organisations to which the Global Reporting Initiative Sustainability Reporting Guidelines apply

Although in the long term the GRI Guidelines are intended to be applicable to all types of organisations, the initial development work of the GRI has been focused on reporting by business organisations. The GRI recognises that smaller organisations may have more difficulty in becoming GRI reporters and, as such, encourages them to adopt an incremental approach to using the Guidelines.

According to Simon Zadek, 'the GRI is most useful for the companies that are not leaders in the [CR] field' (quoted in Maitland 2002). The Guidelines can be used as a complement to many of the codes and standards profiled in this book.

26.4 Questions posed and answered

The questions that GRI asks include:

- How can a company communicate to its stakeholders?

- On what issues should a company report?

- What are the boundaries of a company?

26.5 The promise and the challenge

Verification is one of the greatest challenges facing the GRI. Increasingly, external verification is seen as an important tool for guaranteeing the credibility of a report. External verification is not required by the GRI. However, GRI is convening a multi-stakeholder group to examine verification issues in general (www.globalreporting.org).

The GRI is among the most visionary of the CR tools profiled in this book. It will take decades for the GRI to become mainstream. According to Robert Massie, a GRI board member, they are in 'year 5 of a 30-year process' (quoted in Maitland 2002). In the course of the next few years, GRI is planning to harmonise reporting requirements, develop sectoral supplements and to improve the Guidelines (www. globalreporting.org). The challenge for the GRI is to make sustainability reporting not only mainstream but also useful to stakeholders and to the reporters.

References

Downing, P. (2003) 'The GRI and Corporate Reporting', *Ethical Corporation* 13 (January 2003): 32-35.

GRI (Global Reporting Initiative) (1999) *Sustainability Reporting Guidelines* (Boston, MA: GRI).

—— (2002a) *Sustainability Reporting Guidelines* (Boston, MA: GRI).

—— (2002b) *What Others Are Saying* (Boston, MA: GRI, available at www.globalreporting.org/about/whatothersay0203.pdf).

Maitland, A. (2002) 'Businesses are Called to Account', *Financial Times*, 28 March 2002.

United Nations (2002) *A Historic Collaborative Achievement: Inauguration of the Global Reporting Initiative* (New York: United Nations, 4 April 2002).

Additional resource

Website

Global Reporting Initiative: www.globalreporting.org

GRI Sustainability Reporting Guidelines*

REPORTING EXPECTATIONS AND DESIGN

The issues below are addressed in the following pages:

- core versus additional indicators;

- flexibility in using the *Guidelines*;

- customising a report within the GRI framework;

- frequency and medium of reporting;

- financial reports; and

- credibility of reports.

Core Versus Additional Indicators

The 2002 *Guidelines* contain two categories of performance indicators: core and additional. Both types of indicators have emerged from the GRI consultative process as valuable measures of the economic, environmental, and social performance of organisations. These *Guidelines* distinguish between the two types of indicators as follows:

Core indicators are:

- relevant to most reporting organisations; and

- of interest to most stakeholders.

Thus, designation as "core" signifies general relevance to both reporters and report users. In designating an indicator as "core", however, GRI exercises some discretion. For some core indicators, relevance may be limited to many, but not most, potential reporters. In the same vein, an indicator may be of keen interest to many, but not most, stakeholders. Over time, GRI expects that development of sector supplements will lead to the shifting of a number of core indicators to such supplements.

---

*   Reproduced with the permission of the Global Reporting Initiative. Selected extracts
     only are reproduced here.

Additional indicators are defined as those that have one or more of the following characteristics:

- represent a leading practice in economic, environmental, or social measurement, though currently used by few reporting organisations;

- provide information of interest to stakeholders who are particularly important to the reporting entity; and

- are deemed worthy of further testing for possible consideration as future core indicators.

Reporting organisations are encouraged to use the additional indicators in Section 5 of Part C to advance the organisation's and GRI's knowledge of new measurement approaches. Feedback on these indicators will provide a basis for assessing the readiness of additional indicators for future use as core indicators, for use in sector supplements, or for removal from the GRI indicator list.

Flexibility in Using the Guidelines

GRI encourages the use of the GRI *Guidelines* by all organisations, regardless of their experience in preparing sustainability reports. The *Guidelines* are structured so that all organisations, from beginners to sophisticated reporters, can readily find a comfortable place along a continuum of options.

Recognising these varying levels of experience, GRI provides ample flexibility in how organisations use the *Guidelines*. The options range from adherence to a set of conditions for preparing a report "in accordance" with the *Guidelines* to an informal approach. The latter begins with partial adherence to the reporting principles and/or report content in the *Guidelines* and incrementally moves to fuller adoption. This range of options is detailed below, and in Figure 2.

"In Accordance" Conditions

Organisations that wish to identify their report as prepared in accordance with the 2002 GRI *Guidelines* must meet five conditions:

1. Report on the numbered elements in Sections 1 to 3 of Part C.

2. Include a GRI Content Index as specified in Section 4 of Part C.

3. Respond to each core indicator in Section 5 of Part C by either (a) reporting on the indicator or (b) explaining the reason for the omission of each indicator.

4. Ensure that the report is consistent with the principles in Part B of the *Guidelines*.

5. Include the following statement signed by the board or CEO: "This report has been prepared in accordance with the 2002 GRI *Guidelines*. It represents a balanced and reasonable presentation of our organisation's economic, environmental, and social performance."

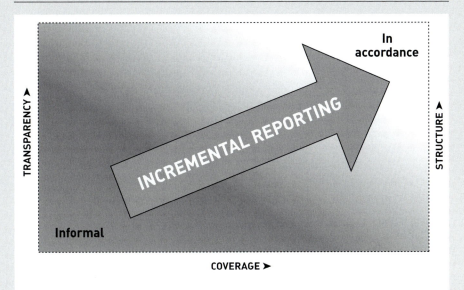

Figure 2: Options for Reporting

Reporting "In Accordance" with the *Guidelines*

The decision to report in accordance with the *Guidelines* is an option, not a requirement. It is designed for reporters that are ready for a high level of reporting and who seek to distinguish themselves as leaders in the field. The growing number of organisations with strong reporting practices demonstrates the ability of numerous organisations to adopt the in accordance option.

The conditions for reporting in accordance with the GRI *Guidelines* seek to balance two key objectives of the GRI framework:

● comparability; and

● flexibility.

Comparability has been integral to GRI's mission from the outset, and is closely tied to its goal of building a reporting framework parallel to financial reporting. The in accordance conditions help to advance GRI's commitment to achieving maximum comparability across reports by creating a common reference point for all reporters that choose to use this option.

While GRI seeks to enhance comparability between reports, also it is committed to supporting flexibility in reporting. Legitimate differences exist between organisations and between industry sectors. The GRI framework must have sufficient flexibility to allow reports to reflect these differences.

The in accordance conditions rely on transparency to balance the dual objectives of comparability and flexibility. Reporting organisations are asked to clearly indicate how they have used the *Guidelines* and, in particular, the core indicators. The evaluation of these decisions is then left to report users.

Reporting organisations that choose to report in accordance must note the reasons for the omissions of any core indicators in their reports, preferably in or near the GRI Content Index. GRI recognises that various factors may explain the omission of a core indicator. These include, for example: protection of proprietary information; lack of data systems to generate the required information; and conclusive determination that a specific indicator is not relevant to an organisation's operations. In providing these explanations, reporting organisations are encouraged to indicate their future reporting plans, if any, relative to each excluded core indicator. Indicators omitted for the same reason may be clustered and linked to the relevant explanation.

GRI emphasises that the exclusion of some core indicators still allows organisations to report in accordance with the *Guidelines* as long as explanations appear. At this time, GRI does not certify claims of in accordance nor does it validate explanations of omitted information. However, reporting organisations that elect an in accordance approach should anticipate that users will compare their reports against the five conditions associated with the in accordance status and make judgements based on such evaluation.

Informal Application of the *Guidelines*

Given the youthful state of comprehensive economic, environmental, and social reporting, GRI recognises that many organisations are still building their reporting capacity. These organisations are invited to choose an informal approach consistent with their current capacity (see Annex 3*). They may choose not to cover all of the content of the GRI *Guidelines* in their initial efforts, but rather to base their reports on the GRI framework and incrementally improve report content coverage, transparency, and structure over time.

For example, a first-time reporter may use a portion of the performance indicators (Part C) without having to provide an indicator-by-indicator explanation of omissions. Gradually, expanding use of the reporting principles and/or indicators will move the organisation toward more comprehensive coverage of economic, environmental, and social performance. Organisations that choose an incremental approach may reference GRI in their report. Such a reference should include a brief description of how the GRI *Guidelines* informed development of the report. However, incremental reporters may not use the term in accordance nor include the prescribed board or CEO statement unless all conditions for the in accordance option are met.

In sum, aware of the wide spectrum of reporter experience and capabilities, GRI enables reporters to select an approach that is suitable to their individual organisations. With time and practice, organisations at any point along this spectrum can move gradually toward comprehensive reporting built on both the principles and content of the GRI framework. Similarly, GRI will continue to benefit from the experiences of reporting organisations and report users as it strives to continually improve the *Guidelines*.

---

*   See footnote 3 on page 426 regarding references to annexes.

Customising a Report Within the GRI Framework

The *Guidelines* set out the basic information for inclusion in a report. However, GRI expects that reporting organisations will take steps to design their report content to reflect the unique nature of their organisation and the context in which it operates. These steps may involve:

- defining reporting boundaries;
- inserting additional content (usually based on stakeholder consultation) such as indicators, and textual discussions; and/or
- adopting a format tailored to the organisation.

Boundaries

In the early years of reporting, most organisations measured and reported on impacts based on the traditional boundary criteria used in financial reporting, that is, legal ownership and direct control. In recent years, companies have begun to experiment with expanding their reporting boundaries to better reflect the unique "footprint" of their organisation and its activities.

The completeness principle in Part B offers brief commentary on boundaries, and GRI is working to develop additional guidance and technical protocols on this issue. Until such guidance is available, the GRI framework emphasises the importance of extensive interaction with stakeholders to determine appropriate reporting boundaries.

Selecting Additional Content Through Engaging Stakeholders

Compared with financial reporting, which is targeted primarily at one key stakeholder—the shareholder—sustainability reporting has a large and diverse audience. Stakeholder engagement plays an important role in helping to ensure that a report achieves its primary purpose: providing information that meets the needs of the organisation's stakeholders. GRI reporters are expected to use these *Guidelines* (Part C, Sections 1 to 3 and core indicators from Section 5) in addition to sector supplements (if available) as the basis for their report.

The reporting elements and indicators in the *Guidelines* were developed through an extensive multi-stakeholder, consultative process. However, the inclusion of information (including performance indicators) identified through stakeholder consultation is a critical additional step in furthering the utility of an organisation's sustainability report; it is also one of the fundamental principles underlying GRI reporting (see Part B on Inclusiveness).

Since stakeholder consultation often involves a range of parallel discussions with different constituencies, it is important to document the interactions that result in the organisation's selection of indicators and to explain these in the report. While GRI emphasises the importance of stakeholder feedback in drafting reports, it does not offer specific guidance on how to conduct stakeholder engagement. Many guidance documents and case studies on this subject are available elsewhere.

Equally important, organisations should maintain a high degree of transparency in their reports regarding the specific reporting boundaries they have chosen.

Content

GRI encourages organisations to go beyond the information requested in Part C of the *Guidelines*, as needed, to present a balanced and reasonable picture of their economic, environmental, and social performance. In applying the *Guidelines*, each reporting organisation will make different decisions regarding the use of the additional performance indicators in Section 5 of Part C. Reporting organisations should also include other content, particularly integrated performance indicators, identified through stakeholder consultation. This information and these indicators may relate to sector- or geography-specific issues pertinent to the organisation. GRI's sector supplements will address some of these needs.

Structure

Part C of these *Guidelines* ("Report Content") is organised in a logical framework. Reporting organisations are encouraged but not required to use this same organisation for their report. GRI believes that completeness and comparability in economic, environmental, and social reporting are best served when all reporting organisations adhere to a common structure. At the same time, it recognises that some reporting organisations will want to choose a different structure based on specific characteristics of the reporting entity. In evaluating alternative approaches to organising their reports, organisations should carefully weigh the need to capture legitimate organisational and sectoral differences against the benefits of standardised structures. Common structures and formats support consistency and comparability. This provides benefits to both reporting organisations and report users by enhancing the clarity of communication and the ease of use of the documents over an extended period of time. In situations where reporting organisations use alternative structures, the Content Index described in Part C becomes even more essential as a tool to help users find and compare the content of reports.

The choice among different media for reporting (e.g., paper, electronic) may also influence decisions on the structure of reports. For example, some organisations might choose to produce a summary paper report and to make a fully detailed report available on the Internet. Where Internet-based reports using the *Guidelines* comprise linked pages, a means to view the report ordered according to GRI sections should be provided, in addition to any other structure.

Frequency and Medium of Reporting

A wide variety of media is now available to prepare and distribute reports, ranging from traditional printing to various multi-media technologies including the Internet and CD-ROMs. This gives organisations substantial freedom in determining the frequency of preparing reports and the mode of distribution. In general, GRI recommends that reporting on economic, environmental, and social performance be timed to coincide, and possibly integrated, with other external reporting, such as annual financial reports and quarterly earnings statements. Such timing will reinforce the linkages between financial performance and economic, environmental, and social performance (see Annex 2).

In the future, information disclosure is likely to involve a mix of annual, quarterly, and even "real-time data" distributed through a range of different media, each chosen based on the timing and nature of the reported information. Internet-based reporting will facilitate frequent updating of some aspects of GRI-based reports. However, continuous reporting should not replace periodic consolidated reports, vetted through an internal procedure and providing a "snapshot" of the organisation at a given point in time. Snapshots are important for supporting comparisons between organisations and between reports. GRI also recommends that such periodic reports be available in their complete form from the reporting organisation's website (e.g., as a down-loadable file).

Decisions regarding frequency and medium of reporting also should take into account their expected use and feedback. Effective reporting is part of a broader dialogue between the reporting organisation and its stakeholders that should result in new actions by both parties. The frequency and medium of reporting potentially may either enhance or detract from the progress of this dialogue.

Financial Reports

Most organisations publish separate financial and sustainability reports; however, a few corporations have begun to experiment with publishing a single annual report including financial, economic, environmental, and social information. GRI believes that both financial reporting and sustainability reporting serve parallel and essential functions that enrich each other (see Annex 2). GRI encourages the coordination of both reporting processes and expects that over time financial performance measurement increasingly will benefit from the measurement of economic, environmental, and social performance.

Credibility of Reports

Stakeholders expect to be able to trust an organisation's sustainability report. To benefit from the process of sustainability reporting, organisations themselves also want to take steps to enhance the credibility of their reports. This contributes to building stakeholder trust and to continual improvement in the quality of reporting systems and processes.

A range of factors influences the perceptions and expectations of users about the credibility of an organisation's sustainability report. It is important for each reporting organisation to ascertain and evaluate the relative importance of each of these factors (see Annex 4 for examples of such factors). Consultation with stakeholders is the best way to ascertain stakeholder perceptions and expectations about building credibility.

In response to stakeholder expectations, reporting organisations have adopted a variety of strategies for enhancing the credibility and quality of sustainability reports. Strategies include stakeholder consultation panels, strengthened internal data collection and information systems, issue-specific audits by appropriate experts, internal audits of data collection and reporting systems, use of the GRI *Guidelines* as the basis for report preparation (and indicating so), reviews and commentaries by independent external experts, and use of independent assurance[3] processes for sustainability reports. In deciding strategy and developing and implementing policies and practices to enhance report credibility and quality, organisations are encouraged to adopt a progressive approach, each stage of which adds to the credibility and quality of their reporting.

In order to address stakeholders' concerns about the credibility of reports on economic, environmental, and social performance, GRI recommends that reports include a statement of:

- the reporting organisation's policies and internal practices to enhance the credibility and quality of its sustainability report; and

- the reporting organisation's policy and current practice with regard to providing independent assurance about the full report.

GRI recognises that providing independent assurance about sustainability reports is, like reporting itself, at an early stage of development. For example, no universal consensus exists on social performance indicators or related assurance approaches. GRI encourages the independent assurance of sustainability reports and the development of standards and guidelines for the assurance process to be followed by assurance providers.

Annex 4 offers practical guidance to reporting organisations on assurance provision and related processes that enhance report quality and credibility. GRI will continue to evolve its policy on independent assurance informed by the feedback and practices of both reporters and report users.

Notes:

[3] The following is a proposed working description of independent assurance: "The provision of independent assurance is a structured and comprehensive process of collecting and evaluating evidence on a subject matter (the sustainability report) that is the responsibility of another party (distinct from management of the reporting organisation), against suitable criteria. As a result of the process, assurance providers express a conclusion that provides the intended users/stakeholders with a stated level of assurance about whether the subject matter (the sustainability report) conforms in all material respects with the identified criteria. Independent, competent experts who maintain an attitude of 'professional scepticism' perform the assurance process."

PART B: REPORTING PRINCIPLES

INTRODUCTION

This section of the *Guidelines* identifies reporting principles essential to producing a balanced and reasonable report on an organisation's economic, environmental, and social performance. The June 2000 *Guidelines* presented a first version of these principles. These were informed by the financial accounting tradition and adapted for reporting on economic, environmental, and social performance with reference to research related to environmental accounting. Now, with the benefit of time and learning through application of the June 2000 *Guidelines*, GRI presents a revised set of principles that combine and extend many of the concepts that appeared under the headings of "underlying principles" and "qualitative characteristics" of GRI-based reports in the June 2000 *Guidelines*.

Those familiar with financial reporting will recognise overlaps between GRI's reporting principles and those used in financial reporting. However, while financial reporting is a key benchmark for developing principles for reporting on economic, environmental, and social performance, significant differences do exist. The principles in this section take these differences into account. They are rooted in GRI's experience over the last four years, blending knowledge from science and learning from practice.

GRI views these principles as integral to its reporting framework, equal in weight to the elements and indicators in Part C of the *Guidelines*. Organisations using the *Guidelines* are expected to apply these principles in their report preparation. Collectively, the principles define a compact between the reporting organisation and report user, ensuring that both parties share a common understanding of the underpinnings of a GRI-based report. They provide an important reference point to help a user interpret and assess the organisation's decisions regarding the content of its report. The principles are designed with the long term in mind. They strive to create an enduring foundation upon which performance measurement will continue to evolve based on new knowledge and learning.

The principles are goals toward which a reporter should strive. Some reporting organisations may not be able to fully apply them in the short term. However, organisations should identify improvement in how rigorously they apply the principles to their reporting process, in much the same way as they identify improvement in the various aspects of economic, environmental, and social performance.

Reports do not need to contain a detailed checklist showing that all principles have been adopted. But they should offer some discussion of how the reporting principles have been applied. This should include both successes and challenges. If a reporting organisation does not seek to apply these principles, it should indicate where such departures exist and why. Discussion of the application (or non-application) of principles may appear in the profile section of the report or in a separate section that addresses the technical aspects involved in preparing the report.

The 11 principles outlined in the following section will help ensure that reports:

- present a balanced and reasonable account of economic, environmental, and social performance, and the resulting contribution of the organisation to sustainable development;

- facilitate comparison over time;

- facilitate comparisons across organisations; and

- credibly address issues of concern to stakeholders.

ORGANISATION OF THE PRINCIPLES

The principles in Part B are grouped in four clusters (see Figure 3). Those that:

- form the framework for the report (transparency, inclusiveness, auditability);

- inform decisions about what to report (completeness, relevance, sustainability context);

- relate to ensuring quality and reliability (accuracy, neutrality, comparability); and

- inform decisions about access to the report (clarity, timeliness).

The principles of transparency and inclusiveness represent the starting point for the reporting process and are woven into the fabric of all the other principles. All decisions about reporting (e.g., how, when, what) take these two principles and associated practices into consideration.

The principles of sustainability context, completeness, and relevance play the key role in determining what to report. Reports should help place the organisation's performance in the broader context of sustainability challenges, risks, and opportunities. The information contained within the report must meet the test of completeness in terms of the reporting boundaries (i.e., entities included), scope (i.e., aspects or issues reported), and time frame. Lastly, reported information should be relevant to the decision-making needs of stakeholders.

The quality and reliability of the report content are guided by the principles of neutrality, comparability, and accuracy. Reports should be comparable over time and across organisations. Information should be sufficiently accurate and reliable to enable its use for decision-making purposes. Equally important, the report should present its content in a balanced and unbiased manner.

The principles of clarity and timeliness govern the access and availability of reports. Put simply, stakeholders should receive easily understood information in a time frame that allows them to use it effectively.

Lastly, the principle of auditability relates to several other principles such as comparability, accuracy, neutrality, and completeness. Specifically, this principle refers to the ability to demonstrate that the processes underlying report preparation and information in the report itself meet standards for quality, reliability, and other similar expectations.

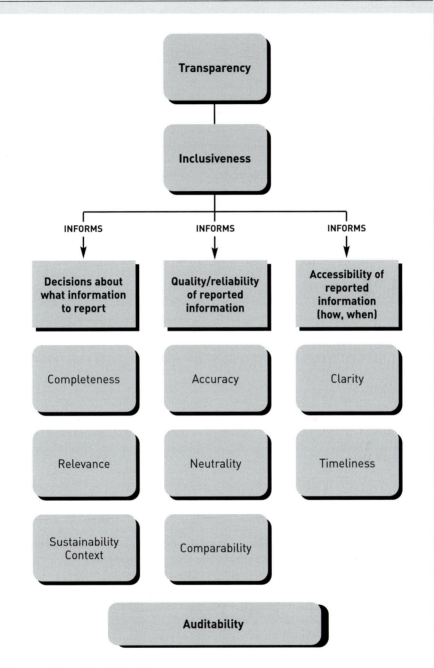

Figure 3: Reporting Principles

Transparency

Full disclosure of the processes, procedures, and assumptions in report preparation are essential to its credibility.

Transparency is an overarching principle and is the centrepiece of accountability. It requires that, regardless of the format and content of reports, users are fully informed of the processes, procedures, and assumptions embodied in the reported information. For example, a report must include information on the stakeholder engagement processes used in its preparation, data collection methods and related internal auditing, and scientific assumptions underlying the presentation of information. This transparency in reporting is an exercise in accountability—the clear and open explanation of one's actions to those who have a right or reason to inquire.

Transparency is central to any type of reporting or disclosure. In the case of financial reporting, over many decades governments and other organisations have created, and continue to enhance, disclosure rules affecting financial reports to increase the transparency of the reporting process. These generally accepted accounting principles and evolving international accounting standards seek to ensure that investors are given a clear picture of the organisation's financial condition, one that includes all material information and the basis upon which this depiction is developed.

GRI seeks to move reporting on economic, environmental, and social performance in a similar direction by creating a generally accepted framework for economic, environmental, and social performance disclosure. As this framework continues to evolve rapidly, general practices will evolve in parallel, based on best practice, best science, and best appraisal of user needs. In this dynamic environment, it is essential that reporting organisations are transparent regarding the processes, procedures, and assumptions that underlie their reports so that users may both believe and interpret reported information. In this sense, transparency transcends any one principle, but affects all.

Inclusiveness

The reporting organisation should systematically engage its stakeholders to help focus and continually enhance the quality of its reports.

The inclusiveness principle is rooted in the premise that stakeholder views are integral to meaningful reporting and must be incorporated during the process of designing a report. Reporting organisations should seek to engage stakeholders who are both directly and indirectly affected. Aspects of reporting enriched by stakeholder consultation include (but are not limited to) the choice of indicators, the definition of the organisation's reporting boundaries, the format of the report, and the approaches taken to reinforce the credibility of the reported information. Characteristics relevant to designing stakeholder consultation processes include the nature and diversity of products and services, the nature of the reporting organisation's operations and activities, and the geographic range of operations. Stakeholder engagement, like reporting itself, is a dynamic process. Executed properly, it is likely to result in continual learning within and outside the organisation, and to strengthen trust between the reporting organisation and report users. Trust, in turn, fortifies report credibility, itself a key goal of GRI's reporting framework.

The principle of inclusiveness also addresses the diverse needs of stakeholders who use sustainability reports. The range of users of a sustainability report is broader than that of financial reports. Inclusiveness is essential to ensuring that the reporting process and content reflect the needs of these diverse users. Each user group has specific information expectations—at times overlapping with those of other groups, at times distinct. Failure to identify and consult with stakeholders is likely to result in reports that are less relevant to users' needs and thereby less credible to external parties. In contrast, systematic stakeholder engagement enhances receptivity and usefulness across user groups. This engagement may also include soliciting views regarding the utility and credibility of sustainability reports issued by the reporting organisation.

GRI recognises that many reporting organisations have a wide range of potential stakeholders. Any systematic approach to inclusiveness will require an organisation to define an approach for grouping and prioritising stakeholders for purposes of engagement. In the spirit of the inclusiveness and transparency principles, it is important for reporting organisations to clearly and openly explain their approach to defining whom to engage with and how best to engage.

Auditability

> **Reported data and information should be recorded, compiled, analysed, and disclosed in a way that would enable internal auditors or external assurance providers to attest to its reliability.**

The auditability principle refers to the extent to which information management systems and communication practices lend themselves to being examined for accuracy by both internal and external parties. Reports using the *Guidelines* contain data that is both qualitative and quantitative in nature. In designing data collection and

---

The Verification Working Group

In response to user requests, GRI formed a working group in 1999 to explore issues and options for strengthening the credibility of sustainability reports through various assurance mechanisms. The results of these consultations are reflected in the statements in Part A (Credibility of Reports) and in Annex 4 on assurance processes. The working group also has prepared an advisory assurance strategy paper (available on www.globalreporting.org) for consideration by the GRI Board of Directors. Beginning in September 2002, the Board will consider options for how GRI might continue to play a constructive role in advancing the assurance of sustainability reports.

---

information systems, reporting organisations therefore should anticipate that internal auditing and external assurance processes may be used in the future.

In preparing reports, organisations should continually ask the question: Is the response to an information query presented in such a way that an internal or external party in the future could examine its accuracy, completeness, consistency, and reliability? Unverifiable statements or data that affect the broad messages contained in a report using the *Guidelines* may compromise its credibility. In addition to accuracy and reliability, the completeness of information may also affect the ability of an auditor to render an assessment.

Completeness

All information that is material to users for assessing the reporting organisation's economic, environmental, and social performance should appear in the report in a manner consistent with the declared boundaries, scope, and time period.

This principle refers to accounting for and disclosing, in sufficient detail, all information of significant concern to stakeholders within the declared boundaries (i.e., operational, scope, and temporal) of the report. Defining whether such information meets the test of significance to stakeholders should be based on both stakeholder consultation as well as broad-based societal concerns that may not have surfaced through the stakeholder consultation process. Such broad-based concerns may derive, for example, from national policy and international conventions.

The completeness principle is three-dimensional:

Operational boundary dimension: Reported information should be complete in relation to the operational boundaries of the reporting organisation, in other words, the range of entities for which the reporting organisation gathers data. These boundaries should be selected with consideration of the economic, environmental, and social impacts of the organisation. Such boundaries may be defined based on financial control, legal ownership, business relationships, and other considerations. The boundaries may vary according to the nature of the reported information. In some cases,

---

Defining Boundaries

Defining boundary conditions for reporting on economic, environmental, and social performance is a complex challenge. Complicating factors include the diverse nature of the information and the intimate relationship between the organisation and the larger economic, environmental, and social systems within which it operates. Boundary research is a high priority in GRI's work programme. Discussion papers, exposure drafts and testable protocols will appear during 2002-2003, leading to more systematic and precise treatment of this critical reporting issue.

the most appropriate boundaries for meeting the expectations outlined by other reporting principles may extend beyond traditional financial reporting boundaries.

Scope dimension: Scope is distinct from boundaries in that an organisation could choose extended reporting boundaries (e.g., report data on all the organisations that form the supply chain), but only include a very narrow scope (e.g., only report on human rights performance). In the context of GRI, "scope" refers to aspects such as energy use, health and safety, and other areas for which the *Guidelines* include indicators and queries. Despite the fact that the reporting boundary may be complete, the scope (e.g., human rights aspects only) may not be complete. The process for determining a complete scope may include, for example, the results of lifecycle analysis of products or services and assessment of the full range of direct and indirect social or ecological impacts of the reporting organisation. Some of these same tools may also influence decisions about the other dimensions of completeness discussed here. The report should disclose all relevant information within the context of the scope (i.e., aspects) covered.

Temporal dimension: Reported information should be complete with reference to the time period declared by the reporting organisation. As far as possible, reportable activities, events, and impacts should be presented for the reporting period in which they occur. This may involve reporting on activities that produce minimal short-term impact, but will have a cumulative effect that may become material, unavoidable, or irreversible in the longer term. Such activities might include, for example, the release of certain bio-accumulative or persistent pollutants. Disclosure of the nature and likelihood of such impacts, even if they may only materialise in the future, comports with the goal of providing a balanced and reasonable representation of the organisation's current economic, environmental, and social performance. In making estimates of future impacts (both positive and negative), the reporting organisation should be careful to make well-reasoned estimates that reflect the best understanding of the likely size, nature, and scope of impacts. Although speculative in nature, such estimates can provide useful and relevant information for decision-making as long as the limitations of the estimates are clearly acknowledged.

Information within the organisation often flows from management systems that operate on a regular, short-term cycle, typically one year. However, a single reporting cycle often is too brief to capture many important economic, environmental, and social impacts. This type of performance, by nature, focuses on the long-term, with forward-looking trends at least as important as lagging, or historical, ones. Thus, reporting organisations should strive to gradually align information systems to account for these forward-looking trends in addition to historical trends.

Relevance

Relevance is the degree of importance assigned to a particular aspect, indicator, or piece of information, and represents the threshold at which information becomes significant enough to be reported.

Relevance in sustainability reporting is driven by the significance attached to a piece of information to inform the user's decision-making processes. Stakeholders use information on economic, environmental, and social performance in a variety of ways, some of which may differ substantially from that of the reporting organisation. The significance of information can be judged from a number of perspectives; however, in any reporting system, the key perspective is that of the information user. The primary purpose of reporting (as opposed to other types of outreach and communication) is to respond to user information needs in a neutral and balanced manner. Reporting must therefore place a strong emphasis on serving users' specific needs.

In considering relevance, it is important to remain sensitive to differences in how users and reporting organisations apply information. Through stakeholder consultation, a reporting organisation can better understand stakeholders' information needs and how best to respond to them. Ideally, reports should contain information that is useful and relevant to both the reporting organisation and the report users. However, in some cases, information may be relevant to the report user, but may not be of the same value to the reporting organisation. It is important to differentiate between situations where reporting expectations differ and those where information is irrelevant.

Sustainability Context

The reporting organisation should seek to place its performance in the larger context of ecological, social, or other limits or constraints, where such context adds significant meaning to the reported information.

Many aspects of sustainability reporting draw significant meaning from the larger context of how performance at the organisational level affects economic, environmental, and social capital formation and depletion at a local, regional, or global level. In such cases, simply reporting on the trend in individual performance (or the efficiency of the organisation) leaves open the question of an organisation's contribution to the total amount of these different types of capital. For some users, placing performance information in the broader biophysical, social, and economic context lies at the heart of sustainability reporting and is one of the key differentiators between this type of reporting and financial reporting. Moreover, while the ability of an organisation to "sustain" itself is obviously important to a range of stakeholders, it is unlikely that any individual organisation will remain in existence indefinitely. This principle emphasises the sustainability of the broader natural and human environment within which organisations operate.

Where relevant and useful, reporting organisations should consider their individual performance in the contexts of economic, environmental, and social sustainability. This will involve discussing the performance of the organisation in the context of the limits and demands placed on economic, environmental, or social resources at a macro-level. This concept is most clearly articulated in the environmental area in terms of global limits on resource use and pollution levels, but may also be relevant to social and economic issues.

The understanding of how best to link organisational performance with macro-level concerns will continue to evolve. GRI recommends that individual reporting organisations explore ways to incorporate these issues directly into their sustainability reports in order to advance both reporting organisations' and users' understanding of these linkages.

Accuracy

The accuracy principle refers to achieving the degree of exactness and low margin of error in reported information necessary for users to make decisions with a high degree of confidence.

Economic, environmental, and social indicators can be expressed in many different ways, ranging from qualitative responses to detailed quantitative measurements. The characteristics that determine accuracy vary according to the nature of the information. For example, the accuracy of qualitative information is largely determined by the degree of clarity, detail, and balance in presentation. The accuracy of quantitative information, on the other hand, may depend on the specific sampling methods used to gather hundreds of data points from multiple operating units. The specific threshold of accuracy that is necessary will depend in part on the intended use of the information. Certain decisions will require higher levels of accuracy in reported information than others.

Application of the accuracy principle requires an appreciation of:

- the intentions and decision-making needs of the users; and

- the different conditions under which information is gathered.

As with other principles, it is important to be transparent in how this principle is applied. Explaining the approaches, methods, and techniques that the reporting organisation uses to achieve satisfactory levels of accuracy will help improve the credibility of the report and the acceptance of the reported information.

Neutrality

Reports should avoid bias in selection and presentation of information and should strive to provide a balanced account of the reporting organisation's performance.

The neutrality principle refers to the fair and factual presentation of the organisation's economic, environmental, and social performance. Embodied in the principle of neutrality is the notion that the core objective behind a reporting organisation's selection and communication of information is to produce an unbiased depiction of its performance. This means presenting an account that includes both favourable and unfavourable results, free from intentional tilt or under- or overstatement of the organisation's performance. The report should focus on neutral sharing of the facts for the users to interpret. Environmental reporting, the precursor to sustainability reporting, has demonstrated this type of gradual evolution from anecdotal and selective disclosure toward a more neutral, factual presentation of data. While reporting practices still vary significantly among reporting organisations, many have recognised that achieving and maintaining credibility among users hinges on the commitment of the reporting organisation to a neutral and fair depiction.

Under the neutrality principle, the *overall* report content must present an unbiased picture of the reporting organisation's performance, avoiding selections, omissions, or presentation formats that are intended to influence a decision or judgement by the user. Where the reporting organisation wishes to present its perspective on an aspect of performance, it should be clear to the reader that such information is separate and distinct from GRI's reporting elements. In the same way that annual financial reports typically contain interpretive material in the front end and financial statements in the back, so too should GRI-based reports strive for a clear distinction between the reporting organisation's interpretation of information and factual presentation.

Comparability

The reporting organisation should maintain consistency in the boundary and scope of its reports, disclose any changes, and re-state previously reported information.

This principle refers to ensuring that reports on economic, environmental, and social performance support comparison against the organisation's earlier performance as well as against the performance of other organisations. This allows internal and external parties to benchmark performance and assess progress as part of supporting rating activities, investment decisions, advocacy programmes and other activities. Comparability and associated demands for consistency are a pre-requisite to informed decision-making by users.

When changes in boundary, scope, and content of reporting occur (including in the design and use of indicators), reporting organisations should, to the maximum extent practicable, re-state current accounts to ensure that time series information and cross-organisational comparisons are both reliable and meaningful. Where such re-statements are not provided, the reporting organisation should disclose such circumstances, explain the reasons, and discuss implications for interpreting current accounts.

Clarity

The reporting organisation should remain cognizant of the diverse needs and backgrounds of its stakeholder groups and should make information available in a manner that is responsive to the maximum number of users while still maintaining a suitable level of detail.

The clarity principle considers the extent to which information is understandable and usable by diverse user groups. In financial reporting, there is an unspoken assumption concerning the general level of background knowledge and experience of the assumed "primary" user group, namely, investors. No such "primary" user group exists for GRI at this juncture. In fact, it may never exist owing to the diversity of user groups that are consumers of economic, environmental, and social performance information. In using the GRI *Guidelines*, it is reasonable to assume that all users have a working knowledge of at least a portion of the economic, environmental, and social issues faced by the reporting organisation. However, not all user groups will bring the same level of experience—or even the same language—to the reading of the report. Thus, reporting organisations, through assessing stakeholder capabilities, should design reports that respond to the maximum number of users without sacrificing important details of interest to a subset of user groups. Technical and scientific terms should be explained within the report, and clear, suitable graphics should be used where appropriate. Providing information that is not understandable to stakeholders does not contribute to successful engagement. Clarity is therefore an essential characteristic of any reporting effort.

Timeliness

Reports should provide information on a regular schedule that meets user needs and comports with the nature of the information itself.

The usefulness of information on economic, environmental, and social performance is closely tied to its timely availability to user groups. Timeliness ensures maximum uptake and utility of the information, enabling users to effectively integrate it into their decision-making. As with financial disclosures, reporting on economic, environmental, and social performance is most valuable when users can expect a predictable schedule of disclosures. Special updates can be issued if and when unexpected developments of material interest to users occur.

Reporting organisations should structure disclosures to accord with the nature of the information. Certain environmental information, for example, may be most useful on a quarterly, monthly or continuous ("real time") basis, while other environmental information is most suitable for an annual report. Similarly, reporting on economic performance may parallel financial reporting: annual disclosures can summarise economic performance during the prior 12 months, while quarterly updates can be issued in parallel with quarterly earnings reports to investors. With the menu of new communications technologies available to reporting organisations, adjusting the timing of disclosures to reflect the varying nature of an organisation's impacts is now more feasible than ever before. However, the degree to which any technology approach can be applied depends on stakeholders having access to the necessary technology.

Although a regular flow of information is desirable for meeting certain needs, reporting organisations should commit to a single point in time to provide a consolidated accounting of their economic, environmental, and social performance. This is necessary to meet the fundamental objective of comparability across organisations. As an example, a yearly consolidated report released on a predictable schedule, accompanied by interim updates using electronic media, represents a standard structure that is consistent with the principle of timeliness.

PART C: REPORT CONTENT

GENERAL NOTES

1. ***Boundaries:*** Organisations using the *Guidelines* may have complex internal structures, multiple subsidiaries, joint ventures, and/or foreign operations. Particular care should be taken to match the scope of the report with the economic, environmental, and social "footprint" of the organisation (i.e., the full extent of its economic, environmental, and social impacts). Any differences should be explained.

2. ***Use of technical protocols:*** In reporting on indicators contained within the *Guidelines*, reporters should use GRI technical protocols whenever available. Drafting of protocols for a limited number of GRI indicators began in 2002, and drafts in progress can be found on the GRI website (www.globalreporting.org). GRI recognises the need for continued development of protocols, and the current set represents the first of many that will follow in coming years. If, for any reason, a reporting organisation does not use an existing GRI protocol, it should clearly describe the measurement rules and methodologies used for data compilation. For situations where a formal GRI protocol is not yet available, reporting organisations should use their professional judgement, drawing on international standards and conventions wherever possible.

3. ***Metrics:*** Reported data should be presented using generally accepted international metrics (e.g., kilograms, tonnes, litres), calculated using standard conversion factors. When other metrics are used, reports should provide conversion information to enable international users to make conversions.

4. ***Time frames and targets:*** Wherever possible, reports should present information for all performance indicators in a manner that enables users to understand current and future trends. At a minimum, reporting organisations should present data for the current reporting period (e.g., one year) and at least two previous

periods, as well as future targets where they have been established. This information provides essential context for understanding the significance of a given piece of information. Comparisons with industry averages, where available, can also provide useful context.

5. ***Absolute/normalised data:*** As a general principle, reporting organisations should present indicator data in absolute terms and use ratios or normalised data as complementary information. Providing only normalised data may mask absolute figures, which is the information of primary interest to some stakeholders. However, if absolute data are provided, users will be able to compile their own normalised analysis using information from Section 2 of Part C (Profile). Nevertheless, GRI does recognise the utility of data presented as ratios. Ratio data may be useful in conjunction with absolute data for communicating performance trends or articulating performance across two or more linked dimensions of sustainability. When ratios are included, organisations are asked to make use of normalising factors from within the report, and from Section 2 of Part C, if appropriate. See Annex 5 for more information on ratios.

6. ***Data consolidation and disaggregation:*** Reporting organisations will need to determine the appropriate level of consolidation (aggregation) of indicator data. For example, indicators could be presented in terms of the performance of the organisation worldwide or broken down by subsidiaries, countries of operation, or even individual facilities. This decision requires balancing the reporting burden against the potential additional value of data reported on a disaggregated (e.g., country or site) basis. Consolidation of information can result in loss of a significant amount of value to users, and also risks masking particularly strong or poor performance in specific areas of operation. In general, reporting organisations should disaggregate information to an appropriate and useful level as determined through consultation with stakeholders. The appropriate level of consolidation/disaggregation may vary by indicator.

7. ***Graphics:*** The use of graphics can enhance the quality of a report. However, care should be taken to ensure that graphics do not inadvertently lead readers to incorrect interpretations of data and results. Care is needed in the selection of axes, scales, and data (including conversion of raw data to ratios and indices for graphic purposes), and the use of colour and different types of graphs and charts. Graphics should be a supplement to—not a substitute for—text and narrative disclosure of information. In general, raw data should accompany graphical presentations, either alongside or in appendices. Graphs should always clearly indicate the source of their data.

8. ***Executive summary:*** GRI encourages the inclusion of an executive summary. In keeping with the reporting principles in Part B, the summary should draw only on material from within the report and be materially consistent with the content of the report.

OVERVIEW OF PART C

Part C of the *Guidelines* specifies the content of a GRI-based report. The report content is organised in what GRI considers a logical order, and reporting organisations are encouraged to follow this structure in writing their reports. See General Notes and Part A for further guidance on report structure. Questions regarding other issues related to application of the *Guidelines* are also addressed in Part A. Please note that Part C is best read in conjunction with Part B.

Part C of the Guidelines *comprises five sections:*

1. *Vision and Strategy*—description of the reporting organisation's strategy with regard to sustainability, including a statement from the CEO.

2. *Profile*—overview of the reporting organisation's structure and operations and of the scope of the report.

3. *Governance Structure and Management Systems*—description of organisational structure, policies, and management systems, including stakeholder engagement efforts.

4. *GRI Content Index*—a table supplied by the reporting organisation identifying where the information listed in Part C of the *Guidelines* is located within the organisation's report.

5. *Performance Indicators*—measures of the impact or effect of the reporting organisation divided into integrated, economic, environmental, and social performance indicators.

The above only covers basic report content as defined by GRI. As noted in Part A, reporting organisations might also have additional sector-specific or organisation-specific information to include in their reports. Organisations that wish to report "in accordance" with the *Guidelines* must meet the five conditions described in Part A.

Major Changes Since June 2000

Since the release of the June 2000 edition of the *Guidelines*, GRI has made a number of major changes to the content of a GRI-based report:

- Following a two-year consultative period, the performance indicators have been substantially revised. The most significant changes are found in the economic and social sections. Aspects and indicators have been reorganised, and new indicators appear. For details on the consultative process, please visit the Global Reporting Initiative website (www.globalreporting.org) to view the Final Report of the Measurement Working Group.

- The requirement for an Executive Summary section has been removed; however, GRI still encourages reporting organisations to include a summary.

- The Vision and Strategy section has been revised to include the CEO statement.

- The 2002 *Guidelines* have new content on governance to describe the significance of economic, environmental, and social issues in top-level decision-making processes.

- Reporting organisations using the GRI *Guidelines* are now expected to include a Content Index within their report, identifying the location of GRI performance indicators and other elements.

- The distinction between "generally applicable" and "organisation-specific" environmental indicators has evolved into the classifications of "core" and "additional." All indicators (not just environmental) are now classified either as "core" or "additional." Core indicators are those relevant to most reporting organisations and of interest to most stakeholders. Additional indicators are viewed as those that have one or more of the following attributes: 1) represent leading practice in economic, environmental, or social measurement aspects, though currently used by few reporting organisations; 2) provide information of interest to stakeholders who are particularly important to the reporting entity; and 3) are deemed worthy of further testing for possible consideration as future core indicators.

- GRI indicators have been revised to better align with major international agreements, including conventions on the environment, labour, and human rights.

- The Performance Indicators sections are now presented in alphabetical order: economic, environmental, social.

Indicators in the GRI Framework

GRI structures performance indicators according to a hierarchy of category, aspect, and indicator. The definitions used by GRI within this hierarchy are aligned with international standards, but adapted to the GRI framework. Indicators are grouped in terms of the three dimensions of the conventional definition of sustainability— economic, environmental, and social. Annex 5 contains further information on GRI's approach to indicators.

In the 2002 *Guidelines*, the hierarchy is structured as follows:

	CATEGORY	ASPECT
ECONOMIC	**Direct Economic Impacts**	Customers Suppliers Employees Providers of capital Public sector

continued over

	CATEGORY	ASPECT
ENVIRONMENTAL	**Environmental**	Materials Energy Water Biodiversity Emissions, effluents, and waste Suppliers Products and services Compliance Transport Overall
SOCIAL	**Labour Practices and Decent Work**	Employment Labour/management relations Health and safety Training and education Diversity and opportunity
	Human Rights	Strategy and management Non-discrimination Freedom of association and collective bargaining Child labour Forced and compulsory labour Disciplinary practices Security practices Indigenous rights
	Society	Community Bribery and corruption Political contributions Competition and pricing
	Product Responsibility	Customer health and safety Products and services Advertising Respect for privacy

An introduction to each set of indicators in Section 5 of Part C briefly describes the reasoning that led to the specific organisation of aspects and indicators in the 2002 *Guidelines*.

Note that within the context of GRI, performance indicators can be either quantitative or qualitative. While quantitative or numerical measures offer many advantages, they may prove unreliable, incomplete, or ambiguous for measuring performance on certain issues. GRI considers qualitative indicators, those indicators requiring textual response, to be complementary and essential to presenting a complete picture of an organisation's economic, environmental, and social performance.

Qualitative measures may be most appropriate when dealing with highly complex economic or social systems in which it is not possible to identify quantitative measures that capture the organisation's contribution—positive or negative—to economic, environmental, or social conditions. Qualitative approaches also may be most appropriate for measurements of impacts to which the organisation is one of many contributors. Wherever possible, qualitative performance indicators have been worded to encourage a response that can be expressed along a scale as opposed to a general descriptive statement (see Annex 5). This, in turn, facilitates comparisons across reporting organisations.

GRI Report Content

The following five sections contain the reporting elements and performance indicators for the 2002 GRI *Guidelines*. Reporting elements are numbered (e.g., 1.1, 2.10) and performance indicators are contained in tables in Section 5. The elements and indicators are listed in **bold type**. Some are supported by additional guidance or explanation in standard type.

---

1 VISION AND STRATEGY

This section encompasses a statement of the reporting organisation's sustainability vision and strategy, as well as a statement from the CEO.

1.1 Statement of the organisation's vision and strategy regarding its contribution to sustainable development.

Present overall vision of the reporting organisation for its future, particularly with regard to managing the challenges associated with economic, environmental, and social performance. This should answer, at a minimum, the following questions:

- What are the main issues for the organisation related to the major themes of sustainable development?
- How are stakeholders included in identifying these issues?
- For each issue, which stakeholders are most affected by the organisation?
- How are these issues reflected in the organisation's values and integrated into its business strategies?
- What are the organisation's objectives and actions on these issues?

Reporting organisations should use maximum flexibility and creativity in preparing this section. The reporting organisation's major direct and indirect economic, environmental, and social issues and impacts (both positive and negative) should inform the discussion. Reporting organisations are encouraged to draw directly from indicators and information presented elsewhere in the report. They should include in their discussion any major opportunities, challenges, or obstacles to moving toward improved economic, environmental, and social performance. International organisations are also encouraged to explicitly discuss how their economic, environmental, and social concerns relate to and are impacted by their strategies for emerging markets.

1.2   Statement from the CEO (or equivalent senior manager) describing key elements of the report.

A statement from the reporting organisation's CEO (or equivalent senior manager if other title is used) sets the tone of the report and establishes credibility with internal and external users. GRI does not specify the content of the CEO statement; however, it believes such statements are most valuable when they explicitly refer to the organisation's commitment to sustainability and to key elements of the report. Recommended elements of a CEO statement include the following:

- highlights of report content and commitment to targets;

- description of the commitment to economic, environmental, and social goals by the organisation's leadership;

- statement of successes and failures;

- performance against benchmarks such as the previous year's performance and targets and industry sector norms;

- the organisation's approach to stakeholder engagement; and

- major challenges for the organisation and its business sector in integrating responsibilities for financial performance with those for economic, environmental, and social performance, including the implications for future business strategy.

The CEO statement may be combined with the statement of vision and strategy.

2 PROFILE

This section provides an overview of the reporting organisation and describes the scope of the report. Thus, it provides readers with a context for understanding and evaluating information in the rest of the report. The section also includes organisational contact information.

Organisational Profile

Reporting organisations should provide the information listed below. In addition, they are encouraged to include any additional information that is needed for a full picture of the organisation's operations, products, and services.

2.1   **Name of reporting organisation.**

2.2   **Major products and/or services, including brands if appropriate.**

     The reporting organisation should also indicate the nature of its role in providing these products and services, and the degree to which the organisation relies on outsourcing.

2.3   **Operational structure of the organisation.**

2.4   **Description of major divisions, operating companies, subsidiaries, and joint ventures.**

2.5   **Countries in which the organisation's operations are located.**

2.6   **Nature of ownership; legal form.**

2.7   **Nature of markets served.**

2.8   **Scale of the reporting organisation:**

- number of employees;
- products produced/services offered (quantity or volume);
- net sales; and
- total capitalisation broken down in terms of debt and equity.

In addition to the above, reporting organisations are encouraged to provide additional information, such as:

- value added;
- total assets; and
- breakdowns of any or all of the following:
  - sales/revenues by countries/regions that make up 5 percent or more of total revenues;
  - major products and/or identified services;
  - costs by country/region; and
  - employees by country/region.

In preparing the profile information, organisations should consider the need to provide information beyond that on direct employees and financial data. For example, some organisations with few direct employees will have many indirect employees. This could include the employees of subcontractors, franchisees, joint ventures, and companies entirely dependent on or answerable to the reporting organisation. The extent of these relationships may interest stakeholders as much or more than information on direct employees. The reporting organisation should consider adding such information to its profile where relevant.

Reporting organisations should choose the set of measures best suited to the nature of their operations and stakeholders' needs. Measures should include those that can be used specifically to create ratios using the absolute figures provided in other sections of the report (See Annex 5 for information on ratios). All information should cover that portion of the organisation that is covered by the report.

2.9   List of stakeholders, key attributes of each, and relationship to the reporting organisation.

Stakeholders typically include the following groups (examples of attributes are shown in parentheses):

- communities (locations, nature of interest);

- customers (retail, wholesale, businesses, governments);

- shareholders and providers of capital (stock exchange listings);

- suppliers (products/services provided, local/national/international operations);

- trade unions (relation to workforce and reporting organisation);

- workforce, direct and indirect (size, diversity, relationship to the reporting organisation); and

- other stakeholders (business partners, local authorities, NGOs).

Report Scope

2.10   Contact person(s) for the report, including e-mail and web addresses.

2.11   Reporting period (e.g., fiscal/calendar year) for information provided.

2.12   Date of most recent previous report (if any).

2.13   Boundaries of report (countries/regions, products/services, divisions/facilities/joint ventures/subsidiaries) and any specific limitations on the scope.

If reporting boundaries do not match the full range of economic, environmental, and social impacts of the organisation, state the strategy and projected timeline for providing complete coverage.

2.14 Significant changes in size, structure, ownership, or products/services that have occurred since the previous report.

2.15 Basis for reporting on joint ventures, partially owned subsidiaries, leased facilities, outsourced operations, and other situations that can significantly affect comparability from period to period and/or between reporting organisations.

2.16 Explanation of the nature and effect of any re-statements of information provided in earlier reports, and the reasons for such re-statement (e.g., mergers/acquisitions, change of base years/periods, nature of business, measurement methods).

Report Profile

2.17 Decisions not to apply GRI principles or protocols in the preparation of the report.

2.18 Criteria/definitions used in any accounting for economic, environmental, and social costs and benefits.

2.19 Significant changes from previous years in the measurement methods applied to key economic, environmental, and social information.

2.20 Policies and internal practices to enhance and provide assurance about the accuracy, completeness, and reliability that can be placed on the sustainability report.

This includes internal management systems, processes, and audits that management relies on to ensure that reported data are reliable and complete with regard to the scope of the report.

2.21 Policy and current practice with regard to providing independent assurance for the full report.

2.22 Means by which report users can obtain additional information and reports about economic, environmental, and social aspects of the organisation's activities, including facility-specific information (if available).

3 GOVERNANCE STRUCTURE AND MANAGEMENT SYSTEMS

This section provides an overview of the governance structure, overarching policies, and management systems in place to implement the reporting organisation's vision for sustainable development and to manage its performance. In contrast, Section 5

(Performance Indicators) addresses the results and breadth of the organisation's activities. Discussion of stakeholder engagement forms a key part of any description of governance structures and management systems.

Some of the information listed in this section may overlap with information in other publications from the organisation. GRI is sensitive to the need to avoid unnecessary duplication of effort. However, for the sake of ensuring full and complete contextual information for users of sustainability reports, it is important to cover the items listed below in combination with other information on the organisation's economic, environmental, and social performance. Organisations may wish to cross-reference between different documents, but this should not be done at the expense of excluding necessary information in a sustainability report.

Structure and Governance

3.1 Governance structure of the organisation, including major committees under the board of directors that are responsible for setting strategy and for oversight of the organisation.

Describe the scope of responsibility of any major committees and indicate any direct responsibility for economic, social, and environmental performance.

3.2 Percentage of the board of directors that are independent, non-executive directors.

State how the board determines "independence".

3.3 Process for determining the expertise board members need to guide the strategic direction of the organisation, including issues related to environmental and social risks and opportunities.

3.4 Board-level processes for overseeing the organisation's identification and management of economic, environmental, and social risks and opportunities.

3.5 Linkage between executive compensation and achievement of the organisation's financial and non-financial goals (e.g., environmental performance, labour practices).

3.6 Organisational structure and key individuals responsible for oversight, implementation, and audit of economic, environmental, social, and related policies.

Include identification of the highest level of management below the board level directly responsible for setting and implementing environmental and social policies, as well as general organisational structure below the board level.

3.7 **Mission and values statements, internally developed codes of conduct or principles, and polices relevant to economic, environmental, and social performance and the status of implementation.**

Describe the status of implementation in terms of degree to which the code is applied across the organisation in different regions and departments/units. "Policies" refers to those that apply to the organisation as a whole, but may not necessarily provide substantial detail on the specific aspects listed under the performance indicators in Part C, Section 5 of the *Guidelines*.

3.8 **Mechanisms for shareholders to provide recommendations or direction to the board of directors.**

Include reference to any policies or processes regarding the use of shareholder resolutions or other mechanisms for enabling minority shareholders to express opinions to management.

Stakeholder Engagement

Stakeholder engagement activities should reflect the organisation's stakeholders as identified in the Profile section.

3.9 **Basis for identification and selection of major stakeholders.**

This includes the processes for defining an organisation's stakeholders and for determining which groups to engage.

3.10 **Approaches to stakeholder consultation reported in terms of frequency of consultations by type and by stakeholder group.**

This could include surveys, focus groups, community panels, corporate advisory panels, written communication, management/union structures, and other vehicles.

3.11 **Type of information generated by stakeholder consultations.**

Include a list of key issues and concerns raised by stakeholders and identify any indicators specifically developed as a result of stakeholder consultation.

3.12 **Use of information resulting from stakeholder engagements.**

For example, this could include selecting performance benchmarks or influencing specific decisions on policy or operations.

Overarching Policies and Management Systems

GRI has included policy indicators in both Section 3 (Governance Structure and Management Systems) and Section 5 (Performance Indicators), using the general principle of grouping information items closest to the most relevant aspect. The broader, overarching policies are most directly related to the governance structure and management systems section of the report. The most detailed level of policy (e.g., policies on child labour) may be captured in the performance indicator section of the report. Where the reporting organisation perceives an overlap in the GRI framework, it should choose the most appropriate location in its report for the information.

3.13 **Explanation of whether and how the precautionary approach or principle is addressed by the organisation.**

This could include an example that illustrates the organisation's approach to risk management in the operational planning or the development and introduction of new products. For reference, see the glossary for text of Article 15 of the Rio Principles on the precautionary approach.

3.14 **Externally developed, voluntary economic, environmental, and social charters, sets of principles, or other initiatives to which the organisation subscribes or which it endorses.**

Include date of adoption and countries/operations where applied.

3.15 **Principal memberships in industry and business associations, and/or national/international advocacy organisations.**

3.16 **Policies and/or systems for managing upstream and downstream impacts, including:**

- supply chain management as it pertains to outsourcing and supplier environmental and social performance; and

- product and service stewardship initiatives.

Stewardship initiatives include efforts to improve product design to minimise negative impacts associated with manufacturing, use, and final disposal.

3.17 **Reporting organisation's approach to managing indirect economic, environmental, and social impacts resulting from its activities.**

See below (under Economic Performance Indicators) for a discussion of indirect economic impacts.

3.18 **Major decisions during the reporting period regarding the location of, or changes in, operations.**

Explain major decisions such as facility or plant openings, closings, expansions, and contractions.

3.19 **Programmes and procedures pertaining to economic, environmental, and social performance. Include discussion of:**

- priority and target setting;

- major programmes to improve performance;

- internal communication and training;

- performance monitoring;

- internal and external auditing; and

- senior management review.

3.20 **Status of certification pertaining to economic, environmental, and social management systems.**

Include adherence to environmental management standards, labour, or social accountability management systems, or other management systems for which formal certification is available.

4 GRI CONTENT INDEX

4.1 **A table identifying location of each element of the GRI Report Content, by section and indicator.**

The purpose of this section is to enable report users to quickly assess the degree to which the reporting organisation has included the information and indicators contained in the GRI *Guidelines*. Specifically, the reporter should identify the location of the following GRI elements:

- *Vision and Strategy*: 1.1 and 1.2

- *Profile*: 2.1 to 2.22.

- *Governance Structure and Management Systems*: 3.1 to 3.20.

- *Performance Indicators*: all core performance indicators and identification of the location of explanations for any omissions.

- Any of the additional indicators from Section 5 of Part C that the reporter chooses to include in the report.

5 PERFORMANCE INDICATORS

This section lists the core and additional performance indicators for GRI-based reports. Reporting organisations that wish to report in accordance with the *Guidelines* should read Part A concerning the requirements for in accordance reporting.

The performance indicators are grouped under three sections covering the economic, environmental, and social dimensions of sustainability. This grouping is based on the conventional model of sustainable development and is intended to aid users of the

Guidelines. However, limiting performance indicators to these three categories may not fully capture the performance of an organisation for a number of reasons. For example:

- changes in one aspect of economic, environmental, or social performance often result in changes to other aspects of sustainability;

- sustainability strategies often use one area of sustainability as a reference point when defining goals for another area; and

- advancing sustainable development requires coordinated movement across a set of performance measurements, rather than random improvement within the full range of measurements.

Therefore, in addition to the economic, environmental, and social dimensions, a fourth dimension of information is necessary: ***integrated performance***.

Integrated indicators are considered first in this section. Following this are the core and additional indicators related to economic, environmental, and social performance.

Integrated Indicators

Given the unique relationship of each organisation to the economic, environmental, and social systems within which it operates, GRI has not identified a standardised set of integrated performance indicators. However, GRI encourages reporting organisations to consult with stakeholders and develop an appropriate shortlist of integrated performance indicators to include in their reports.

Integrated measures are generally of two types:

1. Systemic indicators; and

2. Cross-cutting indicators.

Systemic indicators relate the activity of an organisation to the larger economic, environmental, and social systems of which it is a part. For example, an organisation could describe its performance relative to an overall system or a benchmark, such as a percentage of the total workplace accidents found in the sector within a given country. Similarly, an organisation could present its net job creation as a proportion of the total number of jobs created in a region.

Absolute systemic indicators describe an organisation's performance in relation to the limit or capacity of the system of which it is a part. An example would be the amount of air pollutants of a given type released as a proportion of the total amount allowable in a region as defined by a public authority.

In general, systemic indicators provide an understanding of the degree to which the organisation's performance may influence the performance of a larger system. These types of measures are most useful for organisations that operate within a relatively narrowly defined geographic area.

Cross-cutting indicators directly relate two or more dimensions of economic, environmental, and social performance as a ratio. Eco-efficiency measures (e.g., the amount of emissions per unit of output or per monetary unit of turnover) are the best-known examples (further guidance on ratio indicators can be found in Annex 5). Many organisations have proposed standardised sets of environmental efficiency indicators that measure various types of resource use or pollution emissions against an economic or productivity measure. Cross-cutting indicators effectively demonstrate the size of the positive or negative impact for each incremental change in another value.

In developing and reporting cross-cutting indicators, care should be taken to:

- draw, where possible, on information already reported under these *Guidelines*;
- ensure that the indicators use ratios derived from normalised measures and, when possible, from internationally accepted metrics; and
- supplement, not replace, non-ratio indicators.

ECONOMIC PERFORMANCE INDICATORS

The economic dimension of sustainability concerns an organisation's impacts on the economic circumstances of its stakeholders and on economic systems at the local, national and global levels. Economic impacts can be divided into:

- direct impacts; and
- indirect impacts.

These impacts can be positive or negative. Broadly speaking, economic performance encompasses all aspects of the organisation's economic interactions, including the traditional measures used in financial accounting, as well as intangible assets that do not systematically appear in financial statements. However, economic indicators as articulated in the *Guidelines* have a scope and purpose that extends beyond that of traditional financial indicators.

Financial indicators focus primarily on the profitability of an organisation for the purpose of informing its management and shareholders. By contrast, economic indicators in the sustainability reporting context focus more on the manner in which an organisation affects the stakeholders with whom it has direct and indirect economic interactions. Therefore, the focus of economic performance measurement is on how the economic status of the stakeholder changes as a consequence of the organisation's activities, rather than on changes in the financial condition of the organisation itself. In some cases, existing financial indicators can directly inform these assessments. However, in other cases, different measures may be necessary, including the re-casting of traditional financial information to emphasise the impact on the stakeholder. In this context, shareholders are considered one among several stakeholder groups.

While financial performance indicators are well developed, indicators of organisation-level economic performance as described in the previous paragraph are still evolving.

The indicators in this section are the result of a consultation process that began after the release of the June 2000 *Guidelines* and represent a new approach to reporting on economic impacts. This framework will continue to evolve in future versions of the GRI *Guidelines* as application and learning continue. Such evolution will include an understanding of how economic impacts are linked to the intangible assets of the organisation.

Direct Impacts

The economic indicators on direct impacts are designed to:

- measure the monetary flows between the organisation and its key stakeholders; and

- indicate how the organisation affects the economic circumstances of those stakeholders.

The aspects for this section are organised around stakeholder groups. Each aspect includes a monetary flow indicator, which provides an indication of the scale of the relationship between reporting organisation and stakeholder. Most monetary flow indicators are paired with one or more other indicators that provide insight into the nature of the performance and impact on the stakeholder's economic capacity.

For example, under suppliers, the monetary flow indicator associated with "cost of all goods, materials, and services purchased" provides information on the scale of flows between the reporting organisation and its suppliers. The performance indicator describes one facet of the economic relationship between the suppliers and the reporting organisation.

Indirect impacts

The total economic impact of an organisation includes indirect impacts stemming from externalities that create impacts on communities, broadly defined. Externalities are those costs or benefits arising from a transaction that are not fully reflected in the monetary amount of the transaction. A community can be considered as anything from a neighbourhood, to a country, or even a community of interest such as a minority group within a society. Although often complex, indirect impacts are measurable. However, given the diversity of situations facing reporting organisations, GRI has not at this point identified a single, generic set of such indicators. Thus, each organisation should select performance indicators based on its own analysis of the issues. Information on the reporting organisation's overall approach to identifying and managing indirect impacts is covered under item 3.17 in the Governance Structure and Management Systems section.

Examples of externalities might include:

- innovation measured through patents and partnerships;

- economic effects (positive or negative) of changes in location or operations; or

- the contribution of a sector to Gross Domestic Product or national competitiveness.

Examples of community impacts might include:

- community dependency on the organisation's activities;
- ability of the organisation to attract further investment into an area; or
- the location of suppliers.

Further discussion of indirect economic impacts is available through discussion papers prepared by the Economics Subgroup of the Measurement Working Group. These can be found on the GRI website.

Core Indicators	Additional Indicators
DIRECT ECONOMIC IMPACTS	
Customers	
Monetary flow indicator: **EC1. Net sales.** As listed in the profile section under 2.8. **EC2. Geographic breakdown of markets.** For each product or product range, disclose national market share by country where this is 25% or more. Disclose market share and sales for each country where national sales represent 5% or more of GDP.	
Suppliers	
Monetary flow indicator: **EC3. Cost of all goods, materials, and services purchased.** **EC4. Percentage of contracts that were paid in accordance with agreed terms, excluding agreed penalty arrangements.** Terms may include conditions such as scheduling of payments, form of payment, or other conditions. This indicator is the percent of contracts that were paid according to terms, regardless of the details of the terms.	**EC11. Supplier breakdown by organisation and country.** List all suppliers from which purchases in the reporting period represent 10% or more of total purchases in that period. Also identify all countries where total purchasing represents 5% or more of GDP.
Employees	
Monetary flow indicator: **EC5. Total payroll and benefits (including wages, pension, other benefits, and redundancy payments) broken down by country or region.** This remuneration should refer to current payments and not include future	

continued over

465

Core Indicators	Additional Indicators

DIRECT ECONOMIC IMPACTS (continued)

Employees (continued)

Core Indicators	Additional Indicators
commitments. (Note: Indicator LA9 on training also offers information on one aspect of the organisation's investment in human capital.)	

Providers of Capital

Core Indicators	Additional Indicators
Monetary flow indicator: **EC6. Distributions to providers of capital broken down by interest on debt and borrowings, and dividends on all classes of shares, with any arrears of preferred dividends to be disclosed.** This includes all forms of debt and borrowings, not only long-term debt. **EC7. Increase/decrease in retained earnings at end of period.** (Note: the information contained in the profile section (2.1–2.8) enables calculation of several measures, including ROACE (Return On Average Capital Employed)).	

Public Sector

Core Indicators	Additional Indicators
Monetary flow indicator: **EC8. Total sum of taxes of all types paid broken down by country.** **EC9. Subsidies received broken down by country or region.** This refers to grants, tax relief, and other types of financial benefits that do not represent a transaction of goods and services. Explain definitions used for types of groups. **EC10. Donations to community, civil society, and other groups broken down in terms of cash and in-kind donations per type of group.**	**EC12. Total spent on non-core business infrastructure development.** This is infrastructure built outside the main business activities of the reporting entity such as a school, or hospital for employees and their families.

INDIRECT ECONOMIC IMPACTS

Core Indicators	Additional Indicators
	EC13. The organisation's indirect economic impacts. Identify major externalities associated with the reporting organisation's products and services.

ENVIRONMENTAL PERFORMANCE INDICATORS

The environmental dimension of sustainability concerns an organisation's impacts on living and non-living natural systems, including ecosystems, land, air and water. The environmental dimension of sustainability has achieved the highest level of consensus among the three dimensions of sustainability reporting.

It is particularly important to provide environmental performance information in terms of both absolute figures and normalised measures (e.g., resource use per unit of output). Both measures reflect important, but distinct, aspects of sustainability. Absolute figures provide a sense of scale or magnitude of the use or impact, which allows the user to consider performance in the context of larger systems. Normalised figures illustrate the organisation's efficiency and support comparison between organisations of different sizes. In general, stakeholders should be able to calculate normalised figures using data from the report profile (e.g., net sales) and absolute figures reported in the environmental performance section. However, GRI asks the reporting organisation to provide both normalised and absolute figures.

In reporting on environmental indicators, reporting organisations are also encouraged to keep in mind the principle of sustainability context. With respect to the environmental measures in the report, organisations are encouraged to relate their individual performance to the broader ecological systems within which they operate. For example, organisations could seek to report their pollution output in terms of the ability of the environment (local, regional, or global) to absorb the pollutants.

Core Indicators	Additional Indicators
Materials	
EN1. Total materials use other than water, by type. Provide definitions used for types of materials. Report in tonnes, kilograms, or volume.	
EN2. Percentage of materials used that are wastes (processed or unprocessed) from sources external to the reporting organisation. Refers to both post-consumer recycled material and waste from industrial sources. Report in tonnes, kilograms, or volume.	
Energy*	
EN3. Direct energy use segmented by primary source. Report on all energy sources used by the reporting organisation for its own operations as well as for the production and delivery of energy products (e.g., electricity or heat) to other organisations. Report in joules.	**EN17. Initiatives to use renewable energy sources and to increase energy efficiency.**
	EN18. Energy consumption footprint (i.e., annualised lifetime energy requirements) of major products. Report in joules.

continued over

* A draft protocol is currently under development for this indicator.
Please see www.globalreporting.org for further details.

Core Indicators	Additional Indicators
Energy (continued)*	
EN4. Indirect energy use. Report on all energy used to produce and deliver energy products purchased by the reporting organisation (e.g., electricity or heat). Report in joules.	**EN19. Other indirect (upstream/downstream) energy use and implications, such as organisational travel, product lifecycle management, and use of energy-intensive materials.**
*Water**	
EN5. Total water use.	**EN20. Water sources and related ecosystems/habitats significantly affected by use of water.** Include Ramsar-listed wetlands and the overall contribution to resulting environmental trends.
	EN21. Annual withdrawals of ground and surface water as a percent of annual renewable quantity of water available from the sources. Breakdown by region.
	EN22. Total recycling and reuse of water. Include wastewater and other used water (e.g., cooling water).
Biodiversity	
EN6. Location and size of land owned, leased, or managed in biodiversity-rich habitats. Further guidance on biodiversity-rich habitats may be found at www.globalreporting.org (forthcoming).	**EN23. Total amount of land owned, leased, or managed for production activities or extractive use.**
	EN24. Amount of impermeable surface as a percentage of land purchased or leased.
EN7. Description of the major impacts on biodiversity associated with activities and/or products and services in terrestrial, freshwater, and marine environments.	**EN25. Impacts of activities and operations on protected and sensitive areas.** (e.g., IUCN protected area categories 1–4, world heritage sites, and biosphere reserves).
	EN26. Changes to natural habitats resulting from activities and operations and percentage of habitat protected or restored. Identify type of habitat affected and its status.

* A draft protocol is currently under development for this indicator. Please see www.globalreporting.org for further details.

Core Indicators	Additional Indicators

Biodiversity (continued)

	EN27. Objectives, programmes, and targets for protecting and restoring native ecosystems and species in degraded areas.
	EN28. Number of IUCN Red List species with habitats in areas affected by operations.
	EN29. Business units currently operating or planning operations in or around protected or sensitive areas.

Emissions, Effluents, and Waste

EN8. Greenhouse gas emissions.
(CO_2, CH_4, N_2O, HFCs, PFCs, SF_6). Report separate subtotals for each gas in tonnes and in tonnes of CO_2 equivalent for the following:

- direct emissions from sources owned or controlled by the reporting entity
- indirect emissions from imported electricity heat or steam

See WRI-WBCSD Greenhouse Gas Protocol (www.ghgprotocol.org).

EN9. Use and emissions of ozone-depleting substances.
Report each figure separately in accordance with Montreal Protocol (www.unep.org/ozone/montreal.shtml) Annexes A, B, C, and E in tonnes of CFC-11 equivalents (ozone-depleting potential).

EN10. NO_x, SO_x, and other significant air emissions by type.
Include emissions of substances regulated under:

- local laws and regulations
- Stockholm POPs Convention (Annex A, B, and C)—persistent organic pollutants
- Rotterdam Convention on Prior Informed Consent (PIC)
- Helsinki, Sofia, and Geneva Protocols to the Convention on Long-Range Trans-boundary Air Pollution

EN11. Total amount of waste by type and destination.
"Destination" refers to the method by which waste is treated, including composting, reuse, recycling, recovery, incineration, or landfilling. Explain type of classification method and estimation method.

EN30. Other relevant indirect greenhouse gas emissions.
(CO_2, CH_4, N_2O, HFCs, PFCs, SF_6). Refers to emissions that are a consequence of the activities of the reporting entity, but occur from sources owned or controlled by another entity Report in tonnes of gas and tonnes of CO_2 equivalent. See WRI-WBCSD Greenhouse Gas Protocol.

EN31. All production, transport, import, or export of any waste deemed "hazardous" under the terms of the Basel Convention Annex I, II, III, and VIII.

EN32. Water sources and related ecosystems/habitats significantly affected by discharges of water and runoff.
Include Ramsar-listed wetlands and the overall contribution to resulting environmental trends. See GRI Water Protocol.

continued over

Core Indicators	Additional Indicators
Emissions, Effluents, and Waste (continued)	
EN12. Significant discharges to water by type. See GRI Water Protocol.	
EN13. Significant spills of chemicals, oils, and fuels in terms of total number and total volume. Significance is defined in terms of both the size of the spill and impact on the surrounding environment.	
Suppliers	
	EN33. Performance of suppliers relative to environmental components of programmes and procedures described in response to Governance Structure and Management Systems section (Section 3.16).
Products and Services	
EN14. Significant environmental impacts of principal products and services. Describe and quantify where relevant.	
EN15. Percentage of the weight of products sold that is reclaimable at the end of the products' useful life and percentage that is actually reclaimed. "Reclaimable" refers to either the recycling or reuse of the product materials or components.	
Compliance	
EN16. Incidents of and fines for non-compliance with all applicable international declarations/conventions/treaties, and national, sub-national, regional, and local regulations associated with environmental issues. Explain in terms of countries of operation.	
Transport	
	EN34. Significant environmental impacts of transportation used for logistical purposes.
Overall	
	EN35. Total environmental expenditures by type. Explain definitions used for types of expenditures.

SOCIAL PERFORMANCE INDICATORS

The social dimension of sustainability concerns an organisation's impacts on the social systems within which it operates. Social performance can be gauged through an analysis of the organisation's impacts on stakeholders at the local, national, and global levels. In some cases, social indicators influence the organisation's intangible assets, such as its human capital and reputation.

Social performance measurement enjoys less of a consensus than environmental performance measurement. Through its consultative process, GRI has selected indicators by identifying key performance aspects surrounding labour practices, human rights, and broader issues affecting consumers, community, and other stakeholders in society. The specific aspects for labour practices and human rights performance are based mainly on internationally recognised standards such as the Conventions of the International Labour Organisation (ILO) and international instruments such as the United Nations Universal Declaration of Human Rights. In particular, the labour practices and human rights indicators have drawn heavily on the ILO Tripartite Declaration Concerning Multinational Enterprises and Social Policy, and the Organisation for Economic Co-operation and Development (OECD) *Guidelines for Multinational Enterprises*, which were deemed most relevant to the responsibilities of business during the GRI consultative process.

The aspects of labour practices that relate to human rights have been incorporated into the latter category. This decision was made to avoid treating "labour rights" as something different from, or less important than, "human rights". The decision reflects the strong sentiment that an organisation's contribution in the area of labour practices should not be simply to protect and respect basic rights; it should also be to enhance the quality of the working environment and value of the relationship to the worker. While the aspects under labour practices and human rights are closely related (e.g., collective bargaining and industrial relations), there remains a fundamental difference in the purpose of the indicators, and they have therefore been kept separate. The aspects and indicators under human rights help assess how a reporting organisation helps maintain and respect the basic rights of a human being. The aspects and indicators under labour practices measure ways in which an organisation's contributions go beyond these baseline expectations.

Several of the social performance indicators differ considerably in nature from other economic and environmental performance indicators in the *Guidelines*. Many of the social issues that are the subject of performance measurement are not easily quantifiable, so a number of social indicators are qualitative measures of the organisation's systems and operations, including policies, procedures, and management practices. These indicators relate not to general, overarching policies (as listed in Section 3 of Part C) but to specific, narrowly defined social aspects such as forced or compulsory labour, or freedom of association. Future protocols will help further articulate the specific details associated with these indicators of practice and policy.

While GRI has sought to capture issues of key concern to most stakeholders, the *Guidelines* do not, at present, address the questions of all potential stakeholders. Given the diversity of social situations and issues that confront them, organisations should use stakeholder consultation to ensure that the social impacts on which they report are as complete as possible. Three areas that will require further attention in the future are employee remuneration, working time, and broadening the coverage of community. It is currently felt that these issues are best addressed on a sector-specific basis in GRI's future sector supplements. However, consideration will be given to incorporating appropriate indicators into the core *Guidelines* in future revision cycles.

The social performance indicators that appear in this document represent a significant step forward from the previous version of the *Guidelines* in identifying core issues that are applicable to most organisations. However, GRI social indicators will be continually enhanced over time as the field of performance measurement progresses and GRI receives further feedback on the *Guidelines*.

Labour Practices and Decent Work

Core Indicators	Additional Indicators
Employment	
LA1. Breakdown of workforce, where possible, by region/country, status (employee/non-employee), employment type (full time/part time), and by employment contract (indefinite or permanent/fixed term or temporary). Also identify workforce retained in conjunction with other employers (temporary agency workers or workers in co-employment relationships), segmented by region/country.	**LA12. Employee benefits beyond those legally mandated.** (e.g., contributions to health care, disability, maternity, education, and retirement).
LA2. Net employment creation and average turnover segmented by region/country.	
Labour/Management Relations	
LA3. Percentage of employees represented by independent trade union organisations or other bona fide employee representatives broken down geographically OR percentage of employees covered by collective bargaining agreements broken down by region/country.	**LA13. Provision for formal worker representation in decision-making or management, including corporate governance.**
LA4. Policy and procedures involving information, consultation, and negotiation with employees over changes in the reporting organisation's operations (e.g., restructuring).	

continued opposite

Core Indicators	Additional Indicators

Health and Safety

LA5. Practices on recording and notification of occupational accidents and diseases, and how they relate to the ILO Code of Practice on Recording and Notification of Occupational Accidents and Diseases.

LA6. Description of formal joint health and safety committees comprising management and worker representatives and proportion of workforce covered by any such committees.

LA7. Standard injury, lost day, and absentee rates and number of work-related fatalities (including subcontracted workers).

LA8. Description of policies or programmes (for the workplace and beyond) on HIV/AIDS.

LA14. Evidence of substantial compliance with the ILO *Guidelines for Occupational Health Management Systems*.

LA15. Description of formal agreements with trade unions or other bona fide employee representatives covering health and safety at work and proportion of the workforce covered by any such agreements.

Training and Education

LA9. Average hours of training per year per employee by category of employee.
(e.g., senior management, middle management, professional, technical, administrative, production, and maintenance).

LA16. Description of programmes to support the continued employability of employees and to manage career endings.

LA17. Specific policies and programmes for skills management or for lifelong learning.

Diversity and Opportunity

LA10. Description of equal opportunity policies or programmes, as well as monitoring systems to ensure compliance and results of monitoring.
Equal opportunity policies may address workplace harassment and affirmative action relative to historical patterns of discrimination.

LA11. Composition of senior management and corporate governance bodies (including the board of directors), including female/male ratio and other indicators of diversity as culturally appropriate.

Human Rights

Core Indicators	Additional Indicators
Strategy and Management	
HR1. Description of policies, guidelines, corporate structure, and procedures to deal with all aspects of human rights relevant to operations, including monitoring mechanisms and results. State how policies relate to existing international standards such as the Universal Declaration and the Fundamental Human Rights Conventions of the ILO.	**HR8. Employee training on policies and practices concerning all aspects of human rights relevant to operations.** Include type of training, number of employees trained, and average training duration.
HR2. Evidence of consideration of human rights impacts as part of investment and procurement decisions, including selection of suppliers/contractors.	
HR3. Description of policies and procedures to evaluate and address human rights performance within the supply chain and contractors, including monitoring systems and results of monitoring. "Human rights performance" refers to the aspects of human rights identified as reporting aspects in the GRI performance indicators.	
Non-discrimination	
HR4. Description of global policy and procedures/programmes preventing all forms of discrimination in operations, including monitoring systems and results of monitoring.	
Freedom of Association and Collective Bargaining	
HR5. Description of freedom of association policy and extent to which this policy is universally applied independent of local laws, as well as description of procedures/programmes to address this issue.	
*Child Labour**	
HR6. Description of policy excluding child labour as defined by the ILO Convention 138 and extent to which this policy is visibly stated and applied, as well as description of procedures/programmes to address this issue, including monitoring systems and results of monitoring.	

* A draft protocol is currently under development for this indicator. Please see www.globalreporting.org for further details.

continued opposite

Core Indicators	Additional Indicators

Forced and Compulsory Labour

HR7. Description of policy to prevent forced and compulsory labour and extent to which this policy is visibly stated and applied as well as description of procedures/ programmes to address this issue, including monitoring systems and results of monitoring.
See ILO Convention No. 29, Article 2.

Disciplinary Practices

	HR9. Description of appeal practices, including, but not limited to, human rights issues. Describe the representation and appeals process.
	HR10. Description of non-retaliation policy and effective, confidential employee grievance system (including, but not limited to, its impact on human rights).

Security Practices

	HR11. Human rights training for security personnel. Include type of training, number of persons trained, and average training duration.

Indigenous Rights

	HR12. Description of policies, guidelines, and procedures to address the needs of indigenous people. This includes indigenous people in the workforce and in communities where the organisation currently operates or intends to operate.
	HR13. Description of jointly managed community grievance mechanisms/authority.
	HR14. Share of operating revenues from the area of operations that are redistributed to local communities.

Society

Core Indicators	Additional Indicators
Community	
SO1. Description of policies to manage impacts on communities in areas affected by activities, as well as description of procedures/programmes to address this issue, including monitoring systems and results of monitoring. Include explanation of procedures for identifying and engaging in dialogue with community stakeholders.	**SO4. Awards received relevant to social, ethical, and environmental performance.**
Bribery and Corruption	
SO2. Description of the policy, procedures/management systems, and compliance mechanisms for organisations and employees addressing bribery and corruption. Include a description of how the organisation meets the requirements of the OECD Convention on Combating Bribery.	
Political Contributions	
SO3. Description of policy, procedures/management systems, and compliance mechanisms for managing political lobbying and contributions.	**SO5. Amount of money paid to political parties and institutions whose prime function is to fund political parties or their candidates.**
Competition and Pricing	
	SO6. Court decisions regarding cases pertaining to anti-trust and monopoly regulations.
	SO7. Description of policy, procedures/management systems, and compliance mechanisms for preventing anti-competitive behaviour.

Product Responsibility

Core Indicators	Additional Indicators

Customer Health and Safety

PR1. Description of policy for preserving customer health and safety during use of products and services, and extent to which this policy is visibly stated and applied, as well as description of procedures/ programmes to address this issue, including monitoring systems and results of monitoring. Explain rationale for any use of multiple standards in marketing and sales of products.	**PR4. Number and type of instances of non-compliance with regulations concerning customer health and safety, including the penalties and fines assessed for these breaches.**
	PR5. Number of complaints upheld by regulatory or similar official bodies to oversee or regulate the health and safety of products and services.
	PR6. Voluntary code compliance, product labels or awards with respect to social and/or environmental responsibility that the reporter is qualified to use or has received. Include explanation of the process and criteria involved.

Products and Services

PR2. Description of policy, procedures/management systems, and compliance mechanisms related to product information and labelling.	**PR7. Number and type of instances of non-compliance with regulations concerning product information and labelling, including any penalties or fines assessed for these breaches.**
	PR8. Description of policy, procedures/management systems, and compliance mechanisms related to customer satisfaction, including results of surveys measuring customer satisfaction. Identify geographic areas covered by policy.

Advertising

	PR9. Description of policies, procedures/management systems, and compliance mechanisms for adherence to standards and voluntary codes related to advertising. Identify geographic areas covered by policy.
	PR10. Number and types of breaches of advertising and marketing regulations.

Respect for Privacy

PR3. Description of policy, procedures/management systems, and compliance mechanisms for consumer privacy. Identify geographic areas covered by policy.	**PR11. Number of substantiated complaints regarding breaches of consumer privacy.**

27
ISO 14001

[ISO 14001 is] the gold medal winner among environmental management systems: liked by the market, internationally available
and recognised, not too difficult to achieve (especially if you are a
big company) and it satisfies the users.

*Ruth Hillary, Network for Environmental
Management and Auditing*[1]

Baxter Healthcare's adherence to ISO 14001 will definitely help to
sustain our long-term competitiveness, as discerning customers
around the world are becoming more environmentally conscious.

*Jay Rajangam, Senior Environmental Engineer,
Baxter Healthcare (Singapore)*[2]

Type   Process-oriented standard, certification standard

Strength   Management systems

Keywords Environmental management systems • ISO • Auditors • Certification •
Standard • Overview

27.1 Background

The ISO 14000 series is a family of standards for creating environmental management systems (EMSs; for a definition of an EMS, see Box 27.1).

The International Organisation for Standardisation (ISO) has developed over
13,000 standards, working with standard-setting bodies in 145 countries. The ISO

---

1   Hillary 2001: 11.
2   Quoted in ISO 1998. Also quoted at www.scope4u.com/iso14000-benefits.html.

> ● **Environmental management system**: the part of the overall management system that includes organisational structure, planning activities, responsibilities, practices, procedures, processes and resources for developing, implementing, achieving, reviewing and maintaining the environmental policy.

Box 27.1 **Definition**

Source: www.iso14000.com/Implementation/definitions.htm

9000 and ISO14000 series are among the most well known of the ISO standards. As with all ISO standards, companies that have successfully undergone an ISO 14001 audit by a trained auditor receive an ISO 14001 certificate. The ISO standards can also be used internally, without external auditors.

Since its launch in 1996, the ISO 14000 series has been embraced by the business community, with at least 36,765 companies certified to ISO 14001 in over 112 countries (including certification both to the ISO 9000 series and to the ISO 14000 series).

Companies in compliance with ISO 14001 must develop the following (McIntosh *et al.* 2003: 104):

● An environmental policy

● An assessment of environmental aspects

● An assessment of legal and voluntary obligations

● A management system

● A series of periodic internal audits and reports to top management

27.2 Strengths and weaknesses

The management systems of ISO 14001 provide a useful framework for organisations to address environmental issues. Through training, employees gain an understanding of how to prevent environmental problems. However, one of the most serious shortcomings of ISO 14001 is that it has no performance criteria. Hence, an organisation can implement excellent management systems to address environmental issues yet still cause serious environmental problems. ISO 14001 does not focus on sustainability.

ISO 14001 has attained a critical mass of companies around the world. The advantage for companies of such a well-known and well-accepted certification standard is that companies can opt to work only with certified facilities.

A flexible standard:

> ISO 14001 is not a thoroughbred. It is a workhorse of a standard, designed to get you started and going down the right path . . . it motivates and allows those implementing it to do with it what they want. This is ISO 14001's greatest strength—and weakness (Hillary 2001: 15).

The costs associated with implementing ISO 14001 can be significant (but subsidies are available in some regions to offset the cost—for example, local governments in Japan). However, these costs can be seen as an investment, in that most companies find that such investments lead to business benefits. A survey of 18 Danish companies found that companies received new business as a result of their work on environmental issues. In addition, some companies reported a reduction in their environmental impact, with some negative environmental impacts removed altogether (Pedersen and Nielsen 2000: 37).

In recent years, there have been demands that ISO become more accountable to stakeholders and more transparent. A number of developing countries have complained to the World Trade Organisation that ISO does not take their needs into account when developing standards (ISO 2002). Mike Smith, the ISO Director for the ISO Standard Department, believes that electronic telecommunications will make it easier for enhanced participation at ISO by developing countries (ISO 2002).

27.3 Companies to which ISO 14001 applies

ISO 14001 is well suited to large companies with well-developed management systems.

27.4 Questions posed and answered

ISO 14001 poses the following question:

- How can a company develop management systems to address environmental issues?

27.5 The promise and the challenge

The management systems of ISO have the potential to provide useful analogues for the field of corporate responsibility. Although these management systems are increasingly being modelled in standards such as Social Accountability 8000

(SA8000, Chapter 9), the ISO system will also need to learn from the corporate responsibility (CR) community about multi-stakeholder dialogue. The challenge for ISO will be to find mechanisms for including greater participation of stakeholders in decision-making. Perhaps with this end in mind, ISO has developed a working group (ISO 2003) to assess whether or not ISO should develop a CR standard.

27.6 Compatibility with other standards

ISO 14001 is very compatible with a range of standards, including those within the ISO family of standards, such as the ISO 9000 series. Once a company has developed the management systems for the ISO 14001 certificate, it becomes easier to implement SA8000 as well.

ISO 14001 is also becoming more compatible with the Eco-Management and Audit Scheme (EMAS) of the European Union (see page 209 and footnote 1 on page 202). Developed by the European Union, EMAS is a tool for public and private organisations and requires a company to:

- Conduct an environmental review

- Establish an effective management system

- Conduct an environmental audit

- Write a statement about its environmental performance

In 2001, the Council of Europe and the European Parliament revised EMAS, specifying that organisations should adopt the ISO 14001 management systems to meet the second EMAS criterion listed above.

References

Hillary, R. (2001) 'Introduction', in R. Hillary (ed.), *ISO 14001: Case Studies and Practical Experiences* (Sheffield, UK: Greenleaf Publishing): 9-16.

ISO (International Organisation for Standardisation) (1999) *The ISO 14001 Information Guide* (Geneva: ISO).

—— (2002) 'ISO is no "Sleeping Beauty" says ISO Director of Standards', news item, June 2002, www.iso.ch/iso/en/commcentre/news/ standardspanel.html.

—— (2003) 'ISO weighs up work on social responsibility of organizations', press release 843, 12 February 2003.

McIntosh, M., D. Leipziger and G. Coleman (2003) *Living Corporate Citizenship: Strategic Routes to Socially Responsible Business* (London: FT Pearson).

Pedersen, C., and B. Nielsen (2000) 'Maintaining the Momentum: EMS after the Certifier has Left', in R. Hillary (ed.), *ISO 14001: Case Studies and Practical Experiences* (Sheffield, UK: Greenleaf Publishing): 31-38.

Additional resources

Further reading

ISO (International Organisation for Standardisation) (2003) 'ISO 14000 makes progress in Singapore', *ISO 9000 News*, www.iso.ch/iso/en/ iso9000-14000/feedback.html, 4 February 2003.

Website

International Organisation for Standardisation (ISO): www.iso.ch

ISO 14001:1996
Environmental Management Systems:
Specifications with Guidance for Use*

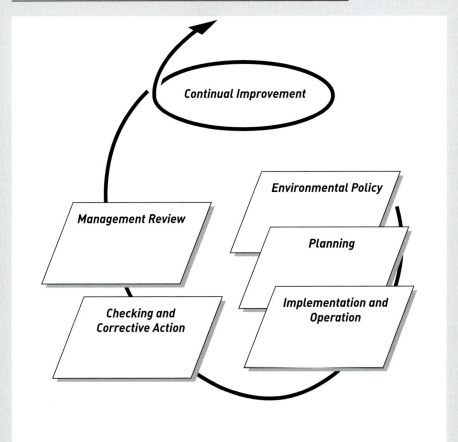

Figure 1: Environmental management system model for this International
Standard

* Selected extracts only are reproduced here. Extracts from BS EN ISO 14001: 1996 reproduced with the permission of the British Standards Institution under licence number
2003SK/069. BSI publications can be obtained from BSI Customer Services, 389 Chiswick
High Road, London W4 4AL. UK (tel: +44 [0]20 8996 9001; e-mail: cservices@bsi-global.
com).

4 ENVIRONMENTAL MANAGEMENT SYSTEM REQUIREMENTS

4.1 *General requirements*

The organization shall establish and maintain an environmental management system, the requirements of which are described in the whole of clause **4**.

4.2 *Environmental policy*

Top management shall define the organization's environmental policy and ensure that it

a) is appropriate to the nature, scale and environmental impacts of its activities, products or services;

b) includes a commitment to continual improvement and prevention of pollution;

c) includes a commitment to comply with relevant environmental legislation and regulations, and with other requirements to which the organization subscribes;

d) provides the framework for setting and reviewing environmental objectives and targets;

e) is documented, implemented and maintained and communicated to all employees;

f) is available to the public.

4.3 *Planning*

4.3.1 Environmental aspects

The organization shall establish and maintain (a) procedure(s) to identify the environmental aspects of its activities, products or services that it can control and over which it can be expected to have an influence, in order to determine those which have or can have significant impacts on the environment. The organization shall ensure that the aspects related to these significant impacts are considered in setting its environmental objectives.

The organization shall keep this information up-to-date.

4.3.2 Legal and other requirements

The organization shall establish and maintain a procedure to identify and have access to legal and other requirements to which the organization subscribes, that are applicable to the environmental aspects of its activities, products or services.

4.3.3 Objectives and targets

The organization shall establish and maintain documented environmental objectives and targets, at each relevant function and level within the organization.

When establishing and reviewing its objectives, an organization shall consider the legal and other requirements, its significant environmental aspects, its technological options and its financial, operational and business requirements, and the views of interested parties.

The objectives and targets shall be consistent with the environmental policy, including the commitment to prevention of pollution.

4.3.4 Environmental management programme(s)

The organization shall establish and maintain (a) programme(s) for achieving its objectives and targets. It shall include

a) designation of responsibility for achieving objectives and targets at each relevant function and level of the organization;

b) the means and time-frame by which they are to be achieved.

If a project relates to new developments and new or modified activities, products or services, programme(s) shall be amended where relevant to ensure that environmental management applies to such projects.

4.4 *Implementation and operation*

4.4.1 Structure and responsibility

Roles, responsibility and authorities shall be defined, documented and communicated in order to facilitate effective environmental management.

Management shall provide resources essential to the implementation and control of the environmental management system. Resources include human resources and specialized skills, technology and financial resources.

The organization's top management shall appoint (a) specific management representative(s) who, irrespective of other responsibilities, shall have defined roles, responsibilities and authority for

a) ensuring that environmental management system requirements are established, implemented and maintained in accordance with this International Standard;

b) reporting on the performance of the environmental management system to top management for review and as a basis for improvement of the environmental management system.

4.4.2 Training, awareness and competence

The organization shall identify training needs. It shall require that all personnel whose work may create a significant impact upon the environment, have received appropriate training.

It shall establish and maintain procedures to make its employees or members at each relevant function and level aware of

a) the importance of conformance with the environmental policy and procedures and with the requirements of the environmental management system;

b) the significant environmental impacts, actual or potential, of their work activities and the environmental benefits of improved personal performance;

c) their roles and responsibilities in achieving conformance with the environmental policy and procedures and with the requirements of the environmental management system, including emergency preparedness and response requirements;

d) the potential consequences of departure from specified operating procedures.

Personnel performing the tasks which can cause significant environmental impacts shall be competent on the basis of appropriate education, training and/or experience.

4.4.3 Communication

With regard to its environmental aspects and environmental management system, the organization shall establish and maintain procedures for

a) internal communication between the various levels and functions of the organization;

b) receiving, documenting and responding to relevant communication from external interested parties.

The organization shall consider processes for external communication on its significant environmental aspects and record its decision.

4.4.4 Environmental management system documentation

The organization shall establish and maintain information, in paper or electronic form, to

a) describe the core elements of the management system and their interaction;

b) provide direction to related documentation.

4.4.5 Document control

The organization shall establish and maintain procedures for controlling all documents required by this International Standard to ensure that

a) they can be located;

b) they are periodically reviewed, revised as necessary and approved for adequacy by authorized personnel;

c) the current versions of relevant documents are available at all locations where operations essential to the effective functioning of the environmental management system are performed;

d) obsolete documents are promptly removed from all points of issue and points of use, or otherwise assured against unintended use;

e) any obsolete documents retained for legal and/or knowledge preservation purposes are suitably identified.

Documentation shall be legible, dated (with dates of revision) and readily identifiable, maintained in an orderly manner and retained for a specified period. Procedures and responsibilities shall be established and maintained concerning the creation and modification of the various types of document.

4.4.6 Operational control

The organization shall identify those operations and activities that are associated with the identified significant environmental aspects in line with its policy, objectives and targets. The organization shall plan these activities, including maintenance, in order to ensure that they are carried out under specified conditions by

a) establishing and maintaining documented procedures to cover situations where their absence could lead to deviations from the environmental policy and the objectives and targets;

b) stipulating operating criteria in the procedures;

c) establishing and maintaining procedures related to the identifiable significant environmental aspects of goods and services used by the organization and communicating relevant procedures and requirements to suppliers and contractors.

4.4.7 Emergency preparedness and response

The organization shall establish and maintain procedures to identify potential for and respond to accidents and emergency situations, and for preventing and mitigating the environmental impacts that may be associated with them.

The organization shall review and revise, where necessary, its emergency preparedness and response procedures, in particular, after the occurrence of accidents or emergency situations.

The organization shall also periodically test such procedures where practicable.

4.5 Checking and corrective action

4.5.1 Monitoring and measurement

The organization shall establish and maintain documented procedures to monitor and measure, on a regular basis, the key characteristics of its operations and activities that can have a significant impact on the environment. This shall include the recording of information to track performance, relevant operational controls and conformance with the organization's environmental objectives and targets.

Monitoring equipment shall be calibrated and maintained and records of this process shall be retained according to the organization's procedures.

The organization shall establish and maintain a documented procedure for periodically evaluating compliance with relevant environmental legislation and regulations.

4.5.2 Nonconformance and corrective and preventive action

The organization shall establish and maintain procedures for defining responsibility and authority for handling and investigating nonconformance, taking action to mitigate any impacts caused and for initiating and completing corrective and preventive action.

Any corrective or preventive action taken to eliminate the causes of actual and potential nonconformances shall be appropriate to the magnitude of problems and commensurate with the environmental impact encountered.

The organization shall implement and record any changes in the documented procedures resulting from corrective and preventive action.

4.5.3 Records

The organization shall establish and maintain procedures for the identification, maintenance and disposition of environmental records. These records shall include training records and the results of audits and reviews.

Environmental records shall be legible, identifiable and traceable to the activity, product or service involved. Environmental records shall be stored and maintained in such a way that they are readily retrievable and protected against damage, deterioration or loss. Their retention times shall be established and recorded.

Records shall be maintained, as appropriate to the system and to the organization, to demonstrate conformance to the requirements of this International Standard.

4.5.4 Environmental management system audit

The organization shall establish and maintain (a) programme(s) and procedures for periodic environmental management system audits to be carried out, in order to

a) determine whether or not the environmental management system

   1) conforms to planned arrangements for environmental management including the requirements of this International Standard; and

   2) has been properly implemented and maintained; and

b) provide information on the results of audits to management.

The organization's audit programme, including any schedule, shall be based on the environmental importance of the activity concerned and the results of previous audits. In order to be comprehensive, the audit procedures shall cover the audit scope, frequency and methodologies, as well as the responsibilities and requirements for conducting audits and reporting results.

4.6 *Management review*

The organization's top management shall, at intervals that it determines, review the environmental management system, to ensure its continuing suitability, adequacy and effectiveness. The management review process shall ensure that the necessary information is collected to allow management to carry out this evaluation. This review shall be documented.

The management review shall address the possible need for changes to policy, objectives and other elements of the environmental management system, in the light of environmental management system audit results, changing circumstances and the commitment to continual improvement.

ANNEX A (INFORMATIVE)
GUIDANCE ON THE USE OF THE SPECIFICATION

This annex gives additional information on the requirements and is intended to avoid misinterpretation of the specification. This annex only addresses the environmental management system requirements contained in clause 4.

A.1 *General requirements*

It is intended that the implementation of an environmental management system described by the specification will result in improved environmental performance. The specification is based on the concept that the organization will periodically review and evaluate its environmental management system in order to identify opportunities for improvement and their implementation. Improvements in its environmental management system are intended to result in additional improvements in environmental performance.

The environmental management system provides a structured process for the achievement of continual improvement, the rate and extent of which will be determined by the organization in the light of economic and other circumstances. Although some improvement in environmental performance can be expected due to the adoption of a systematic approach, it should be understood that the environmental management system is a tool which enables the organization to achieve and systematically control the level of environmental performance that it sets itself. The establishment and operation of an environmental management system will not, in itself, necessarily result in an immediate reduction of adverse environmental impact.

An organization has the freedom and flexibility to define its boundaries and may choose to implement this International Standard with respect to the entire organization, or to specific operating units or activities of the organization. If this International Standard is implemented for a specific operating unit or activity, policies and procedures developed by other parts of the organization can be used to meet the requirements of this International Standard, provided that they are applicable to the specific operating unit or activity that will be subject to it. The level of detail and complexity of the environmental management system, the extent of documentation and the resources devoted to it will be dependent in the size of an organization and the nature of its activities. This may be the case in particular for small and medium-sized enterprises. Integration of environmental matters with the overall management system can contribute to the effective implementation of the environmental management system, as well as to efficiency and to clarity of roles.

This International Standard contains management system requirements, based on the dynamic cyclical process of "plan, implement, check and review".

The system should enable an organization to

a) establish an environmental policy appropriate to itself;

b) identify the environmental aspects arising from the organization's past, existing or planned activities, products or services, to determine the environmental impacts of significance;

c) identify the relevant legislative and regulatory requirements;

d) identify priorities and set appropriate environmental objectives and targets;

e) establish a structure and (a) programme(s) to implement the policy and achieve objectives and targets;

f) facilitate planning, control, monitoring, corrective action, auditing and review activities to ensure both that the policy is complied with and that the environmental management system remains appropriate;

g) be capable of adapting to changing circumstances.

A.2 *Environmental policy*

The environmental policy is the driver for implementing and improving the organization's environmental management system so that it can maintain and potentially improve its environmental performance. The policy should therefore reflect the commitment of top management to compliance with applicable laws and continual improvement. The policy forms the basis upon which the organization sets its objectives and targets. The policy should be sufficiently clear to be capable of being understood by internal and external interested parties and should be periodically reviewed and revised to reflect changing conditions and information. Its area of application should be clearly identifiable.

The organization's top management should define and document its environmental policy within the context of the environmental policy of any broader corporate body of which it is a part and with the endorsement of that body, if there is one.

NOTE: Top management may consist of an individual or group of individuals with executive responsibility for the organization.

A.3 *Planning*

A.3.1 Environmental aspects

Subclause **4.3.1** is intended to provide a process for an organization to identify significant environmental aspects that should be addressed as a priority by the organization's environmental management system. This process should take into account the cost and time of undertaking the analysis and the availability of reliable data. Information already developed for regulatory or other purposes may be used in this process. Organizations may also take into account the degree of practical control they may have over the environmental aspects being considered. Organizations should determine what their environmental aspects are, taking into account the inputs and outputs associated with their current and relevant past activities, products and/or services.

An organization with no existing environmental management system should, initially, establish its current position with regard to the environment by means of a review. The aim should be to consider all environmental aspects of the organization as a basis for establishing the environmental management system.

Those organizations with operating environmental management systems do not have to undertake such a review.

The review should cover four key areas:

a) legislative and regulatory requirements;

b) an identification of significant environmental aspects;

c) an examination of all existing environmental management practices and procedures;

d) an evaluation of feedback from the investigation of previous incidents.

In all cases, consideration should be given to normal and abnormal operations within the organization, and to potential emergency conditions.

A suitable approach to the review may include check-lists, interviews, direct inspection and measurement, results of previous audits or other reviews depending on the nature of the activities.

The process to identify the significant environmental aspects associated with the activities at operating units should, where relevant, consider,

a) emissions to air;

b) releases to water;

c) waste management;

d) contamination of land;

e) use of raw materials and natural resources;

f) other local environmental and community issues.

This process should consider normal operating conditions, shut-down and start-up conditions, as well as the realistic potential significant impacts associated with reasonably foreseeable or emergency situations.

The process is intended to identify significant environmental aspects associated with activities, products or services, and is not intended to require a detailed life cycle assessment. Organizations do not have to evaluate each product, component or raw material input. They may select categories of activities, products or services to identify those aspects most likely to have a significant impact.

The control and influence over the environmental aspects of products vary significantly, depending on the market situation of the organization. A contractor or supplier to the organization may have comparatively little control, while the organization responsible for product design can alter the aspects significantly by changing, for example, a single input material. Whilst recognizing that organizations may have limited control over the use and disposal of their products, they should consider, where practical, proper handling and disposal mechanisms. This provision is not intended to change or increase an organisation's legal obligations.

A.3.2 Legal and other requirements

Examples of other requirements to which the organization may subscribe are

a) industry codes of practice;

b) agreements with public authorities;

c) non-regulatory guidelines.

A.3.3 Objectives and targets

The objectives should be specific and targets should be measurable wherever practicable, and where appropriate take preventative measures into account.

When considering their technological options, an organization may consider the use of the best available technology where economically viable, cost-effective and judged appropriate.

The reference to the financial requirements of the organization is not intended to imply that organizations are obliged to use environmental cost-accounting methodologies.

A.3.4 Environmental management programme(s)

The creation and use of one or more programmes is a key element to the successful implementation of an environmental management system. The programme should describe how the organization's objectives and targets will be achieved, including time-scales and personnel responsible for implementing the organization's environmental policy. This programme may be subdivided to address specific elements of the organization's operations. The programme should include an environmental review for new activities.

The programme may include, where appropriate and practical, consideration of planning, design, production, marketing and disposal stages. This may be undertaken for both current and new activities, products or services. For products this may address design, materials, production processes, use and ultimate disposal. For installations or significant modifications of processes this may address planning, design, construction, commissioning, operation and, at the appropriate time determined by the organization, decommissioning.

A.4 *Implementation and operation*

A.4.1 Structure and responsibility

The successful implementation of an environmental management system calls for the commitment of all employees of the organization. Environmental responsibilities therefore should not be seen as confined to the environmental function, but may also include other areas of an organization, such as operational management or staff functions other than environmental.

This commitment should begin at the highest levels of management. Accordingly, top management should establish the organization's environmental policy and ensure that the environmental management system is implemented. As part of this commitment, the top management should designate (a) specific management representative(s) with defined responsibility and authority for implementing the environmental management system. In large or complex organizations there may be more than one designated representative. In small or medium sized enterprises, these responsibilities may be undertaken by one individual. Top management should also ensure that appropriate resources are provided to ensure that the environmental management system is implemented and maintained. It is also important that the key environmental management system responsibilities are well defined and communicated to the relevant personnel.

A.4.2 Training, awareness and competence

The organization should establish and maintain procedures for identifying training needs. The organization should also require that contractors working on its behalf are able to demonstrate that their employees have the requisite training.

Management should determine the level of experience, competence and training necessary to ensure the capability of personnel, especially those carrying out specialized environmental management functions.

A.4.3 Communication

Organizations should implement a procedure for receiving, documenting and responding to relevant information and requests from interested parties. This procedure may include a dialogue with interested parties and consideration of their relevant concerns. In some circumstances, responses to interested parties' concerns may include relevant information about the environmental impacts associated with the organization's operations. These procedures should also address necessary communications with public authorities regarding emergency planning and other relevant issues.

A.4.4 Environmental management system documentation

The level of detail of the documentation should be sufficient to describe the core elements of the environmental management system and their interaction and provide direction on where to obtain more detailed information on the operation of specific parts of the environmental management system. This documentation may be integrated with documentation of other systems implemented by the organization. It does not have to be in the form of a single manual.

Related documentation may include

a) process information;

b) organizational charts;

c) internal standards and operational procedures;

d) site emergency plans.

A.4.5 Document control

The intent of **4.4.5** is to ensure that organizations create and maintain documents in a manner sufficient to implement the environmental management system. However, the primary focus of organizations should be on the effective implementation of the environmental management system and on environmental performance and not on a complex documentation control system.

A.4.6 Operational control

Text may be included here in a future revision.

A.4.7 Emergency preparedness and response

Text may be included here in a future revision.

A.5 *Checking and corrective action*

A.5.1 Monitoring and measurement

Text may be included here in a future revision.

A.5.2 Nonconformance and corrective and preventive action

In establishing and maintaining procedures for investigating and correcting nonconformance, the organization should include these basic elements:

a) identifying the cause of the nonconformance;

b) identifying and implementing the necessary corrective action;

c) implementing or modifying controls necessary to avoid repetition of the nonconformance;

d) recording any changes in written procedures resulting from the corrective action.

Depending on the situation, this may be accomplished rapidly and with a minimum of formal planning or it may be a more complex and long-term activity. The associated documentation should be appropriate to the level of corrective action.

A.5.3 Records

Procedures for identification, maintenance and disposition of records should focus on those records needed for the implementation and operation of the environmental management system and for recording the extent to which planned objectives and targets have been met.

Environmental records may include

a) information on applicable environmental laws or other requirements;

b) complaint records;

c) training records;

d) process information;

e) product information;

f) inspection, maintenance and calibration records;

g) pertinent contractor and supplier information;

h) incident reports;

i) information on emergency preparedness and response;

j) information on significant environmental aspects;

k) audit results;

l) management reviews.

Proper account should be taken of confidential business information.

A.5.4 Environmental management system audit

The audit programme and procedures should cover

a) the activities and areas to be considered in audits;

b) the frequency of audits;

c) the responsibilities associated with managing and conducting audits;

d) the communication of audit results;

e) auditor competence;

f) how audits will be conducted.

Audits may be performed by personnel from within the organization and/or by external persons selected by the organization. In either case, the persons conducting the audit should be in a position to do so impartially and objectively.

A.6 *Management review*

In order to maintain continual improvement, suitability and effectiveness of the environmental management system, and thereby its performance, the organization's management should review and evaluate the environmental management system at defined intervals. The scope of the review should be comprehensive, though not all elements of an environmental management system need to be reviewed at once and the review process may take place over a period of time.

The review of the policy, objectives and procedures should be carried out by the level of management that defined them.

Reviews should include

a) results from audits;

b) the extent to which objectives and targets have been met;

c) the continuing suitability of the environmental management system in relation to changing conditions and information;

d) concerns amongst relevant interested parties.

Observations, conclusions and recommendations should be documented for necessary action.

28
The 'Sustainability: Integrated Guidelines for Management' (SIGMA) Project

The day-to-day management challenge of handling all the different aspects of sustainable development (environmental management, quality, community investment, heath and safety, HR [human resources] issues, risk and insurance, stakeholder engagement and so on) becomes more and more complex—and more onerous. The SIGMA project has attempted to bring all these together in an integrated management framework specifically to help those 'on the front line' to make better sense of an agenda that currently threatens to overwhelm them rather than liberate them!

Jonathon Porritt, Forum for the Future[1]

Type   Process-oriented initiative

Strength Integration of key standards

Keywords Sustainability • Guidelines • Management • Integration • Core functions

28.1 Background

The 'Sustainability: Integrated Guidelines for Management' (SIGMA) project sets out a framework for companies seeking to become more sustainable. Launched in 1999, the SIGMA project is a partnership between Forum for the Future, Account-

---

1   E-mail to author, 5 August 2003.

Ability and the British Standards Institution (BSI). A fully revised set of guidelines were released on 23 September 2003. The SIGMA Project contains three key elements:

- A set of guiding principles
- A management framework for mainstreaming sustainability into the core functions of a company
- A toolkit

If there is one word that describes the SIGMA project, it is 'integration'. SIGMA integrates social, environmental and economic issues while encouraging organisations to integrate sustainability issues within the organisation. Last, SIGMA is itself a synthesis of several corporate responsibility (CR) initiatives, including key elements of the Global Reporting Initiative (GRI, Chapter 26), ISO standards (on ISO 14001, see Chapter 27) and other models.

The SIGMA Principles are drawn from many existing conventions, treaties and principles, including:

- UN Global Compact (Chapter 4)
- International Chamber of Commerce (ICC)'s Business Charter for Sustainable Development (Part 4, page 204)
- The Rio Declaration on Environment and Development (Chapter 14)
- Global Sullivan Principles (Chapter 3)
- OECD Guidelines for Multinational Enterprises (Chapter 2)
- The Natural Step (Chapter 16)
- AccountAbility 1000 (AA1000) Framework (Chapter 24)
- Other UN and ILO conventions (see www.projectsigma.com)

Like the AA1000 Framework, SIGMA can be used as a stand-alone model or in conjunction with a wide range of other initiatives. Again, as with the AA1000 Framework, the SIGMA framework allows organisations to define their own system based on their own specific needs.

The SIGMA framework assists organisations in:

- Defining the business case for their own organisation
- Benchmarking management issues with a questionnaire
- Devising a sustainability scorecard
- Understanding environmental accounting
- Understanding linkages to other CR initiatives

By using the SIGMA framework, organisations can define the 'sustainability gap', or the difference between their current actions and their targets, as well as the 'sustainability cost', or the resources necessary to reduce or eliminate that gap.

28.2 Strengths and weaknesses

One of the greatest strengths of the SIGMA approach is its linkages with other initiatives, such as GRI, the AA1000 Framework, The Natural Step and ISO 14001. At a time when 'code overload' is a serious problem,[2] the integrationist approach is helpful.

With funding from the UK Department of Trade and Industry (DTI) and developed by three British organisations (BSI, Forum for the Future and AccountAbility), it is not surprising that SIGMA has attracted primarily UK organisations.

28.3 Organisations to which the SIGMA framework applies

SIGMA is designed for use by organisations of all sizes and in all sectors.

28.4 Questions posed and answered

SIGMA asks and answers the following questions:

- What tools and frameworks do organisations need to integrate and promote environmental, social and economic sustainability?

- What synergies exist between SIGMA and existing CR models?

In addition, the SIGMA Management Framework includes four key phases in which companies must address the following questions (see Table 1 on pages 504-505):

- Phase 1: leadership and vision

- Phase 2: planning

- Phase 3: delivery

- Phase 4: monitor, review and report

---

2   The term 'code fatigue' is also used; see Rondinelli 2001.

28.5 The promise and the challenge

The challenge for SIGMA will be to promote the concept of sustainability broadly so as to influence more traditional management systems such as ISO 14001 (see Chapter 27) and the Eco-Management and Audit Scheme (EMAS; see page 209).

References

Rondinelli, D. (2001) *Changing the Way Business Does Business: Promises and Pitfalls of Corporate Self-Regulation* (sponsored by the Carnegie Endowment for International Peace; 24 April 2001, www.ceip.org/files/events/events.asp?EventID=351).

SIGMA ('Sustainability: Integrated Guidelines for Management') (2003) *The SIGMA Project* (London: SIGMA).

Additional resource

Website

SIGMA ('Sustainability: Integrated Guidelines for Management') Project: www.projectsigma.com.

The SIGMA Guidelines*

1.3 SIGMA—helping organisations to take action

A key issue for organisations that want to respond to the challenge posed by sustainable development is how to take effective action.

SIGMA provides a clear, practical, integrated framework for organisations. It allows an organisation to build on what it has, to take a flexible approach according to its circumstances and to reduce duplication and waste by seeing how different elements can fit together. The SIGMA Guidelines point the practitioner towards the important questions to ask and the actions to resolve them.

SIGMA content	How it helps an organisation
SIGMA Guiding Principles	Help an organisation understand how it can contribute to sustainable development and offer a framework to help an organisation develop its own robust principles.
SIGMA Management Framework integrates sustainable development issues into core processes and mainstream decision-making.	Four systematic phases, broken down into detailed sub-phases to allow an organisation to develop, plan, deliver, monitor and report on its sustainable development strategy and performance. The Framework explains clearly and concisely necessary activities, the anticipated outcomes, and lists further resources. It also helps an organisation understand how to build on what it already has in place.
SIGMA Toolkit Available at www.projectsigma.com	Advice and guidance on specific management challenges, e.g. reviewing performance, assessing opportunities and risks, and stakeholder engagement.

---

* Only selected extracts from the SIGMA Guidelines are reproduced here. Reprinted with the permission of Project SIGMA.

1.4 SIGMA Guiding Principles for a sustainable organisation

The SIGMA Guiding Principles consist of two core elements:

1. The holistic management of five different types of capital that reflect an organisation's overall impact and wealth (in the broadest sense).

2. The exercise of accountability, by being transparent and responsive to stakeholders and complying with relevant rules and standards.

The Guiding Principles are shown in Figure 1.

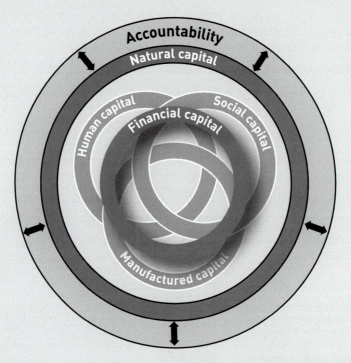

Figure 1: The SIGMA Guiding Principles

The five capitals are:

Natural capital—the environment

Social capital—social relationships and structures

Human capital—people

Manufactured capital—fixed assets

Financial capital—profit and loss, sales, shares, cash etc

Natural capital encompasses the other capitals as natural resources and ecological systems form the basis of life, on which all organisations (and wider society) depend. Social, human and manufactured capitals are critical components of an organisation and its activities. High levels of these capitals deliver value to both organisations and society, not to mention improving the quality of life of stakeholders. Financial capital is crucial to the ongoing survival of an organisation, and is simply derived from the value that the other four capitals provide. All of the capitals are heavily interlinked and there is some overlap between them.

This whole system is then encircled by the principle of **accountability**, representing the relationship that an organisation has with the outside world—with its stakeholders and for its stewardship of the five capitals.

The capitals need to be managed for the long term, not just for immediate return, building up stocks of capital and living off the interest that this creates. They also need to be recognised as interdependent, where changes in one are likely to cause an impact on another. Likewise, one form of capital cannot simply be traded against another.

The SIGMA Guiding Principles are compatible with other approaches that organisations may wish to pursue, most notably the concept of the triple bottom line, which has widespread popularity.

1.5 SIGMA Management Framework

The SIGMA Management Framework describes a four-phase cycle to manage and embed sustainability issues within core organisational processes.

Organisations may enter the cycle at different points and work through the phases at different speeds according to their particular circumstances and existing systems.

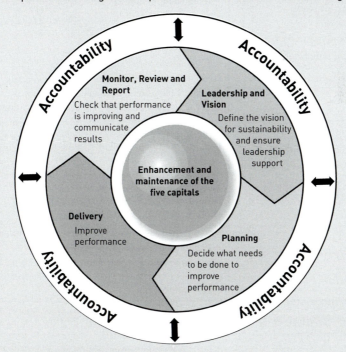

Figure 2: The SIGMA Management Framework

SIGMA Four-phase Management Framework and sub phases	
Management Phase	**Purpose**
Leadership and Vision **LV1** *Business case and top-level commitment* **LV2** *Vision, mission and operating principles* **LV3** *Communication and training* **LV4** *Culture change*	• To develop a business case to address sustainability issues and secure top-level commitment to integrate sustainable development into core processes and decision-making. • To identify stakeholders and open dialogue with them on key impacts and suggested approaches. • To formulate the organisation's long-term sustainable development mission, vision and operating principles and a high-level strategy that supports them, and to revisit them periodically. • To raise awareness of sustainability issues and how they may affect the organisation's licence to operate and its future direction and its training and development requirements. • To ensure that the organisational culture is supportive of a move towards sustainability.
Planning **P1** *Performance review* **P2** *Legal and regulatory analysis and management* **P3** *Actions, impacts and outcomes* **P4** *Strategic planning* **P5** *Tactical planning*	• To ascertain the organisation's current sustainability performance, legal requirements and voluntary commitments. • To identify and prioritise the organisation's key sustainability issues. • To develop strategic plans to deliver the organisation's vision and address its key sustainability issues. • Consult with stakeholders on plans. • To formulate tactical short-term action plans to support the agreed sustainability strategies with defined objectives, targets and responsibilities.
Delivery **D1** *Change management* **D2** *Management programmes* **D3** *Internal controls and external influence*	• To align and prioritise management programmes in line with strategic and tactical planning and the organisation's sustainability vision. • To ensure that identified actions, impacts and outcomes and legal and self-regulatory requirements are managed and appropriate internal controls are in place. • To improve performance by delivering sustainability strategies and associated action plans. • To exercise appropriate external influence on suppliers, peers and others to progress sustainable development.

Table 1: SIGMA Four-phase Management Framework and sub phases
(continued opposite)

SIGMA Four-phase Management Framework and sub phases	
Management Phase	**Purpose**
Monitor, Review and Report **MMR1** *Monitoring, measurement, auditing and feedback* **MMR2** *Tactical and strategic review* **MMR3** *Reporting progress* **MMR4** *Assurance of reporting*	● To monitor progress against stated values, strategies, performance objectives and targets. ● To engage with internal and external stakeholders via reporting and assurance, and by incorporating feedback into effective strategic and tactical reviews culminating in appropriate and timely change.

Table 1 (continued)

Part 10
Visions for the future

29
An emerging consensus

Many of the 32 tools profiled in this book represent a synthesis of different approaches, a crystallising of the visions of companies, non-governmental organisations (NGOs), trade unions and governments into a new paradigm. According to Mark Wade of Shell, a consolidation is necessary among the [bewildering array] of codes and guidelines.[1] Many of the standard-setting bodies have worked in relative isolation:

> A new relationship is evolving between companies, NGOs and governments. The barriers between these sectors is growing more porous, with different actors more willing to step outside the confines of their sector.[2]

This book explores the 'space between' the various sectors, the fertile ground in which convergence can germinate.

The corporate responsibility (CR) movement faces a struggle between the need for convergence among standards and the need to promote innovation. The other key challenge is to develop trust through verification in the face of growing cynicism from a range of stakeholders. In order to reach a critical mass, the initiatives described in this volume will need to demonstrate the business benefits of these codes.

29.1 Pathways to convergence

If the 1990s were the age of codes of conduct, the first decade of the 21st century will be known as the age of convergence. Although the need for convergence of

1 Interview with Mark Wade, Shell Learning–Leadership Development, London, 11 April 2003.
2 *Ibid.*

standards has never been greater, the consensus necessary for achieving convergence can be elusive. Codes of conduct and standards are the result of intense negotiations between stakeholders and strongly reflect the organisation(s) that developed them. As a result, there are important cultural, historical, sectoral and/or geographic nuances to each code that make it unique. These different points of departure can be barriers to convergence. The convergence debate can open up items that have already been debated and decided, causing a need to revisit politically sensitive issues. Furthermore, there is often a strong sense of competition among some initiatives, which can make co-operation unlikely.

There are two types of convergence: convergence of performance standards, and procedural convergence. In the convergence of performance standards, the expectations of companies are harmonised. For example, convergence of CR performance standards might merge requirements and definitions around such issues as use of child labour, or discrimination. Procedural convergence refers to the convergence of processes such as reporting, external verification and accreditation. The first category defines parameters of performance for corporate responsibility; the second defines its new disciplines. The disciplines of corporate responsibility will be established in answering the following types of question:

- What constitutes social auditing?
- What constitutes best practice in social reporting?

It is easier to achieve convergence on procedural issues than it is on performance standards. Whereas performance standards have been negotiated with great difficulty, procedural mechanisms are still evolving, and standard-setters may be more open to sharing lessons learned. Procedural convergence is a key goal in order to increase the transparency of CR initiatives.

There are several initiatives working towards procedural convergence. The International Social and Environmental Accreditation and Labelling (ISEAL) Alliance (see www.isealalliance.org; for the membership of ISEAL, see Box 29.1) includes accreditation bodies covering fair trade, social accountability, organic agriculture and sustainable fishing and forestry. The ISEAL Alliance is working on a common methodology for social and environmental accreditation procedures. Rather than creating a new standard, the goal of the project is to learn from other initiatives through pilot projects and to develop common frameworks, definitions and protocols. The ISEAL Alliance is researching the overlap of standards and is developing a framework for increasing compatibility. Joint training programmes are another priority. The ISEAL Alliance is an excellent model for convergence. Rather than creating a single standard, the goal is to learn and share experiences and to develop common procedures and protocols that will make each of the participating initiatives stronger.

Convergence is also being promoted among the following procedural standards:

- The AccountAbility 1000 (AA1000) Assurance Standard (Chapter 25)
- The Global Reporting Initiative (GRI, Chapter 26)
- The SIGMA ('Sustainability: Integrated Guidelines for Management') project (Chapter 28)

Current members of the ISEAL Alliance are:

- The Fair Trade Labelling Organisation (FLO) (www.fairtrade.net)

- The Forest Stewardship Council (FSC) (www.fscoax.org)

- The International Federation of Organic Agriculture Movements (IFOAM)(www.ifoam.org)

- The International Organic Accreditation Service (IOAS) (www.ioas.org)

- The Marine Aquarium Council (MAC) (www.aquariumcouncil.org)

- The Marine Stewardship Council (MSC) (www.msc.org)

- The Social Accountability International (SAI) (www.cepaa.org)

- The Sustainable Agriculture Network (SAN) (www.rainforest-alliance.org/programs/cap/gan/html)

Box 29.1 Members of the International Social and Environmental Accreditation and Labelling (ISEAL) Alliance

Source: www.isealalliance.org

- The Eco-Management and Audit Scheme (EMAS) of the European Union (see page 209 and footnote 1 on page 202)

- Q-Res[3]

The aim is to develop a common platform and template of key elements. These organisations plan to develop a handbook for companies.

In addition to these multilateral types of convergence, there is an increase in the number of bilateral forms of convergence taking place. For example, the GRI and the UN Global Compact (Chapter 4) have signed a formal statement of mutual recognition. These statements are making it easier for companies to make their CR strategies more coherent, integrated and significant to a broader array of stakeholders. At best, procedural convergence among CR initiatives can lead to forms of accreditation and verification that are widely accepted. This in turn will promote the credibility of corporate responsibility.

---

3 Developed in Italy in 1999 by the Centre for Ethics, Law and Economics at the University of Castellanza in Italy, Q-Res addresses the social and ethical issues facing companies (www.biblio.liuc.it:8080/biblio/liucpap/pdf/95e.pdf).

29.2 **Promoting trust through verification**

We are in an age of accountability, where society holds companies and governments increasingly accountable for their actions. Hence, one of the key challenges within the field of CR relates to the issue of credibility and transparency. How can stakeholders trust what a company says about its social record in social reports? One of the major challenges for the field is the development of institutions and procedures for independent verification of social reports. What types of organisations can verify company reports and statements, and how will this be done? Under what conditions can a facility be termed socially responsible? Initiatives such as SA8000 (Chapter 9) and ISO 14001 (Chapter 27) are using a model of certification at the facility level to demonstrate compliance. Without credible systems for verification and certification, stakeholders may become increasingly cynical about corporate responsibility.

Abbreviations

AA   AccountAbility
AIDS   acquired immunodeficiency syndrome
APEC   Asia–Pacific Economic Co-operation
ASI   Anti-Slavery International
AVE   Außenhandelsvereinigung des
          Deutschen Einzelhandels eV (foreign
          trade association of the German retail
          trade)
BSI   British Standards Institution
CCBIBT   Council on Combating Bribery in
          International Business Transactions
CCC   Clean Clothes Campaign
CEO   chief executive officer
CERES   Coalition for Environmentally
          Responsible Economies
CIME   Committee on International
          Investment and Multinational
          Enterprises (OECD)
COFACE   Compagnie Française pour l'Assurance
          du Commerce Extérieur
CR   corporate responsibility
DESA   Department of Economic and Social
          Affairs (UN)
DJSI   Dow Jones Sustainability Index
DNA   deoxyribonucleic acid
DSD   Division for Sustainable Development
          (UN)
DTI   Department of Trade and Industry (UK)
EMAS   Eco-Management and Audit Scheme
EMS   environmental management system
ETI   Ethical Trading Initiative
FAQ   frequently asked question
FCPA   Foreign Corrupt Practices Act (USA)
FIDH   International Federation for Human
          Rights (Fédération Internationale des
          ligues des Droits de l'Homme/
          Federación Internacional de los
          Derechos Humanos)
FLA   Fair Labor Association
FSC   Forest Stewardship Council
FWF   Fair Wear Foundation
GRI   Global Reporting Initiative
GSP   Global Sullivan Principles
GUF   global union federation
HCHR   High Commissioner for Human Rights
          (UN)
HIV   human immunodeficiency virus
HRW   Human Rights Watch
HSE   health, safety and environment
IBLF   International Business Leaders' Forum
ICC   International Chamber of Commerce
ICCR   Interfaith Center on Corporate
          Responsibility
ICEM   International Federation of Chemical,
          Energy, Mine and General Workers'
          Unions
IFBWW   International Federation of Building

          and Wood Workers
ILD   Institute for Leadership Development
ILO   International Labour Organisation
ILRF   International Labour Rights Fund
IMF   International Monetary Fund
ISEAL   International Social and
          Environmental Accreditation and
          Labelling
ISO   International Organisation for
          Standardisation
ITGLWF   International Garment, Textile and
          Leather Workers' Federation
IUF   International Union of Food,
          Agricultural, Hotel, Restaurant,
          Catering, Tobacco and Allied Workers'
          Associations
LCHR   Lawyers' Committee for Human Rights
LSE   London Stock Exchange
MNC   multinational company
MSC   Marine Stewardship Council
NCP   National Contact Point (OECD)
NGO   non-governmental organisation
NOPEF   Norsk Olje og Petrokjemisk Fagforbund
          (Norwegian Oil and Petrochemical
          Workers' Union)
OECD   Organisation for Economic
          Co-operation and Development
PR   public relations
SA   Social Accountability
SAI   Social Accountability International
SIGMA   Sustainability: Integrated Guidelines
          for Management
SME   small or medium-sized enterprise
SRI   socially responsible investment
TICI   Transparency International Canada
          Inc.
TNC   transnational corporation
TNS   The Natural Step
UDHR   Universal Declaration of Human Rights
UN   United Nations
UNCED   UN Conference on Environment and
          Development
UNCHR   UN Commission on Human Rights
UNDP   UN Development Programme
UNEP   UN Environment Programme
UNICEF   UN Children's Fund
UNIDO   UN Industrial Development
          Organisation
USAID   US Agency for International
          Development
WBCSD   World Business Council for Sustainable
          Development
WCED   World Commission on Environment
          and Development
WRAP   Worldwide Responsible Apparel
          Production
WRC   Worker Rights Consortium